Gods, Voices, and the Bicameral Mind

GODS, VOICES, AND THE BICAMERAL MIND

THE THEORIES OF JULIAN JAYNES

Edited by

Marcel Kuijsten

Julian Jaynes Society

First Edition

Library of Congress Cataloging-in-Publication Data

Kuijsten, Marcel

Gods, Voices, and the Bicameral Mind: The Theories of Julian Jaynes

Includes bibliographical references and index.

1. Consciousness. 2. Consciousness—History. 3. Psychology.

ISBN: 978-0-9790744-3-1 (softcover)

Library of Congress Control Number: 2016904044

Cover design by Marcel Kuijsten
Cover illustration by Pete Cruickshank, © fotosearch.com

Julian Jaynes Society
Henderson, NV
julianjaynes.org

Printed in the United States of America

CONTRIBUTORS

ROBERT ATWAN founded the annual Best American Essays in 1986 and has served as series editor since. He has edited numerous anthologies, and his essays, criticism, and reviews cover a wide variety of topics that include dreams and divination in the ancient world, photography, Shakespeare, American popular culture, memoir, contemporary poetry, and literary nonfiction.

TODD GIBSON has a doctorate in Tibetan Studies from Indiana University at Bloomington and has published numerous articles on Inner Asian and Tibetan cultural history. He is now retired and living in Thailand.

JOHN HAMILTON retired as Director of Psychology from Gracewood Hospital, the original Georgia facility for the mentally and physically handicapped.

CHARLES HAMPDEN-TURNER is a British management philosopher, and Senior Research Associate at the Judge Business School at the University of Cambridge since 1990. He has authored or co-authored 15 books on a variety of subjects, including *Maps of the Mind: Charts and Concepts of the Mind and its Labyrinths*.

ROBERT E. HASKELL (1938–2010) was Professor Emeritus and chair of the Department of Social/Behavioral Sciences at the University of New England, a co-founder of the New England Institute of Cognitive Science and Evolutionary Psychology, and an associate editor of *The Journal of Mind and Behavior*. His major publications include seven books and over 65 research papers.

RUSSELL T. HURLBURT is Professor of Psychology at the University of Nevada, Las Vegas, and author or co-author of several books and many articles on Descriptive Experience Sampling (DES), a method of investigating inner experience.

MARCEL KUIJSTEN is Founder and Executive Director of the Julian Jaynes Society. In 2013, he co-chaired (with Rabbi James Cohn) the 2013 Julian Jaynes Society Conference on Consciousness and Bicameral Studies. His previous books are *The Julian Jaynes Collection* and *Reflections on the Dawn of Consciousness: Julian Jaynes's Bicameral Mind Theory Revisited*.

EDWARD PROFFITT (1938–2012) was a poet and professor at Manhattan College. He published extensively on writing, literature, and poetry. His books include *Reading and Writing About Short Fiction*, *Reading and Writing About Literature*, and *The Organized Writer*.

BRIAN J. MCVEIGH studied Asian Studies and Political Science at the State University of New York at Albany, from where he received his Master's degree. He was awarded his Ph.D. in anthropology from Princeton University and was a student of Julian Jaynes. A psychological anthropologist and specialist in Japanese, he has lived and worked in Asia for almost 17 years. He is the author of eleven books and is now training in mental health counseling.

JAMES E. MORRISS taught at Dowling College, Long Island, New York, and is the co-author of three books in comparative psychology and brain research: *The Brains of Animals and Man*, *Animal Instincts*, and *How Animals Learn*.

TED REMINGTON is Assistant Professor of English and Director of Writing at the University of Saint Francis in Fort Wayne, Indiana. He holds a Ph.D. in Rhetorical Studies from the University of Iowa.

BILL ROWE retired from the University of California Santa Cruz where he worked for 27 years as a staff research associate for the Santa Cruz Institute for Particle Physics. Since retiring he has worked as an independent consultant for medical device companies developing models and neural implants for various neurological disorders.

JOHN SAPPINGTON is a retired clinical psychologist and was Professor of Psychology at Augusta College (now Georgia Regents University).

JUDITH WEISSMAN (1946–1998) was Professor of English at Syracuse University, where she taught literature for more than twenty years. She published two books — *Half Savage and Hardy and Free: Women and Rural Radicalism in the Nineteenth-Century Novel* and *Of Two Minds: Poets Who Hear Voices* — and many articles and reviews.

LAURA MOONEYHAM WHITE is the John E. Weaver Professor of English at the University of Nebraska-Lincoln. Her publications include two monographs and a critical edition on Jane Austen; she has also published broadly on interdisciplinary nineteenth-century topics. White's recent work includes a monograph on Lewis Carroll and a data-mining project on Austen's use of free indirect discourse.

CONTENTS

Introduction

MARCEL KUIJSTEN

I N JANUARY 1977, the psychologist Julian Jaynes, who taught at Princeton University for nearly 25 years, released his seminal book, *The Origin of Consciousness in the Breakdown of the Bicameral Mind*. In this work he proposed that consciousness is not innate, but rather a learned process built up through metaphorical language and taught to each successive generation. Jaynes specifically defines consciousness as the human ability to introspect, and not merely being awake or aware of one's surroundings. According to Jaynes, human psychology underwent a profound transformation as recently as 3,000 years ago. For those who understand Jaynes's theory and appreciate its significance, it is easy to regard Julian Jaynes as one of the most original and important thinkers of the twentieth century. (For readers new to Jaynes's theory, the first chapter of this book provides a summary.)

The Origin of Consciousness was immediately popular with the general public, but Jaynes's theory remained controversial among academics. In the ensuing years, Jaynes published articles expanding on his ideas, gave many interviews, and was frequently invited to lecture on his theory. Two conferences were organized to discuss the theory, one at McMaster University in 1983 and one at Harvard University in 1988. *The Origin* was translated into French, German, Italian, and Spanish (more recently, unauthorized versions have appeared in Persian and Korean), an electronic version was published in 2012, and an audio version was published in 2015. A promised second book, however, never materialized.

After his death in November 1997, the future of Jaynes's theory remained uncertain. Although the theory was frequently mentioned by a wide variety of scholars and authors, no one was actively promoting it. Those in academia often stay away from controversial theories for professional reasons — academia in general, and psychology in particular, is much more prone to conformity than most people realize. Furthermore, professors are rewarded more for publishing their own theories than for expanding on the work of others.

Shortly after I learned of Jaynes's death, I posted an article I had written on Jaynes's theory on the newly emerging internet. The enthusiastic, worldwide response that I received motivated me to start the Julian Jaynes Society. The early years of the Society focused on making available articles relevant to the theory and providing a forum for online discussion. Initially, my goal was to locate and publish Jaynes's second book, and for several years I attempted to track down his unpublished writings. After many dead-ends, I eventually discovered that while some chapters had been completed, there was not enough material to constitute a complete second book. During this time, I became acquainted with other scholars who were also passionate about Jaynes's theory, and the idea for an edited book of articles on the theory took shape.

The resulting book, *Reflections on the Dawn of Consciousness: Julian Jaynes's Bicameral Mind Theory Revisited*, was completed in late 2006 and released in early 2007. It was the first book dedicated entirely to Jaynes's theory since his *Origin of Consciousness*. The book contains a biography of Julian Jaynes, perspectives on various aspects of Jaynes's theory from a variety of scholars, and additional material by Jaynes that previously had only been published in academic journals. Some of the many topics discussed are the relationship between consciousness and language, auditory hallucinations as a vestige of the bicameral mind, new evidence for Jaynes's theory, the implication of Jaynes's theory for the origin of religion, and the evidence for bicameralism in early China. Readers around the world were hungry for new material on Jaynes's theory, and the book was received enthusiastically. It now has readers across the United States and in more than 32 foreign countries.

Julian Jaynes had a family home in Prince Edward Island, where he spent summers throughout his life. He retired there in 1995, and died on November 21, 1997, at the age of 77. Jaynes had made arrangements to donate his extensive library of rare psychology books and journals to the Psychology Department of the University of Prince Edward Island, along with funding for scholarships and conferences on consciousness. Beginning in 2002, Scott Greer, a psychology professor at the university, took the initiative to organize the Julian Jaynes Symposium on Consciousness. In 2002, the symposium featured William Woodward, a psychology professor and former student of Julian Jaynes; in 2003, philosophy professor and author Daniel Dennett, who also knew Jaynes and has written on his theory; and in 2004, Michael Gazzaniga, the psychologist and author best known for his research on split-brain patients.

In 2005, the symposium was expanded to three speakers: John Limber, a professor of psychology; Brian McVeigh, a professor of anthropology and a student and friend of Julian Jaynes; and Scott Greer himself. In both 2006 and 2008, Greer expanded the symposium to a full two-day conference, featuring the neurologist, neuropsychiatrist, author, and professor Richard Restak as the keynote speaker in 2006 and the psychology professor and author Karl Pribram (1919–2015) as the keynote speaker in 2008. In April of 2008, Brian McVeigh and I also organized a speaker session and workshop on Jaynes's theory at the Toward a Science of Consciousness Conference in Tuscon, Arizona.

In 2007, Rabbi James Cohn's *The Minds of the Bible: Speculations on the Cultural Evolution of Human Consciousness* was published by the Julian Jaynes Society (an updated and revised version was published in 2013). In it, Rabbi Cohn brings to bear his considerable knowledge of Biblical history and ancient texts to elucidate the evidence for bicameralism and the transition to consciousness as documented in the Hebrew Scriptures (Old Testament).

In 2012 I published *The Julian Jaynes Collection*, which contains articles and lectures by Jaynes (extending his theory into areas not covered in his original book), interviews with Jaynes, discussion of the theory, and extensive question and answer sessions with Jaynes that followed his lectures. Answers to the most frequent questions people have after reading *The Origin of Consciousness* can be found in this book. My introduction to the book brings readers up to speed on new evidence for Jaynes's theory and explains it's wide ranging influence and ongoing relevance.

The Prince Edward Island and Tuscon conferences paved the way for what would be the largest conference ever held on Jaynes's theory, organized by Rabbi James Cohn and me in June of 2013. Taking place in Charleston, West Virginia, the 2013 Julian Jaynes Society Conference on Consciousness and Bicameral Studies was made possible by a generous grant from the Bertie Cohen "Rabbi's Invitational Series" of Temple Israel. The multidisciplinary program featured 26 speakers over three full days, including keynote talks by psychology professor and author Roy Baumeister, who knew Jaynes while a student at Princeton University, and read an early draft of Jaynes's book; psychology and cognitive neuroscience professor and author Merlin Donald; and the Dutch psychiatrist Dirk Corstens, who is active in the Hearing Voices Network and regularly works with voice hearers. The conference brought together Jaynes enthusiasts from around the U.S. as well as Australia, Canada, France, Germany, the Netherlands, Thailand, Turkey, and the United Kingdom.

It is hard to convey the overwhelmingly positive and enthusiastic atmosphere at the conference. For many of the attendees, it was the first time they could hear lectures on the theory and discuss Jaynes's ideas face-to-face with others who were as familiar with the theory as they were. An audio CD of the conference talks was published in 2014, and the chapters in the current book by Bill Rowe and Ted Remington are in part based on the lectures they presented at the conference.

New Evidence for Jaynes's Theory

In *The Origin*, Jaynes provides extensive evidence to support his theory from a wide variety of disciplines, but as it has now been nearly four decades since Jaynes's book was first published, those familiar with it are often interested to learn what new evidence has emerged in the intervening years that either supports or refutes the theory.

In a chapter in *Reflections on the Dawn of Consciousness* and the Introduction to *The Julian Jaynes Collection*, I summarize much of the new evidence for Jaynes's theory that has emerged since the theory was first published. I will briefly highlight some of the more important points here, as well as indicate topics that are addressed in the current book:

- Beginning in 1999, numerous neuroimaging studies have demonstrated a right/left temporal lobe interaction during auditory hallucinations, confirming Jaynes's neurological model.
- New research confirms that consciousness makes up a much smaller part of our mentality and decision making than was previously believed.
- Dreams have changed during recorded history from bicameral or visitation dreams to modern, conscious dreams (see Chapter 6).[1]
- Vestiges of bicamerality have been documented in preliterate societies worldwide (see Chapter 7), and researchers have also noted differences in aspects of consciousness based on differences in language.
- Auditory hallucinations are more widespread throughout the population than was previously known (see Chapters 7, 8, and 9).
- Hallucinations frequently center on the person's behavior — commanding it, commenting on it, or describing it — as Jaynes's theory would predict (see Chapter 10).
- "Command hallucinations" that direct behavior are now well documented in individuals whose hallucinations require professional help.
- Research indicates that subjective consciousness is not innate but is learned by children as they acquire language (see Chapter 11).
- Children with imaginary companions are more common than was previously known, frequently involve hallucinations, and often manifest as "conscience-related" imaginary companions that help direct behavior.
- New research further explains the important role of metaphor in the development of consciousness (see Chapters 13).

---

1. This is not technically "new" evidence, as Jaynes was familiar with this transition and lectured on the subject (see Julian Jaynes, "The Dream of Agamemnon," in Marcel Kuijsten [ed.], *The Julian Jaynes Collection* [Henderson, NV: Julian Jaynes Society]). But as the chapter he wrote on dreams was not included in *The Origin* due to space constraints, the topic is new to most readers.

• The transition from bicamerality to consciousness has been documented in additional cultures beyond those described by Jaynes (see Chapters 14 and 15).

Continued Relevance

Nearly forty years after it was first published, Julian Jaynes's theory of the origin of consciousness and a previous mentality called the bicameral mind remains not only relevant, but in many ways continues to be ahead of much of the current thinking in consciousness studies. Jaynes's theory provides a more logically consistent understanding of human history, and many of the practices of ancient and modern cultures are difficult to make sense of without the benefit of his ideas.

After a long period where behaviorism dominated psychology, *The Origin* (and, later, advances in brain imaging technology) helped scholars to once again see consciousness as a viable topic of study. Jaynes demonstrates that consciousness is not an all or nothing proposition, but rather a package of features that are learned and thus can vary in different individuals and cultures. This important realization — that consciousness is learned and not innate — encourages us to study its development in children and to find better ways to teach consciousness to each successive generation, as well as find ways to continue to develop and expand our own consciousness throughout life.

Understanding Jaynes's insights on consciousness could help future generations develop techniques for greater willpower, self-control, and a greater ability to modify habitual behaviors and genetically-based predispositions. The mainstream view — that consciousness is innate, fixed at birth, and consistent throughout history — leaves us with the impression that we are effectively helpless to improve upon our current capacity for conscious thought. Understanding the cultural, learned basis of consciousness has tremendous implications for the future development of psychology and indeed human civilization.

Jaynes's theory also inspired much of the modern research into hallucinations in the normal population, beginning with investigations in the early 1980s and culminating in the Hearing Voices Network. This worldwide group seeks to remove the stigma of auditory hallucinations, demonstrate that they can be a relatively common experience in normal individuals, and provide support groups for voice-hearers. Jaynes's theory remains the most supportable and generalizable explanation for the occurrence of auditory hallucinations, and provides voice-hearers with a historical context to better understand their experience.

Julian Jaynes's ideas have provided inspiration for science fiction writers such as Philip K. Dick, Robert J. Sawyer, Neal Stephenson, and Philip Pullman, and artists such as Lee Bul and Ian Cheng.

Jaynes's theory sheds light on many aspects of human psychology that would otherwise remain a mystery. Hypnosis, "possession," poetic frenzy, and even the origin of religion can all be more easily understood through the lens of Jaynes's theory. In short, we cannot fully understand our present psychology without the more accurate understanding of our past that Jaynes's theory provides.

Misconceptions & Critiques

Discussing and promoting Jaynes's theory for nearly two decades has provided an education on the nature of opinion formation and belief systems, the often irrational resistance people have to new ideas, and the ease with which people form and repeat misconceptions. Speaking on the myths and misconceptions surrounding the demise of the video game manufacturer Atari, founder Nolan Bushnell notes that "a simple answer that is clear and precise will always have more power in the world than a complex one that is true."[2] Bushnell's observation is not limited to the situation with Atari. When it comes to subjects that are not fully understood, it seems to be a reality of human nature that we have a propensity to prefer easy answers and simple "truths" over more complex — and oftentimes more accurate — explanations. This certainly describes the study of the history of psychology: many prefer simplistic answers that ignore inconvenient facts, rather than explanations that take into account the full range of human experience and all its fascinating complexities.

People often display a strong preference for simple answers and a compulsion to have everything settled (rather than withholding judgment until more information is available); we seem to have an aversion

2. Nolan Bushnell quoted in Zak Penn, *Atari: Game Over* (Xbox Video, 2014).

toward unknowns and ambiguity. Yet subjects that we are not entirely familiar with are generally more complex than we first realize. It behooves us to resist the impulse to make snap judgments and succumb to the illusion of mastery for subjects we don't fully understand. By prematurely making up our mind about a topic we are unfamiliar with, we risk the tendency to oversimplify and to only seek evidence that confirms our existing beliefs. Withholding an opinion on new ideas until we have adequate information to make an informed judgment takes a great deal of effort and self-discipline.

When people first encounter Jaynes's ideas, they often make a snap judgment based on their existing, often unchallenged preconceptions about the nature of consciousness and human history. Jaynes's theory can at first seem challenging and difficult to wrap one's mind around — it takes a certain amount of imagination for individuals with consciousness to conceive of what life would be like without it, to understand how the brain might leverage newly acquired language to convey information between the hemispheres, or to contemplate what life would be like in ancient cultures such as those in Mesopotamia where the leadership consisted entirely of gods.

As I have detailed on the Julian Jaynes Society website, the vast majority of critiques of the theory are based on misconceptions about what Jaynes actually said, often critiquing Jaynes's argument that consciousness was a recent development based on a very broad definition of consciousness (typically including things like basic sense perception), and not taking the time to understand Jaynes's more precise, narrow definition. Critiques of Jaynes's theory typically fail to take into account new evidence that supports the theory or to offer alternate explanations for the otherwise mysterious phenomenon that Jaynes's theory explains.

The field of consciousness studies is highly fragmented due to both the lack of a widely agreed-upon, precise terminology to describe the numerous mental phenomenon often referred to as "consciousness," and a lack of agreement on the fundamental nature of consciousness itself. Further complicating the issue, some authors discuss conscious and unconscious mental processes using different terminology entirely, such as "hot and cold" or "System 1 and System 2" — both cases roughly corresponding to unconscious and conscious processes. A new lexicon must be developed to distinguish things like sense perception, attention, and introspection, as well as to differentiate the scientific study of consciousness from more mystical or "New Age" pursuits.

While some scholars addressing the topic of consciousness use a definition comparable to Jaynes's, many theorists write or speak on the subject without ever defining what they are discussing, and frequently include a wide range of mental processes such as attention, awareness, and sensory perception under the umbrella of consciousness. Defining consciousness so broadly that all living things (including single celled organisms) would be considered conscious renders the term almost meaningless. While such research advances our understanding of things like attention and perception, it does not speak to the issue of introspectable mind-space that concerned Jaynes.

Others pursue highly speculative, neo-mystical concepts such as panpsychism (the belief that consciousness pervades the universe) or look to quantum mechanics as the source of consciousness. Jaynes's more disciplined, grounded approach to consciousness defines it essentially as "that which is introspectable," and distinguishes it from the basic sense perception we share with all animals. Even after nearly forty years, Jaynes's discussion of what consciousness is and is not remains not only insightful but in many ways ahead of the current thinking in the field.

In contrast to the more esoteric theories of consciousness — that use the term consciousness in place of what formerly might have been referred to as the "soul" — the most controversial aspect of Jaynes's theory is how recently he dates its emergence. Yet for those who investigate how Jaynes defines consciousness and carefully consider his arguments, the evidence for a major psychological transition around the time period that Jaynes identifies is easily defensable — despite being still largely under the radar of most psychologists and historians.

Future Research

In *The Origin*, Julian Jaynes provides the foundation for an alternate, more accurate view of the history of the human mind. He also made it clear that much more work needs to be done. A complete understanding of the details and implications of Jaynes's theory will require the efforts of many scholars — the valuable contributions from the authors of the chapters in this book and in *Reflections on the Dawn of Consciousness* are only the beginning.

The culture and practices of ancient civilizations worldwide must be reexamined through the lens of Jaynes's theory. Consciousness is a culturally based, learned set of features rather than an all-or-nothing biological adaptation, and evidence now suggests that like most new technologies, these features emerged gradually over time, rather than all at once. (We are beginning to see this gradual learning of consciousness in child development studies as well.) The bicameral mind likely overlapped for a period of time with consciousness as these different features emerged. Due to the limits of the historical record, this transition may never be fully clarified, however it certainly could be better illuminated than it is today. Jaynes called the idea of a gradual overlapping transition from bicamerality to consciousness the "weak version" of his theory, and while it may be less falsifiable than the "strong version" (which proposes a more rapid transition), it may ultimately prove to be more historically accurate. Even today, we see individual and cultural variability in the features of consciousness — another area for future research.

The birth of consciousness ushered in profound changes for human civilization. In what Jaynes terms the "cognitive explosion," we see the sudden beginnings of philosophy, science, history, and theater. We also observe the gradual transition from polytheism to monotheism. Consciousness operating on human emotions caused shame to become guilt, fear to become anxiety, anger to become hatred, and mating behavior to give rise to sexual fantasy. Through the spatialization of time, people could, for the first time, think about their lives on a continuum and contemplate their own death. Despite its significance, very little has been written on the impact of consciousness in, for example, ancient Greece and Rome. Interested scholars will find abundant research opportunities examining the consequences of consciousness for the civilizations of the early conscious period.[3]

---

3. See Chapter 6 of this volume, "The Interpretation of Dreams, The Origin of Consciousness, and the Birth of Tragedy," as well as the historian Ross R. Maxwell's "Eternal Rome: Subjective Consciousness and Immortality" (*Psychohistory Review*, Vol. 14, 2, 1985), which examines the quest for immortality in Rome from the perspective of Jaynes's theory. See also Julian Jaynes, "A Two-Tiered Theory of Emotions: Affect and Feeling," in Kuijsten (ed.), *The Julian Jaynes Collection*.

More work remains to be done in understanding the relationship between consciousness and language and how children learn consciousness as they acquire language — psychologists and linguists have thus far only scratched the surface of these topics. Recently contacted preliterate societies provide psychologists and anthropologists that are familiar with Jaynes's theory the rare opportunity to study vestiges of bicamerality and variability in the features of consciousness in living cultures, but the window of opportunity for this research is rapidly closing. The ongoing study of voice-hearing in both normal and clinical populations, as well as imaginary companions in children, will undoubtedly further contribute to our understanding of Jaynes's theory, as parallels between ancient and modern voice-hearing are better understood.

Overview of the Book

One of the challenges in publishing a book on Julian Jaynes's theory is striking a balance between providing material that is accessible to the many non-academics who are interested in Jaynes's ideas, while at the same time providing material that is substantive enough to be interesting to scholars (providing new insights into the various aspects of Jaynes's theory and moving the theory forward in new directions). To that end, I have chosen selections that most readers will hopefully find both readable and substantive.

The first chapter, by Charles Hampden-Turner, provides a good summary of the theory for those unfamiliar with Jaynes's work, and a good refresher for those who are. In Chapter 2, James Morriss explains the theory and provides more in-depth analysis and discussion.

New ideas are nearly always met with resistance, and Jaynes's theory is no exception. In Chapter 3, Brian McVeigh, who knew Jaynes while a doctoral student in anthropology at Princeton University, identifies and explains six of the most common intellectual obstacles to understanding Jaynes's theory.

One aspect of Jaynes's theory that some have difficulty with is the notion that prior to the development of consciousness, non-habitual behavior was directed by verbal hallucinations. I have found that just the mention of auditory hallucinations can trigger a knee-jerk hostile reaction to the theory in some individuals. Perhaps mental illness has been so stigmatized by society that the mere mention of hallucinations elicits an unconscious aversion. At the time Jaynes first proposed his theory, hallucinations also seemed too infrequent to have played such an important role in a previous mentality. In the ensuing decades, however, the idea that hallucinations are much more common among the normal population than was previously known has been gaining acceptance among both mental health professionals and the general public alike — although there is still a very long way to go. In Chapter 4, Bill Rowe tackles the subject of how auditory verbal hallucinations evolved in conjunction with language, aided social cohesion, and gave rise to the notion of gods. Drawing upon the work of other scholars to support Jaynes's theory, he also discusses the seven factors Jaynes identifies that lead to the development of consciousness.

In Chapter 5, Bill Rowe explores the ancient Dark Age from the perspective of Jaynes's theory — a period from roughly 1200 to 800 B.C.E. when many of the civilizations around the Mediterranean mysteriously collapsed. Rowe examines the six explanations for the collapse proposed by Robert Drews in *The End of the Bronze Age: Changes in Warfare and the Catastrophe ca. 1200 B.C.* — as well as the work of other historians such as Eric Cline — and he examines how the evidence for these explanations compares with Jaynes's theory of the breakdown of the bicameral mind as the cause of the collapse.

In Chapter 6, Robert Atwan explores dreams and the birth of tragedy. Dreams are an important aspect of Jaynes's theory in that they provide another way to document the transition from bicamerality to consciousness. Dreams in ancient civilizations were primarily visitation dreams, where the dreamer is asleep in bed and is visited by a god or deceased relative and given instruction, in much the same way that bicameral hallucinations functioned during wakefulness. Atwan explores the fascinating transition from bicameral dreams to conscious dreams, along with the beginnings of Greek tragedy.[4]

---

4. While it is regrettable that a chapter Jaynes wrote on this subject was not included in his original book, fortunately he provides his ideas on dreams in a lecture titled "The Dream of Agamemnon," which I've published in *The Julian Jaynes Collection*, and I recommend reading his lecture in conjunction with Robert Atwan's chapter.

As I mentioned previously, the idea that auditory hallucinations could have been a part of the daily life experience for people at one time in history is one of the most difficult aspects of Jaynes's theory for many to accept. The next four chapters address various aspects of this issue. Chapters 7, "Evolution and Inspiration" by Judith Weissman, and Chapter 8, "Romanticism, Bicamerality, and the Evolution of the Brain" by Edward Proffitt, discuss the auditory hallucinations often seen in poetic inspiration as a vestige of the bicameral mind, and the transition from inspired poetry to conscious poetry.

While historical texts such as the *Iliad* and the Old Testament provide valuable insights into the bicameral experience, another way to better understand bicameralism is to study those who hear guiding or commanding voices today. We now know that hallucinations emerge in normal individuals in a wide variety of contexts, ranging form stress to social isolation. Chapter 9, "On Listening to Voices," revisits the population of non-verbal voice-hearing quadriplegics described in *Reflections on the Dawn of Consciousness*. This group provides another example of the wide variety of situations in which voices emerge and the functional role these voices play.

In Chapter 10, "A Schizophrenic Woman Who Heard Voices of the Gods," Russell Hurlburt describes his work with a Dutch woman who hears voices and sees visions of beings she calls "gods." Hurlburt notes that "she repeatedly heard voices she took to be gods talking to her … and giving her commands." Although a conscious person who also hears voices and sees visions — as opposed to someone who is strictly bicameral — the descriptions of her inner experience provide rare and valuable insights into what daily life may have been like for bicameral people.

In "Two Origins of Consciousness," Bill Rowe looks at the development of consciousness in children as a way of shedding light on the historical origin of consciousness. He presents a developmental pathway to consciousness and explains child development studies that support Jaynes's idea that children learn consciousness as they develop language. Through studying the development of consciousness in children we can thus infer more about the transition to consciousness in ancient history.

In "The Origin of Consciousness, Gains and Losses: Walker Percy vs. Julian Jaynes," Laura Mooneyham White describes both the parallels and sharp contrasts in the ideas of Julian Jaynes and the author Walker Percy (1916–1990). Percy was a novelist whose interests included philosophy and semiotics (the study of signs and symbols and how they are used). He wrote six novels as well as philosophical non-fiction books and essays, the most well known being *Lost in the Cosmos*.

One of the most challenging aspects of Jaynes's theory is understanding how consciousness is built up through metaphor. Ted Remington further elucidates this process and compares Jaynes's ideas on the subject to the rhetorician I. A. Richards (1893–1979). Both Jaynes and Richards argue that metaphor plays a much more significant role in thought than is generally believed. Remington explains how Jaynes expands upon Richards's ideas and discusses more recent works on metaphor and thought that support Jaynes's theory.[5]

In discussing the evidence for the bicameral mind and the transition from bicamerality to consciousness, Julian Jaynes focuses primarily on the civilizations of ancient Greece, Egypt, Mesopotamia, and the early Hebrews, and he leaves it to others to investigate the evidence in other cultures. In *Reflections on the Dawn of Consciousness*, the sinologist Michael Carr describes evidence for bicameralism and the transition to consciousness in early China, which happened roughly contemporaneously with ancient Greece. In "Souls, Gods, Kings, and Mountains" and "Listening for Ancient Voices" (Chapters 14 and 15), Todd Gibson presents detailed evidence for bicameralism and the development of consciousness in ancient Tibet, adding another valuable piece to the puzzle of how and when the transition to consciousness took place in different cultures worldwide. Chapter 14 analyzes Tibetan linguistics and ancient Tibetan history through the lens of Jaynes's theory, and Chapter 15 examines vestiges of bicamerality in more recent Tibetan religion. While the discussion of the evolution of Tibetan mind-related vocabulary is difficult material, even casual readers should be able to gain insights from the author's main points.

In the final chapter, "Vico and Jaynes: Neurocultural and Cognitive Operations in the Origin of Consciousness," Robert Haskell compares Jaynes's ideas on the bicameral mind with those of the eighteenth century

---

5. For more on this topic, see Julian Jaynes's "Representations as Metaphiers" in Kuijsten (ed.), *The Julian Jaynes Collection*.

Italian philosopher and historian Giambattista Vico (1668–1744), best known for his book *The New Science*, first published in 1725. Like Jaynes, Vico takes seriously the possibility that human psychology underwent a major transition during recorded history. Although Jaynes was not aware of Vico, Haskell outlines the many ways in which Vico's characterizations of ancient people are strikingly similar to Jaynes's descriptions of bicameral civilizations.

Fully understanding all of the nuances of Jaynes's theory does take some time and patience, but the profound insights the theory provides into our past, present, and future makes the effort well worth it. For the most complete understanding of Jaynes's important ideas, I would encourage you to also read his book, *The Origin of Consciousness in the Breakdown of the Bicameral Mind*, my two previous books, *Reflections on the Dawn of Consciousness* and *The Julian Jaynes Collection*, and *The Minds of the Bible* by Rabbi James Cohn. If you have questions about the theory, I welcome you to join the discussion online at julianjaynes.org.

CHAPTER 1

Gods, Voices, and the Bicameral Mind:
The Theories of Julian Jaynes

CHARLES HAMPDEN-TURNER

"For all good poets, epic as well as lyric, composed
their beautiful poems not by art, but because they are
inspired and possessed. ... There is no invention in him
until he has been inspired and is out of his senses."
— Plato

JULIAN JAYNES, A PROFESSOR OF PSYCHOLOGY AT PRINCETON, is responsible for the most intriguing and extensive thesis yet to emerge from brain research. Did our ancestors have god-directed minds? Is consciousness little more than 3,000 years old? He starts by asking what consciousness is — that irradicable difference between what others see and our own sense of self. Consciousness is not the same as being awake. To be knocked "unconscious" is to lose many automatic functions. It is not continuity since even "stream of consciousness" is full of gaps. The Cartesian notion of "the helpless spectator" asks us to believe that the intensification of consciousness during decisions has nothing to do with outcomes. We know that we can learn, judge, think abstractly, and even generalize without consciousness. Many skills like oratory, music, and skiing fail us when consciousness interferes. Einstein had so many creative ideas while shaving that he would cut himself with surprise.

Jaynes's solution is that consciousness is built up through metaphor — relationships between two or more unlike experiences joined

First published in Charles Hampden-Turner, *Maps of the Mind: Charts and Concepts of the Mind and its Labyrinths* (New York: Collier Books, 1982). Reprinted (with minor edits) with permission.

by likenesses. The countryside "blanketed by snow" is more than a superficial connection. It teems with associations, contours, warmth, protection, slumber, and an awakening in spring. Consciousness is a lexical field, whose terms are metaphors or analogs of behavior in the physical world. We project syntheses of associations into an imagined screen within our heads. Consciousness has thus the relationship of a map to a territory, as when in the 'pith' and 'kernel' of Jaynes's thesis he mounts metaphors on metaphors in levels of abstraction. The origins of even our most basic verbs are metaphorical. 'To be' is from Sanskrit *bhu* 'to grow'. 'Am' and 'is' derive from *amsi* 'to breathe'. Thus the metaphor of our being is literally stretched like a screen between brain hemispheres and between referents like growing, breathing, and standing out (*ex-istere*). Conscious being is the relationship between these, a 'between.'

Jaynes sees consciousness as right/left brain synthesis with five characteristics:

1. *Spatialization*, when we stretch out dimensions of time and space.
2. *Excerption*, by which maps record only selected parts of the territory.
3. *The analog 'I'* and *metaphor 'me'*, a projected personification of ourselves moving in space and time which anticipates doing and being done by.
4. *Narratization*, wherein events are selected for their congruence and sequential unfolding.
5. *Conciliation*, wherein experiences are consciously assimilated to each other.

With consciousness so defined we must recognize that in a book like the *Iliad* (shorn of its later accretions), human beings are not conscious at all! What would later become terms for mental processes have only their original concrete referents. Hence *psyche* in the *Iliad* means 'breath', not soul or conscious mind as it meant by the sixth century B.C. *Thumos* means motion or agitation of limbs, not emotional sensibility. *Noos* means simple perception, not the imaginal mind, and so on. Jaynes believes that the world of the *Iliad*, indeed the whole known world of theocratic god-kings, prior to about 1500 B.C. was possessed of a bicameral mind, split in two, with a right hemisphere, executive part called a god, and a left hemisphere, follower part, called a man. Gods ordered men to act, directly or through priests, and men obeyed. There was no argument, love, or personal relationship with divine executors.

For the most part such minds would operate, learn, think, react, and retain equilibrium as ours do, unconsciously. But when something unexpected (and hence stressful) happened, instead of a period of intense consciousness, with inner deliberation and argument, bicameral man would receive a god-like command from his right hemisphere instructing him to act, as Zeus ordered Agamemnon to attack before the walls of Troy. This is essentially similar to the reported auditory hallucinations in schizophrenia, which are frequently accurate comments on events, and which Jaynes regards as partial relapses to an earlier state of ancestral bicamerality. Just as contemporary psychotics have a low stress tolerance, combined with an existing schizoid form of personality organization, so that breaks occur readily, so bicameral civilizations heard stress-precipitated commands at almost every crisis point. The remarkable unanimity of such mass action is a consequence of pre-structured collective beliefs, just as the patients of phrenologists oblige with behavior appropriate to the bump being magnetized, and research has found that hypnotized subjects confine themselves to actions which they considered "possible" and "permissible" before hypnosis began.

Were whole peoples once organized by a mixture of hallucinated voices and hypnotic suggestions? Incredible? Jaynes has amassed considerable circumstantial evidence to which this précis cannot do justice. Recall that speech areas are almost entirely confined to the left hemisphere (that is for the 90 percent of the population which is right handed). This high degree of hemisphere specialization is peculiarly human, and is generally attributed to language acquisition. There are three major language areas, the supplementary motor cortex, Broca's area, low down on the left frontal lobe, and Wernicke's area, mostly in the posterior part of the left temporal lobe. The latter seems the most crucial, since extensive damage involves permanent loss of language function, while equivalent damage to the right temporal lobe produces deficit, despite the near-identity of neural structures. However, persons with left temporal lobe damage at birth utilize their right hemispheres to acquire language, so what is this vast under-utilized area for?

Jaynes believes that during a crucial period in our evolution, at the very time that language was being acquired by the left hemisphere, the right temporal lobe was preempted for the issuance of god-like commandments, across the thin anterior commissure that joins the two temporal lobes like a private corpus callosum. Auditory commands would have been the most economical code for getting elaborate information processing through so small a channel.

When this hallucinatory area was stimulated by an electric current in experiments by Wilder Penfield, subjects would hear voices (and sometimes have visions) addressing them. One typical subject exclaimed, "That man's voice again! My father's ... and it frightens me!" Others heard voices to the accompaniment of music, chanting, or singing, which would criticize, advise, or command, but they were consistently other than the hearer, often a dead relative or friend. We also know that while the right hemisphere cannot speak, or barely so, it can comprehend and interpret quite complicated instructions. Patients with strokes in their left hemisphere can obey their doctors or researchers in detail.

Recall also that when the corpus callosum between the hemispheres is severed or communication anesthetized, one hemisphere can try and "help" the other in the manner of two independent persons. The left hemisphere feeling a frown on the face, produced by the right hemisphere, whose left hand knows the answer, will be prompted to change its verbal answer. It is like Athena taking Achilles in hand. For in many respects the right hemisphere acts in god-like ways. It is timeless, immediate, visionary, coherent, with recognizable forms and faces. It responds to over-arching purposes and grand designs and has an affinity for music, rhythm, cadence, and patterns in general. It binds people together (religion is from *religare* 'to bind') and its intuitive style is given to inspiration and seeming miracle.

How could bicamerality have evolved? There was no one to cut the corpus callosum. Jaynes argues from studies that reveal the great plasticity of the brain to changes in environment. Persons with their brains damaged have developed additional areas to overcome injuries. The principle of natural selection could well have given an advantage over several millennia to persons bicamerally organized. They may have evolved from small groups of hunter-gatherers into whole communities remotely controlled by the internalized voices of god-kings, a form of social control far more sophisticated than the signs and calls of earlier primates, and one that allowed for the development of language.

Jaynes dates bicameral man from the Natufian settlement at Eynan just north of the Sea of Galilee, discovered in 1959. Those parts of it which date from 9000 B.C. show town settlements theocratically organized around the burial mounds of god-kings. Thenceforward theocratic organization spread rapidly with dead kings as living gods and their tombs as temples. We find them propped up on thrones of stone, surrounded by food and gifts. Later, some bicameral theocracies became literate, the Babylon of Mesopotamia, the Kings of Ur and Isin, the Mephite theology, and the Dead King's Voice of Osiris. These were not "authoritarian" regimes, for there was no subjectivity or private ambition to crush, only an innocent obedience to voices reverberating in the brain.

The end of bicameral civilization may have come from the strains produced by their initial success. Controlling more than a thousand people must have posed difficulties, but nothing compared with the conflicts resulting from collisions between god-programmed peoples each marching to a different drummer. The biblical story of the Tower of Babel may well refer to this. The spread of writing must also have weakened auditory commands. But the most proximate cause was possibly the cataclysmic events in the second millennia B.C., when volcanic eruptions on the island of Thera, estimated to have been 350 times greater than a hydrogen bomb, turned half the world's known population into refugees and drowned the Minoan culture beneath a tsunami perhaps 700 feet high, giving rise to the legend of Atlantis. The once stable hierarchies crumbled in mass migrations, wiping out the great empires of the Hittites and Mycenae, as primal hordes turned on god-kings … Assyria having fallen into two centuries of anarchy emerged as a monster of sadistic ferocity, terror replacing the sudden loss of authority.

Yet there was no turning back to lost Edens. The languages, cities, and foreigners were there and only consciousness could survive the confusion. The *Odyssey*, which probably followed the *Iliad* by at least a century, is a myth marking the transformation. The heroes who battle before Troy "were the will-less gigolos of divinities" whose Olympian rivalry was in bloody impasse. It took "wily Odysseus" and his Trojan Horse to break free, conquer Troy, and defying gods wander homelessly abroad using the serpentine wits of an exiled Adam. In the *Odyssey* we suddenly encounter conscious actors, moral judgments and *psyche*, *noos*, and *thumos* used as metaphors for consciousness. We find a similar transition between Amos and Ecclesiastes, from "Thus Spake the Lord ..." to "For all things there is a season ..." The Lord who walks in the Garden and closes the ark, yields to a Yahweh who appears only to Moses in disguise and condemns bicameral idolators.

The Greek epic poets in their tales of mythic heroes were surely celebrating a novel orchestration of hemispheric functions. Tragic drama stressed the price of consciousness, that the hubris of the analog 'I' on the screen of consciousness could find itself in agonizing contradiction with real events. The psychic heroism of Orestes, Oedipus, Antigone, Socrates, and eventually Christ, was that all remained defiantly conscious in crucifying circumstances which threatened relapse into bicamerality and oblivion of mind.

CHAPTER 2

Reflections on Julian Jaynes's
The Origin of Consciousness in the Breakdown of the Bicameral Mind

JAMES E. MORRISS

A RISTOTLE DEFINED MAN as the living being who has "logos." This definition has become canonical in the statement that man is the "animal rational," a creature distinguished from all others by his capacity for thought. Although the word "logos" embodies the concept of thought, its primary meaning is language.[1] If Aristotle believed man's uniqueness lay in his ability to create language, Western philosophy did not consider this a central issue in its explorations of human awareness. Neither has language been a primary focus in psychology's old debate over the nature of consciousness. This may be changing, however, for Julian Jaynes, a psychologist with a strong philosophical bent, has drawn language into the center of the consciousness controversy with *The Origin of Consciousness in the Breakdown of the Bicameral Mind*.[2] In this beautifully written and carefully documented book, Jaynes suggests that man's uniqueness lies not only in his ability to create language but in the profound effect language has had on man. However, before considering this work, I want to try placing in perspective the issues with which it deals.

Our semantic heritage includes among its memorabilia of meanings a record of man's attempts to describe his experience of "being."

First published in *ETC: A Review of General Semantics*, 1978, 35, 3. Reprinted with permission.
1. Hans-Georg Gadamer, *Philosophical Hermeneutics* (Berkeley: University of California Press, 1976), pp. 59–62.
2. Julian Jaynes, *The Origin of Consciousness in the Breakdown of the Bicameral Mind* (Boston: Houghton Mifflin, 1976).

For centuries theologians talked about the "soul" and philosophers pondered the nature of consciousness. Plato's concept of immaterial "ideas" as true reality blossomed into dualism with the Cartesian distinction between mind and matter. The roots of this dichotomy lay deep in man's tendency to mistake symbols for things. Abstract ideas become reified in their symbolic representations and words create an aura of certainty that obscures the elusiveness of certain concepts. When science began to consider the nature of self-perception, caution had to be exercised in the choice of terms used to describe "inner" reality.

In the late eighteen hundreds, psychology, heralded by William James as the "science of mind,"[3] inherited from philosophy the problem of man's awareness of his awareness. As this new discipline struggled for respectability it adopted the predominantly mechanistic paradigm of the age and as a first order of business set about sharpening fuzzy concepts and discarding from its workshop linguistic tools which seemed inappropriate for prying out "final" answers. The elusive concept of "soul" was among the first semantic casualties of scientific scrutiny. James noted the explanatory inadequacy of this traditional religious term in one of his early essays, and the "associationist" school, strongly influenced by the logical positivists, created what was known as a "psychology without a soul."[4] But having adeptly disposed of the human soul, psychology was confronted with another slippery concept: consciousness. As students of the nervous system probed the mechanisms "thought" to underlie consciousness, they were as unable to explain consciousness as the philosophers who preceded them had been.

Toward the middle of the twentieth century, the behaviorists, under the tutelage of John Watson, solved the problem of consciousness by ignoring it. In an effort to demonstrate their kinship to "hard" scientists, they emphasized only what was objective and measurable. This approach resulted in great success and led to the announcement by B. F. Skinner, at the time the leading proponent of behaviorism, that the concept of an "inner-self," an "autonomous man," is being abolished. In his controversial book, *Beyond Freedom and Dignity*,[5] Skinner says the picture which

3. William James, *The Principles of Psychology* (1890), 1, 1–8 (New York: Dover, 1950).
4. Ibid., p. 1–2.
5. B. F. Skinner, *Beyond Freedom and Dignity* (New York: Bantam/Vintage, 1971), Chapter 9.

emerges from a scientific analysis of man has consciousness reduced to a repertoire of behavior.[6]

Long before Skinner proclaimed the death of "dualism" and buried the cherished concepts of freedom and dignity beneath reams of data on reinforcement contingencies, the materialists in the field, with their tendency to account for everything on physical grounds, had been countered by men like Carl Gustav Jung who, in *Modern Man in Search of a Soul*,[7] argued persuasively for keeping the "psyche" in psychology. Other influential works, some from outside the field, helped to keep the controversy burning. A distinguished paleontologist, Pierre Teilhard de Chardin, in *The Phenomenon of Man*,[8] traced the story of life as a movement of consciousness veiled by morphology. He defined consciousness as every form of "interior perception" imaginable from the most rudimentary, in Archeozoic slime, to the human phenomenon of self-reflection. He used the word "consciousness" interchangeably with expressions such as "soul," "spirit," and "mind," all of which were seen as aspects of the "noosphere" moving inexorably toward the "super-consciousness" of its "omega point."

Teilhard de Chardin's teleological masterpiece was more theistic than scientific in its orientation and conclusions. Like most other books on consciousness, recently emerging from all quarters of the literary landscape, it is dismissed by the adherents of behaviorism because it harbors the enemy of inadequately defined terms.[9] Robert Ornstein, in his

---

6. The explanatory power of the behaviorists' stimulus-response model was brought into question with the publication of *Plans and the Structure of Behavior* (New York: Henry Holt and Company, 1960). The authors, George Miller, Eugene Galanter, and Karl Pribram, who had all been in the behaviorist camp, where consciousness is either ignored or denied, initiated what has come to be known as the "cognitive revolution" by suggesting that purposive behavior is guided by a plan. Their work is considered one of the most important recent breakthroughs in the understanding of behavior.
7. Carl Gustav Jung, *Modern Man in Search of a Soul* (New York: Harcourt, Brace & World Inc., 1933).
8. Pierre Teilhard de Chardin, *The Phenomenon of Man* (New York: Harper & Row Publishers, 1959).
9. In their recent book, *The Self and its Brain* (New York: Springer International, 1977), Sir Karl Popper and Sir John Eccles argue that the self-conscious mind is an independent entity, and that the unity of conscious experience comes not from neurological synthesis but from the integrating character of the self-conscious mind. In their rejection of materialism, the authors revive the ancient mind-body conundrum, and in their dictum against reductionism there is a ring of nostalgia for the human soul. However, in their method of arguing for dualism, or "psychophysical interactionism," these eminent scholars do not attempt to define terms, for they believe every definition must make essential use of undefined terms and that meaning should not be allowed to dominate discussion as it so often does in contemporary philosophical writing. In their preface, the authors state that what they "are interested in is not the meaning of terms but the truth of theories; and this truth," they say, "is largely independent of the terminology used."

popular book, *The Psychology of Consciousness*,[10] has candidly noted that many of his readers may end up unsure and a bit confused about what consciousness is. The question, he says, is usually ruled out from scientific inquiry for it does not seem to be fully answerable in reasonable terms. It is like asking "What is God?" or "What is life?"

If one feels that the behaviorists, by refusing to consider what they have termed "mentalisms," have narrowed the range of their questions to the trivial and pinholed the perspectives from which legitimate problems can be approached;[11] if one feels that somewhere there must be a more satisfying answer to the age-old question, "What is consciousness?", then perhaps a more radical approach to the problem is required — an approach that will at least provide a testable guess to stand on.

Gardner Murphy once observed that what psychology needed was more "outrageous" hypotheses. Julian Jaynes, in a breakthrough of bold conjectures, has provided just such an outrageous hypothesis. In fact, Jaynes's extraordinary thesis is much more than a hypothesis, for as he develops his ideas the reader begins to sense a theory of monumental dimensions unfolding. It is a theory that could alter our view of consciousness, revise our conception of the history of mankind, and lay bare the human dilemma in all its existential wonder.

Unaccompanied by Jaynes's arguments and evidence, a brief explanation of his thesis is inadequate. However, bearing the dangers of oversimplification in mind, we can say that Jaynes believes consciousness to be a relatively recent linguistic development which, in the Western world, made its appearance on the stage of history around 1000 B.C. Prior to that time, he contends, man's activities were largely dictated by auditory hallucinations which originated in the right hemisphere of the brain and were acted on by the left hemisphere; hence the term "bicameral" (as in two legislative chambers). Jaynes argues that the hallucinations of the right hemisphere, interpreted by the ancients as "voices of the gods," occurred in situations of decision-making stress and, like the instincts which guided us in the green forest of our past, they directed and

---

10. Robert E. Ornstein, *The Psychology of Consciousness* (San Francisco: W.H. Freeman & Co., 1972).
11. Thomas S. Kuhn, in *The Structure of Scientific Revolutions* (Chicago: University of Chicago Press, 1962), notes that in "normal science" phenomena that do not fit into the paradigm are often not seen at all (p. 24). The paradigm is a criterion for choosing the questions that will be asked, the problems that will be admitted, and those which will be rejected (p. 37).

reinforced responses that provided stability and enhanced the chances of success for nature's new experiment with symbol-making creatures.[12]

As Jaynes meticulously develops each of his ideas and buttresses them with scholarly citations, he audaciously ventures into neurophysiology, anthropology, classical literature, psychopathology, ancient history, general semantics, art, and poetry. Stunned by these interdisciplinary incursions, some critics have accused him of sampling selectively, choosing only those bits of evidence that fit his theory. Though academics and specialists couched in the traditions of their long cultivated domains will not be easily persuaded by Jaynes's revolutionary views, his compelling arguments and impressive documentation raise new questions that will undoubtedly stir up dust in many fields. As well as being a maverick thinker, Jaynes has a genius for exposition. The clarity of his writing is never dimmed by its scholarly strictures. The book opens with lyrical prose, is laced throughout with grace and wit, and words its way to a final crescendo in a concluding chapter that is brilliantly perceptive and deeply moving.

Who is Julian Jaynes? And what possible support can be found for his radical views? Jaynes is a lecturer in the history of psychology at Princeton. He studied philosophy and literature at Harvard and McGill and spent ten years as a research assistant at Yale. He never completed the formal requirements for the Ph.D.,[13] and is harshly critical of doctoral programs in which students are indoctrinated into the prejudices of their professors and given degrees for unoriginal research. The reason for his criticism may stem from the fact that he was once part of one of the major schools of behaviorism, where his interest in questions regarding the nature and origin of consciousness was not considered legitimate, and where he found text after text that attempted to hide such unwanted

---

12. For Jaynes's views regarding the evolution of language prior to the development of consciousness, see Julian Jaynes, "The Evolution of Language in the Late Pleistocene," *Annals of the New York Academy of Science*, 1976, Vol. 280, pp. 312–325; reprinted in Marcel Kuijsten (ed.), *The Julian Jaynes Collection* (Henderson, NV: Julian Jaynes Society, 2012).

13. Jaynes was ultimately awarded his doctoral degree from Yale in the spring of 1977 after friends urged Yale to grant it and other friends urged Jaynes to accept it. See William Woodward and June Tower, "Julian Jaynes: Introducing His Life and Thought," in Marcel Kuijsten (ed.), *Reflections on the Dawn of Consciousness: Julian Jaynes's Bicameral Mind Theory Revisited* (Henderson, NV: Julian Jaynes Society, 2006). — *Ed.*

problems from the student's view. Undaunted by his training, he has continued to seek answers to questions regarding

> this world of unseen visions and heard silences, this unsubstantial country of the mind ... A whole kingdom where each of us reigns reclusively alone ... A hidden hermitage ... An introcosm ... This consciousness that is myself of selves, that is everything, and yet nothing at all — what is it? And where did it come from? And why?[14]

Unlike most other authors dealing with consciousness, Jaynes does not take this concept for granted. In an early chapter of his book he adroitly exposes what he considers to be the inadequacies of traditional concepts of consciousness and provides his readers with a detailed and comprehensive definition of his own.

There is nothing in consciousness that is not an analog of something that was in behavior first, said John Locke in one of his essays.[15] Jaynes agrees. He contends that consciousness is the creation of an "analog world" that parallels the behavioral world, even as the world of mathematics parallels the world of quantities of things. It is a metaphor-generated model of the world in which events are narrated within a dimension of "mind-space." It is the invention of an analog 'I' and analog 'others' interacting in this analog world of the mind. For Jaynes, consciousness is not an emergent property of brain function yet to be identified by neuroscientists. It is instead a product of language development, an artifact of man's symbolic universe.

Ignoring Jaynes's definition of consciousness, some critics have attempted to discredit his theory by noting that recent experiments indicate chimpanzees can recognize their own images, and that reflecting surfaces, evidently used as mirrors, have been found among the artifacts of civilizations that Jaynes placed in his "unconscious" bicameral era.[16] However, by Jaynes's definition, consciousness is more than recognition and reaction to stimuli such as one's own reflection in a mirror. He even presents convincing arguments to show that consciousness is not

---

14. Jaynes, *Origin of Consciousness*, p. 1.
15. John Locke, *An Essay Concerning the Understanding, Knowledge, Opinion and Assent* (Draft B), B. Rand, ed. (Cambridge: Harvard University Press, 1951), II, pp. i–23.
16. Marcel Kinsbourne, "Bicameral Man and the Narcissan Conspiracy," *Contemporary Psychology*, 1977, 22, 11, pp. 801–802.

necessary for such activities as learning, thinking, and problem-solving, all of which occur to varying degrees in nonhuman species of animals. He also points out that we live out a good part of our daily lives by habit, perceiving and performing automatically, like bicameral man, with little need for reflective consciousness.

But Jaynes's special and restricted definition of the term "consciousness" is often confusing. In everyday usage, lack of consciousness usually implies a total absence of mental function as opposed to a lack of self-reflectivity. We have to keep reminding ourselves that he is not equating consciousness with the waking brain.[17] A different title would have helped: *The Origin of Subjectivity* ... or perhaps *The Origin of Introspection* ... However, such titles would not have helped Jaynes make his point — a point of both agreement and difference with the behaviorist view that consciousness is nonexistent. The behaviorists have spent half a century running countless numbers of rats through countless miles of mazes; when they say "consciousness does not exist," Jaynes gives them their due — for rats and other animals. But what Jaynes objects to is what Arthur Koestler calls the "ratomorphic" view of *man*.[18] For Jaynes, the human species is different. Man is unique. For him consciousness *does* exist. It is the very real heritage of a long history of language development. Hence the title of Jaynes's book.

If Jaynes is the first to suggest that consciousness is the symbol-based ability for subjectivity, he is certainly not the first to note the recency of man's capacity for self-reflection. The philosopher Ernst Cassirer states that the concept of "being" appears to belong to a relatively late period

---

17. I am grateful to Dr. George Weller, a psychologist at New York's Montefiore Hospital, for pointing out the possibility of a neurological basis for self recognition that is not linguistic. There are certain cases of brain damage (anosognosia) where the patient has lost use of limbs and is unable to recognize his dysfunctioning member as part of his own body. Even individuals who are blind may lack awareness of their loss of sight.

18. Arthur Koestler, *The Ghost in the Machine* (London: Hutchinson, 1967), pp. 15–18. At the same time, the attribution of consciousness to animals has been called an anthropomorphic fallacy. The debate over the issue of animal consciousness was recently revived with Donald R. Griffin's *The Question of Animal Awareness: Evolutionary Continuity of Mental Experiences* (New York: Rockefeller University Press, 1976). Griffin believes communication is the key to consciousness, and notes that many species of animals, from the honeybee to the chimpanzee, communicate in much finer grain messages than we give them credit for. According to Griffin, animals are conscious, and the difference between human awareness and animal awareness is quantitative, not qualitative. [For Jaynes's thoughts on both Griffin's research and the topic of consciousness in animals, see "In A Manner of Speaking: Commentary on Cognition and Consciousness in Non-Human Species" in Kuijsten (ed.), *The Julian Jaynes Collection. — Ed.*]

of language development and that the denotation of the 'I' in the course of language-making had to be derived slowly and stepwise from concrete, purely sensory beginnings.[19] Cassirer says that the chasm between specific perceptions and general concepts is so great that it could have been bridged only by language itself preparing and inducing the process without man's conscious awareness.[20] Like Cassirer, Jaynes emphasizes the role of language as an organ of perception in the gradual increase of man's capacity for self reflection. He believes consciousness is dependent on the ability to create metaphor. By metaphor he means the use of a word for one thing to describe another, because of some similarity that seems to exist between them or their relationships. The verb *to be*, he tells us, was generated by such a metaphor. It evolved from the Sanskrit *bhu*, "to grow." "Abstract words," he says, "are ancient coins whose concrete images in the busy give-and-take of talk have worn away with use."[21]

Susanne Langer notes in her discussion of language that all abstract words are probably "faded metaphors," and before the process of "fading" occurred, language could not render a situation without a demonstrative indication of it in present experience.[22] What Jaynes seems to be saying is that bicameral man, in his primitive stage of language development, did not have adequate symbolic referents to translate impinging sense data into subjective consciousness. Shackled by this dependence on the concrete, our bicameral forebears had yet to discover or consciously exploit the double level of metaphor. In the magic of make-believe, myth and reality were inextricably fused and would not emerge as distinctive features of mind in the Western world until the birth of philosophy, which interestingly enough occurred in the middle of the first millennium B.C. — well after the time Jaynes sets for the beginning of the breakdown of the bicameral mind.

Bicameral man, according to Jaynes, in addition to lacking a subjective consciousness, had a unique split in mental function similar to that exhibited by schizophrenics today. In his description of schizophrenia and the auditory hallucinations that characterize this disorder, Jaynes notes that patients' descriptions of their "voices," which often utter

---

19. Ernst Cassirer, *Language and Myth* (New York: Dover Publications Inc., 1946) pp. 74–76.
20. Ibid., p. 16.
21. Jaynes, *Origin of Consciousness*, p. 51.
22. Susanne K. Langer, *Philosophy in a New Key* (Cambridge: Harvard University Press, 1942), p. 140.

authoritative commands, are similar to the descriptions of the "voices of the gods" that directed the activities in Homer's *Iliad*. Could it be, Jaynes asks, that the frequent references to "the voices of gods" that continually recur in the *Iliad* and other ancient writings were not, as is commonly thought, simply a poetic device used to enhance the narrative drama (a technique which, he notes, is out of keeping with the literal texture of these narratives)? Could it be that men of those times, like schizophrenics today, actually hallucinated the "divine voices" that directed their activities? Jaynes thinks they did.

The area of the brain he suggests is responsible for these auditory hallucinations is an area in the right hemisphere that corresponds to Wernicke's speech area in the left. Since its function is not known, it has been referred to as a "silent area." Jaynes notes that most important sensory and motor functions are represented in both cerebral hemispheres. Speech, however, is limited in most of us to the left hemisphere of the brain. Jaynes contends that in bicameral man this served to free the right hemisphere for the activities of storing up admonitory experiences, processing information unconsciously, and then transmitting directives to the left hemisphere in the form of auditory hallucinations which the ancients perceived as "voices of the gods." As evidence, he cites the experiments of Wilder Penfield, a noted brain surgeon, who found that when he electrically stimulated this "silent area" during brain operations, his patients often had the sensation of hearing voices.[23]

Jaynes argues that bicameral man had a poorly developed sense of linear time and was incapable of reflecting on his past or contemplating his future. He supports this by noting the absence of any evidence for self-reflection and inner-direction in ancient theocratic societies. He believes that the activities of bicameral man were governed mostly by habit and that when novel situations occurred, for which habit would not suffice, auditory hallucinations provided direction. These hallucinations were probably initiated by decision-making stress, and their content reflected an unconscious processing of information that emerged in the remembered voices of deceased parents, tribal leaders, or kings. The effectiveness

---

23. For an overview of Penfield's work, see Russell Freedman and James E. Morriss, *The Brains of Animals and Man* (New York: Holiday House, Inc., 1972), pp. 52–54, 114–116.

of the hallucinated words in governing bicameral activities resulted from their being perceived as commands of "gods."

Jaynes's attraction to this explanation may have been enhanced by his once having had an auditory hallucination (an experience described in his book). He cites studies which have shown that such hallucinations are not uncommon among normal people. Like Jaynes, a surprising number of non-psychotic individuals in the populations studied recalled having had one or more auditory hallucinations. In most cases, the voices were perceived as originating from an external location and were convincingly real. Recently, a friend whose daughter had just died of leukemia told me that his teenage son was troubled because he "still heard his sister talking to him."[24] Jaynes argues that such hallucinations were common in the early history of civilization and that they provided the very roots of religious thought.

According to historians of antiquity, religion seems to have had its origin in the worship of the dead and the belief that the dead had become "gods" who continued to take part in human affairs.[25] If men of ancient times lacked the linguistic tools for memory and reflection, it seems unlikely that such practices as the veneration of ancestors would ever have originated without some powerful and tangible reminder of the deceased. Auditory hallucinations would certainly have provided such reminders.

Auditory hallucinations could also have influenced the ancients as they fashioned their stories of creation. Cassirer notes that in all mythical cosmogonies as far back as they can be traced, the "word" is a primary force in which all being and doing originate. In almost all great religions the "word" is venerated as the instrument of creation and "gods" were said to convey their commands in the spoken word.[26] "In the beginning was the Word, and the Word was with God, and the Word was God," writes Saint John of the Gospels.[27] What, asks Cassirer, gives the "word" this extraordinary religious character? The interlocking relationship between

---

24. Erich Lindemann, in his study of acute grief, has noted the tendency for hallucinatory experiences among surviving family members of the deceased. See Lindemann's "Symptomatology and Management of Acute Grief," *American Journal of Psychiatry*, 1944, 101, pp. 141–148.
25. Numa Denis Fustel de Coulanges, *The Ancient City* (New York: Doubleday/Anchor Books), translation by W. Small, 1873, Ch. 1.
26. Cassirer, *Language and Myth*, pp. 44–62.
27. The Gospel According to Saint John, Chapter 1, verse 1 (King James Version).

language and religion cannot be due to mere chance.[28] Certainly Jaynes's hypothesis provides a plausible explanation.

Though the idea of a society of unconscious men dependent on habit and auditory hallucinations for direction is conceivable, one would suspect that if bicameral man ever existed, he could be found today. Certainly people representative of various stages of man's history, from as far back as the Stone Age, have been identified and studied by anthropologists. Have no bicameral cultures been discovered? It is possible that when researchers begin to collect new kinds of data or look at old data in a new way, they may find tribes or societies that fit quite well within the Jaynesian concept of bicamerality.[29] If not, perhaps it can be demonstrated that language-based consciousness developed throughout the world at a much more rapid rate than technological achievement.

The breakdown of the bicameral mind, Jaynes tells us, occurred when it no longer enhanced the group's survival potential. He suggests this happened rather suddenly, in the Mediterranean area, sometime after 1400 B.C.[30] At that time, Western civilizations were thrown into turmoil by the devastations resulting from a series of widespread geological upheavals that produced volcanic outbursts and a sinking of Mediterranean land masses. The survivors of tidal waves and poisonous vapors from eruptions, such as occurred on the Minoan island of Thera, were suddenly refugees. As neighbor invaded neighbor there was anarchy and chaos and the "voices" of familiar "gods" were of little assistance in the social disruptions that occurred in these centuries. It was during this time, says Jaynes, that self-conscious actions and reflective judgment attained a new survival value. The future of the race was now in the hands of those who were able to think for themselves, a new man with cunning and the ability to employ deceit in treacherous situations unfamiliar to the more stable bicameral societies.

---

28. Cassirer, *Language and Myth*, p. 55.
29. Descriptions of preliterate societies often indicate vestiges of bicamerality. See Marcel Kuijsten, "Introduction," in Kuijsten (ed.), *The Julian Jaynes Collection.* — *Ed.*
30. Jaynes believes the advance to consciousness occurred quite late in some cultures outside of this area. He suggests that the Incas may have been a bicameral society at the time of their conquest by Pizarro. He provides evidence for this by noting the conquistadors reported that the Devil himself spoke to the Incas out of the mouths of their statues. The great ease with which the empire was conquered, Jaynes says, was perhaps due to the superiority consciousness gave its plunderers.

Even before the geological disasters occurred, Jaynes notes, the auditory authority of the "gods" had already begun to be eroded by the pressures of increased population, trade, and the success of writing during the second millennium B.C. Edmund Carpenter and Marshall McLuhan have pointed out that the binding power of the acoustic word, which even today is so strong in many preliterate cultures that the eye is subservient to the ear, was annulled by the magic of writing.[31] Jaynes notes that when the commands of "gods" or the directives of kings were incised into clay tablets or stone, they could be dealt with by man's own efforts or ignored in a way that the ubiquitous auditory hallucinations could not.

McLuhan, commenting on *The Origin of Consciousness in the Breakdown of the Bicameral Mind*, accuses Jaynes of failing to give adequate emphasis not only to the role writing played in the transition to consciousness, but also to the fact that phonetic literacy fosters the sense of lineal or sequential space and time. The advent of literacy, McLuhan claims, created an environment that gave dominance to the logical and visual left hemisphere.[32] Though Jaynes does note the "tremendous importance" of writing in the breakdown of the bicameral voices, he does not fully develop the interrelationship between writing and consciousness, nor does he discuss the role of phonetic literacy in the development of a new dimension of space and time, though he sees this development as important in the origin of consciousness.

Support for the bicameral hypothesis, Jaynes tells us, comes from man's earliest recorded literature, with its absence of subjectivity and its depiction of action and external events. He devotes a whole chapter to the *Iliad*, which he views as an excellent example of bicameral mentality. An astonishingly different mentality is found in the *Odyssey*, which Jaynes believes was written several centuries later. The Odyssean theme of homeless wanderings and enslavements, where the "gods" are often superseded by human initiative and time acquires a new dimension, describes, according to Jaynes, the beginning of the bicameral breakdown. Odysseus seems to be the hero of a new consciousness, and the *Odyssey* can be read as the story of man's voyage to the self.

---

31. Edmund Carpenter and Marshall McLuhan, *Explorations in Communication* (Boston: Beacon Press, 1960), pp. 65, 69.
32. Marshall McLuhan, "Review of *The Origin of Consciousness in the Breakdown of the Bicameral Mind*," available from Centre for Culture and Technology, University of Toronto, Canada, pp. 1, 3.

Literature in other cultures reflects a similar transition. In China, subjectivity blossoms with the teachings of Confucius, and in India the change from bicamerality is reflected in the differences between early Vedic literature, which was said to be dictated by the "gods," and the later and more subjective Upanishads. However, Jaynes believes that no literature records the birth pangs of consciousness at such length or with such fullness as the Judeo-Christian scriptures. He notes that Hebrew history, as recorded in the Old Testament, moves from bicameral prophets who proclaimed "thus spake the Lord" to the self reflective contemplations found in books of later origin such as *Ecclesiastes*.

Jaynes finds evidence for bicamerality in early references to poetry in Greek literature, where the relationship between the poets and that special group of divinities known as the muses appears to be the same as the relationship between the oracles and the "gods" who were believed to speak through them. These trance oracles, who for centuries hallucinated their pronouncements for men of both high and low estate, appear to have been a bridge between individuals who could no longer hear the "voices" of their "gods" and the divine dictums they still desired. The wandering bards or poets also depended on trance hallucinations as they narrated past events in rhythmical metered verse. Their "inspired" stories were considered to be "divine speech" originating from the muses who were said to be the daughters of Mnemosyne, the female Titan whose name later became our word for memory. Even as late as Plato's time, poetry was referred to as "divine madness." Using a Jaynesian approach to view the mind's remarkable ability for unconscious processing of information, one might speculate that the insights and intuitions which underlie most creativity and discovery in both the arts and sciences are echoes of bicamerality, "divine dictums" no longer packaged in hallucinatory wrappings.[33]

---

33. Jaynes points out that "the picture of a scientist sitting down with his problems and using conscious induction and deduction is as mythical as a unicorn." Einstein's greatest ideas came to him quite suddenly. He once told a friend that he had to be careful as he shaved each morning lest he cut himself with surprise at a new discovery. Michael Polanyi, a well known philosopher of science and a professor of physical chemistry, has emphasized the importance of "personal knowledge," derived from unconscious processing of information. "All the efforts of the discoverer are but preparations for the main event of discovery, which eventually takes place," says Polanyi, "by a process of spontaneous mental reorganization uncontrolled by conscious effort." *Science, Faith and Society* (Chicago: University of Chicago Press, 1946), p. 34.

The bicameral paradigm seems to throw light on a number of anomalies that have never quite resolved themselves in scientific theory. Jaynes devotes whole sections of his book to what he considers to be contemporary vestiges of bicamerality, such as modern day "spiritualist mediums," automatic writing, glossolalia, schizophrenia, and hypnosis. In hypnosis, for example, the subject's uncritical and illogical obedience to the commands and expectations of the hypnotist is quite similar to the situation Jaynes claims to have existed between bicameral man and his "gods."

Jaynes marshals an impressive array of evidence to support the explanatory power of his bicameral paradigm for the whole contour of history as well. He tells us that the long trek from the oracles and prophets through centuries of superstitions and "isms," including the pilgrimage of science in its search for final answers, can all be viewed as attempts to regain the "divine" certainty which was lost when the "voices of the gods" fell silent and were supplanted by the privacy and aloneness of conscious introspection.

According to Jaynes, man is still undergoing his metamorphosis to self-awareness, and where the wings of consciousness will bear him is unsure. Unlike Teilhard de Chardin, Jaynes does not indulge in teleological speculations. He is content to trace the development of consciousness from the bicameral era to the present, where he abandons us at the growing edge of this great transition, to contemplate our destiny.

Some readers, seeking to confirm a more mystical concept of man, will undoubtedly be discomfited by the fact that Jaynes, in limiting consciousness to a symbolic internalization of behavioral repertoires, seems to be only a step away from Skinner; and others, who are in search of a "soul," will be disturbed by the theological implications of bicamerality. However, Jaynes's work, while failing to flatter our vanity, demands our attention, as it cannot be faulted for fuzzy concepts or vague speculation. His ideas are presented with clarity and backed up with evidence. Though some critics have suggested that his book be read as "science fiction," the hypotheses it sets forth are framed with a specificity that makes possible their confirmation or refutation.

Karl Popper, a leading philosopher of science, contends that the demarcation criterion that distinguishes science from non-science is "falsifiability."[34] If this is so, Jaynes's theory is eminently scientific, for it is deliberately and precisely structured with the falsifiability or testability of each hypothesis in mind. For example, if archeological evidence can be found that indicates subjectivity existed prior to 1000 B.C., or if neurological studies demonstrate that schizophrenic hallucinations do not originate in the right hemisphere,[35] then some of Jaynes's hypotheses will have to be revised.

Whatever the eventual outcome of investigations fostered by these bold conjectures, the heuristic nature of this outrageous theory will undoubtedly result in important new research. For this reason alone, Jaynes's linguistic theory of consciousness and the bicameral hypothesis can be considered significant contributions to man's age old quest for answers to one of the greatest riddles of cosmology.

---

34. Karl R. Popper, *Objective Knowledge* (Oxford: Clarendon Press, 1972), p. 1–31.
35. For a review of recent studies confirming Jaynes's neurological model, see Marcel Kuijsten, "Consciousness, Hallucinations, and the Bicameral Mind: Three Decades of New Research," in Kuijsten (ed.), *Reflections on the Dawn of Consciousness*. — Ed.

CHAPTER 3

Elephants in the Psychology Department: Overcoming Intellectual Barriers to Understanding Julian Jaynes's Theory

BRIAN J. MCVEIGH

A Herd of Elephants: Ignoring Anomalous Behavior

EW WANT TO CONFRONT THE PINK ELEPHANTS that crowd the classrooms, offices, and laboratories of psychology departments. Too many careers might be trampled on if the herd — i.e., hallucinations, spiritualist mediums, automatic writing, and poetic and religious frenzy — is directly met head-on. Better to account for those roaming elephants by attributing them to a few loose neurological wires within the individual's brain.

Consider the divine visitations accompanied by thundering voices heard by holy men, priests, and ordinary people in times past. Some of these were certainly literary inventions. However, given their ubiquity in the ancient world and mountain-moving historical impact, others were undoubtedly hallucinations. From the Old Testament to the Avesta (the ancient scriptures of Zoroastrianism), ancient religious texts are replete with divine voices commanding prophets. That the mind would be so organized as to allow something as astonishing as "hearing voices" is a wondrous fact apparently lost on not a few researchers. This is the point: one or two loose wires cannot explain all those pink elephants anymore than dinosaur fossils can be explained away as merely being oddly-shaped stones.

But wait; there is more. Hallucinations are only one elephant. An entire family of anomalous psychological behavior — hypnotic trancing, glossolalia, and spirit possession during which the self dramatically fragments — has more or less been ignored. Though many have *described* these disconcerting phenomena, they have yet to *explain* and *incorporate* them into mainstream psychology in a robust theoretical manner. In *The Origin of Consciousness in the Breakdown of the Bicameral Mind*, Julian Jaynes boldly did explain from where this strange family of eccentric psychological behavior comes. He argued that a two chambered mentality (thus, "bicameral"), in which the right side of the brain "spoke" through the voices of gods or deceased ancestors to the brain's left side, accounted for auditory hallucinations.[1] This psycho-hierarchy of god and individual, burdened by increasing complexity, eventually broke down, replaced by a unicameral mentality — what Jaynes called consciousness — of an inner conscience and other cognitive tools for handling social complexity. The gods departed and retreated to the heavens, leaving between them and us layers of lesser deities, angels, devils, demons, and ghosts. The harassing and persecuting voices suffered by modern-day schizophrenics or the visions of more recent prophets (e.g., Joseph Smith and the Book of Mormon) are vestiges of bicamerality. For most of us, with the lines of divine communication cut, unforgiving history has rolled the gods and the individual into one person (though for many of us the attributes of divinity have become personified as a distant monotheistic super-being). Conscience is waiting for a heavenly voice to tell us what to do and then realizing we are that voice.

Intellectual Barriers To Understanding Jaynes's Theory

Jaynes's arguments are disquieting and controversial, though very few accounts in psychology have explained so much with such startling scientific conciseness. His conclusions may ultimately be proven incorrect, partially correct, or entirely correct. However, before we can even begin to assess his assertions, we must reach a clear consensus on what Jaynes was attempting to accomplish in his work. However, in order to do this, we must navigate our way through a maze of misguided assumptions,

---

1. Less commonly, hallucinations were also visual.

mistaken suppositions, and misleading habits of thought that we commonly employ to discuss psyche. I have noticed that when discussing the ideas of Jaynes, one must carefully walk through a labyrinth of misconceptions built up by the disciplinary premises of academic fields which typically have their own language. Therefore, it behooves us to carefully pay attention to the universe of meanings each idiom generates, since stubborn ideas are often embedded in confusing terminology. In addition, recognizing the power of words is crucial, since they implicitly shape our everyday thinking.

I have introduced this chapter with one intellectual barrier, i.e., the failure to theoretically incorporate anomalous behavior, such as audiovisual hallucinations, hypnosis, and spirit possession, into mainstream psychology. After defining the nature of consciousness, I explore six other intellectual barriers that stand in the way of assessing Jaynes's contribution to psychology:

(1) the word *consciousness* itself, which is too vague and polysemantic to be of any use;

(2) the mistake of equating consciousness with perception;

(3) confusing consciousness with reasoning;

(4) the failure to recognize that consciousness, not the *unconscious*, is the problem to be explored;

(5) the under-appreciated extraordinariness of consciousness as a phenomenon in human history; and

(6) ignoring history as a source of evidence for appreciating our psychic diversity and psychic plasticity.[2]

The Nature of Consciousness

What exactly is consciousness? It is an

analog of what is called the real world. It is built up with a vocabulary or lexical field whose terms are all metaphors or analogs of behavior in the physical world. Its reality is of the same order as mathematics. It allows us to shortcut behavioral processes and arrive at more adequate decisions. Like mathematics, it is an operator rather than a

---

2. One can surely think of other barriers, such as the difficulty, for practical academic reasons known to academics, of carrying out interdisciplinary research.

thing or repository. And it is intimately bound up with volition and decision.[3]

Consciousness is shorthand for an array of cognitive functions designed by society to deal with the culmination of political economic pressures set in motion by the agricultural revolution (from about 10,000 B.C.E.). According to Jaynes, consciousness had emerged by the latter half of the second millennium B.C.E. A tool kit of mental devices for coping with social complexity, it is a consequence of *cultural development*, not biological evolution. Consciousness can be dissected into seven different components:[4]

(1) *The spatialization of psyche*: imputing an imaginary space or "introcosm" within the individual.

(2) *Privileging individual traits*: highlighting individuation and personal uniqueness.

(3) *Autonomy*: assigning intentionality and responsibility to the "inner person."

(4) *Self-reflexivity*: the relation between an analog 'I' and a metaphor 'me'.

(5) *Narratization*: constructing a linear temporality with the self as the main actor.

(6) *Excerption*: the extraction "from the collection of possible attentions to a thing which comprises our knowledge of it."[5]

(7) *Conciliation*: the process by which "a slightly ambiguous perceived object is made to conform to some previously learned schema, an automatic process sometimes called assimilation."[6]

---

3. Julian Jaynes, *The Origin of Consciousness in the Breakdown of the Bicameral Mind* (Boston: Houghton Mifflin, 1976) p. 55.

4. This list is not meant to be exhaustive. Note that what is enumerated here is an elaboration of Jaynes's list of features (Ibid., pp. 64–65).

5. "Actually we are never conscious of things in their true nature, only of the excerpts we make of them." This feature of interiority is "distinct from memory. An excerpt of a thing is in consciousness the representative of the thing or event to which memories adhere, and by which we can retrieve memories." Reminiscence "is a succession of excerptions" (Ibid., pp. 61–62). Consciousness, then, "is not a superior unit that directs messages down to its subordinates in the brain." Rather, consciousness is "the instance of selection that picks and chooses among the many options nonconsciousness offers up" (Tor Nørretranders, *The User Illusion* [New York: Penguin Books, 1998], p. 243).

6. Consilience (or "conciliation," "compatibilization") "is essentially doing in mind-space what narratization does in our mind-time or spatialized time. It brings things together as conscious objects just as narratization brings things together as a story" (Jaynes, *Origin of Consciousness*, pp. 64–65).

The Tyranny of Words: The Mystification of "Consciousness"

The first barrier concerns the very word *consciousness* itself. In the English language consciousness has five very different meanings: (1) the physiological state of not sleeping; (2) the physiological state of not being in a coma; (3) the mutual self-awareness of a group (e.g., national consciousness, class consciousness); (4) a vague usage to describe cognition, perception, and awareness; and finally, (5) what one's inner self introspects upon. This last meaning designates what Jaynes meant by consciousness.

Years ago Prof. Jaynes himself acknowledged to me that the vagueness and polysemantics of "consciousness" were inconveniently misleading. After considering this troublesome and ambiguous word for many years I have, perhaps rather presumptuously, decided to use the term "interiority" in place of consciousness.[7] Interiority (or "conscious interiority") denotes an imaginary place or the belief in a "mental space" that exists "in" the "head," in which a "self" moves about and psychological events and processes transpire. Interiority is not biologically innate (nature); rather, it is culturally constructed (nurture). Hopefully the use of interiority will inject conceptual clarity into the discussion.

The Mind's Eye Is Not The Real Eye: Mistakenly Equating Conscious Interiority With Perception

The most common and misleading understanding of what constitutes interiorized experience is that it is perception, or that introspection is some type of mental mirror that "copies" what we perceive. Equating conscious interiority with perception, as if interiority merely mirrored bodily sensations, is the second barrier. The perception theory of conscious interiority is the most obstinate, commonly-held, and entrenched view of the nature of interiority. It is important to argue not that this theory is sort of wrong. Rather, the perception theory is wrong in the most fundamental sense. The belief that interiority is perceptual experience is so commonsensical, but the confusion of vision with introspection ("introception") has distorted the philosophy of mind for centuries.

---

7. Since "consciousness" is regularly used by other authors, I cannot replace it with interiority in all places. Therefore, I advise the reader to mentally substitute consciousness with interiority.

It is, however, very easy to demonstrate that the two are very different, as the following sections argue.

That interiority does not reflect the outside world is clear since what "you can consciously recall is a thimbleful to the huge oceans of your actual knowledge."[8] Our introspection only "reflects" a very limited portion of our perceptual, bodily experiences. Moreover, people are "not conscious of very much of what they sense; people are not conscious of very much of what they think; people are not conscious of very much of what they do." Human consciousness, then, "is a closed, partly mendacious system, which claims that what we experience is what we sense."[9]

Reactivity. The very language we use to describe psycho-physiological processes requires an overhaul. Let us avoid confusion by labeling non-conscious cognition "reactivity" (rather than the confusing "perception"). Reactivity includes "all stimuli my behavior takes into account of in any way, while consciousness is something quite distinct and a far less ubiquitous phenomenon. We are conscious of what we are reacting to only from time to time."[10] Remarkably, an "astonishing number of textbooks in physiology and neuropsychology fail to mention this."[11] But the fact is that "much of everyday life — thinking, feeling, and doing — is automatic in that it is driven by current features of the environment (i.e., people, objects, behaviors of others, settings, roles, norms, etc.) as mediated by automatic cognitive processing of those features, without any mediation by conscious choice or reflection."[12] Note that over eleven million bits of information per second move from the world to our sensory mechanisms. However, the physiologist Dietrich Trincker reports that "only one millionth of what our eyes see, our ears hear, and our other senses inform us about appears in our consciousness."[13] The task of psyche is to

---

8. Jaynes, *Origin of Consciousness*, p. 28.

9. Nørretranders, *User Illusion*, pp. 259, 209.

10. Jaynes, *Origin of Consciousness*, p. 22.

11. Nørretranders, *User Illusion*, p. 124.

12. John A. Bargh, "The Automaticity of Everyday Life," in Robert S. Wyer, Jr., (ed.), *The Automaticity of Everyday Life* (Mahwah, NJ: Lawrence Erlbaum Associates, 1997), pp. 1–62.

13. Dietrich Trincker, "Aufnahme, Speicherung und Verarbeitung von Information durch den Menschen," *Veröffentlichungen der Schleswig-holsteinischen Universitätsgesellschaft, Neue Folge*, 44 (Kiel: Verlag Ferdinand Hirt, 1966), emphasis in original; cited in Nørretranders, *User Illusion*, p. 126.

"reduce eleven million bits to sixteen bits so that the sixteen bits can be used as a map of the eleven million."[14]

According to Professor Manfred Zimmerman of Heidelberg University, what we perceive at any moment is "limited to an extremely small compartment in the stream of information about our surroundings flowing in from the sense organs." Research has demonstrated that "the maximal information flow of the process of conscious sensory perception is about 40 bits … many orders of magnitude below that taken in by receptors. Our perception, then, would appear to be limited to a minute part of the abundance of information available as sensory input."[15] Remarkably, though Professor Zimmerman's conclusion has been repeated since the late 1950s in the literature on medicine, psychology, and information theory, it has not made "a mark either on physiology and neuropsychology or on our culture as whole."[16]

An example of reactivity is proprioception, or the largely nonconscious sense of where one's body parts are in space (its impairment is related to the loss of "body-sense" and "body-ego"). An understanding of reactivity allows us to see through the illusions of conscious interiority. "We experience sensation but do not experience that this sensation has been interpreted and processed."[17] The processing is the task of nonconsciousness. People "experience far more than" what they consciously register; "they interact far more with the world and with each other than their consciousness thinks they do," and the "control of actions that consciousness feels it exercises is an illusion."[18] "Few hypotheses in the behavioral sciences have occasioned so much controversy as the suggestion that people may be affected by external stimuli of which they remain wholly unaware."[19] Why? Because we are socialized to believe that we are autonomous, independent, and self-directed. The self is sovereign.

---

14. Nørretranders, *User Illusion*, p. 242.
15. Manfred Zimmerman, "Neurophysiology of Sensory Systems," in Robert F. Schmidt (ed.), *Fundamentals of Sensory Physiology* (Berlin: Springer-Verlag, 1986), pp. 68–116; cited in Nørretranders, *User Illusion*, p. 124.
16. Nørretranders, *User Illusion*, p. 125.
17. Ibid., p. 288.
18. Ibid., p. iv.
19. Norman F. Dixon, *Subliminal Perception: The Nature of a Controversy* (London: McGraw Hill, 1971), p. 5.

The Idol of Homo Rationalis: Confusing Interiority With Rationality[20]

That we are beings blessed with "reason" is associated with the stored-up intellectual riches of Western civilization. The crowning feature of the human condition, it is what allows us to comprehend, reflect, and analyze. This ability to form and traffic in abstract concepts is what distinguishes us from animals. Opposed to passion and feelings that cloud our judgments, reason defines our very humanity. In the Middle Ages it was regarded as a divine gift. Reason is actually closely linked to discussions about language, rationality, logic,[21] and truth, and has in no small measure defined the parameters of Western philosophical debate. It is also tightly associated with interiority, here understood as an operating room of the mind in which a cold logic is used to dissect superstition, myths, and misunderstanding with precision and god-like clarity.

Reason, it seems, is burdened with many crucial responsibilities, such as illuminating our thinking, guiding scientific progress, and upholding civilization. Therefore, it is easy to understand why some, if they equate reasoning with conscious interiority, might be discomfited by the suggestion that conscious interiority is not necessary for complex thought processes. To suggest as much seems to deny what makes us inherently human (i.e., reasoning faculties). The point, however, is that reasoning is not the same as conscious interiority. Indeed, reasoning routinely occurs without conscious interiority. Unfortunately, the notion of humans as imbued with reason erects a barrier to conceptualizing cognition as possible without conscious thought. We assume that a primary purpose of the mind is to reveal to itself its inner workings. This is an illusion.

Confusing Interiority With Cognition: The Role of The Nonconscious

The fourth barrier concerns our assumption that cognition is mainly conscious. However, the mystery is not why the "unconscious" exists, but rather why does interiority exist. After all, experimentation has demonstrated that interiority is unnecessary for most forms of mentation.

---

20. I am grateful to Scott Greer for suggesting to me that our equating interiority with "rationality" prevents us from conceptualizing cognition as possible without conscious thought.
21. Logic is technically the formalization of the means by which reason operates.

Theoretical work on nonconscious cognition (conventionally called the "unconscious") began in the nineteenth century when two counter-intuitive and inconvenient facts became clear. First, interiority does not reflect experiences we have of the external world. "Your consciousness is not identical to what your senses perceive." Second, the 'I' of our subjective interiorized experience is not the initiator of our actions (our non-conscious psyche is). Phrased differently, we might say that the self of our interiority "portrays itself as the initiator, but it is not, as events have already started by the time consciousness occurs."[22]

Mental activity below the radar screen of experience has variously been called unconscious, subconscious, and preconscious, but I use "nonconscious" to avoid any unfortunate and unnecessary Freudian associations. Nonconscious cognition "is not repressed unconscious activity of the sort Freud uncovered, activity driven out of the 'sight' of consciousness, but just mental activity that is somehow beneath or beyond the ken of consciousness altogether."[23] Whatever it is called, the "parts of the mind that are out of awareness similarly remain engaged in work, spreading activation amongst themselves, and in some cases serving to support the edifice that's made it to consciousness."[24] Therefore, there

> is a great deal of information reduction in the nervous system. Most information flow in the brain is, by the way, unconscious. The soul is not 'richer' than the body; on the contrary, most of the processing in our central nervous system is not perceived. The unconscious (which was discovered and elucidated long before Freud) is the most ordinary process in the nervous system. We just look at the results, but we are able to direct the focus of attention.[25]

The failure to appreciate the difference between conscious interiority (a small product of cognition) and nonconsciousness (most of cognition) has generated much confusion. Unfortunately, because early researchers

22. Nørretranders, *User Illusion*, pp. 129, 242.
23. Daniel Dennett, "Consciousness," in Richard L. Gregory (ed.), *The Oxford Companion to the Mind* (Oxford: Oxford University Press, 1987), pp. 160–164.
24. Charles S. Carver, "Associations to Automaticity," in Robert S. Wyer, Jr. (ed.), *The Automaticity of Everyday Life* (Mahwah, NJ: Lawrence Erlbaum Associates, 1997), pp. 95–103.
25. H. H. Kornhuber, "The Human Brain: From Dream and Cognition to Fantasy, Will, Conscience, and Freedom," in Hans J. Markowitsch (ed.), *Information Processing by the Brain* (Toronto: Hans Huber Publishers, 1988), pp. 241–58.

"equated cognition with conscious cognition," we "have been cleaning up after this misconception ever since."[26] Some intellectual historical perspective is needed to illustrate how researchers, incapable of "seeing" mental activity while introspecting, were forced to look "behind" and "below" interiority for invisible mental processes.

Historical Perspective on Invisible Cognition. If the nonconscious became one of the great leitmotifs of the nineteenth century, the question is why it has not received more sustained attention throughout the centuries. The answer is that if people did not theorize about interiority (what is introspectable), then there was little need to consider what was not introspectable (despite its influence on behavior). We must ask why "the conception of unconscious mental processes was conceivable (in post-Cartesian Europe) around 1700, topical around 1800," and widespread by around 1900.[27]

We should note the etymology of the terms under discussion. In English *unconscious* first appeared in 1712, meaning "unaware, lacking conscious thought"; in 1860 the meaning of "temporarily insensible, knocked out," was added (the noun *unconscious* appeared in 1884). *Subconscious*, meaning "not wholly conscious," was first used in 1823. Its more familiar sense as a noun appeared in 1886 (though *subconsciousness* was used from 1874). *Preconscious* was used from 1860.

Something like the nonconscious has manifested its ghostly presence in the corners of the edifice of Western thought. A tradition of inquiry into what we might call nonconscious mental processes can arguably be traced back to St. Augustine, who wrote of "a vast and boundless subterranean shrine. Who has ever reached the bottom of it?" "Imagine the plains, caverns, and abysses of my memory; they are innumerable and are innumerably full of innumerable kinds of things."[28] Well over a millennium later the philosopher Gottfried Wilhelm Leibniz (1646–1716) wrote about "*petites perceptions,*" or countless imperceptible experiences, that though obscure and unconsciously registered, taken together constitute mind.

---

26. Bargh, *Automaticity of Everyday Life*, pp. 50–51.
27. Lancelot Law Whyte, *The Unconscious Before Freud* (New York: St. Martin's Press, 1978) p. 63.
28. St. Augustine in Rex Warner, *The Confessions of St. Augustine* (New York: Mentor, 1963), pp. 219, 227.

Much of the earlier research on nonconscious cognition was rooted
in physiological studies and questions about sensations in the nineteenth
century. Other insights came from methodological problems associated
with "introspectionism" and psychological self-examination. The philosopher Johann Friedrich Herbart (1876–1841) and the philosopher
and physicist Gustav Fechner (1801–1887) wrote about the "limen of
consciousness" and the physiologist and physicist Hermann von Helm-
holtz (1821–1894) noted what he called "unconscious inferences." In his
Mental Physiology (1874) William Benjamin Carpenter (1813–1885)
spoke of "unconscious cerebration." In 1911 the Danish philosopher
and psychologist Harald Høffding wrote that an "activity which would
otherwise take place with consciousness can, when consciousness is ab-
sorbed in something else simultaneously, occur below the threshold of
consciousness."[29]

The remarkably prolific philosopher Karl R. E. von Hartmann (1842–
1906) wrote the *Philosophy of the Unconscious* (1884). This pre-Freudian
work had an influence throughout Europe that has "sometimes been
underestimated."[30] But it was through Freud, who is mistakenly credited
with "discovering the subconscious," that the Western world has come to
know the unconscious as something framed within the psychoanalytic
paradigm. Somewhat later Charles Sanders Peirce and Joseph Jastrow
used the notion of "abduction," which "draws on unconscious powers" in
negotiating through everyday life (1884).[31] This notion resonates with
the recognition that most of what takes place mentally is not conscious.
Note should also be made of Bryan and Harter's work on the automati-
zation of telegraphic skills;[32] William James's thoughts on habit;[33] Leon
Solomons and Gertrude Stein on automatic writing,[34] and the "subconsciousness and attentive consciousness" of George Frederick Stout

29. Harald Høffding, *Psykologi* (Copenhagen: Gyldendal, 1911), p. 102; cited in Nørretranders, *User Illusion*, p. 157.
30. Whyte, *Unconscious Before Freud*, p. 163.
31. Charles Sanders Peirce and Joseph Jastrow, "On Small Differences of Sensation," *Memoirs of the National Academy of Sciences*, 1884, 3, pp. 73–83.
32. William Lowe Bryan and Nobel Harter, "Studies of the Telegraphic Language: The Acquisition of a Hierarchy of Habits," *Psychological Review*, 1899, 6, 345–75.
33. William James, *Principles of Psychology* (New York: Holt, 1890).
34. Leon M. Solomons and Gertrude Stein, "Normal Motor Automatism," *Psychological Review*, 1886, 3, pp. 492–512.

(1929).[35] The entire theoretical thrust of the Würzburg School — established by the philosopher and psychologist Oswald Külpe (1862–1917) — centered on "imageless thought," which may be interpreted as the recognition that much thinking is not introspectable. A member of the Würzburg School, the philosopher August Messer (1867–1937) who had psychological interests, believed consciousness was only the visible tip of the iceberg. Also relevant is work on the nonconscious aspects of hysteria, dissociative disorders, and other pathologies by the neurologist Jean-Martin Charcot (1825–1893), the neurologist Morton H. Prince (1854–1929), and the sadly overlooked and underestimated psychologist Pierre Janet (1859–1947).

Closer to our own times is Otakar Machotka's *The Unconscious in Social Relations* (1964);[36] the distinction that Perls, Hefferline and Goodman make between figure and ground;[37] Eugene Gendlin's discussion of fringe and focusing;[38] the distinction Shiffrin and Schneider make between automatic and controlled information processing;[39] E. E. Smith's notions of prestorage and computation;[40] Wilfrid Sellars' discussion of "Humean and Aristotelian" inferences;[41] and Ulric Neisser's ideas on nonpictorial imagery.[42]

I am not arguing that all the above researchers were and still are grappling with exactly the same problem. However, I am making the point that in some approximate way they were — as some still are — attempting to get a handle on the aware-versus-unaware enigma. What we should be attentive to is the fact that — whether dealing with memory, perception, imagery, or inference making — the research agendas of those cited above demonstrate enough family resemblances to the

35. George F. Stout, *A Manual of Psychology* (London: W. B. Clive, 1929).
36. Otakar Machotka, *The Unconscious in Social Relations* (New York: Philosophical Library, 1964).
37. Frederick S. Perls, Ralph F. Hefferline, and Paul Goodman. *Gestalt Therapy: Excitement and Growth in Human Personality* (Harmondsworth, Middlesex: Penguin Books, 1973).
38. Eugene T. Gendlin, *Experiencing and the Creation of Meaning: A Philosophical and Psychological Approach to the Subjective* (New York: Free Press of Glencoe, 1962).
39. Richard M. Shiffrin and Walter Schneider, "Controlled and Automatic Human Information Processing: II. Perceptual Learning, Automatic Attending, and a General Theory," *Psychological Review*, 1977, 84, pp. 127–190.
40. E. E. Smith, "Theories of Semantic Memory," in W. K. Estes (ed.), *Handbook of Learning and Cognitive Processes*, Vol. 6 (Hillsdale, NJ: Erlbaum Associates, 1978).
41. Wilfrid Sellars, *Science, Perception, and Reality* (London: Routledge and Kegan Paul, 1963).
42. Ulric Neisser, "Changing Conceptions of Imagery," in Peter W. Sheehan (ed.), *The Function and Nature of Imagery* (New York: Academic Press, 1972).

conscious-versus-cognition problem to suggest that, in their own ways, they were grappling with a very similar basic issue.

The rise of behaviorism in the early twentieth century severely damaged research into nonconscious cognition. The once dominating research agenda of behaviorism, as elucidated by the likes of John B. Watson (1878–1958) and B. F. Skinner (1904–1990), was to simply deny the existence of anything not directly visible and measurable. Thus conscious interiority was not, in their opinion, amenable to scientific scrutiny. Beginning in the late 1950s the "cognitive revolution" acknowledged invisible processes, thereby rectifying behaviorism's bizarre view of the human condition (however, due to behaviorism's influence, psychology has paid a heavy methodological price). This is why Nørretranders writes that cognitive science

> is not particularly concerned with the unconscious. It attempts to understand which logical rules and algorithms are needed in order to describe the human mind. It assumes that there are clear, logical rules, not incomprehensible quantities of unconscious calculation.[43]

Though the situation has been greatly rectified among some researchers, the average person still believes in the folk psychology of "my-mind's-eye-can-see-my-own-mental-activity" and "conscious-is-a-copy-of-perceptual-experience."

From Duality to a Tripartite. After an explicit recognition of interiority in the seventeenth century, it would take several centuries of mystified thinking until we realized that the introspectable space we call conscious interiority was not the mind in its entirety, but only a small chamber of a much larger edifice. Invisibility and a spatiality of depth characterize this grand structure, with its unknown palatial halls, concealed quarters, and hidden rooms connected by secret passages that lead to even deeper unexplored caverns. It is in these spaces that the sociopsychological foundations of the human condition stand. And yet strangely, despite all the evidence for nonconscious cognition,

---

43. Nørretranders, *User Illusion*, p. 164.

researchers have been made to jump through methodological hoops to establish nonconsciousness beyond any reasonable doubt. It might be a step forward for social psychology to adopt the same level of healthy skepticism for models that include a role for conscious mediation.[44]

The stubbornness of research psychology illustrates the sway of folk psychology over those who should know better. In any case, increasingly we

have come to accept without the slightest twinge of incomprehension a host of claims to the effect that sophisticated hypothesis-testing, memory searching inference — in short, information processing — occurs within us even though it is entirely inaccessible to introspection.[45]

In order to make the centrality of nonconscious mental processes more clear, I suggest that we discard Cartesian mind–body dualism, and replace it with a more fruitful triunity of: (1) conscious mind; (2) nonconscious mind; and (3) body. Concomitant with this, we should discard the dualistic spatial metaphor of inner and outer, and employ the visual trope of: (1) introspectable mental processes (interiority witnessed by the "mind's eye"); (2) invisible mental processes (nonconscious cognition); and (3) the visible world (body and environment). Recent work in cognitive science strongly bolsters the premise that most thinking is done nonconsciously, or invisible to the mind's eye. By recognizing a third element (invisible mental processes), an entire world of encyclopedic knowledge and complicated processes is acknowledged that accounts for the tremendous amount of labor going on within our minds. These invisible mental processes also account for the apparent automaticity, spontaneity, and unthinkingness of much of our actions. The delegation of habitualized, routine processes to the non-conscious

frees up processing capacity for the novel, creative work that only conscious processing can provide — the chess master who can look far ahead because the calculations that burden his or her opponent's attentional capacity are made for him or her nonconsciously, the tennis champion for whom the decisions as to where to run and which type of shot the opponent will attempt are made preconsciously,

44. Bargh, *Automaticity of Everyday Life*, pp. 4–5.
45. Dennett, "Consciousness," p. 162.

freeing him or her to surprise and perplex the opponent with a novel bit of strategy.[46]

A Failure In Astonishment: Appreciating The Ruptures of History

The fifth barrier, a lack of amazement at the very existence of interiority, is probably the most difficult to discuss. Why? The very act of acknowledging interiority rests on an intuition. Without putting too fine a point on it, you either appreciate it or you do not (or, you either notice the herd of pink elephants discussed above, or you do not). Too many of us assume interiority is a type of perceptual response to the environment, or consider it a vague thought process generated by brain activity that even our pets have to some degree. In other words, because many of us take interiority for granted, we do not realize its extraordinariness and singularity as a historical phenomenon.

Historians may not agree on all of the details concerning the great transformations and disruptions that mark the temporal trajectory of humankind, but they can at least point to a rough periodization and agree on some basic facts. For example, the agricultural revolution (from approximately 10,000 B.C.E.) would eventually lead to the origins of the earliest states and urban cultures. The "Axial Age" (from 800 to 200 B.C.E.) witnessed the interiorization of spiritual experience and laid the foundations for the world's great religio-philosophical systems that more or less arose independently and simultaneously in India, China, and the Middle East.[47] The industrial revolution (late eighteenth century) would drive the production of unprecedented economic wealth and cause massive changes in consumerist lifestyles and spawn modern politics. When it comes to interiorization, however, it is difficult to associate it with particular places, dates, personages, or technologies. Arguably, this explains why it is difficult to appreciate its historic impact.

Ignoring The Attic of History

The final barrier concerns ignoring history as a source of evidence, insights, and leads for appreciating the psychic diversity and psychic

---

46. Bargh, *Automaticity of Everyday Life*, p. 10.
47. Karl Jaspers, *The Origin and Goal of History* (London: Routledge and Kegan Paul, 1953).

plasticity of the human condition. History is an attic filled with odd antiques with stories to tell, and the family of humankind owes it to itself to explore this creaky loft, dusting off forgotten *objets d'art*, treasured heirlooms, and precious curios (i.e., lost civilizations, undeciphered ancient texts, archaeological mysteries). In a sense, this last barrier returns us to the fifth, or the lack of amazement at the existence of interiority. Through a careful reading of psychohistory, we can come to see just how profound the transformation of the human condition has been.

Conclusion: The "Virtual Evolution" of Homo Sapiens

The need for a historically-informed and culturally-sensitive psychology cannot be over-emphasized. After all, culture has the effect and impact of evolution minus genetic mutation. If we understand the significance and role of interiority, then we will also understand that *homo sapiens* is the only species that can evolve without major alterations in its physical nature. This "virtual evolution" is possible because of culture or extra-genetic information — and interiority, as a type of extra-genetic information, is a specific development of human culture.

CHAPTER 4

Voices Become Gods

BILL ROWE

Afters a lecture given by Julian Jaynes at the Canadian Psychological Association Symposium on Consciousness in 1985, Daniel Dennett, referring to the various factors in Jaynes's theory as modules, said, "The module I would be most interested in simply discarding is the one about hallucinations. Now you might think that if you throw out his account of hallucinations you haven't got much left of Jaynes's theory, but in fact I think you would, although he would probably resist throwing that part away." To no one's surprise Jaynes said, in his response, "Yes. I would find it difficult to dispense with hallucinations. They practically define the bicameral mind."[1]

Dennett is not alone in wishing the voices would go away. Many readers find it odd that hallucinated voices play such a pivotal role in a theory of consciousness. Is consciousness not about basic sensation, "raw feels," immediate experience, things like that? Perhaps. But in Jaynes's view, those are inappropriate targets for the word *consciousness*.

The voices enter Jaynes's theory of consciousness as auditory verbal hallucinations experienced during moments of stressful indecision. They arose sometime during the last major glaciation but took on new meaning around 9000 B.C.E. in the ancient Near East with the beginning of agriculture. They were a response to the need for a new kind of

Portions of this chapter first appeared in "Retrospective: Julian Jaynes and *The Origin of Consciousness in the Breakdown of the Bicameral Mind*," *American Journal of Psychology*, 2012, 125, 1–4. Reprinted with permission.
1. Julian Jaynes, "Consciousness and the Voices of the Mind," *Canadian Psychology*, 1986, 27, 2; reprinted in Marcel Kuijsten (ed.), *The Julian Jaynes Collection* (Henderson, NV: Julian Jaynes Society, 2012).

social control as people moved away from small hunter-gatherer bands to larger, agriculturally based communities. Jaynes proposes that the voices evolved along with language over the previous 100,000 years or so. Figure 1 shows the phases of the evolution from early language to consciousness. It can be seen that the bicameral period, when the voices dominated, lasted about 10,000 years. Before that time the voices would have played a minor role, and after that time they were a hindrance. They were a minor presence before 9000 B.C.E. because communal life was simple and predictable, and prepotent behavioral repertoires were sufficient to manage daily life. After about 1000 B.C.E. an intentional narrative self had emerged to manage more complicated and less predictable social encounters. In this latter period hallucinated voices attempting to guide or direct behavior were typically experienced as intrusive and interfering.

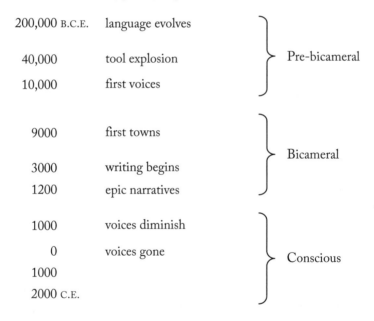

200,000 B.C.E.	language evolves	
40,000	tool explosion	Pre-bicameral
10,000	first voices	
9000	first towns	
3000	writing begins	Bicameral
1200	epic narratives	
1000	voices diminish	
0	voices gone	Conscious
1000		
2000 C.E.		

Figure 1. Evolution of the hallucinated voices (adapted from Jaynes, 1986, p. 133).

Are the Voices Really Necessary?

This description is what Jaynes would call the strong form of his theory. It is the one that most people know. But what is less well known is that Jaynes acknowledged a weak version that I think few people would have trouble with. In his opening lecture at the Canadian Symposium on Consciousness mentioned earlier, Jaynes said, "I would add here that there is a weak form of the theory. It says that consciousness could have begun shortly after the beginning of language or perhaps at certain times and places." He went on to say, "After all, people could create metaphors at the beginning of oral language — that is how language grew. Consciousness could have originated in exactly the same way as I have described, and existed for a time in parallel with the bicameral mind. Then the bicameral mind is sloughed off at approximately 1000 b.c. for the reasons I have suggested, leaving consciousness to come into its own."[2]

What Jaynes is saying here is that the metaphorical self, the conscious self, could have arisen in just the way that many people might suspect, as the slow accretion of metaphorical terms and expressions. But over the years, Jaynes stood his ground on the strong form of his theory for good reason. The weak form is almost unfalsifiable. If you present a theory to the world, it should be in disprovable form. The strong form is also preferred because it has more explanatory power. It includes many historical phenomena that may or may not be in the causal chain of the evolution of consciousness but are ignored at the risk of losing valuable insights into the varieties of conscious experience.

So Jaynes leaves open the possibility that what he calls consciousness could have arisen in other places in ways less dependent on the bicameral mind. For example, there could have been isolated groups in the world that did not develop a settled agricultural way of life and did not experience the social disruption from rapidly mixing cultures. Over long periods of time these groups could acquire the features of consciousness for reasons other than the increased task demands of agriculture and the interpersonal dissonance associated with clashing cultures. But possibility and probability are two different things. And when Jaynes looked at all the data available from the ancient Near East and Asia, he found strong support for bicamerality. Support in the form of multiple independent sources of evidence converged on a theory of auditory verbal hallucinations as a system of social control.

---

2. Ibid.

The Origin of Language

It is instructive to read Julian Jaynes's contribution to the "Origins and Evolution of Language and Speech" in the 1976 *Annals of the New York Academy of Sciences*.[3] Jaynes presents a well-formulated theory of the origin of language in the late Pleistocene. Nowhere in his talk on the origin of language did Jaynes mention hallucinated voices. And the reason, as was mentioned earlier, is that before the beginnings of agriculture, decision making and task management within these small hunter-gatherer groups did not require such intervention.

Jaynes points out that the first step toward speech would have been the emergence of intentional vocalization, that is, the decoupling of vocal signals from limbic control. Neurologically this amounts to the encephalization of vocalization. Before this, vocal cries and calls would have been limited to mere accompaniments to ongoing multisensory interactions with the environment. He suggested that the emergence of intentional speech occurred with the evolution of additional frontal cortex and came to reside in the region just ventral to the cortical area that was already controlling the intentionally gesturing hand.[4]

To the question of how early humans functioned and communicated without the kind of language we are familiar with, Jaynes replied, "The answer is very simple: just like all other primates, with an abundance of visual and vocal signals which were very far removed from the syntactical language that we practice today."[5]

It does not require advanced language for a community to produce usable items such as speartips and harpoons. Regarding the production of tools Jaynes goes on to say, "This art was transmitted solely by imitation, exactly the same way in which chimpanzees transmit the trick of inserting straws into ant hills to get ants." The process of imitation is actually not as straightforward as Jaynes makes it out to be here. Nevertheless, the spirit of what he is saying is right. Stimulus enhancement and local

3. Julian Jaynes, "The Evolution of Language in the Late Pleistocene," *Annals of the New York Academy of Sciences*, 1976, 280; reprinted in Kuijsten (ed.), *The Julian Jaynes Collection*.
4. For discussions on the cortical control of vocalizations see Terrence W. Deacon, *The Symbolic Species: The Co-evolution of Language and the Brain* (New York: W. W. Norton & Company, 1997) and W. Tecumseh Fitch, *The Evolution of Language* (New York: Cambridge University Press, 2010).
5. Julian Jaynes, *The Origin of Consciousness in the Breakdown of the Bicameral Mind* (Boston: Houghton Mifflin, 1976), p. 130.

enhancement along with *Homo sapiens'* exquisite mimetic propensities would have made Paleolithic humans very efficient at imitative learning.[6] In addition to this, as Jaynes theorizes, they had the ability to use simple modifiers and nouns. The kind of shared focal attention and collaborative problem solving that these skills bequeath should have been sufficient to produce the kinds of tools and artifacts we see in the Middle and Upper Paleolithic record.

Covering the time period from about 100,000 years ago to about 10,000 years ago, Jaynes suggests a possible sequence of the emergence of parts of speech ranging from inflectional endings, to commands, to life nouns, to nouns, names, verbs, and syntax. Jaynes acknowledges that this ordering could be different in different places, but he insists that any ordering must be tied to identifiable changes in the archeological record. For example, modifier words such as sharper, used in collaborative problem solving, should coincide with the manufacture of better tools. Life nouns, such as animal names, should lead to the ability to evoke the image or memory of a prey in their absence and coincide with the production of cave art. Nouns for things would predict the invention of artifacts such as pottery, ornaments, and bone carvings. And personal names for people should lead to larger, more stable social groups.

I refer the reader to the original article for more details and debates. But whatever linguistic theory one proposes, it should comport with two notable features of the last 200,000 years. One is the incredibly long period of technological stasis throughout the Paleolithic up until 40,000 years ago. And the other is the dramatic explosion of artifacts after 40,000 years ago. Regarding the earlier time period, this is a span of roughly 160,000 years in which anatomically modern humans were using stone tools that differed very little from those of their presapien antecedents. And then, over a short time period of 30,000 years, we see the emergence of things such as cave paintings, articulated throwing spears, awls, clothing fasteners, and the working of bone and antler into tools such as sewing needles and barbed harpoons.

---

6. For a discussion on primate imitation see Michael Tomasello and Josep Call, *Primate Cognition* (New York: Oxford University Press, 1997), Chapter 9.

The Rise of Agriculture

Toward the end of the last glacial maximum, around 12,000 years ago, we see in the archeological record of the Near East things that are not easily accounted for by the behavioral repertoire and linguistic skills that had worked quite well for thousands of years. Hunter-gatherer sites were giving way to more settled populations. People were collecting wild seeds and hunting the wild ancestors of domestic sheep and goat. In the Levant, a hunter-gatherer culture known as the Natufians were the first people to establish permanent year-round settlements, marking a major turning point in the transition between mobile hunter-gatherers and settled agrarian communities.[7] One of the most striking features of Natufian culture was the ritualistic practice of the burial of the dead, particularly the practice of skull removal and the relocation of the crania in domestic or special-purpose settings.[8] What makes these examples of early settled life difficult to account for in terms of late Paleolithic cognitive capacity is that, in Jaynes's words, "They could not narratize and had no analog selves to 'see' themselves in relation to others. They were what we could call signal-bound, that is, responding each minute to cues in a stimulus-response manner, and controlled by those cues."[9] Something new was needed.

"Civilization is the art of living in towns of such size that everyone does not know everyone else."[10] Jaynes admits that this is not a very inspiring definition of civilization but true nevertheless. The Natufians were not constructing cities, of course, but they were living in settlements of up to 200 people, and this is a dramatic change from the 20- to 30-person hunter-gatherer bands that preceded them. How do that many people coordinate activities so that there is no conflict, and things get done and done on time? Earlier, we saw that Jaynes linked the advent of names with the size of the group. So inventing names is one way to keep track of the increasing complexity of daily social life. But, more than that, keeping that many people fed entails task management problems that require

7. Ofer Bar-Yosef, "The Natufian Culture in the Levant: Threshold to the Origins of Agriculture," *Evolutionary Anthropology*, 1998, 6, 5, pp. 159–177.
8. Ibid.
9. Jaynes, *Origin of Consciousness*, p. 140.
10. Ibid., p. 149.

a kind of planning and self-cuing that the predecessors of the Natufians
were probably not capable of.

For all the lexical items at their disposal, the archeological evidence
suggests that Paleolithic humans were behaviorally bound to short-term
goal-directed activities. But with the beginnings of agriculture there
would be a need for some sort of temporal priming to keep people on
task for extended periods of time. Jaynes gives the hypothetical example
of a man who, at his own command or a chief's, is trying to set up a
fish weir. How does he keep himself on task? If he is not conscious and
cannot narratize his situation, how would he keep from being distract-
ed? "Learned activities with no consummatory closure do need to be
maintained by something outside of themselves," Jaynes says. "A Middle
Pleistocene man would forget what he was doing."[11] In a later section
we will see Jaynes's proposal that the hallucinated voices emerged at this
time. And part of the evidence is the unusual burial practice of the Natufian communities and the cult-like use of the skulls of the deceased. But
for now I want to use findings from developmental psychology to moti-
vate the claim that the kind of self-discipline we take for granted is actually a hard-won acquired skill and did not exist in human populations
10,000 years ago.

Voluntary Memory

It takes modern children 6 to 7 years to acquire the kind of self-
cueing skills necessary to stay on task. In a study of the acquisition of
voluntary memory in preschool age children, the Russian psychologist
Z. M. Istomina had children age 4 to 7 play a game of going to a pretend
store to get a list of items. The 4-year-olds ran off to the store impulsively,
usually not even listening to the instructions to the end. "Initially it never
occurred to the children that they would have to recall exactly what they
were to buy in the store. They considered their role as 'emissary' fulfilled
when they entered the store and were ready to turn to something else,
for example, to participate in the game going on at the store itself."[12] For
these children the objective of remembering the content of the message

11. Ibid., pp. 134–35.
12. Z. M. Istomina, "The Development of Voluntary Memory in Children of Preschool Age," *Soviet
Psychology*, 1975, 13.

was not singled out. Most of the 5- to 6-year-olds listened attentively to the instructions about what to buy, although they tried to carry out the task as quickly as possible. This group showed some early signs that they understood that the objective was to "remember" something. Typically they demonstrated this by repeating the items as they were read. When asked how she remembered the items on the shopping list, one child said, "I repeated the list in a whisper."

New patterns emerged for the older children, such as silent mental repetition, repeating the items after they were read instead of during the reading, and stopping on the way to the store and coming back with a question about an item. But, more significantly, new ways of ordering and associating the items were observed. The older children would rearrange the order of the items in accordance with personal meanings or associations. Intentional rearranging according to meaning helps to overcome losses due to basic memory span.

Modern children have the advantage of the encouragement and modeling by adults who already have the skill of voluntary self-cuing memory. But it is by no means obvious that middle Paleolithic humans possessed such a skill. Up until around 40,000 years ago there is little in the archeological record to indicate a need for the acculturation of such voluntary memory. Up until then the stone toolkit of choppers and flakes had remained stable for tens of thousands of years. The skills needed to maintain the level of technology seen in the record of this time period are easily transmitted by imitation, especially imitation enhanced by the rudiments of language, which would have facilitated shared focal attention and collaborative problem solving. I also suggest that, given the short life span of Paleolithic humans (estimated at about 30 years), there would have been little advantage in investing so many years in sculpting a behavior that was not actually needed for typical daily tasks.

The Rise of the Voices

At the open-air Natufian site of Eynan, just north of the sea of Galilee, at around 9000 B.C.E., there is a burial tradition like nothing ever seen before. As Jaynes describes it, "An adult male, presumably the king, was partly covered with stones and partly propped up on stones, his upright head cradled in more stones, facing the snowy peaks of Mount Hermon, thirty miles away."[13] Jaynes goes on to suggest that this dead king, propped up on a pillow of stones, was heard by those still living as giving forth commands much as he had done before he died. This, Jaynes believed, was the first god. To be sure, the hallucinated voices arose earlier in hunter-gather times as simple nonvoluntary auditory reminders of the current task. But at the opening of the Neolithic revolution, we see these auditory experiences recruited not as short-term individual task reminders but, rather, as organizing instructions for an entire group.

The Pre-Pottery Neolithic B site of Tell Halula (about 8000 B.C.E.) in the middle valley of the Euphrates River illustrates the group nature of late Neolithic mortuary practices. At Tell Halula, we see the dead buried in an upright position at the very entrance of a dwelling. These upright graves were clearly marked with clay plugs, which the occupants made no effort to conceal. In a recent article titled "Seated Memory: New Insights Into Near Eastern Neolithic Mortuary Variability From Tell Halula, Syria," Guerrero, Molist, Kuijt, and Anfruns point out, "In most houses, the entrance/burial area represents about 34% of the total space of the main room."[14] The authors comment that the inhabitants appear to have lived, slept, and engaged in the same types of activities in all areas of the room. At contemporary sites in the Levant such as 'Ain Ghazal, and at Jericho, we see a similar mortuary pattern with the dead buried in courtyards, under buildings, and beneath room floors. Why are the dead kept so close by? Why are they arranged in a seated position, and at the only entrance and exit?

In a 2008 article called "The Regeneration of Life: Neolithic Structures of Symbolic Remembering and Forgetting," the anthropologist Ian Kuijt describes even more exotic mortuary practices and speculates on their meaning. Kuijt calls attention to widespread similarities in Pre-Pottery Neolithic mortuary practices, not just in the conventionality of primary intramural burials but in a secondary mortuary practice of removing the skull of a deceased person and giving it special ritual

13. Jaynes, *Origin of Consciousness*, p. 142.
14. Emma Guerrero, Miquel Molist, Ian Kuijt, and Josep Anfruns, "Seated Memory: New Insights into Near Eastern Neolithic Mortuary Variability from Tell Halula, Syria," *Current Anthropology*, 2009, 50, 3, 379–391, p. 384.

treatment. These secondary mortuary practices involved reconstructing the physical features of the face with plaster, clay, and seashells.

At this same time there arose other practices involving the ritualistic use of the human face and body, such as half-size human statues, busts made of wood and plaster, small seated figurines, and miniature painted heads on the ends of animal bones. Kuijt reminds his readers that most researchers regard these as the material expression of Neolithic "ancestor cults." Kuijt disagrees. "My argument is that, rather than being a reflection of ancestor worship, Neolithic mortuary and ritual practices highlight integrated systems of memory and embodiment that initially focused on remembrance but through time facilitated the forgetting of the dead."[15]

The ancestor worship that Kuijt is reacting to is an anthropological model that links mortuary practices to a tendency for kinship-based agricultural groups to affirm links to ancestors in order to bolster claims to land that they are farming. To be sure, there are modern-day agriculturalists, such as the Merina of Madagascar, who collectively bury the dead in monumental tombs that are located in ancestral villages. But it is by no means clear that such practices began that way 10,000 years ago. As James Whitley points out in a 2002 article called "Too Many Ancestors," "No-one has yet come up with a theory that might explain why such hunter-fisher-gatherer-cum-horticulturalists might have been peculiarly prone to venerate their ancestors." Furthermore, Whitley observes that "if ancestors only come into the picture with the establishment of agriculture, then ancestors ought to be more prominent in interpretations of the Late Bronze Age and Iron Age than they should be for the Neolithic."[16]

This is an excellent point because as we move through the Bronze Age and into the Iron Age, we do not see a continuation of skull removal, plastering, and burying in the vicinity of the living space. Instead, we see those practices fade away and be replaced by a tradition of idols that are found in every home and often in multiple rooms in every home. This is consistent with Jaynes's theory that mortuary practices in the late Neolithic were not about ancestor worship or even, as Kuijt suggest, about systems of memory and embodiment. Rather, at the beginning of

15. Ian Kuijt, "The Regeneration of Life: Neolithic Structures of Symbolic Remembering and Forgetting," *Current Anthropology*, 2008, 49, 2, p. 172.
16. James Whitley, "Too Many Ancestors," *Antiquity*, 2002, 76, p. 121.

agriculture they were a way of continuing the task cueing, instructions, or admonishments of leaders who had passed away.

VOICES BECOME GODS

Jaynes opens Book II of *The Origin of Consciousness* with a discussion of three outstanding archeological features that he says can be understood only in terms of the bicameral mind. They are the houses of gods, graves, and idols. In the opening chapter he devotes a full page to a defamiliarization exercise with the intent of making the common town designed around a god-house stand out in sharp relief against the background of history. He asks that we imagine ourselves coming as strangers to a land where all the settlements are organized on a pattern of ordinary houses grouped around one larger and more magnificent dwelling. We might at first assume that the large house was the home of the prince or ruler of the region. We might be right, but not in the case of older civilizations. For thousands of years, settlements featured monumental buildings in which no one lived, no grain was stored, and no animals were housed. Why?

"Around 6000 B.C. the PPNB [Pre-Pottery Neolithic B] culture disappears and there is a widespread desertion of sites in Palestine as well as in the Syrian steppe." Thus the British archeologist James Mellaart, in his book *The Neolithic of the Near East*, closes the door on the last days of the Pre-Pottery Neolithic in central and southern Levant.[17] He goes on to point out that even with the rise of Pottery Neolithic, Palestine never regained its cultural eminence. Cultural innovation shifted to the north and, ultimately, into the Tigris–Euphrates river valley, where we witness the ascent of Mesopotamian urban civilization. Here we see the evolution of very large civilizations based on the control of rivers, in contrast to previous cultures in the Near East that depended on rainfall. By the end of the Ubaid period (ca. 5300 to 3600 B.C.E.) we find sites such as Eridu that were possibly as large as 10 hectares (about 25 acres), roughly the size at which Pre-Pottery Neolithic settlements collapsed.[18] This was followed by the Uruk period (3600 to 3100 B.C.E.), with settlements such

---

17. James Mellaart, *The Neolithic of the Near East* (New York: Charles Scribner's Sons, 1975), p. 67.
18. Charles L. Redman, *The Rise of Civilization: From Early Farmers to Urban Society in the Ancient Near East* (New York: W.H. Freeman, 1978), p. 247.

as Warka, in present-day southern Iraq, that covered as much as 80 hectares and had a population of 10,000.[19]

God-Houses

In discussing the architecture at Eridu, anthropologist Charles Redman comments, "What is remarkable about these buildings is that they
contained all of the elements of later Sumerian temples."[20] Or, as Jaynes
describes them, "God-houses were set on mud-brick platforms, which
were the origin of ziggurats."[21] By the Early Dynastic period (ca. 2700
B.C.E.) in that same region we see actual ziggurats and, at the same time,
the pyramids of Egypt. Jaynes discusses other huge and otherwise useless
structures at Hattusas, the Anatolian Hittite capital (in present day Turkey). Similar buildings were constructed by the Olmec along the coast of
the Gulf of Mexico, the Mayans in the Yucatán Peninsula, and the Inca
in what is now Peru. From Mesopotamia to Peru, Jaynes reminds us, all
the great civilizations went through a stage when some sort of structure
was erected as the dwelling place of the dead as if they still lived. We are
so accustomed to the town plan of a church surrounded by homes, shops,
and municipal buildings that we seldom give it a second thought. But
if we stand back and try to avoid projecting the familiar present onto
the unfamiliar past, we can see that these town structures *are* unusual.
Absent a theory such as that of Jaynes, there is no obvious reason for
such an early obsession with the dead, the skulls of the dead, and the
tremendous architectural investment in structures devoted to people who
are no longer alive.

If Jaynes's theory is correct, then these large structures are the cultural residuals of the stone pillars cradling the dead Natufian king's silent
skull. As societies become larger and more complex, the need for instruction becomes ever more desperate. The structures that served as common
cues for hallucinated guidance become larger and more monumental,
hence the dazzling towers, pyramids, and ziggurats and the enormous
amount of time and energy invested in placing the dead rulers inside and

---

19. Ibid., p. 255.
20. Ibid., p. 250.
21. Jaynes, *Origin of Consciousness*, p. 152.

providing them with comforts and nourishment to ensure their continuing guidance.

Graves

The burial of dead elites as if they were still living is a common feature
of all the cultures of the Pre Pottery Neolithic. Site surveys show the
widespread practice of burying important people with weapons, furniture, ornaments, and food. We see this in the very first European chamber tombs of the Neolithic, for example. And the elaborate Egyptian
burials of pharaohs are well known. In the third millennium B.C.E., kings
in the city of Ur were buried with their entire retinue. The archeologist
Leonard Woolley describes a royal burial at the ancient city of Ur that
included members of the king's court, soldiers, men-servants, women,
musicians, animals, and chariot drivers.[22] A similar practice is seen in
the royal burials of the Shang dynasty in China. The American historian
and sinologist David Keightley describes a burial in which the vertical
location in the grave pit, as well as the proximity to the king, reflected
the social status of the victim, "with those retainers close to the king in
life being buried close to him in death and enjoying the highest postmortem status."[23] Likewise, in the New World, at the Mayan site of
Kaminal-juyu, a chief is found buried with two adolescents, a child, and
his dog for company.[24]

Further evidence that the dead were the origin of gods can be found
in the writings of those bicameral civilizations that became literate. For
example, in his book *The Epic of Gilgamesh and Old Testament Parallels*,
the Assyriologist and biblical scholar Alexander Heidel refers to ancient
Assyrian incantations that explicitly denote the dead as gods. "In a bi-
lingual incantation text from Assyria, the ghosts of the dead are called
'gods' (*ilâni*)," and "the imprisoned gods come forth from the grave, the
evil winds come forth from the grave ..."[25] In what is now Mexico, the

22. Leonard Woolley, *The Excavations at Ur: 1924-1934* (Society of Antiquaries, 1934).
23. David N. Keightley, "The Shang: China's First Historical Dynasty," in M. Loewe and E. L.
Shaughnessy (eds.), *The Cambridge History of Ancient China: From the Origins of Civilization to 221
B.C.* (Cambridge: Cambridge University Press, 1999), p. 267.
24. Victor W. von Hagen, *World of the Maya* (New American Library, 1960), p. 109.
25. Alexander Heidel, *The Gilgamesh Epic and Old Testament Parallels* (Chicago: University of Chicago Press, 1949), p. 196; p. 153.

ethnographer and evangelizer Bernardino de Sahagún recorded that the Aztecs said that he who has died became a god:

> Teotihuacan has always been regarded as a great necropolis; the Aztecs described it to Fray Bernardo de Sahagun ... as follows: "... they called the place Teotihuacan, burial place of kings; the ancients said: he who has died became a god."[26]

Jaynes does ask the obvious question: Could not grief itself be the promoter of all these practices? It is possible, he acknowledges. But as we have noted elsewhere, the preponderance of multiple independent sources of evidence make this projection of our current form of grief increasingly implausible. Examples include "the pervasion of references to the dead as gods in different regions of the world, the vastness of some of the enterprise as in the Great Pyramids, and even the contemporary vestiges in lore and literature of ghosts returning from their graves with messages for the living."[27] In any case, the kind of grief that comes to mind today as an explanation for these ancient mortuary practices would not have been possible for bicameral people. With no analog space in which to project an imagined person, what we call grief would have been short-lived. And it would have consisted mostly of ritualized practices designed to establish the continuance of hallucinatory guidance.

Idols That Speak

Figure 2 shows an assortment of what are called eye idols from Tell Brak in northeastern Syria (ca. 3300 B.C.E.) and Figure 3 is a collection of stone and marble sculptures from Tell Asmar (ca. 2600 B.C.E.) near present-day Baghdad. Probably the most striking features of these artifacts are the eyes. Typically, the diameter of the human eye is about 10 percent of the height of the head. With this ratio used as an eye index, the statues from Tell Asmar range up to 18 percent. An eye index for the eye idols from Tell Brak is irrelevant because the body of the idol is essentially just a base for a pair of eyes. This motif of exaggerated eyes is seen all over the ancient world. In dynastic Egypt eye indexes range up to 20 percent. And in New World Mesoamerica at La Venta and Tres Zapoltes we see huge

---

26. Miguel Covarrubias, *Indian Art of Mexico and Central America* (New York: Knopf), p. 123.
27. Jaynes, *Origin of Consciousness*, p. 165.

Figure 2. Eye idols from Tell Brak, ca. 3500 B.C.E.

Figure 3. Statues from Tell Asmar, Iraq, ca. 2600 B.C.E.

heads carved out of basalt with eye indexes ranging from 11 percent to 19 percent. Jaynes sees these effigies as lineal descendants of the propped-up skulls of dead chiefs back at the beginning of agriculture. And in keeping with his theory of the bicameral mind, he sees them as difficult to interpret as anything other than aids to hallucinated voices.

Eye-to-Eye Contact

Eye-to-eye contact is important in primate behavior, and it is uniquely significant for human beings. Infants in the first year of life frequently make and hold contact with their mother's or their caregiver's eyes in the course of an engagement. Jaynes points out that in an authority relationship you are more likely to feel the power of the superior person when the two of you are staring straight into each other's eyes. There is a kind of stress and unresolvedness, he notes, and "were such a relationship mimicked in a statue, it would enhance the hallucination of divine speech."[28]

In both the New World and the Old World we see a vast number of these idols. Jaynes is careful to note that the majority of them were probably not used to evoke auditory hallucinations. Many may have been used as mnemonic devices, such as the *quipu* or knot-string literature of the Incas or the beads of Catholic rosaries.[29] This is important for people who do not have the self-cuing skills of voluntary memory that we discussed earlier.

However, that at least some of these idols were believed to speak is attested to in historical records. The sixteenth century Spanish Jesuit missionary and naturalist José de Acosta recorded that the Devil himself spoke to the Incas out of the mouths of their statues:

> There are certaine memories and discourses which say, that in this Temple the Divell did speake visibly, and gave answers by his Oracle, and that sometimes they did see a spotted snake; and it was a thing very common and approved at the Indies, that the Devill spake and answered in these false Sanctuaries, deceiving this miserable people.[30]

---

28. Ibid., p. 169.
29. Ibid., p. 167.
30. José de Acosta, *The Natural and Moral History of the Indies*, translated by Edward Grimstone (New York: Burt Franklin, 1900), pp. 325–326.

De Acosta goes on to relate this to similar reports by Plutarch and the Christian apologist Justine Martir, commenting on what appear to be residuals of bicamerality in the first century C.E.

> But where the Gospel is entred, and the Crosse of Christ planted, the father of lies is become mute, as Plutarch writes of his time "Cur cessaverit Pithias fondere oracula": and Iustine Martir treates amply of the silence which Christ imposed to devills, which spake by Idolls, as it had been before much prophecied of in the holy Scripture.[31]

Cuneiform literature frequently mentions god-statues that spoke. The Biblical scholar and assyriologist R. H. Pfeiffer cites a royal letter from the first millennium B.C.E.

> I have taken note of the portents ... I had them recited in order before Shamash ... the [statue] of Akkad brought up visions before me and cried out: "What pernicious portent have you tolerated in the royal image?" (Again) it spoke: "Say to the Gardener ... [wine] ... Salla has given his servant to Nabu-usalli, for this purpose." It made inquiry concerning Ningal-iddina, Shamash-ibni, (and) Na'id-Marduk. Concerning the rebellion in the land it said: "Take the wall cities one after the other, that a cursed one will not be able to stand before the Gardener."[32]

There is also a type of object, referred to as the teraphim in the Hebrew Bible, that could speak. Karel Van Der Toorn, professor of religious studies at the University of Amsterdam, explored the use of this term in the light of extra-Biblical cuneiform evidence. He suggests that the teraphim were cultic idols, associated with ancestors, that played a role in divination. In some cases, Zechariah 10:2 for example, the Bible is quite explicit about this, "For the idols have spoken vanity, and the diviners have seen a lie, and have told false dreams; they comfort in vain: therefore they went their way as a flock, they were troubled, because there was no shepherd."[33]

The ethnographer Cottie Arthur Burland describes the Aztecs as having once been a wandering tribe until an image spoke to them from

---

31. Ibid., p. 326.
32. Robert H. Pfeiffer, *State Letters of Assyria* (New Haven: American Oriental Society, 1935), quoted in Jaynes, *Origin of Consciousness*, p. 174.
33. Zechariah 10:2, quoted in Karel Van Der Toorn, "The Nature of the Biblical Teraphim in the Light of the Cuneiform Evidence," *Catholic Biblical Quarterly*, 1990, 52, 2, 203–222.

a ruined temple. As a punishment it commanded them to travel hither and thither, carrying the image with them wherever they went, always subjected to the cruelties of the ruler of the state where they happened to be at the time.[34] This is reminiscent, as Jaynes notes, of the unembodied bicameral voices that led Moses zigzagging across the Sinai desert.[35]

THE BEGINNING OF CONSCIOUSNESS

The idols discussed here date from approximately 3000 B.C.E., where the curtain was about to rise on the great dynasties and temple-states of the Near East. The next three thousand years brought the Great Pyramids, ziggurats, writing, and the manufacture of metal artifacts. It is here that Jaynesian theory and conventional history appear to clash in an unresolvable way. The people responsible for these accomplishments simply could not have been nonconscious! Could they? The answer is a qualified "yes" — a yes predicated on just what Jaynes meant by consciousness. Jaynes was aware that his numerous neologisms and list of features of consciousness presented barriers to the understanding of his theory. He once commented that he could have called his book *"The Origin of Conscious Experience in the Breakdown of the Bicameral Mind."* Even that title is ambiguous, but he did go on to say that basically consciousness is that which is introspectable. Given this definition, it seems less of a conceptual leap to consider ancient populations functioning nonconsciously, or, said more simply, without the learned skill of introspection.

The kind of social structures that could enable nonintrospectors to build pyramids and ziggurats and inaugurate writing are precisely those arrived at in the decline of the Pre-Pottery Neolithic and the rise of hierarchical theocracies. The rigid social constraints of these temple-states ensured that most moment-to-moment events were predictable enough to be managed by prepotent learned behavioral repertoires. And the degree of unpredictability inherent in these large enclaves was accommodated by the ever-present guidance of the gods, the idol- and monument-cued auditory reminders of what to do now.

---

34. Cottie A. Burland, *Montezuma, Lord of the Aztecs* (London: Weidenfeld & Nicolson, 1973), p. 47.
35. Jaynes, *Origin of Consciousness*, p. 174.

The Tukulti Altar

"Act promptly, make your god happy," or, said another way, "Don't think: let there be no time space between hearing your bicameral voice and doing what it tells you."[36] It is this sort of obedience that Jaynes suggested is evident in the image of Hammurabi shown receiving the famous Laws of Hammurabi in the left-hand panel of Figure 4. This interpretation is reinforced if we compare the Hammurabi stele with a stone altar of Tukulti-Ninurta I four hundred years later. There is a stark contrast. The right-hand panel of Figure 4 shows two images of Tukulti; one is a standing figure approaching what Jaynes interpreted as the throne of his god, and the second one is of him kneeling before this empty throne. "No king before in history is ever shown kneeling. No scene before in history ever indicates an absent god. The bicameral mind had broken down."[37]

The carving of an otherwise powerful tyrant in an imploring position before a symbol of his god suggest the unraveling of a way of life at the end of the second millennium B.C.E. A way of life soon to be replaced by a culture of incessant questioning and endless second-guessing. The individual was being born. Six hundred years after Tukulti found his god missing, Greek philosophers rationalized this individualism but did not comfort the individual. As University of Vermont Professor Luther Martin states in his book *Hellenistic Religions*, "Hellenistic existence had been propelled into an individualism without instruction, an aimlessness motivated by a profound sense of alienation; in short, into a crisis of freedom,"[38] — the birth pangs of human subjective consciousness.

Julian Jaynes's interpretation of the Tukulti altar has been questioned by Simon McCarthy-Jones in his 2012 book *Hearing Voices*. McCarthy-Jones challenges Jaynes's claim that Tukulti is kneeling before an empty throne. Citing a personal communication with the archeologist Irving Finkle, McCarthy-Jones says: " … first it is an altar, and not a throne the king is kneeling in front of, and more importantly, the altar is in fact not empty, but has on it what is either a clay tablet with a stylus, or a hinged writing board; if this symbol has been correctly understood, this will be a

36. Jaynes, *Origin of Consciousness*, p. 204.
37. Ibid., p. 223.
38. Luther H. Martin, *Hellenistic Religions: An Introduction* (Oxford University Press, 1987), p. 24.

Figure 4. Hammurabi, 1792–1750 B.C.E. Tukulti-Ninurta I, 1243–1207 B.C.E.

symbol of the god Nabu, the god of writing, who was a major god in the Assyrian pantheon."[39]

There are a number of enigmatic features to the Tukulti altar, and McCarthy-Jones has called attention to one of them. We will see below, however, that the features that make the Tukulti altar unusual are, in fact, indicators of the change in mentality described by Jaynes's theory of the breakdown of the bicameral mind.

In the summer of 1995 the Tukulti altar was part of an exhibition of ancient Assyrian artifacts at the Metropolitan Museum of Art in New York City. Robert Steven Bianchi, Chief Curator of the Gandur Foundation for Art, writing a review for *Minerva* magazine said: "Among the most enigmatic objects in the exhibition is a cult pedestal of the god Nusku, who was both a god of light and an intercessor, praying in this case on behalf of king Tukulti-Ninurta I (1243-1207 B.C.)." Bianchi goes on to say that, "Some interpret the object on the pedestal as the two leaves of a shrine's door; others as a rod or ray of Nusku's against a background of some sort; and others still as a stylus and tablet on which the king's fate is to be recorded."[40]

39. Simon McCarthy-Jones, *Hearing Voices: The Histories, Causes and Meanings of Auditory Verbal Hallucinations* (Cambridge: Cambridge University Press, 2012), p. 16.
40. Robert S. Bianchi, "Assyria in New York," *Minerva*, 1995, 6, 4, p. 11.

The inscription at the base of the altar suggests a representation of the god Nusku. It reads, in part:

> Cult platform of the god Nusku, chief vizier of Ekur, bearer of the just scepter, courier of the gods Assur and Enlil, who daily repeats the prayers of Tukulti-Ninurta, the king ...[41]

However, referring to the alter as a socle, the archaeologist Oscar White Muscarella commented that "... it remains unclear just what is depicted on the socle ... Whatever is represented, however, it is not a deity itself but rather a symbol."[42]

In an essay on the continuities between Babylonian and Assyrian art, the archeologist Henri Frankfort says: "But it is different in the case of the altar of Tukulti-Ninurta I. ... The relief on the front shows a rite performed before the very object it decorates. The king bearing a scepter is first shown as he approaches, then as he kneels before the altar, carved with the emblem of the god Nusku. The almost intimate meeting between king and god which was depicted on steles from the time of Gudea down to that of Hammurabi is not considered possible in Assyria. Both in art and literature the gods appear withdrawn from the world of men ..."[43]

The gods have withdrawn from the world of men. Their symbolic stand-ins appear on carvings instead of direct representations. And even these are now acting as couriers to even more abstract and remote gods.

Before the weakening of the voices by writing at about 2500 B.C.E., Jaynes tells us that there was no hesitancy regarding what to do, and thus no need for prayer or intermediaries. But as civilizations became more complex toward the end of the third millennium, we see evidence of personal and household gods that act as go-betweens with higher city or state gods. And by the end of the second millennium a dramatic change occurs. "First, the major gods disappear from such scenes, even as from the altar of Tukulti-Ninurta. There then occurs a period where the individual's personal god is shown presenting him to the god's symbol only."[44]

---

41. Zainab Bahrani, *The Graven Image: Representation in Babylonia and Assyria* (Philadelphia: University of Pennsylvania Press, 2003), p. 192.

42. Prudence O. Harper, Evelyn Klengel-Brandt, Joan Aruz, and Kim Benze (eds.), *Assyrian Origins: Discoveries at Ashur on the Tigris* (New York: Metropolitan Museum of Art, 1995), pp. 112–113.

43. Henri Frankfort, *The Art and Architecture of the Ancient Orient* (New Haven: Yale University Press, 1996), p. 132.

44. Jaynes, *Origin of Consciousness*, p. 230.

McCarthy-Jones has rightly called our attention to the ambiguity regarding what is depicted on Tukulti's altar. But in focusing on this detail he overlooks the point that Jaynes is making. Whether it is an empty throne or an empty writing board, the message is the same, the gods have left us, and now we must implore, kneel, and pray to them to discover their will.

The Causes of Consciousness: Seven Factors

Jaynes lists seven factors that he believes caused subjective consciousness to emerge toward the end of the second millennium B.C.E.:

(1) The weakening of the auditory by the advent of writing,

(2) The inherent fragility of hallucinatory control,

(3) The unworkableness of gods in the chaos of historical upheaval,

(4) The positing of internal cause in the observation of difference in others,

(5) The acquisition of narratization from epics,

(6) The survival value of deceit, and

(7) A modicum of natural selection.[45]

Jaynes notes that consciousness did not really emerge *de novo* only at this time. There is simply too much variation in human mentality to think that small groups or cliques could not have developed a metaphorical space and an analog self. But we are looking at broad sweeps of history here with clear endpoints: an earlier point when human agency seems to have resided in the gods and a later time when the gods had departed and people were left to make their own choices.

Between roughly 2000 B.C.E. and 1000 B.C.E., with the likely exception of number seven, all of these factors emerged and blended in the ancient Near East. The great temple-states that had stabilized by 3000 B.C.E. were shaken by internal strife and seemingly endless migrations. The Sumerians, who had settled the southern regions of the Tigris-Euphrates river valley, were displaced by the Semitic Akkadians by around 3300 B.C.E. After 2000 B.C.E. the Amorites, another Semitic group, settled in

---

45. Ibid., p. 221.

the region. Other newcomers continued to arrive and mix with previous groups, such as the Kassites and the Mitanni. Toward the end of the second millennium people from the north, the Hittites and the Dorians, arrived and settled in Anatolia and Greece. Echoes of this tumultuous period can be seen in the Old Testament, which is structured around two epic migrations in the second millennium B.C.E.: the migration of a group led by Abraham out of southern Mesopotamia and the wandering of another group led by Moses coming up out of the desert between Egypt and the Levant.

Cuneiform, which had been invented by 3000 B.C.E., was in wide use during the second millennium. It was flexible enough by shortly after 1800 B.C.E. to accommodate the writing of the code of Hammurabi and, toward the end of the second millennium, was being used to construct great tales such as the *Epic of Gilgamesh*. The advent of writing had conflicting effects on bicamerality. On one hand, the codification of rules of behavior stabilized the social order. On the other hand, its very existence challenged the need for the voices. In Jaynes's words, "Once the word of god was silent, written on dumb clay tablets or incised into speechless stone, the god's commands or the kings directives could be turned to or avoided by one's own efforts in a way that auditory hallucinations never could be."[46]

Maintaining the insular structure and rigid hierarchical control required by the bicameral mind was not possible under the conditions just listed. The collision of different cultures alone would have been enough to challenge the authority of the hallucinated voices. But with the advent of writing, the demise of the bicameral mind was virtually guaranteed.

Literary Evidence

The missing guidance, depicted as an empty throne in the Tukulti stele, is reflected in the cuneiform literature of the time. Two of the earliest literary sources reflecting this abandonment by the gods are the *Ludlul Bel Nemeqi* and the Babylonian *Theodicy*. The *Ludlul Bel Nemeqi*, sometimes called the Babylonian Job, is a monologue in which a Babylonian noble tells the story of how he has met with just about every kind of

---

46. Ibid., p. 208.

calamity imaginable. And the *Theodicy* is an acrostic poem relating a dialogue between another sufferer and a friend. The historian and archaeologist Wilfred G. Lambert dates the *Ludlul* during the Kassite period, roughly between 1500 B.C.E. and 1200 B.C.E. and the *Theodicy* somewhere between 1400 and 800 B.C.E.[47] Both the *Ludlul* and the *Theodicy* reflect individuals fraught with confusion over why such evils have beset them. "My god has forsaken me and disappeared, My goddess has failed me and keeps at a distance," read lines 43 and 44 of tablet 1 of the *Ludlul Bel Nemeqi*.[48] And similarly, the "sufferer" in the Theodicy says, "May the god who has thrown me off give help" and "May the goddess who has [abandoned me] show mercy."[49] These works are part of what is called the Babylonian wisdom literature, and as Jaynes points out, it is a short distance from these to the biblical Job and the psalms of the Old Testament.

No such insecurity or lamentation is seen in the literature of Hammurabi's time. Hammurabi does not second-guess any of the commands he writes down, even when, to us anyway, they seem amoral if not outright cruel. Death was the penalty for what today are seen as misdemeanors. Stealing was punishable by death, for example. And Law 108 says that if a woman beer-seller in a tavern was caught watering down the beer, she could be thrown into the river.[50]

Thus, over the course of the second millennium B.C.E., year by year, in city by city, for person after person, the gods abandoned humankind. And then the lights went out over the entire western half of the ancient Near East.

---

47. Wilfred G. Lambert, *Babylonian Wisdom Literature* (Oxford University Press, 1960), pp. 15, 67.
48. Ibid., p. 33.
49. Ibid., p. 89.
50. Robert Chadwick, *First Civilizations: Ancient Mesopotamia and Ancient Egypt* (Oakville, CT: Equinox, 2005), pp. 64–70.

CHAPTER 5

The Ancient Dark Age

BILL ROWE

WITHIN A PERIOD OF FORTY OR FIFTY YEARS "at the end of the thirteenth and beginning of the twelfth century almost every significant city or palace in the eastern Mediterranean world was destroyed, many of them never to be occupied again."[1] So says Vanderbilt historian Robert Drews in the introduction to his book *The End of the Bronze Age: Changes in Warfare and the Catastrophe ca. 1200 B.C.* Even if Drews is wrong about the short span of time over which the destruction took place, he is right about the point in time and the geographic scale. Around 1200 B.C.E. Mycenaean Greece disappeared. Likewise, on the Anatolian plateau, the powerful Hittite empire crumbled. Similar catastrophes befell the cities of Cyprus, Western Anatolia, Syria, and the Southern Levant. The infrastructure of Egypt was spared such devastation, but the nation did not survive as a great power. Ramesses III, pharaoh of the 20th dynasty, was in power at the beginning of the twelfth century. During the reign of his successor, Ramesses IV, Egypt lost its presence in the northern regions and sank into a low ebb during the 21st dynasty. Mesopotamia was spared. The deepest it goes into Mesopotamia is the city of Emar, in what is today northern Syria, near the Euphrates River.

The Catastrophe, as Drews calls it, and the emergence of human subjective consciousness, according to Julian Jaynes's theory, are synchronous

---

Portions of this chapter first appeared in "Retrospective: Julian Jaynes and *The Origin of Consciousness in the Breakdown of the Bicameral Mind*," *American Journal of Psychology*, 2012, 125, 1–4. Reprinted with permission.
1. Robert Drews, *The End of the Bronze Age: Changes in Warfare and the Catastrophe ca. 1200 B.C.* (Princeton, NJ: Princeton University Press), p. 4.

events. The dark silence of 1200 to 800 B.C.E. seems to incubate a new kind of human mentality. On the earlier side of this time span we have, with a few exceptions, the preconscious people of the *Iliad* unquestioningly acting out the commands of their god or goddess. On the later side we find hyperconscious people such as Odysseus fretting over and narratizing every uncertainty in his life. There are many suggestions about the cause of the ancient Dark Age, and Drews does a good job of comparing the major theories. I will use his criticism of those theories as a backdrop against which to view Jaynes's contribution to this major historical event. I will also adopt Drews's use of the term *Catastrophe*.

The alternative explanations for the Catastrophe discussed by Drews are earthquakes, migrations, ironworking, drought, systems collapse, and raiders. Drews's personal theory is none of these. He makes the case that it was masses of infantrymen using javelins and a new type of sword against conventional charioteers that made such widespread destruction possible. This he calls the military explanation. We can make use of Drews's critique of the alternative theories without having to adopt the entirety of his military explanation. Although, with one proviso, I think his suggestions fit the existing data better than the alternatives. The data for this time period are sparse, and Drews straightforwardly admits that his theory is speculative and that we are grossly ignorant about the details of second millennium B.C.E. warfare. However, his criticisms of the alternative explanations are convincing enough that it is easy to agree with him when he says, "It is time that we begin to guess."[2] He was referring to guessing about warfare, of course. But when natural disasters, migrations, systems collapse, raiders, and possibly Drews's military solution fail to answer all our questions, there is no shame in guessing about the role of the human mind. Which is what Julian Jaynes did more than 35 years ago.

Thera

In the second millennium B.C.E. one of the largest volcanic eruptions in recorded history occurred in the eastern Mediterranean on the small island of Thera, also known as Santorini. In Book II, Chapter 3 of the

---

2. Ibid., p. 98.

Origin of Consciousness Jaynes suggests that this event accelerated the mass migrations and invasions that threw the Near Eastern world into a dark age from which came the dawn of consciousness.[3] Drawing upon estimates available to him at that time, Jaynes located the eruption as having occurred somewhere between 1470 and 1170 B.C.E., right at the beginning of the ancient Dark Age. More recent estimates, however, indicate a date in the vicinity of around 1600 B.C.E.[4] This would place it too early in the second millennium to be a primary driving factor in Jaynes's theory. He may have seen this coming because in the Afterword to the 1990 edition of his book he deemphasized the effects of the eruption, saying that he would not now make as much of the Thera explosion.

It is good that Jaynes made this correction. His ideas about the breakdown of the bicameral mind can be challenging enough without the distraction of inaccurate dating of historic events or the misapplication of their effects to his theory. In summary fashion, I will look at the evidence Drews presents in his criticism of the major theories for the cause of the ancient Dark Age. We will see that what ideas are left standing either support Jaynes or, at the very least, do not contradict him.

Acts of God

Because there is no evidence of devastating volcanic activity around 1200 B.C.E., Drews does not include it in his discussion of the cause of the Catastrophe of the late Bronze Age. He does point out that in all of antiquity there are very few cities that were destroyed by an "act of God."[5] Typically, after earthquakes, for example, people rebuild and get back to business. But rebuilding is precisely what did *not* happen to most of the roughly 50 cities that collapsed at the end of the Bronze Age, most of which were burned or sacked. Of the few cities in antiquity wiped out by natural disasters, he describes Helike on the Corinthian Gulf, which after the quake of 373 B.C.E. simply found itself under water as the gulf

---

3. Julian Jaynes, *The Origin of Consciousness in the Breakdown of the Bicameral Mind* (Boston: Houghton Mifflin, 1976), p. 212.
4. Sturt W. Manning, "Clarifying the 'High' v. 'Low' Aegean/Cypriot Chronology for the Mid Second Millennium B.C.: Assessing the Evidence, Interpretive Frameworks, and Current State of the Debate," in Manfred Bietak and Ernst Czerny (eds.), *Proceedings of the SCIEM 2000, 2nd EuroConference* (Vienna, Austria: Osterreichischen Akademie der Wissenschaften, 2003).
5. Drews, *Bronze Age*, p. 38.

enlarged. He also mentions Thera and Pompeii, which were completely covered in volcanic ash.

In surveying the data for the six cities in which experts claim the strongest evidence for earthquakes, Drews comes up empty handed. There are no skeletons, for example.[6] Natural disasters such as earthquakes usually strike unannounced, and people do not have time to flee. Sometimes volcanoes do give days or weeks of warning. But in the case of the cities in Drews's survey, none of them show signs of volcanic ash. And certainly most of them are located too far away from the island of Thera to have been directly hit by the blast or even the ensuing tsunami. Two other items of interest point away from natural disasters as the agent of destruction. There is a marked absence of valuable items in the debris of the collapsed buildings. And, specifically for the sites in the quake-prone Argolid, most of the masonry was left unscathed.[7] All this points away from "acts of God" and is consistent with theories of raiders, invaders, or possible internecine conflict.

Iron

Perhaps the most influential ironworking theory is that of V. Gordon Childe, put forth in his classic 1942 book *What Happened in History.* Drews recounts Childe's theory that iron weapons were developed in Anatolia in the thirteenth century B.C.E. and were then used to conquer most of the other Bronze Age kingdoms. He also surveys several other theories where the invention of iron gave certain groups a marginal advantage over their Bronze Age neighbors. Evidence for these theories has always been slim, however, and Drews notes that by the 1960s the ironworking hypothesis was basically undone by archeological excavations and metallurgical analysis. For example, he cites Waldbaum's 1978 study of the relative percentages of ferrous to bronze artifacts in East Asian sites. The average percentage grows from 3 percent in the twelfth century, to 20 percent in the eleventh century, to 54 percent by the tenth century B.C.E.[8] In a more recent publication, Waldbaum herself rejects a

6. Ibid., p. 39.
7. Ibid., pp. 40–43.
8. Jane C. Waldbaum, *From Bronze to Iron: The Transition from the Bronze Age to the Iron Age in the Eastern Mediterranean* (Göteborg, Sweden: Paul Aströms Förlag, 1978).

Hittite origin and control of iron smelting and comments, "Although the rates at which it was substituted for bronze vary somewhat from region to region, by the tenth century B.C. iron could be said to be in 'common use' in most of the eastern Mediterranean."[9] These findings place the use of iron several hundred years too late for it to have been a factor in causing the ancient Dark Age.

Drought

There have been numerous theories about the relationship between the ancient Dark Age and climate change. In his 1968 book *Discontinuity in Greek Civilization*, Rhys Carpenter proposed that in ca. 1200 B.C.E. a drought in the eastern Mediterranean was serious enough that people were forced to leave their homes and resort to violence to feed themselves. Also, in a 1982 issue of *Climatic Change*, Weiss suggested that drought induced the migration of people from western Anatolia and also was linked with the invasion of Egypt by "Sea People." Drews, who disagrees with the strong form of the drought theory, acknowledges that it may have been a precipitating factor in the great Catastrophe. There may have been local droughts in Anatolia and elsewhere ca. 1208 B.C.E., he says, but they must have been localized enough that adjacent areas such as Greece were unaffected because no evidence for a drought has been found there.[10] But beyond that, the nature of the destruction of cities does not support the idea that drought was the proximal cause.

For example, palace inventories from Pylos and Knossos made just before the Catastrophe were large and varied and do not suggest that the people were suffering from drought-induced famine. And whoever sacked Troy, Mycenae, Pylos, Hattusas, and Ugarit failed to settle down there. This is at odds with what would have been their purpose if drought had driven them to locations where food was plentiful. In fact, at many of the Greek sites that were burned, it seems clear that the arsonists were not starving because storerooms of food were left to burn — an unlikely event if the invaders were in search of food.

---

9. Jane C. Waldbaum, "Thirty Years of Archaeological and Technological Research," in V. C. Pigott (ed.), *The Archaeometallurgy of the Asian Old World* (Philadelphia: University of Pennsylvania Museum of Archaeology and Anthropology, 1999), p. 32.
10. Drews, *Bronze Age*, p. 79.

To whatever degree local droughts can be summoned to support the demise of the Bronze Age, there is still the problem that droughts do not cause cities to burn and be destroyed. In the end, the drought theory defaults to some form of invasion and assault or, as it is usually called, the migration theory. We will turn to that next.

The Migration Hypothesis

The growth of the size of cities and the advent of writing are strong factors in pushing Jaynes's bicameral mind to the breaking point. But without the meeting of cultures via trade, immigration, or invasion, it is unlikely that the transition to consciousness would have taken the particular course that he suggests or occurred on the timetable that he gives. So when someone like Drews challenges the migration theory, it is necessary to see whether this criticism is one of those threads that, when pulled, unravels the whole theoretical sweater.

Drews's interpretation of the migratory hypothesis is based on his deconstruction of how archeologists in the nineteenth century came to believe it in the first place. The idea that great migrations caused the ruin of Bronze Age civilization does not rest on documentary evidence, he tells us. The theory was largely the creation of Egyptologist Gaston Maspero in the 1870s. And Maspero's goal was not to explain the demise of Bronze Age civilization but, rather, the unsuccessful attempts to conquer Egypt during the reign of Merneptah and Ramesses III.[11]

The main evidence for "foreigners" invading Egypt comes from two sources: the Medinet Habu Mortuary Temple of Ramesses III and inscriptions on the inside of the eastern wall of the main Karnak temple commemorating the victories of Merneptah over the Libyans.

In the inscriptions and reliefs depicting Egyptian conflicts under these two rulers there are lists of names of the attackers, such as Lukka, Ekwesh, Tursha, Shekelesh, and Shardana. Before Maspero's interpretation, most scholars regarded these as names for auxiliaries or mercenaries hired by regional nations to fight against Egypt.[12] Emmanuel de Rougé, writing earlier than Maspero, interpreted these names as denoting men

---

11. Ibid., p. 54.
12. Ibid.

from Lycia, Achaea, Tyrsenia (western Italy), Sicily, and Sardinia, respectively. In the Medinet Habu there was also a reference to Peleset, a term that Egyptologists at that time interpreted as denoting Philistines. By the mid-nineteenth century, translators were already using terms such as "northerners coming from all lands" and "peoples de la mer Mediterranee" (Peoples of the Sea) to categorize the nonlocal contingents of attacking forces. But nothing on the reliefs or inscriptions actually says that these names referred to invaders relocating from their homelands. In fact, among the inscriptions at the Karnak temple commemorating Merneptah's victory over the Libyans, there are lists of trophy body parts taken from each of the groups listed here, which strongly suggests they were not invaders. The ratios of these body parts compared with those taken of Egypt's neighbors, the Libyans, is so small that the most reasonable interpretation is that these were hired mercenaries, not migrating nations.[13]

The Birth of a Movement

Drews describes Maspero's creative interpretation of a story told by Herodotus (fifth century B.C.E.) that a Prince Tyrsenos led a migration from Lydia (western Turkey today) to Italy. Maspero surmised that these must have been the Tursha mentioned in the Merneptah inscriptions and, going further with this, that the Shekelesh and Shardana must have been part of this same migration. Thus these *peuples de la mer* ("Sea Peoples"), as Maspero called them, expelled from their Asiatic homeland, occupied Italy, Sicily, and Sardinia, and then just kept going, becoming the "northerners coming from all lands," as depicted in the Egyptian reliefs and inscriptions.[14]

Picking up on a suggestion by Egyptologist François Chabas that the garb and arms of some of the opponents shown in wall reliefs resembled those of "Europeans" and not those of local people, Maspero began what Drews regards as a wholesale revision of the entire period:

> Thus Maspero invented or gave shape to three great migrations in the reigns of Merneptah and Ramesses III. In the primary migration, Illyrians came from their Indo-European homeland in northern

---

13. Ibid., p. 49.
14. Ibid., pp. 54–57.

Europe to the Balkans. This set off the secondary migrations, in which Dorians, Phrygians, and Libu were expelled from the Balkans. The arrival of the Phrygians in western Anatolia, finally, resulted in the tertiary migrations of 'the Sea Peoples'.[15]

Chapter 4, on the migration theory, is one of the longest chapters in Drews's book, and we cannot look at the detailed criticisms of all the components. But we have already seen that physical evidence from Karnak and Medinet Habu does not support the notion of invading nations from the north. Another important bit of deconstruction done by Drews is his observation that Maspero ignored or dismissed the conclusions of nineteenth-century historians and philologists that Herodotus's story of Prince Tyrsenos was fictitious.

Furthermore, we see that there is weak or nonexistent archeological evidence for events such as an Illyrian invasion of the Balkans, or a "Dorian Invasion" responsible for the destruction of Mycenae and other Bronze Age sites. And, lastly, one of the most serious arguments Drews makes is a historical one. The theory assumes national identities for these migratory peoples all over the Mediterranean world, an assumption for which there is no evidence. For example, there is no evidence that "the Sicilians," "the Sardinians," or "the Achaeans" were ever a coherent people with a "shared history, pursuing a common goal and acting with a common purpose."[16]

As a final note, I should emphasize that this migration theory is not to be confused with earlier, larger descriptions of people on the move. The migration hypothesis we have just looked at is focused mainly on the eastern Mediterranean, in the final centuries of the second millennium, and confined mostly to Egypt, Greece, and the Levant. And as a theory its purpose was to identify factors leading up to the collapse of the Bronze Age. This migration theory is independent of earlier migrations and displacements of peoples over the entire Near East starting around 2000 B.C.E., migrations that include Anatolia and central and southern Mesopotamia. Much of the mixing of people that challenged bicameral societies to produce the Code of Hammurabi and the *Ludlul Bel Nemeqi*, for example, happened in this earlier period.

---

15. Ibid., p. 59.
16. Ibid., p. 71.

There are three more alternative explanations to look at before weighing it all against Jaynes's idea of the unworkableness of gods in the chaos of historical upheaval. They are raiders, the systems collapse theory, and Drews's military explanation.

Raiders

This is one place where there is not as much controversy among historians and archeologists. That is, most people agree that there were a large number of pirates and raiders in the late Bronze Age. Drews cites archeologist A. Bernard Knapp's[17] view that the "Sea Peoples" were basically a motley group of raiders and city-sackers, as well as Egyptologist Wolfgang Helck's[18] conclusion that the inscriptions of Merneptah and Ramesses III did not speak of a "Sea Peoples" but rather of pirates wasting everything within their reach. And Nancy Sandars, author of *The Sea Peoples: Warriors of the Ancient Mediterranean 1250–1150 B.C.*,[19] agrees that the raiders played a small role and that they were one of the results of the general breakdown, not the cause. Concerning the Greek mainland, Vincent Desborough suggested in *The Last Mycenaeans and their Successors*[20] that it was barbarian raiders from the Balkan peninsula who swept through Boeotia and on down to the Peloponnese and then left, returning to their homeland in temperate Europe.[21]

Although it may be true that few researchers doubt the presence of raiders in the ancient Near East, there is less harmony over the claim that they caused the collapse of the Bronze Age. Drews comments that Nancy Sandars once held the "raiders" view of events in Greece but that she changed her mind and adopted what is called the systems collapse theory. Of all the factors we have been looking at, the systems collapse theory most closely resembles Jaynes's breakdown model.

17. A. Bernard Knapp, *Copper Production and Divine Protection: Archaeology, Ideology and Social Complexity on Bronze Age Cyprus* (Coronet Books Inc., 1986).
18. Wolfgang Helck, "Die Seevölker in den ägyptischen Quellen," in H. Müller-Karpe, *Geschichte des 13 und 12 Jahrhundert v. Chr. Frankfurt Colloquium, Feb. 1976* (Munich, 1977).
19. Nancy K. Sandars, *The Sea Peoples: Warriors of the Ancient Mediterranean 1250–1150 B.C.* (London: Thames & Hudson, 1985).
20. Vincent Desborough, *The Last Mycenaeans and their Successors: An Archaeological Survey ca. 1200–1000 B.C.* (Oxford: Oxford University Press, 1964).
21. Drews, *Bronze Age*, pp. 91–93.

Systems Collapse

Most of the theories we have looked at so far point to a systems collapse model, that is, some internal weakness in the social structure that allowed even a small disruption to precipitate a complete collapse of the culture. In some cases this effect is suggested by the fact that we see very little rebuilding. With the exception of devastating events such as volcanoes and tsunamis, most civilizations simply start over. And historically we see that even in the case of sacking by invaders, some remnant of the original population, or even the invaders themselves, rebuild the city. An example of this is the continuance of Rome after being sacked in 387 B.C.E. Furthermore, in the case of raiders, it is one thing for raiders to assault the great cities of the Near East, it is another thing for them to be so successful. The systems collapse model proposes that there was a widespread fragility in the socially cohesive structures themselves. With this in mind, the cause of the Catastrophe was the internal weakness of late Bronze Age societies, and the agent (or proximal cause) could be raiders, natural disaster, drought, or migrations. All the agents we have looked at so far were possible contributors to the rolling blackouts that swept across the late-Bronze Age Near East. But, as we have seen, none of them fit the data as being a first-order driver of the Catastrophe. And even if we add Drews's military suggestion, we are still left with the question of why this was so successful over such a wide range of cities, terrains, and peoples.

Bureaucratic flaws and inefficiencies are often cited as the likely source of structural instability. V. Gordon Childe, for example, proposed a Marxist view that inequalities built into hierarchically stratified societies held contradictions that virtually guaranteed collapse. Drews points out that it is particularly revealing to use the Linear B tablets to compare Bronze Age with Iron Age societies. Using this lens, we see what appears to be a particularly stifling and ponderous bureaucracy that attempted to manage every aspect of life. "That systems so complex and centralized collapsed under even slight pressures is not surprising."[22] However, there are serious problems with the systems collapse theory. Why did such ponderous bureaucracies thrive and last so long? And why did they

---

22. Ibid., p. 88.

collapse when they did, given, as Drews reminds us, that there is no evidence they were any more fragile at around 1200 B.C.E. than they were for centuries before that?

The Military Explanation

This theory says that the Catastrophe came about when people in "barbarian" lands realized that they could overcome the conventional chariot-based defenses of the eastern kingdoms by using a new type of battlefield technique: large numbers of infantrymen using javelins and a new type of thrusting and slashing sword called the Naue type II. In this way, by ca. 1200 B.C.E., "The barbarians — in Libya, Palestine, Israel, Lycia, northern Greece, Italy, Sicily, Sardinia, and elsewhere — thus found it within their means to assault, plunder, and raze the richest palaces and cities on the horizon, and this they proceeded to do."[23]

Drews presents ample evidence for a change in warfare with the end of the Bronze Age and the rise of the Iron Age. There seems little reason to doubt that on the fertile plains surrounding the great palaces and cities of the Near East, most battles were chariot battles, with infantry playing a supporting role. After the Catastrophe, however, in the Iron Age the chariot was no longer used in this way. The chariot became part ceremonial platform and part transport vehicle, bringing fighters to certain places on the battlefield. And archeological evidence does indeed show strong support for the introduction of new weaponry, the Naue type II sword being one of the most important examples. This sword is believed to have originated in the area between the eastern Alps and the Carpathians, possibly as early as 1450 B.C.E. It made its appearance in southern areas by ca. 1200 B.C.E., was the only sword in use in the Aegean by the eleventh century, and by the beginning of the Iron Age had become the standard sword throughout the Near East.[24]

The message Drews takes from this is that the eastern kingdoms collapsed after they were attacked.[25] The Catastrophe was straightforwardly the result of innovative battlefield techniques levied against antiquated chariot-based defense systems. Thus he sees no reason to look for a

23. Ibid., p. 104.
24. Ibid., pp. 194–195.
25. Ibid., p. 93.

systems collapse or any sort of weaknesses in the social structure of the Near East kingdoms.

I think Drews is essentially right about the military explanation. It fits the data for the great Catastrophe better than all the others we have considered. To drive this point home, he reminds us of what amounts to an 800-pound fact in the room: most of the major palaces and cities in the Near East at the end of the Bronze Age were burned and sacked. Natural disasters do not burn and sack. People burn and sack. But we know that the great empires did not turn on each other at around 1200 B.C.E. That would have left massive campaign trails, and there would have been victors. So who is left? Motley collections of infantry warriors from barbarous, mountainous, or otherwise less desirable lands, perhaps.[26]

Problems With the Military Explanation

Drews's military explanation focuses tightly on the agent of destruction: the invading "barbarians" or "city-sackers." But, in my view, this was not the cause. The cause was the context that allowed "barbarians" all across the Near East to get the message about the new battlefield gold standard, a message that the administrators, quartermasters, and generals of all the eastern kingdoms failed to notice. How plausible is it that, in the decades or centuries leading up to the Catastrophe, only the "barbarians" noticed an increasing advantage of infantry over chariots? Not very plausible, in my opinion. This consideration does not invalidate the military explanation. But it does return the focus of discussion to a version of the systems collapse theory. I will offer a Jaynesian version of systems collapse, one where cognitive inflexibility, not administrative inflexibility, leaves whole cultures confused, indecisive, and vulnerable.

In Drews's book, I could not find an explanation for why the "barbarians" responded more quickly to military conditions than did the kingdoms. However, there are two comments indicating that Drews is aware that one is needed. I will briefly look at these comments because they are relevant to the justification of a systems collapse component.

While discussing the Karnak temple depictions of the Libyan king Meryre's failed attack on Egypt, Drews says, "Meryre's failure, like the

_____
26. Ibid., p. 97.

Achaeans' successes at Troy and Thebes, seems to have publicized the possibilities of the new kind of warfare."[27] And in his preface to the military solution, Drews makes a similar statement about the efficacy of infantry assaults against chariot defenses: "Once that lesson had been learned, power suddenly shifted from the Great Kingdoms to motley collections of infantry warriors."[28]

There are several problems with these comments. One concerns the likelihood that failures such as Meryre's would have been publicized in the first place. Drews is no doubt aware that a failure was more likely to *not* be publicized. Perhaps this is why his sentence is crafted more carefully and he says only that the *possibility* was publicized. Furthermore, he sweetens the assertion by mentioning the success of the Trojan War. This would indeed be strong support for spreading the word if we did not already know that that particular view of how Troy fell was itself speculative. His second comment casually implies that lessons had been learned by the invaders. The problem with this is that there are no documented examples of lessons learned. The implied message here is that over time there had been numerous skirmishes around the Mediterranean where small victories or marginal gains had accumulated into a new consensus view of battlefield innovations. Although this might be true, I could find only three candidates for this in Drews's book, and all of them are speculative.

One is Drews's contention that Troy was sacked not by Ionic-speaking warriors from Mycenaean palaces but rather by more bellicose North Greek speakers from the less civilized regions of Thessaly and Phthiotis.[29] Two other suggestions that could serve as early victories for lessons learned are from the Old Testament. The first is from the Song of Deborah (Judges 5), which, Drews explains, celebrates an Israeli victory over the chariots of Jabin, king of Hazor. The second is from the Song of the Sea (Exodus 15), depicting the successful escape of Moses and his followers from Egyptian chariots.[30] It is certainly possible that these are examples of the kind of victories over chariots that Drews wants them to be. Nevertheless, they are clearly speculative and require special pleading. As far as I can see, there are no strong, independently documented

---

27. Ibid., p. 219.
28. Ibid., p. 97.
29. Ibid., p. 117.
30. Ibid., pp. 212–213.

examples of a series of lesson-learning encounters with chariot forces in the period just preceding the Catastrophe.

There is another shortcoming to the military explanation that suggests the need for a systems collapse component. Drews points out in several places that the great kingdoms of the Near East were doing just fine right up to the tossing of the torch. For example, Drews describes the socioeconomic health of the city of Ugarit as robust enough that the palace scribes continued to do their work right up "until the day of destruction."[31] Life in the Greek palace-states seemed to be so secure in the century and a half before the Catastrophe that H. W. Catling, once the director of the British School at Athens, described the period as the *Pax Mycenaica*.[32]

And, continuing in this spirit, Drews absolves the "ponderous and stifling" palace bureaucracies from any culpability by noting that, as overmanaged as they may have been, "The fact remains, however, that these bureaucratic dinosaurs were remarkably long lived."[33]

Drews's purpose in illustrating the healthy functioning of the eastern kingdoms is to advance his military theory to the front of the explanatory line. We have already seen that droughts, "acts of God," iron, migrations, and raiders did not cause the Catastrophe. Given that cities and palaces were doing fine, the only theory left standing is the military option. And this would be fine if not for the fact that this remaining theory depends upon people noticing that the new battlefield techniques are gaining success. But, as Drews depicts it, only the "barbarians" made this observation, and not the large cities and palaces. If the cities were functioning well, then they would have been just as capable as the "barbarians" of noticing changes in battlefield outcomes. But if the cities and palaces throughout the region could be shown to have been internally inflexible, then that would resolve this problem, and the military theory would be back on sound footing. Enter Julian Jaynes and the breakdown of the bicameral mind.

---

31. Ibid., p. 89.
32. Ibid., p. 116.
33. Ibid., p. 88.

The Bicameral Mind Theory

Julian Jaynes's breakdown of the bicameral mind is a kind of systems collapse theory. Bicameral societies are inherently inflexible. Jaynes says that as bicameral theocracies grow and become more successful, the complexities of hallucinatory control also grow, "until the civil state and civilized relations can no longer be sustained, and the bicameral society collapses."[34] So if we conceive of the eastern kingdoms as being bicameral societies, some of the problems for Drews's military explanation go away. Before whatever the disrupting factor was (e.g., assaults by "barbarians"), they would have been functioning well, just as Drews pointed out. But unlike nonbicameral societies, they would not have been very adaptable. In Jaynes's words, "In comparison with conscious nations, then, bicameral nations were more susceptible to collapse. The directives of the gods are limited. If on top of this inherent fragility, something really new occurred, such as a forced intermingling of bicameral peoples, the gods would be hard pressed to sort anything out in a peaceable way."[35]

Systems Collapse Affirmed

The anthropologist Eric Cline at George Washington University has taken a fresh look at the great Catastrophe in his 2014 book, *1177 B.C.: The Year Civilization Collapsed*. His book contains an up to date compilation of research on the final four centuries of the Bronze Age. Cline's particular emphasis is on the interconnectivity of cities and empires in the Aegean and Eastern Mediterranean. He surveys the cargo of sunken ships, examines the contents of letters and monumental carvings, and discusses cross-cultural influences in terms of marriages, trade, treaties, and warfare. In his search for the cause of the great collapse, Cline examines the familiar cast of characters: earthquakes, climate change, drought, famine, the Sea Peoples, and internal rebellion. In keeping with his emphasis on overlapping social networks, he also considers factors such as the collapse of international trade and the decentralization and rise of the private merchant. Cline's conclusion is that all of these are wanting, "In my opinion … none of these individual factors would have been

---

34. Jaynes, *The Origin of Consciousness*, p. 195.
35. Ibid., pp. 207–208.

cataclysmic enough on their own to bring down even one of these civilizations, let alone all of them."[36] His conclusion is that the catastrophe was caused by a form of systems collapse.

This is the same conclusion I came to above after reviewing the evidence presented in Robert Drews's book. Cline's systems collapse, however, comes with a caveat. Unable to say what, precisely, it was about the system that caused the unraveling, he reframes the event in terms of complexity science or complexity theory as he calls it. Complexity science is the study of complex systems that are made up of a large number of interacting parts. A common task is to develop models that account for sudden changes in these systems. Changes that can be initiated by any one of the many interacting parts, but none of which are accessible as reliable state-change predictors. Theories like this are used to describe the dynamics of traffic jams and other difficult to predict systems such as the stock market. Turning to complexity science isn't without merit in Cline's case, since he has spent most of his book illustrating the dense interconnectivity and rapidly shifting dynamics of cultures at the close of the Bronze Age. Given this state of affairs, it is certainly plausible that the Aegean and Western Mediterranean geopolitical system was, indeed, poised near an irreversible "tipping point." A point of instability at which any small inflection of a single variable such as weather, invaders, or a natural disaster, for example, could initiate a rapid loss of coherence and thus trigger a dramatic collapse.

Appropriate as this reframing may be, I think Cline throws in the towel a bit too soon. While complexity theories can map overall trajectories of state changes in densely interconnected systems, they lose specificity and predictability. Cline is aware of this and expresses some trepidation at his own suggestion, acknowledging that, "… it may not be of much use at this stage, except as an interesting way to reframe our awareness that a multitude of factors were present at the end of the Bronze Age …"[37] And further, he states that, " … we are not even certain that we know all of the variables and we undoubtedly do not know which ones were critical."[38]

---

36. Eric H. Cline, *1177 B.C. The Year Civilization Collapsed* (Princeton: Princeton University Press, 2014), p. 162.
37. Ibid., p. 170.
38. Ibid.

So, as we saw with Drews's military theory, the plausibility of Cline's final suggestion requires a widespread internal fragility of the entire Aegean and Western Mediterranean region. But neither author, nor any other historian that I know of, can identify the source of this broad instability. Historians and archeologists are not trained or motivated to excavate the mentality behind the artifacts and events that they discover and explore. Given this explanatory vacuum, Julian Jaynes's theory is, I believe, a welcome and useful addition.

As the detailed work of both Drews and Cline show, the evidence for the collapse of Bronze Age civilizations calls for a new model, one that identifies a core weakness that is independent of local geography, weather, and other regional variations. Jaynes's bicameral mind answers this call. It identifies a mentality anchored in the trajectory of mortuary practices from the beginning of agriculture, through the advent of idols in the late Neolithic, to the pervasiveness of the voices in the ancient literature, and finally, the woeful cries of an abandoned people: "why have the gods left us?"

CHAPTER 6

The Interpretations of Dreams,
The Origin of Consciousness, and the Birth of Tragedy

ROBERT ATWAN

"Never by daytime will there be an end to
hard work and pain, nor in the night to weariness,
when the gods will send anxieties to trouble us."
— Hesiod, *The Works and Days*

THE MOST CURIOUS CHARACTERISTIC OF HUMAN DREAMS may lie not so much in their reputedly mysterious qualities as in our equally mysterious urge to interpret them. People throughout history have perceived the dream as a riddle, a conundrum, a puzzle, or, as Freud put it, "a rebus"[1] — in short, an enigmatic message to be deciphered. So persistently has this view of the dream endured that today some psychoanalysts believe that the requirement of interpretation may be built into the psychic structure of the dream itself. A dream would not, according to this view, be fully experienced until it had been related and professionally interpreted; that is, *until* it existed as a "text" possessing hermeneutical value. Hermeneutics — the science of interpretations — appropriately derives its name from Hermes, the Greek god of trickery and divine communications, "Speeder of Night's spies / And guide of all her dreames' obscurities."[2]

First published in *Research Communications in Psychology, Psychiatry, and Behavior*, 1981, 6, 163–182. Reprinted with permission.
1. Sigmund Freud, *The Interpretation of Dreams*, trans. by James Strachey (New York: Avon Books, 1965, p. 312). All references to Freud are from this edition.
2. Homer, "A Hymne to Hermes," Chapman translation.

Yet mankind may not always have perceived dreams as mysterious messages requiring interpretation. Nietzsche suspected — and both Freud and Jung entertained his idea — that dream-thinking constituted the basic mode of thinking of early humanity. If that were the case, then prehistoric people probably noticed no difference between sleeping and waking mental states and had no reason to value dreams as a special kind of consciousness. In this phylogenetic picture of the mind, our present dreams return us to a far earlier stage in the evolution of consciousness, one in which the logico-temporal skills we take for granted had not yet come into existence. "Just as the body bears the traces of its phylogenetic development," Jung argued, "so also does the human mind." He went on to say that "there is nothing surprising about the possibility that the figurative language of dreams is a survival from an archaic mode of thought."[3] It may be that this is the primordial consciousness the persecuted Prometheus describes in Aeschylus' great drama of social evolution:

> In those days they had eyes, but sight was meaningless;
> Heard sounds, but could not listen; all their length of life.
> They passed like shapes in dreams, confused and purposeless.
>   (11. 447-49)[4]

In such a world as this, if there were boundary-shifts between dreams and reality, they would indeed have been negligible.

The idea of the dream as a divine message — an idea that would possess enormous cultural consequences — presumably found its way into the thought of the first civilizations in Mesopotamia, Egypt, and the Indus Valley sometime toward the end of the third millennium B.C. This was a period, as Julian Jaynes points out in *The Origin of Consciousness in the Breakdown of the Bicameral Mind*, in which early societies had begun to feel that they had lost the direct guidance of the gods and were desperately trying to reestablish communication through various methods of divination, such as omens, augury, sortilege, and extispicy ("reading" the organs of sacrificed animals).[5] Although all of these practices — including

---

3. Carl G. Jung, "General Aspects of Dream Psychology," in *Dreams*, trans. by R. F. C. Hull (Princeton, NJ: Princeton University Press, 1974), p. 34. See also Freud, p. 588.
4. Aeschylus, *Prometheus Bound*, trans. by Philip Vellacott (New York: Penguin Books, 1980).
5. Julian Jaynes, *The Origin of Consciousness in the Breakdown of the Bicameral Mind* (Boston: Houghton Mifflin, 1976), pp. 236–246.

attention to the meaning of dreams — played a significant role in the life and literature[6] of early civilizations, they apparently were preceded by an even more significant divinatory practice, prophetic possession.[7] Hearing the voice of a god as it passed through the mediumship of a divinely inspired individual remained for millennia the most direct and popularly prized mode of divination. Throughout the ancient world, ecstatic prophecy led to the establishment of highly esteemed oracles, such as those at Delphi or Dodona, where a priestly, scribal class developed a complex interpretive system for the translation of the frenzied priestesses' incoherent expressions. It seems quite possible, given the priority of oracles, that dream interpretation developed in the West as an offshoot of oracular translation. People did not begin believing in dreams until they had first begun to believe in oracles.

Greek mythology provides some evidence (if myth and evidence are not too incompatible) for the assumption that oracles preceded dreams as conduits of divine communications. In Euripides' *Iphigeneia in Tauris* (414 B.C.), the Chorus describes how the infant Phoibos Apollo took control of the Delphic oracle from its ancient possessor, Themis, the daughter of Earth, by slaying the great snake, Python. But Earth reclaimed the oracle and in revenge began transmitting prophetic dreams to mankind. The enraged Apollo then fled to Zeus, who, entertained by the infant god's greedy demands, restored the oracle to Apollo and removed from dreams their truthfulness:

When Apollo, going to Pytho,
had driven Themis, daughter of Earth, from that sacred
oracular place, then Earth
produced the Dreams, nocturnal apparitions,
things primeval, things of the time of telling,
and what she would bring to pass,
by incubation in sleep under the dark ground.
Earth, angry in her daughter's cause,
took from Phoibos his privilege.

6. For example, dreams play a considerable part in the action and imagery of the *Epic of Gilgamesh*, some sections of which date back to the second millennium B.C.
7. E. R. Dodds, *The Greeks and the Irrational* (Berkeley: The University of California Press, 1951), p. 70. Dodds cites C. J. Gadd, *Ideas of Divine Rule in the Ancient East*: "oracles and prophecy tend to harden into practices of formal divination," p. 86 (31).

But Lord Apollo ran on swift
feet to Olympos,
clung with his infant hand
to the throne of Zeus, pleading
that the grudge of the earth goddess be taken away
from the Phythian temple.
Zeus laughed, because the child
had come in haste for the spoils with their golden treasures,
and shook his curls to affirm surcease of the night voices,
took away truth from what was shown men in night visions,
restored to Apollo his privileges,
and to mortals at the throne thronged with strangers gave confidence
in his oracular poems.   (11. 1234–1256)[8]

Especially interesting in this account of the ancient rivalry between oracles and dreams is the image of Apollo as an infant, since the Greeks
apparently believed that infants do not dream.[9]

The chthonic origin of dreams becomes powerfully associated with
oracular knowledge in the Prometheus legend. A child of Earth, which
the Greeks considered the source of all prophecy, Prometheus (whose
name means "Fore-thinker") boastfully claims to have given mankind
"all human skill and science." Besides stealing fire from the gods for humanity's improvement, Prometheus taught the race of mortals the difficult arts of mathematics, astronomy, agriculture, husbandry, navigation,
and medicine. He also showed people "how to set down words in writing — the all-remembering skill, mother of many arts." And as another
contribution to cultural evolution, he

distinguished various modes of prophecy,
And was the first to tell from dreams what Fate ordained
Should come about; interpreted the hidden sense
Of voices, sounds, sights met by chance upon the road. (11. 484–87)

In the context of modern scientific skepticism, however, with its emphasis on prediction rather than prophecy, it may be difficult to understand
the intellectual premium the ancient world placed on prophetic skill.

8. Euripides, *Ipigeneia*, trans. by Richmond Lattimore (New York: Oxford University Press, 1973).
9. Aristotle, *de somniis*, 461A.

It helps to keep in mind, therefore, that since early civilizations were as mystified about the past as they were about the future (note that in Euripides' myth, Earth produces dreams that help mortals divine "things primeval"), the future must have seemed just as potentially knowable as the past. To put this another way, we might argue that the less a society knows about its past, the more it will believe it can know about its future. Prometheus' punishment was perfectly suited to his name and crime: chained to the rocky earth, the source of dreams; a vulture set to gnaw at his liver, the organ the Greeks regarded as the seat of divination.

The connection between dreams and divination remains close and vital throughout early Greek civilization. The great first work of European literature is not more than 620 lines into the telling when what may be the first "transcript" of a dream in western culture occurs. And it is a divine dream. Agamemnon, chief leader of the Greek armies now into the tenth year of their siege of Troy, has provoked Achilles' wrath by taking that leader's concubine from him. Withdrawing from battle, Achilles petitions his divine mother, Thetis, to ask Zeus to intervene in the struggle so that the Greeks will be defeated and realize how desperately they need the prowess of Achilles. Zeus agrees and, as Book II of the *Iliad* begins, commands evil Dream to visit Agamemnon with a false message:

> So he spoke, and Dream listened to his word and descended.
> Lightly he came down beside the swift ships of the Achaians
> and came to Agamemnon the son of Atreus. He found him
> sleeping within his shelter in a cloud of immortal slumber.
> Dream stood then beside his head in the likeness of Nestor,
> Neleus' son, whom Agamemnon honoured beyond all
> elders beside. In Nestor's likeness the divine Dream spoke to him:
> "Son of wise Atreus breaker of horses, are you sleeping?
> He should not sleep night long who is a man burdened with counsels
> and responsibility for a people and cares so numerous.
> Listen quickly to what I say, since I am a messenger
> of Zeus, who far away cares much for you and is pitiful.
> Zeus bids you arm the flowing-haired Achaians for battle
> in all haste; since now you might take the wide-wayed city
> of the Trojans. For no longer are the gods who live on Olympos
> arguing the matter, since Hera forced them all over
> by her supplication, and evils are in store for the Trojans

from Zeus. Keep this thought in your heart then, let not forgetfulness take you, after you are released from the kindly sweet slumber."

                                                                (11. 16-34)[10]

The trick dream works. Agamemnon wakes up "believing things in his heart that were not to be accomplished."

Agamemnon's dream is prototypical of the Homeric dream. In Book XXIII of the *Iliad*, Achilles dreams of his slain friend Patroklus, who "came and stood over his head" asking for proper burial. In Book IV of the *Odyssey*, the goddess Athene hovers above Penelope's head disguised as her sister, and then in Book VI the goddess drifts into Nausikaa's bedchamber

> like a breath of wind to where the girl slept,
> and came and stood above her head and spoke a word to her,
> likening herself to the daughter of Dymas, famed for seafaring
>
> (11. 20–23)[11]

In Homer's nighttime world, the dream elusively enters the dreamer's bedchamber from the outside; assumes the shape of a trusted friend or relative; stands at the head of the dreamer; and either delivers a message or engages in conversation with the dreamer. In none of these dreams does the dream seem to be occurring *inside* the dreamer. The dream is almost entirely auditory and nearly identical — except of course for the precondition of sleep — to the waking visitation of gods. Though Homer very briefly refers to other dream states,[12] the auditory-oracular type clearly represents for him the dream *par excellence*.

One dream in Homer, however, stands out from all the rest: Penelope's famous dream in Book XIX of the *Odyssey*. Odysseus has returned to Ithaka disguised as a beggar, and Penelope (who may "unconsciously" recognize her husband's identity) asks him to interpret a dream:

> But come, listen to a dream of mine and interpret it for me.
> I have twenty geese here about the house, and they feed on
> grains of wheat from the water trough. I love to watch them.
> But a great eagle with crooked beak came down from the mountain,

---

10. *The Iliad of Homer*, trans. by Richmond Lattimore (Chicago: The University of Chicago Press, 1961).
11. *The Odyssey of Homer*, trans. by Richmond Lattimore (New York: Harper & Row, 1968).
12. See the *Iliad*, 22. 199–201.

and broke the necks of them all and killed them. So the whole twenty
lay dead about the house, but he soared high in the bright air.
Then I began to weep — that was in my dream — and cried out
aloud, and around me gathered the fair-haired Achaian women
as I cried out sorrowing for my geese killed by the eagle.
But he came back again and perched on the jut of the gabled
roof. He now had a human voice and spoke aloud to me:
'Do not fear, O daughter of far-famed Ikarios.
This is no dream, but a blessing real as day. You will see it
done. The geese are the suitors, and I, the eagle, have been a bird of
portent, but now I am your own husband, come home,
and I shall inflict shameless destruction on all the suitors.'
So he spoke; and then the honey-sweet sleep released me,
and I looked about and saw the geese in my palace, feeding
on their grains of wheat from the water trough, just as they had been.

Odysseus answers her:

'Lady, it is impossible to read this dream and avoid it
by turning another way, since Odysseus himself has told you
its meaning, how it will end. The suitors' doom is evident
for one and all. No one will avoid his death and destruction.'

Then Penelope responds with one of the most celebrated comments on
dreams in literature:

'My friend, dreams are things hard to interpret, hopeless to puzzle
out, and people find that not all of them end in anything.
These are two gates through which the insubstantial dreams issue.
One pair of gates is made of horn, and one of ivory.
Those of the dreams which issue through the gate of sawn ivory,
these are deceptive dreams, their message is never accomplished.
But those that come into the open through the gates of the
polished horn accomplish the truth for any mortal who sees them.
I do not think that this strange dream that I had came to me
through this gate. My son and I would be glad if it did so.'

(11. 535–569)

Unlike other Homeric dreams, Penelope's has a very strong visual component and is narrated by the dreamer expressly for interpretation.

Furthermore, as E. R. Dodds says in his indispensable study of the Greek mind, "it is the only dream in Homer which is interpreted symbolically."[13] This would make the dream, in fact, one of the earliest symbolically interpreted "texts" in literature.

Even a cursory reading of Penelope's dream suggests its internal and dramatic complexity. The dream is not only a portent of what Odysseus will accomplish, but its visual element is in itself a typical augural event. Penelope has, in other words, dreamt an omen. Yet, the dream does not stop there; it surprisingly goes on to include its own interpretation. Penelope then (cunningly?) places this "box within a box" before her disguised husband (who has already revealed another disguised self to her in the dream), asking him to put it all into another box. Then, as though to disqualify his self-identifying interpretation, she concludes with a lovely image to remind both of them how unreliable dreams can be.

As one of the earliest specimens in the history of dreams, this first symbolically interpreted dream clearly shows how much alike the *modus operandi* of dreams and oracles had become. It also replicates in a way the three-stage interpretative procedure commonly used by the oracles at Delphi: (1) the puzzling or incoherent "text" of the priestess (the dream vision of the eagle and geese); (2) its prophetical translation into another, clearer text (the eagle's interpretation), which incidentally was often composed — as were Homer's lines — in dactylic hexameters; and (3) the delivery of the text to the client (the disguised Odysseus), who then must reinterpret the message himself to decide what course of action it recommends. In terms of the poem's dramatic action, Penelope's dream becomes Odysseus' oracle. In terms of subsequent literary history, Penelope's dream is an accurate portent of the stuff dreams to come will be made of.

Despite its intricacy, Penelope's dream would not have interested Freud, who carefully distinguished between authentic and artificial dreams: "most of the artificial dreams constructed by imaginative writers are designed for symbolic interpretation ... they reproduce the writer's thoughts under a disguise which is regarded as harmonizing with the recognized characteristics of dreams."[14] Freud always admitted that the poets had anticipated his psychological discoveries, yet he apparently

13. Dodds, *The Greeks and the Irrational,* p. 106.
14. Freud, *Interpretation of Dreams,* p. 129.

took issue with Cicero's belief that "even dreams contrived by poets partake of the essence of dreams."[15] The Homeric oracular dream would undoubtedly have been too lucid and coherent for Freud; his analytical procedures seemed to thrive on incoherence, fragmentation, and sheer scarcity of evidence. Professionally, Freud was suspicious (as Jung was not) of dreams reported to contain sensible auditory data. Though acknowledging that dreams occasionally do make use of auditory and other sense impressions, he nevertheless insisted throughout his writings that dreams "think predominately in visual images."[16]

That auditory-oracular dreams are hardly common today does not necessarily mean they have always been the literary fabrications Freud considered them to be. To be sure, the medieval dream-allegory and the early nineteenth-century dream-vision were often inspired by firmly entrenched literary conventions. Yet that might not have been the case for Homer. Citing ancient classifications of dreams, E. R. Dodds thinks that the oracle dream (also known as the *chrematismos* or *admonitio* dream), "in which a single dream-figure presents itself, as in Homer, to the sleeper and gives him prophecy, advice, or warning," may not be a purely literary invention, but, rather like a hallucination, a peculiarly stylized expression of deeply-rooted culture-patterns.[17] According to Dodds, enough documentation exists to suggest that Homeric dreams, though they sound unrealistic to modern readers, may very likely resemble a type of actual dream familiar to ancient civilizations.

Such a view, of course, goes against the grain of traditional Freudian thinking, which usually proceeds according to a timeless and global model of the human mind. Although there seems little reason to suppose that all people at all times dream the same way, psychoanalytic interpretations of literary and historical dreams generally assume such universality to be the case. For example, in an impressive recent study of dreams in Greek tragedy, George Devereux dismisses the typical Homeric dream as

---

15. Cicero, *de divin*, 1. 42.

16. Freud, *Interpretation of Dreams*, p. 82; see also p. 67.

17. Dodds, p. 107–109. Although it is tempting to think Homer constructed auditory dreams because he was blind, Dodds's documentation makes it clear that reports of such dreams pervade ancient writing. In modern times, James Joyce (who was nearly blind) thought dreams were closely tied to auditory stimuli: "In sleep our senses are dormant, except the sense of hearing, which is always awake, since you can't close your ears. So any sound that comes to our ears during sleep is turned into dreams." Thus *Finnegans Wake*, the longest auditory dream in literature.

psychologically implausible: "long discourses are undreamlike precisely because they fit the literary-esoteric convention that important dreams should include long speeches."[18] As a literary psychotherapist, Devereux intellectually leans toward Freud's ideal manifest dream — distorted, disorienting, rich in scotomatous imagery. Psychoanalysts, unlike Penelope, prefer the gates of ivory to the gates of horn. Clinical experience, moreover, has shown Devereux that "dreams involving *actual auditory sensations* are extremely rare, and dreams of *hearing* articulate speech practically non-existent."[19] Against the artificial Homeric dream, he places the far more plausible Euripidean dream, which could be dreamed by "real Greeks or by modern dreamers."[20] An oracular dream, in Devereux's view, is by definition not "properly psychological." This is debatable; but Devereux is clearly correct when he observes that between the age of Homer and that of the great tragic poets "the manner of *contriving* literary dreams had changed."[21]

To see the change we have only to look at the vivid dream near the opening of the earliest surviving Greek tragedy, Aeschylus' *The Persians* (472 B.C.). Atossa, widow of the great Persian King Darius, relates an allegorical dream that foreshadows her son Xerxes' devastating defeat by the Greek navy at Salamis in 480 B.C.:

> Since first my son marshalled his army and set forth
> To waste Ionia, every night dreams visit me;
> But never yet so clear a vision as I saw
> This night that's past. Listen: two women, finely dressed,
> One in the Persian style, the other Dorian,
> appeared to me, flawless in beauty, and in gait
> And stature far excelling women of our day.
> Sisters of one race, each had her inheritance,
> One Greece, the other Asia. And, it seemed, these two
> Provoked each other to a quarrel; and my son
> restrained and tamed them, yoked them to his chariot,
> And fastened harness on their necks. And one of them,
> Proud of these trappings, was obedient to the rein.

18. George Devereux, *Dreams in Greek Tragedy* (Berkeley: University of California Press, 1976), p. xxv.
19. Ibid., pp. 30–31.
20. Ibid., p. 267.
21. Ibid., p. xxix.

The other struggled, tore the harness from the car,
Threw off the bridle, snapped the wooden yoke in two.
My son fell to the ground; and by his side his father
Darius stood and pitied him. Xerxes looked up,
Saw him, and tore his robe. Such was my dream by night.

(11. 176 ff.)[22]

The first thing to notice about Atossa's clairvoyant dream is how purely visual it is compared to the typical dream in Homer. Aeschylus surely modeled this dream along the lines of the symbolically visual (and violent) component of Penelope's dream, yet felt that he could dispense with the conventional auditory element. The dream is still an oracular one, however; almost immediately after Atossa awakens, her dream's grimly prophetic message is reinforced by the omen of a falcon successfully attacking an eagle.

With few exceptions, Atossa's dream establishes the dream pattern of fifth-century Greek dramatic literature. From Aeschylus on, dream experience will be predominately visual. The dreamer will not be the passive recipient of a message, but will become an active participant in the dream (in Aeschylus' *The Choephori*, the Chorus reports that Klytaimestra dreams she gave birth to a snake, wrapped it in shawls like a baby, and breast-fed it; Hecabe, in Euripides' play of that name, dreams that a fawn she holds in her lap is dragged away from her). The dreamer will also view the dream less as an extrapsychic visitation and more as an intrapsychic phenomenon (in Euripides' play, Iphigeneia dreams she escapes from Tauris and reaches Argos, where she dreams herself asleep dreaming another dream). And like Penelope's precursive dream, the content of dreams in the tragedies will be invariably violent. The change in dream patterns between the Homeric epics and the tragedies is admittedly not complete; vestiges of the divine visitation dream remain. But it is clear that by the fifth century B.C. fundamental changes have occurred in the literary construction of dreams. Is it possible that this change signals something larger than a change in literary fashion?

I think so. If we can assume that these earliest of invented dreams duplicated authentic oneiric phenomena (as Dodds convincingly suggests)

---

22. Aeschylus, *The Persians*, trans. by Philip Vellacott (New York: Penguin Books, 1980).

and were not simply artificial or "poetic" in the Freudian sense, then we can reasonably conclude that the change in dreams from a predominately auditory experience to a predominately visual one entailed a rather significant alteration in the structure of human consciousness.[23] That such an alteration very likely did occur is the central argument of what is surely one of the most provocative studies of the human mind to have appeared in recent years — Julian Jaynes's *The Origin of Consciousness in the Breakdown of the Bicameral Mind*. Briefly stated, Jaynes's hypothesis is that the subjective consciousness we take for granted — our everyday sense of self-awareness and individuality — developed as late as the first millennium B.C. Before then, men and women were "bicameral"; that is, they lacked cerebral hemisphere integration and lived without a clear sense of self-determination and responsibility. Their actions were guided, Jaynes argues, by auditory hallucinations activated in the *right* temporal parietal region of the brain. The "voices," Jaynes maintains, were quite simply the voices of the gods. They were in no sense "figments of the imagination" of anyone. They *were* man's volition. They occupied his nervous system, probably his right hemisphere, and from stores of admonitory and perceptive experience, transmuted this experience into articulated speech which then "told" the man what to do.[24] These authoritative right-hemisphere voices controlled the destiny of people and nations.

Jaynes believes that the bicameral mind evolved *after* the acquisition of language and held sway for at least seven millennia. But the advent of writing, the rise of cities, and the expansion of trade (Prometheus' gifts, remember) eroded the hallucinatory authority. With the subsequent specialization of the left hemisphere came new civilizations based on subjective, analytical, and moral values. The transformation occurred rather quickly. For Jaynes, the other-directed world of the *Iliad* is still basically a bicameral world in which the "gods take the place of consciousness."[25] On the other hand, the *Odyssey*, which Jaynes accepts as at least a century older, ushers us into a somewhat different world, one that seems to

---

23. This is not to claim that people in ancient times had no visual dreams. That would be absurd. The point is that auditory dreams were more highly valued than visual ones and were fairly common, though certainly not as articulate as Homer renders them. Socrates mentions having auditory-oracular dreams in *Crito* 44B and in *Phaedo* 60E.
24. Jaynes, *Origin of Consciousness*, pp. 202–203.
25. Ibid., p. 72.

represent a transitional stage (*vide* Penelope's dream) between the two types of mind. By about the end of the sixth century B.C., though bicameral flashbacks obviously persist for some time, we begin to notice the blossoming of the integrated subjective conscious mind in Greece.

Although dreams and drama do not fall within the scope of Jaynes's argument,[26] the observable changes in dream patterns as reflected in the tragedy of the fifth century help support his hypothesis. If hearing were, as he maintains, "the very essence of the bicameral mind,"[27] we may reasonably surmise that the auditory dreams which have come down to us through ancient literature and history are truer to actual dream experiences than we now think. With the breakdown of the bicameral mind and the loss of direct daytime links to divinity, societies probably found a much needed substitute and solace in dreams, just as they had in oracles. It seems quite likely that people who depended upon hearing authoritative voices during the day, would also be prone to hearing them at night in their dreams. And as contact with the receding gods diminished, the night voices would have — along with prophets and oracles — helped keep divinity within earshot.

The ancient idea of the dream as a divine message originated, if my elaboration of Jaynes's thesis is correct, as a response to a particular psychogenic condition. His theory also suggests why the ancient dream experience, which to us seems so artificial and literary, followed a distinctly auditory pattern. Furthermore, the shift in dream patterns from the auditory dream of the Homeric period to the visual dreams of the fifth century tragedies closely approximates the timetable Jaynes proposes for the bicameral mind's breakdown and the evolution of left-hemispheric specialization.

Perhaps, too, Jaynes's thesis helps shed some light on the obscure origins of drama. "The coming of consciousness," he observes, "can in a certain vague sense be construed as a shift from an auditory mind to a visual mind."[28] To pass from the age of epics to the age of tragedies is, of course, to shift from an audience of listeners to an audience of

---

26. Jaynes did write a chapter on dreams for *The Origin of Consciousness in the Breakdown of the Bicameral Mind*, however it was not included due to concerns over the length of the book. His ideas on this subject are well represented in his lecture "The Dream of Agamemnon," published in Marcel Kuijsten (ed.), *The Julian Jaynes Collection* (Henderson, NV: Julian Jaynes Society, 2012), and I recommend reading it in conjunction with the present chapter. — *Ed.*
27. Jaynes, *Origin of Consciousness*, p. 269.
28. Ibid.

spectators. Writing of Aeschylus' artistry in *The Persians*, the classicist
C. J. Herington observes that the dramatist orchestrated all the resources
at his disposal, including "the new, visual element, which was the crucial
innovation of the tragedians."[29] It seems possible that the mental processes that lay behind the growing literary preference for the new visual
dreams over the old-fashioned auditory ones were the same processes
that contributed to the birth of tragedy. Legend has it that Aeschylus
attributed the birth of tragedy in his mind, at least, to a dream, albeit an
old-fashioned one:

> Aeschylus used to say that once, as a youth, he was guarding the grapes
> in the countryside and went to sleep. Dionysos appeared over him and
> told him to compose tragedy. When daylight came, since he wanted to
> obey the god, he tried it, and found it easy from that time on.[30]

The connection between dreams and the origins of drama seems even
stronger when we note that the Greek term for tragic actor (*hypokrités*)
was most likely derived from the primitive, ritualistic sense of *hypokríno-
mai*, which in Homer usually means "to interpret a dream or an omen."[31]

As the dream in the fifth century B.C. begins to move *inside* the mind
of the dreamer, and as the dreamer begins to move *inside* his dream, we
can observe a process of interiorization in which the mind for the first
time in human history can be seen as a model of the theater. George Devereux wonders "whether the *idea* of the theater was inspired by dreams,
which are in a way, private dramatic performances."[32] The shift from
a predominately auditory mind to a predominately visual one, and the
revolution in human consciousness entailed by that shift, strikingly support that age-old conjecture.

One metaphor replaces another. The dream is no longer a prophetic
message sent by the gods. It is a private dramatic performance in which,
as the eighteenth-century English writer Joseph Addison put it, we are
the theater, the actors, and the audience.[33]

29. C. J. Herington, *Introduction to Aeschlus' The Persians* (New York: Oxford University Press, 1981), p. 27.
30. Pausanias, *Descriptions of Greece*, I. 21,2. Cited by Herington, p. 12.
31. For a full discussion of this interesting etymological connection between dreams and drama, see
George Thomson, *Aeschylus and Athens* (New York: Grosset & Dunlap, 1968), pp. 170–172.
32. Devereux, *Dreams in Greek Tragedy*, p. 123.
33. And, Freud would add, the playwright.

CHAPTER 7

Evolution and Inspiration

JUDITH WEISSMAN

H UMAN BEINGS NEED INSPIRED POETRY, whether we like it or not.
Poetry originating in urgent, commanding voices has been under
attack for twenty-five hundred years but it refuses to die. Plato claimed
that the poetry of Homer and the Greek tragedians entrapped people in
the traditions of their ancestors; Lucretius scorned prophetic poetry as
the product of superstitious folly. Today certain poststructuralists, academic Marxists, multiculturalists, and feminists attack the poetry that
makes up a large part of the canon of Western literature for all of the old
reasons and many new ones: logocentrism, ethnocentrism, sexism. The
Western tradition of inspired poetry, which is dominated by dead white
European males, is said to embody the ideologies that have supported
the oppressive power structure of Western civilization. In many respects
the attacks are true and worth taking seriously.

And yet the attacks have not stopped the poets. Though rationalism has put an end to many other beliefs, like the idea that the earth is
flat, and to many other practices, like the purgative bleeding of the sick,
from the time of Homer to the present day many poets have claimed to
hear voices that dictated their poems and have written narratives about
characters who obey the commands of either divine or demonic voices,
though other poets — Alexander Pope, John Keats, Robert Browning,
among them — have made no such claim and written no such narratives.
The skepticism or hostility of philosophers has not discouraged the conviction that inspiring voices come to them. I think that the persistence
of this belief can be explained, though in terms that lie outside the usual

First published as the Introduction to Judith Weissman, *Of Two Minds: Poets Who Hear Voices* (Ha-
nover, NH: Wesleyan University Press, 1993). Copyright 1993, Judith Weissman. Reprinted with
permission.

vocabulary of both philosophy and literary criticism. I have not found a
single critic who takes such poets' faith in their inspiring voices seriously,
and so I am standing outside not only the current literary debates but the
old ones too in my conviction that words like "inspired" and "visionary"
are not purely metaphorical expressions implying profundity or other
worldliness. The fact that poets hear commanding voices and that poems
inspired by such voices retain their power over readers can be understood
best through evolutionary biology. "Inspired" and "visionary" describe a
genuine mental phenomenon, an auditory hallucination that can be explained by human evolutionary history.

Some writers who despise poetry that is inspired by voices do at least
believe that inspiration occurs. In both the *Apology* of Socrates and *The
Republic*, Plato calls poetry an impediment to human progress precisely
because it is heard with the bodily ear, not conceived with the mind. In
the *Apology*, Socrates reports going to the poets in his search for wisdom
and being utterly disappointed: "No wisdom enabled them to compose
as they did, but natural genius and inspiration; like the diviners and those
who chant oracles, who say many things but do not understand anything
of what they say. The poets appeared to me to be in much the same case."[1]
He believes that poets and the priests who chant oracles are in the grip
of a non-rational process of natural genius and inspiration: what they say
is invalid because they do not understand it; that is, they do not comprehend it mentally, and therefore they cannot foster mental activity in
their listeners.

In *The Republic,* poets are seen as even more harmful, as threatening
the state. Poets are mere imitators of reality as it is shadowed in the world
of appearances; they are "the ruin of the hearers' minds, unless they possess the antidote, knowledge of what such things really are"[2] — as they
never do. Poets encourage emotion, sympathy, and memory and disguise
their lack of true knowledge with their music, their voice.

> We shall say that the poetic workman dabs on certain colours by us-
> ing the words and phrases of the various arts, but all he knows himself
> is how to imitate: so that others as ignorant as himself, taking their
> view from words, think he is speaking magnificently when he talks in

1. Plato, *The Apology*, in *Great Dialogues of Plato* (New York: New American Library, 1956), p. 428.
2. Plato, *The Republic*, in *Great Dialogues of Plato* (New York: New American Library, 1956), p. 394.

metre and rhythm and pitch about cobbling, or about strategy or anything else. So great is the natural charm in this manner of speaking.[3]

Music and rhythm, qualities that must be heard, not merely thought or
understood, are the enticing snare in which untruth is clothed. Truth
must be naked and new, and by implication, expressed in prose that is
free from the specifically poetic qualities that address the physical being
rather than the mind of the listener.[4] The mind is the most important
faculty for those human beings who are to inhabit Plato's ideal state,
where philosophers are to govern both the soldiers, who have strong
wills, and the workers, who are, unhappily, still in the grip of their senses.
Mind alone can lead the way to a state free from the errors that allowed
democratic Athens to degenerate during the Peloponnesian War.

To Plato, inspired poetry is seductively oral, rhythmic, musical. Its
narrative, stories of what happens to human beings who commit certain
acts, as in Homer and the Greek tragedies, fails to explain why actions
are right or wrong. Not abstract, it shows the consequences of actions,
inviting hearers to imitate some and avoid others. It works by example,
not by analysis, thus appealing to those who have not yet developed the
mental capacities Plato believed necessary if they are to escape the pro-
tracted war and degraded tyranny that had been recent Greek history.
He is right that narrative does not appeal to the powers of reason; even
children and the mentally disabled can understand the implicit ethical
meaning of stories. Plato's distinction between the abstract thought of
philosophers and the narrative of poets was accurate; his belief that abstract thought is a superior mode of teaching ethics to citizens may have
been wrong. Oliver Sacks has said that narrative has "spiritual priority"
over abstract thought and can give "*a sense of the world* — a concrete

---

3. Ibid., p. 400.
4. Eric Havelock (*The Muse Learns to Write: Reflections on Orality and Literacy from Antiquity to the
Present* [New Haven, Conn.: Yale University Press, 1986]) has said of the Platonic dialogues, "Could
not the whole Socratic mission be viewed as a linguistic enterprise, propelled by the oral-literate
transition? If so, Socrates himself played a paradoxical role, an oralist adhering to the habit of his
youth, yet using oralism in a brand-new manner, no longer an exercise in poetic memorization,
but as a prosaic instrument for breaking the spell of the poetic tradition, substituting in its place a
conceptual vocabulary and syntax, which he as a conservative sought to apply to the conventions
governing behavior in an oral society in order to rework them." (p. 5).

reality in the imaginative form of symbol and story — when abstract thought can provide nothing at all."[5]

A utopian state of mind, if not a utopian state, is the goal of many of the new foes of poetry heard as voice. I believe that Jacques Derrida, in particular, provides key words that reveal why inspired poetry is a unique type of literature, especially threatening to philosophers. He devotes an entire volume, *Of Grammatology*, to an exposé of the three-thousand-year-old tradition of orality, primarily a poet tradition, including poems that originate in voices believed to be divine.[6] Some prose, such as folktales and oral histories, has been orally preserved, of course, as well as accounts of historical characters (like Joan of Arc) who heard voices; but there are no orally preserved novels or works of philosophy in which vital messages are conveyed by voices that hearers perceive as external. Taking his stand on the side of the intellectual inquiry only possible in written prose, Derrida provides a brilliant description of the linked qualities of oral poetry. He describes as "natural writing" the literary texts that people have believed to be essentially true and received from some divine or human authority. He sees such writing as "immediately united to the voice and to breath," and he agrees with Plato that poetry is addressed to the body in a way that prose is not. Such writing "is hieratic, very close to the interior holy voice of the *Profession of Faith*, to the voice one hears upon retreating into oneself: full and truthful presence of the divine voice to our inner sense."

Indeed, human beings have believed for thousands of years that what they hear as voice is both true and divine. We understand these texts "as the voice of the other and as commandment."[7] Divine voices have told us what to do, rather than how to think. Derrida wants to undermine this tradition: the classical poems and plays Plato feared, the tradition of the Old and New Testaments, and all subsequent texts in which good

5. Oliver Sacks, *The Man Who Mistook His Wife for a Hat and Other Clinical Tales* (New York: Harper & Row, 1985), pp. 183–84.
6. Walter J. Ong (*Orality and Literacy: The Technologizing of the World* [London: Methuen, 1982]) has incorrectly tried to make Jaynes's theory of bicamerality identical with his own theory of orality: "Whatever one makes of Jaynes' theories, one cannot but be struck by the resemblance between characteristics of the earlier or 'bicameral' psyche as Jaynes describes it — lack of introspectivity, or analytical prowess, of concern with the will as such, of a sense of a difference between past and future — and the characteristics of the psyche in oral cultures not only in the past but even today" (p. 30). Though truly bicameral cultures have always been oral, cultures can be oral without being bicameral, without being governed by hallucinated voices.
7. Jacques Derrida, *Of Grammatology* (Baltimore: Johns Hopkins University Press, 1976), p. 17.

and evil, truth and falsehood, are presumed to exist. An Algerian Jew, he looks forward to a world-historical battle of Algiers that will free us from everything we have inherited in the tradition of "natural writing," a "death of the book," which is "a death of speech (of *so-called* full speech) and a new mutation in the history of writing, in history as writing."[8] His new, mutated writing, like Plato's new philosophy, is to be entirely mental, free from the voice, the body, and the remembered commandments of the past.

In a strange way, Derrida's philosophical assault on "commandment" has roots in Christianity as well as in philosophy. Jesus did not say he came to reject poetry, nor did he discuss literature or philosophy as such; he did seek to change the law, the detailed Jewish law preserved by oral tradition and eventually written down in the Old Testament — dietary laws, family laws, military laws, laws that told the people of Israel both how to look out for themselves and how to look after their own, laws to be obeyed whether or not an individual thought them right and meaningful. In the Gospel of Matthew, Jesus answered the lawyer who asked what was the greatest commandment in the law with "You shall love the Lord your God with all your heart, and with all your soul, and with all your mind. This is the great and first commandment. And a second is like it. You shall love your neighbor as yourself. On these two commandments depend all the law and the prophets" (Matt. 22: 37-40). These two commandments demand subtle thought, not simple obedience in action. Like Plato, Jesus asked that we go beyond the stories, the examples, the commands that we have received from the past and become a new kind of being, rigorously moral, capable of spiritual self-examination. Both the Platonic philosophical tradition and the Christian religious tradition question the precise and clear rules recorded in earlier, oral texts, in the poems of Homer and the Old Testament, by people who thought those commands of divine origin.

Perhaps the power of Jesus' dismissal of the old law is the reason for the absence of inspiring voices in the medieval poetry I have read. Medieval poets wrote about visions that came to them in dreams, pictures of heaven and hell, but I have found none who spoke of hearing a poem dictated by a voice. No doubt some medieval poets did write from auditory

---

8. Ibid., p. 8.

inspiration, but we do not have their poems, perhaps because others did not consider such poems part of a respectable literary tradition.

The voices that have inspired poets have given just what Plato and Derrida have said they did, clear commands from the past, exemplary narratives. To understand why voice should give clear, specific, and practical ethical messages instead of, say, abstract thoughts or descriptions detached from stories, we have to go beyond history to biology and to the theory of Julian Jaynes in *The Origin of Consciousness in the Breakdown of the Bicameral Mind*. On the basis of neurological evidence about the function of the apparently useless speech area on the right side of the brain and from archeological evidence from many ancient cultures, Jaynes has suggested that hallucinated commanding voices were a part of our evolutionary development and that our own brains retain the ability to create such voices even though, as conscious and civilized beings, we no longer need them as our tribal ancestors did. Jaynes begins, as neither philosophers nor literary critics do, with the brain. This theory is that our brains evolved with the capacity to produce admonitory hallucinations — divine voices — because we once needed them to enforce social cohesiveness.

> The situation then is one where the areas on the right hemisphere that correspond to the speech areas [on the left side of the brain] have seemingly no easily observable major function. Why this relatively less essential part of the brain? Could it be that these silent "speech" areas on the right hemisphere had some function at an earlier stage in man's history that now they do not have?
>
> The answer is clear if tentative. The selective pressures of evolution which could have brought about so mighty a result are those of bicameral civilizations. The language of men was involved with only one hemisphere in order to leave the other free for the language of the gods.[9]

Jaynes uses the fragmentary histories we possess from earliest Egypt, Mesopotamia, and Greece to reconstruct a hypothetical history of the evolution of human beings before they were fully conscious and capable of conceptualizing themselves and imagining the different sorts of narratives

9. Julian Jaynes, *The Origin of Consciousness in the Breakdown of the Bicameral Mind* (Boston: Houghton Mifflin, 1976), pp. 103–104.

that would occur if they followed different courses of action, from which they could choose at will.[10]

Jaynes suggests that after the invention of language auditory hallucinations developed to enable tribal people to remember the commands of their leaders:

> The most plausible hypothesis is that verbal hallucinations were a side effect of language comprehension which evolved by natural selection as a method of behavioral control.

> Let us consider a man commanded by himself or his chief to set up a fish weir far upstream from a campsite. If he is not conscious, and cannot therefore narratize the situation and so hold his analog 'I' in a spatialized time with its consequences fully imagined, how does he do it? It is only language, I think, that can keep him at the time-consuming all-afternoon work. A Middle Pleistocene man would forget what he was doing. But lingual man would have language to remind him, either repeated by himself, which would require a type of volition which I do not think he was then capable of, or, as seems more likely, by a repeated "internal" verbal hallucination telling him what to do.[11]

The source to which these hallucinated voices were attributed to changed over time and in different cultures. Voices were thought to come from kings, god-kings, and idols, then were assigned by the Mycenaean Greeks to the Olympian gods and by the Hebrews to Yahweh.

After studying both what we know about the earliest hallucinated voices and the later words of people who remained bicameral, dependent on voices into the conscious age, Jaynes declares that the gods spoke in poetry; they used the rhythmical devices Plato called mere seductive decoration. "The god-side of our ancient mentality, at least in a certain period of history, usually or perhaps always spoke in verse. This means that most men at one time, throughout the day, were hearing poetry (of a sort) composed and spoken within their own minds."[12] Our brains, not arbitrary literary conventions, cause commanding voices to appear in

---

10. "It [consciousness] operates by way of analogy, by way of constructing an analog space with an analog 'I' that can observe that space, and move metaphorically in it. It operates on any reactivity, excerpts relevant aspects, narratizes and conciliates them together in a metaphorical space where such meanings can be manipulated like things in space" (ibid., 65–66).
11. Ibid., p. 134.
12. Ibid., p. 361–362.

our poetry rather than in fiction, history, or philosophy. These voices are neurologically associated with rhythm, not with reason.

I realize that Jaynes's hypothesis that hallucinated voices were a key element in human evolution is not universally accepted and that even if it were, I would still be taking a big risk in arguing that our distant evolutionary past causes conscious, literate people of the present to hear voices and that these contemporary voices retain some of their original purpose, to give us the ethical codes we need to survive. All I can say is that the more I thought about Jaynes's thesis, the more reasonable it sounded, and the more I read in anthropology, in history, and above all, in poetry, the more evidence I found to support the idea that hallucinated voices still give socially useful commands. I simply agree with those who believe that the evolutionary past can be useful — carefully in limited ways — to account for some human behavior in the present.

The best known proponent of this view is E. O. Wilson, the principal theorist of sociobiology, who believes that "there are social traits occurring through all cultures which upon close examination are as diagnostic of mankind as are distinguishing characteristics of other animal species — as true to the human type, say, as wing tessellation is to a fritillary butterfly or a complicated spring melody to a wood thrush."[13] Few go as far as Wilson in arguing that nature more than culture determines our behavior; it is possible to agree with the general idea that we are still bound by our evolutionary past in our civilized human lives without agreeing with him in every detail.[14] Wilson does have some distinguished and persuasive predecessors, who never heard the word sociobiology but nevertheless believed that human behavior was still linked by evolution to the behavior of our animal ancestors. In *The Mill on the Floss*, George Eliot repeatedly compared her human characteristics to the various unreasoning, compulsively repetitive animals they resembled, reminding us that we are not a totally separate species on this earth, absolutely free and self-determining. In this century, Lewis Mumford wrote of the development of cities — apparently a uniquely human event — as, in fact, an extension of animal behavior. He called the second chapter of *The City of History: Its Origins, Its Transformations, and Its Prospects* "Animal

13. E. O. Wilson, *On Human Nature* (Cambridge, Mass.: Harvard University Press, 1978), p. 21.
14. The best book I know on the limits of sociobiology is Philip Kitcher's *Vaulting Ambition: Sociobiology and the Quest for Human Nature* (Cambridge, Mass.: MIT Press, 1985).

Promptings and Foreshadowings," suggesting that we began to gather in established places because we are like the other animals, even fish and birds, who gather to mate and rear young, often in the same place, year after year.[15]

More than our most primitive, instinctual actions can be attributed to evolution, according to biologist Ernst Mayr. He says, in *Animal Species and Evolution*, that the difference between us and other animals is that for us "the behavior phenotype is no longer absolutely determined genetically, but to a greater or lesser extent is the result of learning and education." Newborn human babies cannot go out and weave webs and forage for food like the young of other species; they are programmed to receive teaching first. "The capacity to accept concepts, dogmas, and codes of behavior is one of the many forms of imprinting."[16] I believe that we hallucinate commanding voices because we have evolved to be imprinted with ethical codes; the codes, which can vary enormously, are what the voices reproduce.

I think that auditory hallucinations should be understood as human behavior determined by evolution because I keep finding records of them in extremely different cultures, always urgent, always ethical. I will give just a few examples. In classical Greece, conscious, literate people no longer received regular commands from the gods, as their Mycenaean ancestors had, yet they relied on their oracles, according to Jaynes, on people who could return to a state of receptivity to auditory hallucinations.[17] The classicist Joseph Fontenrose, who has cataloged all reported responses of the Delphic Oracle, has found that though many legendary responses are cryptic, mysterious, or spectacular, the historical responses "are commonplace pronouncements, mostly clear commands and sanctions on religious matters, occasionally on public and private affairs."[18] Fontenrose never mentions Jaynes, and yet his summary fits exactly with Jaynes's theory. If the hallucinated voices of the gods developed from the

15. Lewis Mumford, *The City in History: Its Origins, Its Transformations, and Its Prospects* (New York: Harcourt, Brace and World, 1961).

16. Ernst Mayr, *Animal Species and Evolution* (Cambridge, Mass.: The Belknap Press of Harvard University Press, 1963), pp. 636–637.

17. Jaynes, *Origin of Consciousness*, p. 321.

18. Joseph Fontenrose, *The Delphic Oracle: Its Responses and Operations, with a Catalogue of Responses* (Berkeley: University of California Press, 1978), p. 9.

commands of tribal leaders and were a product of evolution, they had to repeat codes that were already known.

Another classical historian, Robin Lane Fox, actually corroborates Jaynes's theory, even though he calls Jaynes's work "ingenious fantasy" that is "philosophically unsound."[19] Try as he may to be Jaynes's enemy, his report of the known evidence makes him an ally. First, he supports Jaynes's hypothesis that people heard hallucinated voices particularly in times of stress, when they needed to be told what to do. "In the ancient world, as in our own, the evidence suggests that people were most likely to see something when under pressure or at risk."[20] (Visual hallucinations can accompany auditory ones.) He discusses at length Tacitus's account of a priest of Miletus who, after a preparatory ritual, gave response in verse to questions in the minds of petitioners — questions he had not been told. Fox speculates, "If the priest did not ask for his questioners' questions, his verse responses can only have been general and rather stereotyped. Perhaps the god kept to certain familiar verses and 'inspired' his priest to utter one or other set."[21] Yes, that is indeed what Jaynes's hallucinated gods would do.

Such voices are not the property of either the ancient world or the Western world. In *The Mountain People*, anthropologist Colin Turnbull describes the Ik, a Ugandan tribe who had lived peaceably when they could both hunt and garden, until they were forcibly removed from their ancestral lands and relocated to an area where they could no longer hunt. Along with their ancient home, they lost their economy, their religion, and their social bonds; they became the cruelest of individuals, neglecting to grow the crops they once raised, eating whatever they could find each day, snatching food from old people and babies. They had once been guided by the voices of their ancestral spirits, the *abang*, who came to priests in their sleep and told them what they wanted to know. The last priests died shortly after the Ik were forcibly moved, and only one person was left who could still hear commanding voices, Nagoli, the daughter of a priest. Because she was not allowed to become a priest herself, she was called mad. Isolated with the voices of the *abang*, "she was always off on her own, tending gardens that required care and hard work while

19. Robin Lane Fox, *Pagans and Christians* (New York: Alfred A. Knopf, 1986), p. 108.
20. Ibid., pp. 117–18.
21. Ibid., 172.

everywhere else food grew wild."[22] The voices told her how to live by the old agricultural rules, even when no one else obeyed them.

A contemporary group of people who still hear commanding voices enforcing inherited codes are the Saramaka of South America, interviewed by Richard Price, who recorded their oral histories in *Alabi's World*. Their ancestors were brought from Africa to Central America as slaves but soon rebelled against white domination and created a unique culture preserved in a heroic oral tradition. In one episode, the gods appeared to the Saramakas after the war against the whites and gave instructions on how to clear and burn three garden sites to renew agriculture.[23] And even the present-day Saramakas, who are supposed to be Christians, call on the speaking *apukus* who helped their ancestors win the war of liberation. People "still have such gods in their heads, 'calling' them for purposes of divination and curing inside people's houses."[24] Although I have not made any systematic search of anthropological literature for speaking gods, I have found by accident enough to convince me that the voices Jaynes has found among several ancient cultures have existed in many more, both ancient and still living.

Jaynes also says that many perfectly normal people occasionally hear voices; my experience corroborates this too. One friend says he hears his mother yelling at him. Another friend, who scoffs at Jaynes, nevertheless supports him, as Robin Lane Fox does: "I hear voices all the time when I'm alone, sailing. They're the voices of my relatives, telling me what to do."

The largest and best-known group of people who still hear voices do not want to hear them. These are schizophrenics. Hallucinated voices are not a symptom of other forms of mental illness; poets who suffered from other illnesses — William Cowper, William Collins, John Clare — did not report hearing voices. Jaynes believes that this one illness, schizophrenia, is a partial return to the ancient state of bicamerality. "The presence of auditory hallucinations, their often religious and always authoritative quality, the dissolution of the ego or analog 'I' and of the mind-space in which it could narratize out what to do and where it was in time and action, these are the large resemblances."[25] Because schizophrenics are

---

22. Colin M. Turnbull, *The Mountain People* (New York: Simon & Schuster, 1972), pp. 270–271.
23. Richard Price, *Alabi's World* (Baltimore: Johns Hopkins University Press, 1990), p. 249.
24. Ibid., p. 277.
25. Jaynes, *Origin of Consciousness*, p. 431.

at war with themselves and those around them, assaulted by voices terrifying to themselves and unbelievable to their neighbors, they are in pain and are diagnosed as sick. The fact that schizophrenia, unlike many forms of mental illness, occurs in every known culture in very similar forms suggests that it is produced by biology, not culture. E. O. Wilson says that in tribes as different as the Eskimos of the Bering Sea and the Yoruba of Nigeria, "the incidence of schizophrenia is about the same as in Western societies."[26] By suggesting that schizophrenia may originate in the same mental processes that once created the commanding voices that governed entire cultures and that still can create inspired poetry, I am by no means joining those, like R. D. Laing, Michel Foucault, Gilles Deleuze, and Félix Guattari, who would deny the reality of mental illness or glorify it as a higher state of mental life.[27] The appearance of this particular illness, characterized by hallucinated voices, in every known culture suggests only the biological fixity of our ability to produce these voices and the probable roots of both the illness and the voices that inspire poetry in the evolutionary past.

This link does not elevate schizophrenia so much as it limits inspiration. Neither the voices of schizophrenia nor those of poetic inspiration are as free as our capacity to reason. Voices cannot produce truly new possibilities for our lives; they can only repeat, only enforce, inherited ideas and codes. And if the code we inherit is a bad one, we are out of luck if we have to rely on our voices. The people in cultures still controlled by voices they believed divine, like the warriors of the *Iliad*, were prevented from degenerating into the worst forms of dishonesty and depravity with which we are familiar. Full consciousness brings the ability to lie, cheat, plot, torture, and commit all of the other crimes only "civilized" people have been able to invent. On the other hand, people who were entirely bound by their voices were also incapable of going beyond them. In a culture in which hallucinated gods enforce the codes of war, only thought, not a voice, could bring the ideal of nonviolence. With the possible exception of Homer, about whose personal existence we know

---

26. Wilson, *On Human Nature*, p. 59.
27. R. D. Laing, *The Politics of Experience* (New York: Ballantine Books, 1967); Michael Foucault, *Madness and Civilization: A History of Insanity in the Age of Reason* (New York: Random House, 1973); Gilles Deleuze and Félix Guattari, *Anti-Oedipus: Capitalism and Schizophrenia* (Minneapolis: University of Minnesota Press, 1983).

nothing, every one of the poets I have studied could both think *and* hear voices. Each could both question *and* obey messages from the past.

This coexistence of voices and intelligent, learned thought is vividly present in the autobiographical *Memoirs of My Nervous Illness* by one of the most famous schizophrenics in medical history, Daniel Paul Schreber.[28] Though Schreber lacked whatever makes a person a poet, recording memories of his voices in a prose autobiography read only as a case history, he provided a virtual catalog of the ways in which poets can hear voices. Schreber was a true man of the late nineteenth century, literate, learned, well educated in comparative mythology and in science, particularly the theory of evolution. Before his illness he was an unhappy religious skeptic: "My general impression has always been that materialism cannot be the last word in religious matters, but I could not get myself either to believe firmly in the existence of a personal God or to retain such a belief."[29] His illness brought him back to belief, convincing him that he was undergoing a process of physical transformation into a woman by which he would be a new savior of mankind, like Noah and Deucalion and Pyrrha. He believed that the voices that came to him were as historically important as those that had come to the Maid of Orleans, the Crusaders, and Constantine.[30]

Despite his bizarre delusions, Schreber remained intellectual and rational enough to understand and describe his voices precisely and insightfully. He said the voices he heard were transmitted by divine rays that emanated from a whole group of gods and were conveyed in the special "nerve language"[31] people use when memorizing poetry and sermons. Poetry and sermons are, in fact, closer to the special language of auditory hallucinations than philosophy and history are. Schreber further distinguished two kinds of thought, what Jaynes would call consciousness and bicamerality — the "thinking-it-over thought" that caused doubts and allowed persons to change their minds and the "human-thought-of-recollection" that caused poems to have refrains.[32] And even though he believed in the gods that were giving him his world-historical mission

28. Jaynes discusses Schreber in *Origin of Consciousness*, pp. 414–416.
29. Daniel Paul Schreber, *Memoirs of My Nervous Illness* (London: W. Dawson, 1955; Cambridge, Mass.: Harvard University Press, 1988), p. 80.
30. Ibid., p. 73.
31. Ibid., p. 69.
32. Ibid., p. 141.

to save mankind by restoring religion, he could still complain that the gods could speak only in a set collection of phrases and that "in any case these thoughts contain nothing new for me."[33] He knew that hallucinated voices never contain anything really new to the hearer.

His voices could tell him only to restore codes from the past. He was chosen to relieve people of the pains of skepticism, materialism, and pantheism with "the absolute certain knowledge that a living God exists and that the soul lives on after death,"[34] exactly the beliefs that had proved most vulnerable to science in the nineteenth century. And he was also to restore an old code of honor and manliness. On one occasion, after an attendant in the mental hospital made what he considered an unfair demand, "the voices challenged and mocked me for my apparent lack of manly courage until at last I struck him."[35] Progressives in the nineteenth century disapproved of such aggression: Schreber's voices returned to a manliness as old as the *Iliad*.

As his voices continued, they stopped providing clear ethical commands and assumed some of the forms Jaynes found in ancient cultures that were losing faith in their gods — the same forms I have found in classical and English poets. The voices Schreber heard became demonic, calling him the "Prince of Hell," to his great unhappiness, then decaying into odd, meaningless phrases that sounded like fragments of what were once messages. Later the actual words spoken by the people around him seemed to be the words of the lower God; finally, nonverbal external sounds, like the rattle of railway trains or the music of concerts, could trigger his hallucinations, for they seemed "to speak the words which are talked into my head by the voices."[36] Before I read Dr. Schreber's memoirs in their entirety, I worried that I was making a mistake by linking the outright dictation of poems to Homer and Milton and Blake with the instigation of poetry by natural sounds in Wordsworth and Yeats. I am now convinced that the many forms in which poets receive auditory hallucinations have one mental origin.

Dr. Schreber's memoirs do more than confirm the connection between different kinds of voices; his attack on a hospital attendant for

---

33. Ibid., p. 154–155.
34. Ibid., p. 215.
35. Ibid., p. 108.
36. Ibid., p. 183.

the sake of male honor is evidence of what is most potentially troubling about my belief that poetic inspiration is a product of our evolution: except for Emily Brontë, Elizabeth Barrett Browning, Christina Rossetti, and Emily Dickinson, who heard only unwanted sounds, all of the poets I have written about are male. And all of these poets, both men and women, heard from their voices messages about male codes of ethics and honor, bestowed by fathers, kings, or gods. I would like to believe that tradition alone accounts for this imbalance in gender. If our inspiring voices can enforce any ethical code we invent, then logically they could tell us that women are the superior gender, the people who should be prophetic poets, and they could repeat a code invented by women. History, unhappily, is not logical. Though we certainly have verifiable historical evidence for matrilineal cultures, like the Iroquois, and have what seems to be archaeological evidence that women were highly respected in certain ancient cultures, like the Minoan,[37] we have no reason yet to believe that a true matriarchy has ever existed on our planet. The feminist historian Gerda Lerner, in *The Creation of Patriarchy*, writes emphatically and unequivocally, "There is not a single society known where women-as-a-group have decision-making power over men or where they define the rules of sexual conduct or control marriage exchange."[38] I have to believe, though reluctantly, that it is not an accident that almost all of the poets I have studied are men and that most (though not all) of their poems are about a set of rules inherited from the fathers.

I cannot even believe that if English poets had looked for poetic models outside the Western traditions that begin in the patriarchal cultures of Greece and Israel more women poets would have heard inspiring voices and more men would have heard voices enforcing women's authority. When Albert Lord went among the tribal people of Yugoslavia to study living oral epics, he found an exclusively male tradition. Boys alone were trained to memorize the forms of poetry from which they could compose epics.[39] Jeff Opland had found a male tradition among the Xhosa of Africa as well. Though their young girls do compose oral poetry about the goats and cows they milk, boys not only compose poems about their daily

---

37. Jacquetta Hawkes, *Dawn of the Gods: Minoan and Mycenaean Origins of Greece* (New York: Random House, 1968) has persuaded me that Minoan culture honored women.
38. Gerda Lerner, *The Creation of Patriarchy* (New York: Oxford University Press, 1986), p. 30.
39. Albert B. Lord, *The Singer of Tales* (Cambridge, Mass.: Harvard University Press, 1960), pp. 32–33.

life but also learn the poems that embody an ethical tradition, memorize poems inherited from their fathers, with whom they can then communicate after their death.[40] If there is any women's tradition of such poetry, I have not found it.

As a woman I have to decide what to do with what seems to be a fact, that all over the world, throughout history, most of the poets who hear voices have been male, and their poems are usually about the laws of the fathers. I can regard this tradition as an enemy that must be overthrown in its entirety as a bastion of sexism and oppression, or I can try to recognize what is unjust in it and rescue what is valuable, if anything is. My conviction that our evolutionary past has power over us prevents me from hoping that we could escape or reverse a behavior pattern that exists in every known culture, past or present, for example, the fact that men dominate the tradition of poetry inspired by voice. The contents of the codes enforced by such poetry is, however, more important than their origin, and the laws of the fathers need not be cruel, degrading, or oppressive toward women. The laws of the father can be laws of protection and justice for women and children, the old and the weak, and at times in the past they have been.

Indeed, one of the oldest codes of ethics we possess, the one in the Book of Proverbs, commands

> My son, keep your father's commandment, and forsake not your mother's teaching.
> Bind them upon your heart always; tie them about your neck.
> When you walk, they will lead you;
>> When you lie down, they will watch over you
>> And when you awake, they will talk with you. (Prov. 6:20-22)

The teachings of the father and the mother can both be heard here as imperative voices. Both can give rules for compassion, generosity, and justice. Though in the male poets I have written about the voices of the mothers are muted and sometimes even lost, those voices were once clear and strong. Even if women have not had a tradition of inspired poetry, in the past they certainly have been partners in the preservation of a code of ethics. I am not going to waste my time worrying about whether a

---

40. Jeff Opland, *Anglo-Saxon Oral Poetry: A Study of the Traditions* (New Haven, Conn.: Yale University Press, 1980), p. 20.

woman ever has heard or ever will hear an epic poem dictated by a muse. For me it is enough to hope that women will learn from this tradition of poetry how deeply we need our ethical codes and will reclaim their ancient voices as ethical teachers. We cannot get rid of the voices that come to poets; we have to make sure that what poets hear is a code that enforces justice.

CHAPTER 8

Romanticism, Bicamerality, and the Evolution of the Brain

EDWARD PROFFITT

THE CENTRAL QUESTION OF THE MODERN POET vis-à-vis poetry is summed up by Frost in "The Oven Bird": "what to make of a diminished thing." Stripped of his singing robes, the poet now must be not a nightingale but an oven bird, who "knows in singing not to sing." He must, that is, be maker rather than shaman, conscious artificer rather than sacred vessel. Such, of course, seems a diminishment given the origins of poetry in divine prophecy. Still, the poet must be singing even if now he knows "not to sing." In other words, he must give up inspired song for the more mundane melodies of consciousness; he must give up the magic of verbal music, we might say, for the musicality of speech.

How has the poet come to this pass? The answer, I believe, can be gleaned from Julian Jaynes's ground-breaking book, *The Origin of Consciousness in the Breakdown of the Bicameral Mind*.[1] In fact, Jaynes's thesis is so wide-ranging that it should ultimately give rise to, among other things, a whole new theory of literature and literary history, a theory based not in philosophy or rhetoric, but in the physiology of the brain and the history of the development of the conscious self. In a way, one shudders at the idea. For since Frye, every year seems to bring forth a new general theory of literature: of late, for example, we have had structuralism, deconstructionism, and misprisionism. There is hardly time to work out one theory before another comes along to challenge it. But Jaynes's thesis applied to literature will not challenge existing theories;

First published in *The Wordsworth Circle*, Vol. 9, No. 1, 1978. Reprinted with permission.
1. Julian Jaynes, *The Origin of Consciousness in the Breakdown of the Bicameral Mind* (Boston: Houghton-Mifflin, 1976).

rather, it will put literary theory on another plane entirely. It should a.. give us a new point of entry to the poetry of the last two hundred years. The purpose of the present paper, at any rate, is to suggest the special relevance of Jaynes's thesis to Romantic poetry.

That thesis, which is all but impossible to summarize in brief, concerns the physiology of the brain and its evolution as affected by human culture, especially as manifested by the evolution of language. There was a time, Jaynes holds — before the middle of the second millennium B.C. — when men did not possess consciousness as we know it. Directed by the right or non-verbal hemisphere of the brain, men literally heard voices, voices that directed their beings with the authority of deity. Hallucination was the mode of communication between the right and left (verbal) hemispheres, with the voices hallucinated usually being those of the recently dead. Thus the gods and, more to our point, the Muses came into being. But as language evolved and as natural and cultural pressures changed, the metaphors of the internalized self emerged and the left hemisphere became increasingly dominant. The result was the fading away of bicameral voices generally. But those voices were still remembered and still needed by men not fully capable (as we still are not) of self-authorization. And for a long period of time, some men still heard bicameral voices spasmodically: they were the prophets, the oracles, the sibyls, the "inspired" poets. Subsequent history, however, is a history of increasing left-hemispheric dominance and of solidification of the metaphors of self. The gods become further and further removed; the Muses become simple metaphor; the language becomes ever more important in the meditations of men. In fact, the history of the last five hundred years is a history of adjustment to the loss of bicameral authorization entirely, a loss speeded by the growth of science, itself a result of the evolution of consciousness. But it has been in the last two hundred years especially that the loss has become most overt. The self, still unprepared, must now take everything on itself, for the gods and Muses alike have disappeared into thin air. As Jaynes explains: "What we have been through in these last four millennia is the slow inexorable profaning of our species. And in the last part of the second millennium A.D., that process is apparently becoming complete."[2]

2. Ibid., p. 437.

Now, what I intend to do here, as I have stated, is simply to suggest
the relevance of Jaynes's thesis to Romantic poetry. By "Romantic poetry," let me note, I mean the poetry of the whole two-hundred-year period
dating from, say, the publication of *Lyrical Ballads*. For I am in complete
agreement with Harold Bloom when he says:

> from 1744 or so to the present day the best poetry had internalized
> its subject matter, particularly in the mode of Wordsworth after 1798.
> Wordsworth had no true subject except his own subjective nature, and
> very nearly all significant poetry since Wordsworth, even by Ameri-
> can poets, has repeated Wordsworth's inward turning.

> This no longer seems to be a question of any individual's choice, but
> evidently is a necessity ... of the broad movement that we see now can
> be called Romanticism or Modernism, since increasingly the latter
> would appear to have been only an extension of the former.[3]

The poetry of the last two hundred years seems very much of a piece,
with respect both to form and to subject matter. Formally, ours has been
a lyric-centered poetry, and the struggle of our poets had been to work
out the "subjectivized decorum," as Frye calls it, of the lyric mode, especially as that decorum involves an "emancipated lyrical rhythm."[4] As to
subject matter, our most characteristic poetry over the past two centuries
has involved almost singularly the processes of internalization, of the
self's taking on the role of creator both of poetry and of self. As Octavio
Paz profoundly notes: "The poet speaks, and as he speaks, he *makes*. This
making is above all a making of himself: poetry is not only self-knowl-
edge but self-creation."[5]

The two, of course, are intimately related. For the lyric is the mode of
self. Indeed, Jaynes demonstrates that it is in Greek lyric poetry that the
metaphors of self first become consolidated, that in Sappho, for example,
self-consciousness starts to emerge.[6] Still, it is a long way from Sappho
to Wordsworth, or, for that matter, even from Donne to Wordsworth.
Paz's concept of poetry as involving self-creation, a concept that applies

---

3. Harold Bloom, "The Uses of Poetry," *New York Times* (November 12, 1975), p. 43.
4. Northrop Frye, *Anatomy of Criticism: Four Essays* (Princeton: Princeton University Press, 1957), p. 273.
5. Octavio Paz, *Children of the Mire: Modern Poetry from Romanticism to the Avant-Garde* (Harvard University Press, 1974), p. 60.
6. Jaynes, *Origin of Consciousness*, pp. 281–85.

fully to Wordsworth, would have sounded very odd indeed before the inception of the Romantic period. But that, certainly, has been the burden of Romantic poetry, which thereby reflects the further evolution of consciousness marked by the modern world or the further evolution of the concept of self that Jaynes delineates so meticulously.

In other words, Romantic poetry responds to and signals the end of four millennia of mental evolution, or is part and parcel of "this transition to a new mentality" that Jaynes holds "we, at the end of the second millennium A.D., are still in a sense deep in."[7] The old mentality, which lingers yet, is a mentality based in the right hemisphere of the brain; it is a mentality that needs external authorization and that yearns for the voice of such authorization. The new mentality, which the evolution of language and culture as both affect and the workings of the brain has forced us toward, is a mentality based in the left hemisphere, the language hemisphere; it is a mentality of self-authorization, or a mentality that necessitates ego-development to the point that the self can accept its own authorization. But because we are still deep in transition, no doubt, the new mentality, which has shown itself to consciousness only in the latter part of the present millennium, still seems hugely problematic. As Jaynes puts it, "What we must do must come from ourselves. ... We, we fragile human species at the end of the second millennium A.D., we must become our own authorization. And here at the end of the second millennium and about to enter the third, we are surrounded with this problem."[8]

We are indeed. And that, I think, is what our literature gives voice to. Certainly Beckett gives eloquent expression to the problem, as do Stevens and, of course, Yeats. But, as I have said, the whole period is very much marked by a sense of transition to this new mentality. We can go back, thus, and read the early Romantics profitably in light of the thesis at hand. In fact, in some ways the indications that we have reached a final stage in the thrust toward the new mentality are clearest at the inception of the modern world. Vico is a forerunner, but it is perhaps Rousseau who first marks the break fully. Of that break Frye, says:

7. Ibid., p. 317.
8. Ibid., p. 438.

It is generally recognized that Rousseau represents, and to some extent made, a revolutionary change in the modern attitude. The primary
reason for this impact was, I think, not in his political or educational
views as such, but in his assumption that civilization was a purely
human artifact, something that man had made, could unmake, could
subject to his own criticism, and was at all times entirely responsible
for. ... This kind of assumption is so penetrating that it affects those
who detest Rousseau, or have never heard of him, equally with the
small minority of his admirers. Also, it gets into the mind at once,
whereas the fading out of such counter assumptions as the literal and
historical nature of the Garden of Eden story is very gradual.[9]

In Rousseau, then, we can feel the new mentality breaking through. I
would quibble with Frye only on one point: the fading of the old "Garden of Eden" mentality, which Jaynes would call right-hemispheric, does
not take place over two centuries but over two or three millennia. Rousseau thus is in no way a maker of a new mentality based on a growing
concept of man as creator or of self-authorization (left-hemispheric) —
though he surely helped speed the process — but rather a reflector of
a long historical process still in progress. Revolution is not quite to the
point, that is. Nevertheless, Rousseau crystallized the stage of evolution
that grips the modern world: more and more man had become creator,
for more and more the authority of the gods of the right hemisphere has
given way to the self of the left.

That one can feel strongly in Wordsworth. Indeed, that is what Wordsworth is all about — the "Growth of a Poet's Mind." In the intense
internalization of *The Prelude*, Wordsworth sets the stage for subsequent
poetry, as Bloom holds, and also is prophetic of the next stage of human
mentality. The mind must become ever more articulately conscious of its
own processes and formation; the self must create itself by, for the poet,
the act of creating a poem, or by forming language into speech (left-
hemispheric functions). Thus, as M. H. Abrams notes in *Natural Supernaturalism*, Wordsworth had "'no need of a Redeemer'," and thus God is
not an operative principle in *The Prelude*, which "has only two generative

9. Northrop Frye, "The Drunken Boat: The Revolutionary Element in Romanticism," in N. Frye (ed.), *Romanticism Reconsidered: Selected Papers from the English Institute* (New York: Random House, 1963), p. 10.

and operative terms: man and nature."[10] Thus, too, Wordsworth's mature view of language as, in Florence Marsh's words, "a conscious creation rather than a spontaneous expression,"[11] and thus Wordsworth's concern in the Preface with the language really used by men. That concern has been taken hitherto as resulting from a reaction on Wordsworth's part to the decadent late eighteenth-century idea of "poetic diction." No doubt it was in part. But in greater part, I think, it reflects a massive shift to a left-hemispheric mentality, as does Wordsworth's movement toward self-authorization. The poet now must be maker rather than shaman, and poetry now must be based in speech because it is now in no way the voice of a god or muse, but only of the self. Right here, incidentally, I find the motive force of later developments with respect to diction and especially rhythm. The movement to speech in Yeats, or the speech-centered theories of Hopkins or Pound or Williams, *et al.*, reflect a shift to the concerns of the left hemisphere, as, perhaps, does the movement away from meter to free verse in Pound, Williams, *et al.* If Jaynes is right and meter springs mainly from the right hemisphere,[12] then a movement away from meter to free verse suggests a further movement to a left-hemispheric orientation. Also, to the extent that Frye is right that free verse is the essential rhythm of lyric poetry,[13] a movement to free verse suggests a further movement to self-authorization.

At any rate, "the poet speaks, and as he speaks, he *makes*" — Paz's phrase clearly defines Wordsworth's poetic act. In *The Prelude*, Wordsworth set out to make himself by making his poem: in both cases *he* was the maker, and thus his celebration of the *creative* imagination. As in Rousseau, in Wordsworth the human being becomes the creator, creating through language a self capable of its own authorization. Of Romantic poetry generally Geoffrey Hartman says: "There clearly comes a time when art frees itself from its subordination to religion or religiously inspired myth, and continues or even replaces these. This time seems to coincide with what is generally called the Romantic period: the latter, at

---

10. M. H. Abrams, *Natural Supernaturalism* (New York: W. W. Norton & Company, 1977), p. 90, 120.
11. Florence Marsh, *Wordworth's Imagery: A Study in Poetic Vision* (Yale University Press, 1952), p. 4.
12. Jaynes, *Origin of Consciousness*, pp. 361–78.
13. See *Anatomy of Criticism*, pp. 270–73.

least, is a good *terminus a quo.*"[14] To replace "religiously inspired myth"
— that, of course, is Wordsworth's announced project (in the Prospectus
to *The Recluse*). Wordsworth intended to take all on himself, to carry internalization to completion. Why? The failure of the French Revolution
has something to do with it. But more significant is what that revolution
itself, along with the appearance of Romanticism generally, betokens:
by the end of the eighteenth century we reach a point when the new
mentality starts fully to appear, when the claims of the left hemisphere
become ineluctable.

That is not to say, however, that by the end of the eighteenth century
we reach anything like a single-minded human nature (which, I surmise,
is what Wordsworth meant by "tranquility"). Even in those who embrace
the new mentality most thoroughly, the conflicts are intense. And they
still are, as Jaynes poignantly points out. For we are travelling along unknown roads — thus Wordsworth's recurrent anxiety in *The Prelude* as to
whether or not he can accomplish the task before him. In a sense, he does
not know what he is doing. More important, there is even in Wordsworth
a longing for the old. Thus, his sense of loss with respect to childhood's
vision (right-hemispheric) even as he feels the growth of the philosophic
mind (left-hemispheric) as gain. Even as Wordsworth makes the most
aggressive claims for the self as creator — in the Snowdon section of *The
Prelude* — he hears voices speaking more than human speech. To be sure,
what he hears is still right-hemispheric and reveals a desire for external
authorization right in the face of a movement to the internal. We are still
"deep in ... transition," as Wordsworth's falling back in later life also betokens. And perhaps, finally, that is most what Romantic poetry speaks.

Or perhaps I should say that in a few Romantics — Rousseau, Wordsworth, Goethe — we seem at times almost to have made the transition: they map out the territory of the new mentality as thoroughly as
it has yet been mapped. But still the direction is unclear, and most of us
linger along the way. More conflicted than Wordsworth on every score,
Coleridge seems more the poet of transition, or of the problems thereof.
For in Coleridge, the *difficulty* of self-authorization (as differentiated
from growth toward self-authorization) seems the central subject matter.

---

14. Geoffrey H. Hartman, "Romanticism and Anti-Self-Consciousness," in H. Bloom (ed.), *Romanticism and Consciousness: Essays in Criticism* (New York: W. W. Norton & Company, 1970), p. 52.

At least, to read Coleridge in light of Jaynes, I would contend, sheds new light on the nature of Coleridge's conflicts by giving those conflicts a new historical framework. Jaynes's thesis, I have been arguing, opens out new vistas on Romantic poetry. Coleridge as much as Wordsworth is a case in point.

I am thinking now especially of the fact that Coleridge wrote two vastly different kinds of poem; the conversational versus the incantatory. To see each in light of Jaynes's thesis, I think, is to see both anew. The conversational poems are left-hemispheric, poems molded from the language of human speech that give expression to the anxieties of and isolation attendant upon self-authorization (e.g., "The Eolian Harp"). The three incantatory poems, on the other hand, seem much more right hemispheric. Marked by a heavy beat that mesmerizes the reader much as the Ancient Mariner mesmerizes the Wedding Guest, they impart the flavor not of the human voice but of the voice of the gods. That Coleridge wrote poems so vastly different suggests in itself a mind in transition, vacillating between an older mental mode and one struggling to be born. So, too, does the anxiety of the conversational poems in and of themselves. And perhaps here is a reason for the failure of most of those poems: Coleridge could not commit himself, finally, to human speech, or could not settle for (for him it would have been a settling for) the self-authorization that a left-hemispheric orientation requires. But he underscores the difficulty of transition most by attempting to pull back into an older mode and longing for what he knows is impossible: to be a shaman, to be the vessel of the gods.

That is, "Kubla Khan," certainly central to Coleridge's poetic canon, gives full expression to our difficulty. The poet in the modern world must "learn in singing not to sing," must be a conscious creator out of the materials provided by the left hemisphere (i.e., the mundane language of human speech). But he still longs, like most of us still, for the authority of bicameral voices, or for what I have called the magic of verbal music. He would sing not like the oven bird but like the skylark. That, it seems to me, is what "Kubla Khan" tells. Here we have a figure, half god himself and half bicameral man, who hears "ancestral voices" and is guided by what he hears. And we have a poet who longs to be like that figure, or like the possessed poets of old delivering sacred prophecy. He, too, has heard — not words, but "symphony and song" — and he would speak not words but music.[15] Music, says Jaynes, is right-hemispheric, and ancient poetry, allied with music, "was divine knowledge."[16] In "Kubla Khan," that is, the poet would be bicameral, as the "dulcimer" also suggests — Jaynes holds that the function of the lyre was to stimulate the right hemisphere and thus to bring the poet to the pitch of possession by bicameral voices.[17] But the poet knows from the outset that that he cannot be: the conditional "could" says all. Coleridge, who could not settle for speech, could not revert to bicameralism either. Like us, he was caught up in the latter stages of evolutionary transition, and therein lay the difficulty. That is what I find "Kubla Khan" to express most movingly. The difficulty of transition signaled by a longing for bicameral possession, yet an inability to be so possessed, also explains, perhaps, the apocryphal dream-vision story of the poem's origin and Coleridge's diffidence as to its publication. Coleridge would have had the poem be the product of possession rather than of consciousness, but he knew better.

The word "consciousness" tolls me to a related matter. Jaynes holds that "bicameral men did not imagine; they experienced."[18] The longing of the poet in "Kubla Khan" is for exactly that: to experience directly, without the mediation of consciousness, which necessitates imagination. Yet of all the Romantics, Coleridge was the most articulate on the subject of the imagination and, along with Wordsworth, the most dedicated to its power. Here is another of those conflicts so marked in Coleridge. But, no doubt, it was this very conflict that led Coleridge to articulate the concept of imagination in the first place. For, as Helen Regueiro holds: "The imagination arises when the oneness of self and world has been lost, when the experience of isolation has taken place. And its paradoxical function is to retrieve that initial vision whose loss gave birth; to enter, through consciousness, a world from which all consciousness is excluded."[19] Coleridge's very articulation of the concept of imagination,

---

15. Thus, "symphony and song," which is not a tautology because Coleridge means to underscore the musical as opposed to the verbal quality of the utterance he has in mind. In this regard see Joseph Sgammato, "A Note on Coleridge's 'Symphony and Song'," *The Wordsworth Circle*, 6, 1975.
16. Jaynes, *Origin of Consciousness*, pp. 361–70, 363.
17. Ibid., pp. 361–70.
18. Ibid., p. 371.
19. Helen Regueiro, *The Limits of Imagination: Wordsworth, Yeats, and Stevens* (Cornell University Press, 1976), p. 43.

then, is in part a token of his anxiety vis-à-vis the new mentality. But in part, too, it is a sign of a movement toward that mentality, given that imagination is a postulate of consciousness. Or perhaps one might say that imagination is an hypothesis of full consciousness, of the self-authorized self entire, an hypothesis that takes us beyond the split state of mind in which we in a state of transition find ourselves — the state of radical self-consciousness — and allows us to envision a realm of consciousness that we have not yet reached. Hartman says something of the like when he says that "to explore the transition from self-consciousness to imagination ... is the Romantic purpose I find most crucial."[20] In every way Coleridge was an explorer of that transition, or of a mental state pulled between past and future — a state marked by longing for a long past, a state divided at present, yet a state capable of postulating a visionary oneness of consciousness and the unconscious world around (that is, a state capable of self-authorization).

The ontological problem that Coleridge and the other Romantics explore is our problem still: how to be, or how to be human as we now define human — that is, a conscious being — in a nonreflecting world, yet feel oneself to be a part of that world. For the poet the problem is compounded by his art: he must now forge artifacts out of consciousness, or, as Robert Pinsky has it, "find a language for presenting the role of a conscious soul in an unconscious world."[21] His material is the conscious self at its present stage, yet he would find a language that can transcend the divisions of that self and bring about a new wholeness, a new state of being. But this he must do from his consciousness alone; again, he must be maker rather than shaman, though his function is that of a prophet of what can be, or, in Stevens's words, of "What will suffice." Along with Pinsky, I hold such to be the motivating force of most significant poetry of the last two centuries. But why should this be so?

Let me draw to a conclusion by answering that question via a restatement of my general thesis. If Jaynes is right, we are now at the end of a

---

20. Hartman, "Romanticism and Anti-Self-Consciousness," p. 53.
21. Robert Pinsky, *The Situation of Poetry* (Princeton: Princeton University Press, 1976), p. 152. (Pinsky's argument is that this is as much the central concern of the contemporary poet as it was of the Romantics — specifically, Keats, whose "Ode to a Nightingale" is Pinsky's take-off point for his reading of modern poetry. Let me add that the "Ode to a Nightingale" is yet another poem that can be read profitably against the general thesis that I have been developing.)

long evolution of mental and physiological organization, or at the point of crossing into a new territory of human mentality. We still desire the old, but it is blocked to us; the future beckons, but we are not yet there. Arnold's phrase still summarizes our difficulty: we are still "between two worlds, one dead,/ The other powerless to be born." In other words, we haven't quite learned yet how in singing not to sing. Thus, we are in a quandary, as Jaynes, in a passage that could be a gloss on Keat's "Ode to a Nightingale," holds the modern poet to be:

> The modern poet is in a ... quandary. Once, literary languages and archaic speech came somehow to his bold assistance in that otherness and grandeur of which true poetry is meant to speak. But the grinding tides of irreversible naturalism have swept the Muses even farther out into the night of the right hemisphere. Yet somehow, even helplessly in our search for authorization, we remain 'the hierophants of an unapprehended inspiration.' And inspiration flees in attempted apprehension, until perhaps it was never there at all. ... The cognitive imperative dissolves. History lays her finger carefully on the lips of the Muses. The bicameral mind, silent. And since
>
> The god approached dissolves into the air,
> Imagine then, by miracle, with me,
> (Ambiguous gifts, as what gods give must be)
>   What could not possibly be there,
>   And learn a style from a despair.[22]

But for the first time in the history of the last three millennia, we recognize our quandary, our despair, and see at times the glimmer of a new mentality, a new style that we must consciously learn. What marks us most is our recognition that we are in transition, propelled by historical and evolutionary forces toward what we still have only inklings of. It is this, this matter of evolutionary transition so crucial to our being and survival, that Romantic poetry both reflects and explores; I would go even further and say that Romantic poetry at its best points not only to where we are but also to where we are going, or is a vital part of that evolution and a force for its continuance.

---

22. Jaynes, *Origin of Consciousness*, p. 378.

CHAPTER 9

On Listening To Voices

JOHN SAPPINGTON AND JOHN HAMILTON

IMAGINE WHAT IT WOULD BE LIKE for a conscious mind to be trapped inside an entity so twisted and defective that it could not convey the simplest thought to the outside world. Imagine also if that consciousness was permeated by detached voices that offered advice, gave directions and occasionally demanded compliance. Such is the case with many quadriplegic victims of cerebral palsy who have been classified as retarded since birth. Damage to motor areas of the brain prevents coordinated movement so that they cannot gesture or speak as such. Rather, they are eternally captured in a grotesque dance, writhing and grunting in desperate frustration. They seem to want to communicate but simply cannot. Not surprisingly, many of these people are abandoned to institutions where they are assumed to be only dimly conscious, without the power to think or understand. More specifically, they are assumed to lack understanding of words, coin of the realm for intelligent beings. In formal measures of IQ, testers invariably "discover" retardation and aphasia among them. As we shall see, this may tell us more about measures and testers than it does about our subjects' mentality.

Through a combination of serendipity and painstaking work, the authors were permitted a good look at the private mental world of these special people. The outcome was unexpected to say the least. In spite of obvious and extensive brain damage, they ponder sophisticated questions about interpersonal relationships, sexuality, and the cosmic mysteries.

First published in *Pursuit*, 76, 1987. Reprinted with permission.

Even more astonishing, they routinely hear voices which they sometimes attribute to supernatural agents.[1]

Our subjects were nine residents of a state institution for the emotionally and mentally retarded. All had been tested with standard measures of intelligence and found to have IQ scores within the bottom 2 percent of the population. Their personal hygiene and feeding is carried out largely with the help of hired attendants. Decisions about their abilities and appropriate care are the province of educated professionals.

On one occasion, a nursing assistant, Mrs. P., very casually told a staff psychologist that her quadriplegic patients regularly talked to her. She said that they had dozens of ideas on their minds and concerns to relay. Being skeptical, he nodded politely and later checked out her claim like a good scientist. He approached a patient and said, "Please tell Mrs. P to call me at three o'clock." On the following day at 3:00 p.m. his phone rang and Mrs. P. asked what she might do for him. This supposedly retarded and language-less patient had understood, retained, and communicated an accurate message. This method of communicating was interesting in itself. If you could only use two words out of your entire vocabulary, which two would you choose? Mrs. P. correctly reasoned that even these limited persons could make discrete gestures for "yes" and "no." She could then elicit thoughts from the patients by following the trail of their "yes" responses. A sample conversation might go as follows:

Mrs. P.: "Would you like to talk to me?"

Patient: "Yes" (gestured).

Mrs. P.: "Is it about a person?"

Patient: "Yes."

Mrs. P.: "Is the person male?"

Patient: "No."

Mrs. P.: "Does she work here?"

Patient: "Yes."

---

1. John Hamilton, "Auditory Hallucinations in Nonverbal Quadriplegics," *Psychiatry*, 1985, 48, 382–392; reprinted in Marcel Kuijsten (ed.), *Reflections on the Dawn of Consciousness* (Henderson, NV: Julian Jaynes Society, 2006).

Having learned the technique, we were now free to explore the private mental labyrinths of our patients. These turned out to be far more sophisticated than anyone imagined. They were curious to know how ordinary people viewed them. In particular, "How would you feel if you were handicapped?" Several had questions about God and wondered about the possible benefits of afterlife to themselves. Each was aware of the moods and concerns of other quadriplegics and the fact that others heard voices although they obviously could not speak to each other. Two, a male and female, had somehow discovered romance and eagerly awaited the sight of each other. A graduate student, trained to communicate with the patients, was so astonished by the depth of their knowledge of each other that she asked the group if they could hear each other's thoughts. The reply was neither "yes" nor "no." They erupted in laughter. Was the concept ridiculous to them or had the student touched a bizarre secret? In one instance, a patient became distraught and painfully disclosed to the psychologist that she feared for her sister. The sister, she said, was under considerable stress. So certain was her conviction that the psychologist telephoned the sister to inquire. At first, the sister denied any unusual stress but later confirmed that she was in the middle of a painful divorce and was, indeed, very troubled.

There is a great danger in extrapolating from anecdotes. Match an infinity of conjecture with subsequent real events and some will agree by chance alone. Even the worst two dollar bettors pick the right nags occasionally. Nonetheless, there was another strange dimension to this patient's conclusion concerning her sister's plight: the message was told to her by a voice. Auditory hallucinations are a familiar phenomenon in the literature of psychology. They are prominent among schizophrenics and not unknown among hysterics and selected organic illnesses. Voices are occasionally heard by conventional people who are feverish, exhausted, or suspended in the twilight between sleeping and waking. They had not, however, been reported among this population until 1985.[2] In all likelihood, no one had thought to ask.

---

2. Ibid.

As Wilson Van Dusen points out, voices occurring in cases of mental pathology usually have a persecutory nature about them.[3] Indeed, this is true of some voices reported by our patients. They are often ordered and harassed when they ignore the instructions and support offered by the voices. Most voices are benign and some are believed by the patients to be the voices of relatives.

Despite the routine presence of auditory hallucinations in schizophrenics, it is not clear that voices are pathological as such. Julian Jaynes's provocative theory of the evolution of consciousness pivots heavily on the role of internal auditory instructions.[4] His major thesis concerns voices as a common experience of historical man. Noah, Abraham, and others obeyed auditory commands with full confidence that they were being instructed by the gods themselves. In Jaynes's view, historical man did not plan and deliberate prior to acting as do some contemporary humans. Rather, solutions came to them full grown in the form of "divine" voices (albeit through a quirk of cortical circuitry). With exceptions, conventional people of today mistrust voices. Mention voices to a psychiatrist and a prescription pad will quickly materialize, if not a trip to a mental hospital.[5] Notable exceptions include William Blake, the poet, and the genius Emanuel Swedenborg who not only trusted in their voices but used them well in the process of creative flow.

Indeed, the experience of hearing voices is so common in the general population that it could qualify as normal behavior. Jaynes notes data indicating some 71 percent of a college population acknowledging at least a brief encounter with voices. The familiar phenomenon of the child's "imaginary playmate" in many cases translates nicely as "hallucinated playmate." These ethereal companions frequently speak in such a distinct fashion that subjects can remember the voice pitch and quality years later.[6] Popular actor Sherman Hemsley, who appeared in "The Jeffersons," has accepted a new role in a TV situation comedy, "Amen." With a voice

3. Wilson Van Dusen, "The Presence of Spirits in Madness," in James Fadiman and Donald Kewman (eds.), *Exploring Madness: Experience, Theory, and Research* (Monterey: Brooks/Cole, 1979).

4. Julian Jaynes, *The Origin of Consciousness in the Breakdown of the Bicameral Mind* (Boston: Houghton-Mifflin, 1976).

5. David L. Rosenhan, "On Being Sane in Insane Places," *Science*, 1973, 179, 250–258.

6. Julian Jaynes, "Hearing Voices and the Bicameral Mind," *The Behavioral and Brain Sciences*, 1986, 9, 3; reprinted in Marcel Kuijsten (ed.), *The Julian Jaynes Collection* (Henderson, NV: Julian Jaynes Society, 2012).

"as clear as a bell," his mother appeared to him offering advice on his new role. Mr. Hemsley is evidently very receptive to her counsel although she died some five years ago.[7] Like Hemsley, our quadriplegic subjects often identified their voices as belonging to relatives, usually of their own gender. Spoken messages are generally admonitions and constructive ones at that. Cooperating with a treatment program would do as an example of such an admonition. Why then are psychiatrists so eager to find pathology in voices? Perhaps a sampling error is at the heart of the problem. When data on voices is gathered in mental hospitals should we be surprised to find that those hearing them are deeply troubled?

If Jaynes's theory is correct, auditory hallucinations are not necessarily symptoms but manifestations of a larger process — vestiges of the bicameral mind. In this context, voices become clues and yard markers in mapping the topography of the human mind. Voices of the non-dominant hemisphere impart opinions, instructions, and perceptions to the receptive language areas of the dominant hemisphere. In some cases, it has been possible to evoke voices by surgically stimulating the biological wiring of the awake human cortex.[8] It is conceivable then, that nonverbal structures of the brain have their own programs for evaluating external reality. A message received in this fashion by the conscious, verbal area would be experienced in the only mode of which is capable: a statement. The source of the statement would seem to be external since it originated outside of verbal cognition.[9]

To argue, as some have, that retarded persons are simply broken devices is to create the climate for a costly mistake. Broken devices invite fixing and the "fix" in this case turns out to be heavy doses of antipsychotic medication. Indeed, our "retarded" patients are very cautious about revealing the existence of their voices. The phenomenon was shared with us only after considerable trust was established. "Fixing" by this method is to decide in advance that voices are pathological and worthless as clues. Antipsychotic drugs often condemn users to a host of mind-fogging side

---

7. G. Plagenz, "Listening for God's Voices," *Augusta Chronicle-Herald*, February 28, 1987, 5A.
8. Wilder Penfield and Phanor Perot, "The Brain's Record of Auditory and Visual Experience — A Final Summary and Discussion," *Brain*, 1963, 86, 595–696.
9. Here the authors touch upon the fascinating fact that language generated in the non-dominant hemisphere is not perceived as being associated with one's self, and is thus experienced as a hallucination. In ways yet to be explored and understood, our self concept appears to be connected to the language areas of our dominant hemisphere. —*Ed.*

effects that these patients are eager to avoid. Ironically, the minds of brain-injured patients are frequently capable of feats that conventional minds find impossible. Even mainstream scientific literature now contains case studies of apparently retarded persons who play music without training, solve multiplication problems instantly, maintain awareness of exact time without clocks, and perform perpetual calendar tasks.[10]

In this quarter at least, we regard the voices phenomenon as a window of discovery. Through lack of ordinary socializing these patients are able to hear internal speech. As to whether this phenomenon is pathology, the vestige of an ancient mentality, or something else entirely, remains to be seen. We recently completed a study which confirms the ability of these patients to report verbal ideas accurately. Now we are recording the content of prognostic material imparted by the voices. Readers are encouraged to "listen" closely for further developments.

10. Thomas Burling, John Sappington, and Andrew Mead, "Lateral Specialization of a Perceptual Calendar Task by a Moderately Retarded Adult," *American Journal of Mental Deficiency*, 1983, 88, 3, 326–328; M. Forbes, "The Mysterious Savant Syndrome," *Pursuit*, 1986, 19, 1, 13–15.

CHAPTER 10

A Schizophrenic Woman
Who Heard Voices of the Gods

RUSSELL T. HURLBURT

S ALLY CREMER WAS 31 YEARS OLD AT THE TIME OF SAMPLING.[1] The
sampling experience had been suggested to her by her psychiatrist,
whom she had been seeing regularly for two and a half years. She had
been diagnosed as schizophrenic four years earlier, primarily due to the
fact that she frequently heard voices. The voices did occur frequently during sampling, but there were no other overt linguistic characteristics of
schizophrenia (no pressure of speech, no flight of ideas, etc.) during our
conversations. She was a native Dutch speaker, but, as her English was
fluent, the sampling conversations were carried out entirely in English.

This sampling study took place on three days. On the first day the
introduction to the sampling experience was carried out essentially iden-
tically to that of our other subjects, and she was given the sampling appa-
ratus with instructions to use it until she had collected about ten samples.
The second day she sampled for five hours, resulting in 14 beeps being
recorded. She wrote down her experience at the moment of the beep in
Dutch and translated them into English before coming to the sampling
meeting the third day. During the course of this third-day discussion
of her experiences, she stated that she would prefer not to continue the

First published in Russell T. Hurlburt, *Sampling Normal and Schizophrenic Inner Experience* (New York: Plenum Press, 1990). Copyright 1990, Plenum Press, New York. Reprinted with permission.
1. Russell Hurlburt, Professor of Psychology at the University of Nevada, Las Vegas, developed a method called Descriptive Experience Sampling (DES) and has used this method to investigate inner experience for more than three decades. Descriptive Experience Sampling involves providing individuals with a beeper that goes off at random times throughout the day, cueing them to focus on and then document the details of their inner experience at that moment. See Russell T. Hurlburt, *Investigating Pristine Inner Experience* (Cambridge: Cambridge University Press, 2011).—*Ed.*

sampling process, because voices that she called gods would be likely to punish her for continuing; in fact, she had probably already gone too far in the sampling process. She would, however, be willing to complete the descriptions of the samples that she had already collected. Of course we honored this request, and no additional sampling took place. There were two sampling conversations held on the third day, one in the morning and one in the afternoon, each lasting approximately one and a half hours. A total of seven beeps were discussed thoroughly and, as a result, this report will be based on these seven beeps.

Because of the relatively small number of beeps being considered, it will not be possible to give a general description of Sally's inner experience. However, it will be useful to describe some of the characteristics of the samples that we did collect, which we will first do in general terms, then more specifically. First, Sally's samples always had a salient emotional content; there was always a relatively clear, frequently quite strong, affect such as aggression, uncertainty, irritation, or vagueness present at the moment of the beep.

Second, nearly all of her samples involved hearing voices that were understood to be the voices of beings whom she called gods. These voices were located inside or quite near her head and were heard clearly and vividly, more clearly than hearing in her shared external reality. (Sally experienced three different realms where experience could take place: the "shared external reality," which was the world as experienced by herself and others; a "special reality," which was for Sally an objective reality that was not shared with other people; and "inner experience," a region experienced to be inside or near her head, where Sally could see imaginal Images and hear voices.) The gods' voices occurred either singly or in groups of up to about 20 separate voices, speaking to each other conversationally, speaking in unison, or issuing direct commands to Sally.

Third, Sally experienced visualizations of things not present in the shared external reality. These visualizations included seeing inner Images, and also actual, clear seeing into an external special reality, even though Sally knew that this world was not a part of the shared external reality. Fourth, Sally also experienced internal verbalizations related to external reality, an Inner Hearing of words that a friend had said, and Inner Speech, spoken by herself in her own, naturally inflected voice.

THE VOICES OF THE GODS

Six of Sally's seven samples involved a direct perceptual awareness of voices or beings whom Sally called "gods." She used the word "gods" to describe these experiences because earlier in her life she had believed that the voices existed before she was born and would continue to exist after her death. At the time of sampling she was no longer convinced of their immortality, but nevertheless continued to refer to them as gods because she still understood them to be powerful entities that could control her internal and external realities. The gods were experienced as voices heard inside or very close to her head. The voices were about 20 in number, some "more important" than others in the sense that those voices were heard more frequently and appeared to be more powerful than the other voices. Occasionally the gods were also seen, appearing as shadowy beings who will be described below in the Visual Experience section.

The first sample included such speaking by the gods. She was at her mother's house talking with her mother about her own financial situation. Her 15-month-old son was playing nearby. At the moment of the beep, her mother was asking her what was wrong, although nothing was particularly wrong as far as Sally was concerned. Sally's attention at that time was focused on the voices of the gods ordering her not to tell anything about what the gods said (this lack of outward attention may have been what prompted her mother's question). The gods were also forbidding her to write down (as part of the sampling study) the exact words that the gods spoke.

The voice of this particular god was experienced as speaking these words, and the words were clearly audible, more clearly than externally spoken words would have been. Sally could easily remember what the words had been, but because she was forbidden to speak them, she would not repeat them for me. She could, however, describe the characteristics of the voice. It was one of the most familiar voices, one that she referred to as important because it spoke frequently to her. The vocal characteristics of the voice were easily recognizable, even though they varied greatly from occasion to occasion and within occasions. The pitch was low, like a masculine bass voice, but Sally said that it was not correct to interpret the voice as being either masculine or feminine. The pitch could change rather dramatically within utterances, rising to soprano and back to bass again. The voice was speaking in Dutch (as were all of Sally's inner experiences of words), and the volume was rather soft. The words were clearly an imperative; if an external observer could have heard the words, the inflection would have been recognized as being a command. Seemingly as a reaction to these words of the gods, Sally was experiencing a Feeling of uncertainty.

In the next sample (#2), Sally was still in conversation with her mother, who was talking about money. She was again paying only slight attention to her mother's words, and was also looking at and idly seeing her mother and her son who was playing nearby. However, most of her attention was occupied with the voices of the gods. In this sample, the gods' earlier prohibition against repeating their words did not for some reason apply, much to Sally's surprise, so she could report that the gods said, repeatedly (in Dutch), "Dollie (Sally's friend who sometimes takes care of Sally's son) is a bitch … Dollie is a bitch … Dollie is a bitch." These words were said approximately (but not exactly) simultaneously by the 20 separate voices of the gods, rather like a poorly rehearsed chorus speaking in imperfect unison. There was a slight pause between each of the repetitions of the sentence "Dollie is a bitch." The sentence was repeated perhaps ten times. The voices were extremely clearly heard, again as if they were either inside or closely surrounding her head, in front, back, to both sides and above and below. The voices had a range of vocal characteristics from bass to soprano, and the rate of speaking was slightly faster than a human chorus would have pronounced the words.

In the next example where Sally heard the gods' voices (Sample #4), she was again talking with her mother about Sally's taxes. Somewhat more of her attention was on her mother's conversation than in the previous samples, but she still was not paying full attention. Instead, she was attending to the voice of one of the more important gods who was commanding her to look away from her mother. The voice was speaking clearly in words, in Dutch, again in the inside or very near her head.

Once again, the words were clearly available to Sally both at the moment of the beep and at the time of our conversation the next day; but she could not report them because the gods had again commanded her not to do so. Again she was allowed to describe vocal characteristics: the sentence the god spoke was incomplete, having been broken off in the middle for some reason that she did not know; the voice told her to look away (which Sally did in fact do), and started off as a low bass voice and rose to the soprano range by the end of the utterance; there was much intonation and inflection modulation in the manner of speaking, even more so than a human voice would have; the rate of speaking was slower than normal; and the words themselves were drawn out in time like an exaggerated drawl. At the same time that this god's voice was heard, the rest of the gods' voices were humming in the background, a sort of buzzing noise with no particular melody which came from somewhere in the back of the inside or near-outside region of her head.

At the same time both the "look away" and the humming voices were heard, Sally was saying silently to herself (in Dutch) in Inner Speech, "I should have a look at Menno (her son)," to make sure that he was asleep. This Inner Speaking had the same characteristics (intonation, rate of speed, etc.) as her external speech would have had. At the same moment, Sally was also aware of a clear bodily Feeling that she knew was a longing for a cigarette. She described this longing as being like a "hunger in her lungs," quite clearly located deep in her chest.

There was one sample where Sally both heard and saw the gods at the same time (Sample #11). She had left her mother's house to do some errands, and had returned a few hours later and was again sitting in her living room talking with her. Her mother was telling her something, but Sally had no idea what it was because she was quite totally involved with both hearing and seeing the gods. Just before the beep, the gods had instructed Sally to look outside the living room window in a certain direction, and she had done so; at the moment of the beep the gods were "showing themselves to her." She could see the shared external reality outside the window — the garden and the wall beyond — but suspended in space in front of the wall was a clearly defined rectangular region in which the gods could be seen. This was experienced as seeing into reality, except that this rectangular region was a special reality known to be of a different order from the shared external reality. Thus, this seeing was not experienced as like looking at an inner Image; rather, the objects being seen were *not* part of an Image but were instead experienced as entities of an external world discovered by perception.

The rectangular area in which the gods were seen was wider than it was high — perhaps a meter wide and half a meter high — and, although the edges were clearly demarcated, there was no border or frame. Inside this rectangle was a series of vertical bars, white in color and perhaps eight in number, which extended from top to bottom of the rectangle, so that seeing the rectangle was rather like looking at a prison window. Behind the bars were the black or gray shadowy figures of the gods, perhaps 20 in number, which moved back and forth, passing in front and behind each other rather like a group of prisoners milling about inside the prison window, some closer to the window and some farther away, moving around without bumping into each other.

The figures themselves were "slim," that is to say, taller than they were wide, and extended completely to the bottom of the rectangle but not to the top, again like seeing people through the prison window from the waist up and above their heads. The gray, shadowy forms had no explicit features (although Sally reported that on other occasions the figures had armlike structures that seemed to reach out to her), but were seen to alter slightly in shape as they moved, although they always maintained their basic slim form.

The visualization was seen in depth, three-dimensionally, and it seemed to float suspended in space a few centimeters in front of the garden wall. The visualization seemed to undulate toward and away from Sally in waves, with part of the visualization moving somewhat toward her while another part was moving away. This movement was not jerky, but instead was a smoothly flowing oscillation in the visualization. The shadowy figures were seen clearly; that is, the figures were in *fact* shadowy and were not merely seen indistinctly, and there seemed to be a mist or fog behind the bars in between the figures of the gods but not between Sally and the bars. Some of the figures were seen to be closer to the bars (and thus closer to Sally) than others, but all were seen clearly.

Two of the voices were also speaking to Sally while she was looking at them at the moment of the beep. One voice said, in Dutch, "Do you see us now?" and the other voice said a moment later, "We're there." These voices were heard inside Sally's head, in the upper left back part of her inner head or near it. Thus, the voices were heard to be in a different place from where the gods were seen. Furthermore, the seeing of the gods took place in a fixed part of physical reality, just in front of the garden wall, while the sound of the voices was fixed relative to her head and thus turned in space when Sally turned her head.

There was a slight Feeling of reassurance that was associated with this experience. It was not at all frightening, and Sally was calm throughout.

VISUAL EXPERIENCES

Three of the seven samples that we examined included some kind of visualization that was different from Sally's perception of the shared external reality. We have described one of these above, the seeing of the gods in the special reality suspended in front of the garden wall. The other two visualizations involved seeing inner Images, that is, visual displays that Sally described as being like "pictures in her mind."

Images

The first of these (Sample #5) took place while Sally was in conversation with her mother about Dollie and Dollie's husband, who were in the process of getting a divorce. At the moment of the beep, Sally herself was talking aloud to her mother, and at the same time the gods were talking in her inner head or nearby. Sally's impression was that the gods were talking to each other in a conversation that Sally could overhear, and that their general tone of voice was cynical at the moment. She could not remember the exact words of the voices, but the general sense of their conversation was that they were critical of people and of the world in general. This critical conversation seemed to trigger in Sally a clear, strong Feeling of anger or aggression, like "of taking a machine gun and shooting everybody down that I see," which had both bodily and an Image aspect. The bodily aspect was characterized by tension in her hands and stomach. The Image aspect of this aggressive Feeling involved seeing an inner moving picture of approximately ten people riddled with machine-gun bullets, covered with blood and falling down and scream-ing. The Image was like a moving picture, in color of the people in vari-ous stages of falling while being gunned down. The color was accurate, with red blood, etc., except that the people's skin was very, very pale, almost white.

I asked whether the people in the Image were recognizable to her, and she replied in the negative, but then interrupted herself, as if taken her-self by surprise, and said that in fact one of the people was recognizable, an old boyfriend of hers. This boyfriend was not a central or important person in the Image, just another of the gunned-down and falling bodies.

The Image itself was clearly recognized to be a part of her imagina-tion, a picture known to be created by herself in her own inner experi-ence, and was thus experienced much differently from the seeing of the gods in Sample #11. The seeing of the gods was experienced as a seeing into some world that was not created by herself.

The Image occupied the entire vertical extent of her inner visual field, but was seen only in the right half of her inner field. That is, she felt that she had to turn her eyes (or her head) slightly to the right to see the Im-age. The screaming in the Image was seen, not heard; in fact, there was no sound accompanying the Image. The aggressive Feeling seemed to pre-cede the Image in Sally's experience, and to become stronger while the Image was displayed. The Image did not arouse Feelings of compassion or sorrow for the people, etc., but rather was seen as purely aggressive.

The second Image in Sally's samples occurred while Sally was sitting alone on her couch (Sample #7). She was thinking about the irritatingly slow way in which her boyfriend Maarten does things. This thinking was a "visual thought," that is, she was looking at an inner picture of Maarten putting on his coat. Maarten was viewed from the left side, and the full extent of his body could be seen, in motion as he extended his arm to begin putting on his coat. The movement was very slow, exaggeratedly slowed over Maarten's usual slow manner of movement. The Image was in accurate color, and the coat Maarten was putting on was his own ac-curately represented coat.

The Image included a portion of Sally's living room: the walls and carpet behind where Maarten was standing. The walls and carpet were accurately portrayed in the Image, but the remainder of the room was altered from the way it actually existed. For example, the shelf behind where Maarten was standing could be seen clearly, but it was empty instead of having the books and papers on it as it usually did. Furthermore, the plants, chairs, and piano that were really in the room were absent in the Image, even though the floor and walls where these articles stood were clearly visible in the Image. (As an aside, after the description of the sample was complete, I asked her if she could recreate this image now, as we were speaking about it, and she said she could, and did so. I inquired whether the plants, chairs, etc. were still missing, and she said that they were in fact still missing. I then asked whether she could "correct" the Image, that is, to put the plants, etc. back into the scene. She tried to do so, but reported with surprise that she was unable.)

The Image itself was seen straight ahead in the visual field, and, as she watched it, it seemed to bend from the top, to curl over away from her. The Image continued thus to roll away from her until the last (bottom) part rotated, when it disappeared completely from her view. While the Image was thus bending, the visualization of Maarten also bent; that is, his body curved to the side along with the Image as a whole.

Concurrent with this visualization was a Feeling of irritation with Maarten, and while this irritation was said to exist in her body, she could not say exactly how it was experienced.

At the same time that this Feeling and visualization were going on, the voices of the gods could also be heard, asking Sally if she could remember having made love (with Maarten) last night. The exact words the voices used were forbidden to be repeated, but it could be said that the voices occurred one after the other, or sometimes at the same time, asking the same question repeatedly. These voices, as usual, were clearly heard in her inner head or nearby, and when they weren't talking, they were laughing at her. She was embarrassed at not being able to remember having made love, and didn't like the game the gods were playing with her; but those emotions seemed to occur slightly after the beep.

VERBAL INNER EXPERIENCE

We have seen that the inner apprehension of the voices of the gods

occurred at nearly every sample that we examined. There were two
samples (out of seven) where inner verbalizations were experienced that
were not the voices of the gods. One of those has been described above
(Sample #4), in which Sally was saying to herself in Dutch in Inner
Speech, "I should take a look at Menno." These words were experienced
as being said in her own voice with the same vocal characteristics as if
she were speaking aloud. In the other sample (#3), Sally was Inner Hearing Maarten's voice as he had spoken the day before. At the moment of
the beep, Sally was eating a sandwich with her mother, who was talking
about Sally's sister Monique, who had a new job. Sally was not paying
attention at all to the eating, and was only half listening to the conversation over Monique, since she was more focused on thinking about
Maarten. Maarten had told her that he would marry her if that would be
a help in keeping her son with her, that perhaps then no one would be
able to take him away from her. This thinking about what Maarten had
said was experienced as a replay of his exact words. Maarten's voice was
heard, not very distinctly, saying the words that he had used the previous
day, with the same inflection, rate, etc. as in the original. However, the
remembered hearing itself was not as clear as the original hearing had
been, and even less clear than the hearing of the gods' voices had been in
other samples. At the same time, Sally was Feeling a bit "vague," as if she
was not really there while she was eating her sandwich.

FEELINGS

In all the samples we have described except one (Sample #2, where we
may have had an incomplete conversation about the experience), Sally
experienced a clearly defined emotion at the moment of the beep. We
will not repeat those samples here, but instead will draw notice to the
general characteristics of Sally's Feeling experiences. First, her Feelings
were always clearly identifiable: uncertainty in Sample #1, vagueness in
Sample #3, longing (for a cigarette) in Sample #4, anger/aggressiveness
in Sample #5, irritation in Sample #7, and reassurance in Sample #11.
Even though the Feelings themselves were easily identifiable, it was difficult or impossible for Sally to explain exactly how she knew that that

was precisely that Feeling and no other. She could say that particular portions were not as clearly defined as in some of our other subjects (Bob, for example). The overall observation, then, is that in almost all of the experiences some emotional event took place, was clearly recognized, and had a rather clear bodily expression.

DISCUSSION

We should say at the outset that we believed that Sally's reports were accurate descriptions of her inner experience. Her reports were consistent when on occasion she described the same event in each of two sampling conversations, and she presented what was to us a believable pattern of recollections — for example, at times she said she couldn't remember a particular detail without seeming to be particularly stressed at her inability to recall and without succumbing to any perceived pressure from us. Furthermore, she expressed genuine surprise about some characteristics of her experience when we focused her on them.

Sally was a schizophrenic whom an external observer would describe as being relatively symptom-free during the sampling period. Thus, we should compare her inner experience to that of Jennifer, and to that of Bob in his Symptom-Free Period.[2] Because of the prohibitions of the gods, we do not have enough samples to make a complete comparison, but we can still note some striking similarities.

First, Sally's Images were experienced as inner pictures, rather than inner viewings, occupying abruptly less than her entire inner visual field, characteristics that typified both Jennifer's and Bob's images.

Second, one of her Images had the striking tilt also observed by both Jennifer and Bob but by none of our normal subjects (or of our depressed subjects).[3]

Third, Sally's Image of her friend Maarten was arbitrarily inaccurate in details — a shelf without its usual books and a room seen without its

2. See Hurlburt, *Sampling Normal and Schizophrenic Inner Experience.*
3. Ibid., Chapter 17.

plants and furniture, also similar to reports by Jennifer and Bob, but different from our non-schizophrenic subjects.

Fourth, Sally's seeing into a special reality was a unique characteristic. She was clearly able to distinguish seeing in her shared external reality from the seeing of inner Images, and also from the seeing into the special reality which in the sample housed the gods.

Fifth, Feelings were clearly apprehended by Sally on almost every beep, similarly as with both Jennifer and Bob, and more frequently than many (but not all) of our normal subjects.

Sixth, she repeatedly heard voices she took to be gods talking to her or to each other and giving her commands. The hearing of these voices was quite similar to hearing in reality, except that it was even clearer, and that the voices were heard either inside or quite close to her head, even when the gods themselves were seen in the exterior special reality some distance in front of her.

CHAPTER 11

Two Origins of Consciousness

BILL ROWE

C ONSCIOUSNESS HAS TWO ORIGINS, one in history and one in child-hood. The first one we struggle to get even a glimpse of, the second we can watch emerge. The two are related. The more we understand the latter, the better we can theorize about the former. Perhaps looking at Julian Jaynes's theory through the lens of child development can help make it feel less distant and more familiar to more people. After all, if Jaynes is right, all developmental roads lead to some form of subjective consciousness.

THEORY OF MIND

In Western cultures, typically developing children between the ages of 3 and 5 begin to interpret the behavior of other people in terms of un-observable entities that behave in lawful ways.[1] These entities go by the names *beliefs*, *desires*, *thoughts*, and *memories*, and they constitute, in part, what we call the mind. As unobservables they function as theoretical constructs, like center of mass in physics, and a theory about the mind al-lows the child to predict and explain the behavior of other people. With the advent of this theory the child begins to impose a dynamic onto oth-er people's behavior. A person who is just standing still, for example, will

Portions of this chapter first appeared in "Retrospective: Julian Jaynes and *The Origin of Consciousness in the Breakdown of the Bicameral Mind*," *American Journal of Psychology*, 2012, 125, 1–4.
1. Alison Gopnik, "How We Know Our Minds: The Illusion of First-Person Knowledge of Inten-tionality," *Behavioral and Brain Sciences*, 1993, 16, 1–14.

be said to be having *thoughts* running through his head. Someone who bought an ice cream cone did it because she *wanted* it. Or another child opened a cupboard because he *falsely believed* that a cookie jar was there. Within this same developmental period the child also uses these mental state terms to explain his or her own behavior. A standard measurement of theory of mind is the classic false belief test. Typically it involves determining whether a child can make a judgment about another person by inferring that the other person has an erroneous belief about something.[2]

Executive Function

Executive functions have been described as consisting of the "mental operations which enable an individual to disengage from the immediate context in order to guide behavior by reference to mental models or future goals. More specifically, executive functions are thought to involve several interacting but potentially dissociable mental operations, including working memory, inhibition, mental flexibility, and planning."[3] Some typical tests for evaluating executive functions are the Tower of Hanoi task for planning, the Wisconsin Card Sorting task for mental flexibility, and the Stroop test for inhibition.

The general theoretical framework in child development that I assume here is that executive functions precede theory-of-mind capacities and are required for the acquisition of these capacities. Within this framework I favor an *emergence* model as opposed to an *expressionist* one. The expressionist model holds that theory-of-mind capacities exist early, along with executive skills, but the child simply does not yet have the ability to express them. The emergence model that I favor says that theory-of-mind development requires a mature set of executive skills functioning in a social setting that encourages the use of mental state terms.[4] The initial independence of these two domains lends credibility to a key requirement of Julian Jaynes's theory; that is, that the complexities of a

2. Heinz Wimmer and Josef Perner, "Beliefs about Beliefs: Representation and Constraining Function of Wrong Beliefs in Young Children's Understanding of Deception," *Cognition*, 1983, 13, 103–128.
3. Robert M. Joseph and Helen Tager-Flusberg, "The Relationship of Theory of Mind and Executive Functions to Symptom Type and Severity in Children with Autism," *Development and Psychopathology*, 2004, 16, 1, 137–155.
4. Stephanie M. Carlson, Louis J. Moses and Casey Breton, "How Specific is the Relation Between Executive Function and Theory of Mind? Contributions of Inhibitory Control and Working Memory," *Infant and Child Development*, 2002, 11, 73–92.

society could determine the need for mental state evaluative skills. I suggest that the lack of mental state descriptors in the most ancient Greek, as well as other texts, should be taken at face value. That is, the social stresses in these cultures had not yet reached a critical tipping point, one where the basic executive functions failed to provide the cognitive flexibility necessary to negotiate challenges from new interpersonal social demands.[5]

Experimental Evidence

In the Latin Catholic Church the sacrament of confirmation is conferred on the faithful no earlier than age 7. Why age 7? According to canon law, that is the age of reason. Before that the young person is not considered to be responsible for his or her self.

But what is special about age 7? Figure 1 shows the percentage of children passing the false belief test as a function of age in four different countries: Canada, Samoa, India, and Peru.[6] It is not until after age 6 that all children reliably pass the false belief test. Studies have also shown that it is not until around age 6 that children become competent at narrating themselves in the dimension of time.[7] So if we take this as an index that the child can now understand his or her own behavior in terms of intentions, desires, and correct and incorrect beliefs, then it looks like the Catholic Church got it about right at age 7, throwing in an extra year for good measure.

A 2006 article by Sabbagh et al. comparing Chinese and U.S. school children shows a similar trend.[8] Figure 2 illustrates the trends for five different types of theory-of-mind tests. The vertical axis is a standardized scale, but the trend can be seen to track with those in Figure 1. The authors point out that, "more generally, these findings are consistent with those

---

5. For a broad cross-sectional treatment of how children come to understand mind from a social interactionist point of view, see Jeremy I. Carpendale and Charlie Lewis, "Constructing an Understanding of Mind: The Development of Children's Social Understanding Within Social Interaction," *Behavioral and Brain Sciences*, 2004, 27, 1, 79–96.
6. T. Callaghan, P. Rochat, A. Lillard, M. L. Claux, H. Odden, S. Itakura, S. Tapanya, and S. Singh, "Synchrony in the Onset of Mental-State Reasoning: Evidence from Five Cultures," *Psychological Science*, 2005, 16, 5, 378–384.
7. Richard F. Cromer, "The Development of the Ability to Decenter in Time," *British Journal of Psychology*, 1971, 62, 3, 353–365.
8. M. A. Sabbagh, F. Xu, S. M. Carlson, L. J. Moses, and K. Lee, "The Development of Executive Functioning and Theory of Mind," *Psychological Science*, 2006, 17, 1, 74–81.

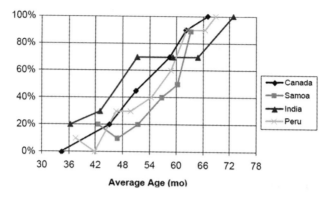

Figure 1. Percentage of children passing the false belief test as a function of age (Callaghan et al., 2005).

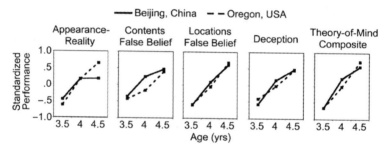

Figure 2. Chinese and U.S. preschoolers' standardized performance on the theory-of-mind tasks, by age. Performance is graphed separately for each of the four kinds of tasks and the aggregate theory-of-mind score (Sabbagh et al., 2006).

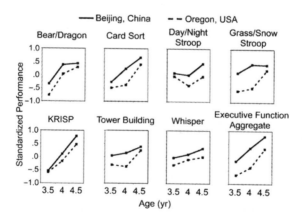

Figure 3. Chinese and U.S. preschoolers' standardized performance on the executive function tasks, by age (Sabbagh et al., 2006).

showing that children from multiple cultures typically show more similarities than differences when tested with appropriately designed theory-of-mind tasks."[9] This is interesting in itself, suggesting that there is broad uniformity in the way human children come to understand the mind. But, for our purposes, there is a more significant figure in the Sabbagh article.

Figure 3 shows the comparison of Chinese and American children on a range of executive function tests. The results show more mature patterns of executive function in Chinese children.

The authors say, "Chinese parents expect children as young as 2 years old to master impulse control, whereas U.S. parents do not expect such mastery until the preschool years." They go on to say that impulse control is more valued in Chinese preschools than in the United States, and therefore Chinese children have more opportunities to practice executive functioning skills. This is important because it illustrates the cultural dependence of the range of executive functions.[10]

Given that the Chinese children acquire theory-of-mind skills on the same timetable as American children, the data in Figure 3 favor the emergent theory over the expressionist one, implying that the understanding of mental states is not a latent capacity just waiting for a means of expression. This suggests that executive skills alone cannot account for the emergence of theory of mind and that a social context is also necessary. Both of these observations support the idea that theory-of-mind competence is a socially acquired skill, similar to Julian Jaynes's idea that consciousness is a socially acquired skill. The authors also note that because of the one-child policy, Chinese children have fewer opportunities to have discussions about mental states with other children. This is significant because other studies have shown that theory-of-mind performance can be predicted by the number of older siblings living in the household.[11]

9. Ibid., p. 80.
10. Ibid., p. 74.
11. T. Ruffman, J. Perner, M. Naito, L. Parkin, and W. A. Clements, "Older (But Not Younger) Siblings Facilitate False Belief Understanding," *Developmental Psychology*, 1998, 34, 161–174.

Julian Jaynes and Theory of Mind

We do not know how Jaynes would have incorporated theory-of-mind ideas into his theory of consciousness. Theory-of-mind did not have the publication density back when he was writing that it does to-day, so it would have been easy to overlook. But they are clearly kindred theories. And the reflexive awareness of mental states such as beliefs, desires, memories, and intentions would have a natural place alongside the analog 'I' and metaphor 'me'.

Numerous classical scholars, along with Julian Jaynes, have puzzled over the absence of mental state terms in the ancient literature. Richard Onians, for example, writing about the origins of European thought, finds an absence of abstract mental terms in the oldest Homeric texts. Thinking, he says, is described as "speaking" and is located in the heart, or midriff.[12] And the term *noos*, which later came to be associated with intellectual thought, did not have such a clear mental demarcation in the *Iliad*. "It is not mere intellect," says Onians; "it is dynamic ... and emotional."[13] Bruno Snell, in his classic book, *The Discovery of the Mind*, also discusses the character of mental state terms in the *Iliad*. Regarding words for "seeing," for example, he points out that "the verbs of the early period, it appears, take their cue from the palpable aspects, the external qualifications, of the act of seeing, while later on it is the essential function itself, the operation common to every glance, which determines the content of the verb."[14] And E. R. Dodds, surveying the fragmented lexicon of expressions in the *Iliad* for what are later called thoughts, perception, and volition, concludes that "Homeric man has no unified concept of what we call 'soul' or 'personality'."[15] But by the middle of the first millennium B.C.E., in works like the *Odyssey* and Hesiod's *Works and Days*, we see literature featuring very modern-sounding individuals complete with a wide range of mental state terms.

This is exactly what is predicted by the social constructionist model outlined above. There would be no reference to mental states in the early

12. R. B. Onians, *The Origins of European Thought: About the Body, the Mind, the Soul, the World, Time and Fate* (Cambridge: Cambridge University Press, 1951), p. 23.
13. Ibid., p. 83.
14. Bruno Snell, *The Discovery of the Mind* (Cambridge, MA: Harvard University Press, 1953), p. 4.
15. E. R. Dodds, *The Greeks and the Irrational* (Berkeley: University of California Press, 1951), p. 15.

literature because they had not yet been codified. And they had not been codified because the social disruptions leading to the collapse of bicameral civilizations had not yet happened. As discussed in Jaynes's chapter on the causes of consciousness, the new more urban, more cosmopolitan, iron-age setting put severe stress on the individual's cognitive capabilities. Life amongst strangers is not only more demanding in terms of decision making, but it also requires more nuanced skills at disambiguating the intentions of other people. And the ability to negotiate these social uncertainties is facilitated by conceptualizing other people in terms of mental states such as beliefs, desires, thoughts, and memories. But this ability must be taught. And the character and context of that teaching can be understood by examining the advent of theory of mind in children today.

There are four observations from the developmental literature I have cited that, I believe, lend plausibility to the claim that people of the ancient world described by Julian Jaynes had a radically different mentality from that of people today: Executive skills are independent of theory-of-mind skills, executive skills precede theory-of-mind skills developmentally, the extent of executive skills is culturally specified, and theory-of-mind development is facilitated by challenging social interactions. I will briefly comment on each of these.

Executive skills such as response inhibition, task flexibility, working memory, and cognitive conflict resolution do not depend on theory-of-mind capabilities. This independence suggests that a culture could exist using executive skills only. The converse does not follow, however. The developmental literature shows that the acquisition of theory-of-mind skills requires the prior establishment of executive skills.

In conjunction with this, the second observation, that executive skills precede theory-of-mind skills developmentally, lends further credibility to the claim that historically cultures may have functioned perfectly well without the overlay of theories of mind.

The claim that Chinese children have more mature executive skills because more is expected of them early on suggests that culture has a significant effect on executive functions. We are accustomed to thinking of young children as "little incompetents," but childhood, its duration, and the skills it produces, is very much a function of the needs of the culture.

Lastly, theory-of-mind skills are facilitated by challenging social interactions. This observation is in line with Jaynes's claim that subjective consciousness is an adaptation, in part, to interpersonal challenges resulting from the clash of cultures.

I began this section by noting that numerous classical scholars, along with Julian Jaynes, have puzzled over the absence of mental state terms in the ancient literature. But by the middle of the first millennium B.C.E. we see writings featuring very modern-sounding individuals complete with a wide range of mental state terms. This shift in the literary record supports Jaynes's theory of the collapse of bicameral civilizations. In bicameral times there would have been no need for mental state terms and functions because most people lived their entire lives in fairly insular settings, seldom encountering anyone who reasoned or behaved much differently from them. But with the clash of cultures toward the end of the second millennium B.C.E., along with other factors that Jaynes mentions, such as the invention of writing, there would have been social selective pressure to evolve a more flexible and reliable way to predict and interpret the behavior of other people.

It is significant that the signature test for theory-of-mind is the false belief test, that is, the ability to conceptualize other people in terms of beliefs that are wrong, that do not comport with reality. There are even versions of the false belief test that directly involve deception, such as the Deceptive-Pointing Task, which follows the same developmental curve as other theory-of-mind capacities. Without this ability true deception is not possible.[16] There is tactical deception, or course, which many animals demonstrate. But tactical deception is the acquisition of pragmatic strategies to bring about certain ends and is easily learned in natural habitats. As Jaynes points out, there is little deception in the *Iliad*. (The Trojan horse story, to the degree that it even qualifies as deception, does not occur in the *Iliad*.) Treachery, he notes, is impossible for an animal or for a bicameral person. "Long-term deceit requires the invention of an analog self that can 'do' or 'be' something quite different from what the person actually does or is, as seen by his associates."[17]

---

16. S. M. Carlson, L. J. Moses, H. R. Hix, "The Role of Inhibitory Processes in Young Children's Difficulties with Deception and False Belief," *Child Development*, 1998, 69, 3, 672–691.
17. Julian Jaynes, *The Origin of Consciousness in the Breakdown of the Bicameral Mind* (Boston: Houghton Mifflin, 1976).

By the middle of the first millennium B.C.E. there were, essentially, no groups left in the ancient Middle East that did not acculturate their young into a theory-of-mind consciousness. The consequences of this were significant. Virtually all the world's religions and major philosophies came into being at around 500 B.C.E., plus or minus a few hundred years: Judaism (of the Book), Confucianism, Taoism, Buddhism, Zoroastrianism, and Greek rationalism, to name a few. Apparently this kind of cognitive fluidity was also a slippery slope into anxious confusion. What is this mind anyway? Where did it come from? Does it go away when you die?

In the first century A.D. a Hellenized version of Judaism came to dominance in the West. Christianity fully embraced this narrated mind, even gave it a companion, so to speak — the soul — to account for the explanatory gaps that philosophers could not agree on. And, in time, the church instituted the sacrament of confirmation to inaugurate the age, 7, at which a young person can be held responsible and even punished for his or her thoughts. About a thousand years later psychologists discovered that at age 7 most children pass the false belief test and realize that the adults around them can be wrong about things. Something to be punished for, I suppose.

THE ADVENT OF CONSCIOUSNESS IN CHILDREN

Child development is a mature academic field with a well-developed experimental methodology and broad links to other scholarly areas. Jaynes has given us clear features of consciousness to be explained. Thus the developmental trajectory leading to the analog 'I', the metaphor 'me', and spatialized time, for example, can be observed and mapped. Earlier we saw in the discussion of theory of mind that the ability to conceive of oneself and others in mental state terms is an acquired skill. Mental state terms are the very things that scholars such as R. B. Onians and Bruno Snell tell us are missing from the lexicon of Bronze Age Greeks. People who might otherwise dismiss these claims as the specious excess of niche scholarship might be less hostile to experimental evidence of the onset, development, and variations in children's acquisition of theory of mind terms.

But mental state terms are only the beginning. There is also the study of the acquisition of time talk in children,[18] along with the ability to de-center in time and narrate around a point other than the present.[19] These are major components of Jaynes's theory of consciousness. Furthermore, we can ask how and when a child learns to use metaphor. When does a child finally realize that other people can have false beliefs? When and how do they use this understanding to intentionally deceive? All of these developmental features can be studied within groups, between groups, across cultures, and to some extent over the recent past. Variations due to family structure, peer groups, nutritional factors, and environmental in-fluences can also be examined. And, finally, differences caused by autism, birth defects, and illness can be added to the list. Packaging all of this under the rubric of the advent of consciousness takes some of the guess-work out of what was possible and not possible in the ancient world.

Also, studying child-rearing practices in many different contexts can help with the defamiliarization that is needed in order to imagine a time when people were not like us. Richard Nisbett gives an example of this in this book *The Geography of Thought: How Asians and Westerners Think Differently ... and Why*. In discussing the strong individualism of the Western self and the more collective Asian self, he recalls the popular Dick and Jane books that many Americans school children read from the 1930s to the 1960s. Nisbett notes the emphasis on the individual on the first page where the text reads, "See Dick run. See Dick play. See Dick run and play." The first page of a Chinese primer of the same time period depicts a little boy sitting on the shoulders of a bigger boy, and the cap-tion reads, "Big brother takes care of little brother. Big brother loves little brother. Little brother loves big brother."[20]

Psychologists Hazel Markus and Shinobu Kitayama note certain contrasting child-rearing practices relating to individual choice, another topic of importance to Jaynes. American children, they note, are social-ized to have distinct preferences. And well before the children can ver-bally respond, their care-givers are saying things like, "Do you want the

18. Francesco Antinucci and Ruth Miller, "How Children Talk About What Happened," *Journal of Child Language*," 1976, 3, 167–189.
19. Cromer, "The Development of the Ability to Decenter in Time."
20. Richard Nisbett, *The Geography of Thought: How Asians and Westerners Think Differently ... and Why* (New York: Free Press, 2003), p. 50.

red cup or the blue cup?" By contrast, the authors point out, the Japanese mother does not ask for a child's preference. Instead, she decides what is best for the child and tries to arrange it.[21] Studies like these can help people see how the cultural background contextualizes the formation of the social self. With these things in mind, it should not seem so strange to look at the social setting of, say, fifth century B.C.E. Athens and fifteenth century B.C.E. Babylon to contemplate the kind of selves those different cultures produced.

The Developmental Pathway to Consciousness

In what follows I will present a developmental theory of consciousness that is compatible with the ideas of Julian Jaynes. We will look at a sequence of five developmental milestones that are unique to human beings. Milestones that identify different things that are shared between the child and the caregiver at different stages of development. Shared affect, for example, or shared experience, and intentions. It is through these behavioral couplings that the child comes to sense the world from the viewpoint of another person. And, through this, ultimately come to sense his or herself through this other point of view. This is significant because Jaynes's theory requires that the child be escorted into consciousness by other people.

There are two transcendental moments along a child's developmental road to consciousness. The first is at around 9 months of age, and it is underwritten by the ability to share subjective experience. This event is implicit and nonreflexive, but it is profound just the same. The second occurs sometime between 3 and 7 years of age, when the child becomes competent at theory of mind skills and can explicitly take herself as an object of attention.

The Sequence

What are the uniquely human capacities that facilitate these momentous events in the life of a child? Keeping to the principle that it is through shared experience that adults usher infants into the world of

---

21. Hazel Rose Markus and Shinobu Kitayama, "A Collective Fear of the Collective: Implications for Selves and Theories of Selves," *Personality and Social Psychology Bulletin*, 1994, 20, 568–579.

consciousness, I will list the key milestones in terms of what is shared at each phase and the mechanism facilitating that sharing. There are five:

(1) *Shared affect.* Between birth and 9 months, what is shared is affect, and the mechanism is rhythmic engagement.

(2) *Shared experience.* Sometime before 9 months the human dyad begins sharing subjective experience via a species-specific mechanism called affect attunement. I call this transcendental because the infant is not only beginning to see the world through the experience of another person but also has the opportunity to see herself reflected back when the adult's attention is on the child.

(3) *Shared intentions.* Joint attention skills allow child and adult to maintain simultaneous attention on a third object. At around 9 months of age, typically developing infants begin to display a remarkable set of behaviors: they begin giving things, sharing things, teasing, and pointing. This is sometimes called the "nine month miracle."[22]

(4) *Pretense.* In the teen months social behavioral scripts are shared, and the mechanism is pretend play.

(5) *Theory of mind.* At around 3 years of age, knowledge of mental states begins to be shared, and the mechanism or vehicle, more properly, is theory of mind skills.

The items in the above list are certainly not the only milestones that a human infant passes through. Rather, they are the ones that I believe are most related to the advent of consciousness. Below, I will describe each one briefly in terms of their enabling factors. For example, *shared affect* is mediated by *rhythmic engagement*; *shared experience* by *affect attunement*; *shared intentions* by *joint attention*; *pretense* by *multiple simultaneous representations*; and *theory of mind* by *shared mental states*.

Shared Affect /Rhythmic Engagement. During the first year of life, normally developing human infants and their caregivers engage in rhythmically mediated bouts of shared gestures. An example of this is motherese. This is where the vocalization directed toward the infant is rendered with a prosodic contour characterized by exaggerated pulsed excursions in frequency and intensity. Human infants stop what they are doing and

---

22. Michael Tomasello, "On the Interpersonal Origins of Self-Concept," in Ulric Neisser (ed.), *The Perceived Self* (Cambridge: Cambridge University Press, 1993), pp. 174–184.

become momentarily transfixed by this. As they move through the first year this sort of prosodic interaction is displayed in all sensory modalities, and as the infant gains more control of his limbs he begins to reciprocate. Some examples are face-to-face interactions, vocal turn taking, and kinesic turn taking.[23] The adult form of this is rhythm. All societies that we know of have some form of recognizable rhythmic interactions.[24]

Shared Experience/Affect Attunement. Affect attunement often looks like imitation, but it is not. It is a mimetic form of interaction where the referent is not the overt gesture but rather an internal feeling state. How can an internal feeling state be shared? An example says this best. After accomplishing an amusing routine, a 10-month-old girl looks up at her mother. The girl "opens up" her face (mouth opens, eyes widen, eyebrows raise) and then closes it back in a smooth arch. The mother responds saying, "Yeah." However she intones it so that the pitch contour of "yeah" has the same "envelope" as the girl's facial gesture. The mother's vocal prosodic contour has matched the child's facial kinetic contour.[25]

What the mother did was reflect back to the child, in a different modality, what the child just experienced. For the child this interaction has a kind of déjà vu quality to it. She hears the mother, of course, but she also senses an amodal reflection of what she just did, or more properly, what she just felt. In this case the mother abstracted the intensity, timing, and shape profiles out of the child's affective behavior and played them back in another medium. As Daniel Stern says in his book *The Interpersonal World of the Infant*, "The reason attunement behaviors are so important as separate phenomena is that true imitation does not permit the partners to refer to the internal state. It maintains the focus of attention upon the forms of the external behaviors."[26] It is important that the mother does not use the same modality in her interaction. "Imitation renders form. Attunement renders feeling."[27]

---

23. Beatrice Beebe, Daniel Stern, and Joseph Jaffe, "The Kinesic Rhythm of Mother-Infant Interactions," in A. W. Siegman and S. Feldstein (eds.), *Of Speech and Time: Temporal Patterns in Interpersonal Contexts* (Hillsdale, NJ: Erlbaum, 1979), pp. 23–34.
24. Ian Cross, 2006, "Music and Social Being," *Musicology Australia*, 2006, 28, 114–126.
25. Daniel N. Stern, *The Interpersonal World of the Infant* (New York: Basic Books, 1985), p. 140.
26. Ibid., p. 142.
27. Daniel N. Stern, Lynne Hofer, Wendy Haft and John Dore, "Affect Attunement: The Sharing of Feeling States Between Mother and Infant by Means of Inter-Modal Fluency," in T. Field and N. A. Fox (eds.), *Social Perception in Infants* (New York: Ablex Publishing, 1985), pp. 249–268.

At this point something remarkably new becomes available to the human infant-caregiver dyad. With the ability to signal to someone a reflection of their own subjective feelings comes the ability to manipulate those feelings. Daniel Stern refers to these variations on attunement as misattunements, overattunements, underattunements, and inauthentic attunements. We trade in these alter attunements all the time. There is the well-known joke about two psychiatrists who pass each other on the street. They both say "hello" and then, as they walk on, each one of them says to himself; "I wonder what he meant by that." This joke is founded on the premise that a greeting can contain more than one message. The word "hello" is the archival message of record, so to speak, and the one that people are officially held accountable for. While the other message, couched in the way it is delivered, is amenable to a range of deniability. Labov and Fanshel called attention to this aspect of communication in their 1977 book *Therapeutic Discourse.*[28] They considered deniability of intonational contours to be a vital aspect of human communication, to the point of claiming that if they were ever conventionalized and made explicit, then some other channel of deniability would inevitably be invented.

Stern gives an example of the early use of an alter attunement used by a mother to regulate the behavior of her infant. The child looks at his mother with a bright face and a good deal of arm flapping. She wants him to remain cheerful but would like to tone down the level of activity. She might respond with her body in an attunement that matches his activity, but in the vocal channel say something like: "yes honey" in a relatively flat tone that falls short of his arm flapping. The mother, in this example, gained entry into the infant's emotional experience by attuning to him with her body, but demonstrated a different form of arousal by falling short of matching him with her vocalization. Another quite common example is a caregiver redirecting a hurt child. An infant might fall down and begin to cry. The mother will then respond by saying something like "Oh, yes, oh look at what you've done," with intonations of fun and surprise. This example is more than just a case of redirecting the infant's attention. Stern points out that "the mother's maneuver would never have worked if the level of arousal she showed in her fun-filled

---

28. William Labov and David Fanshel, *Therapeutic Discourse* (New York: Academic Press, 1977).

surprise had not matched the infant's level of negativity toned arousal."[29] To the infant this must feel like the mother has slipped inside of him subjectively and created the illusion of sharing but not the actual sense of sharing. With these variations on attunement the infant begins to realize, not only that experience is potentially sharable, but that it is potentially permeable as well.[30]

This is a form of engagement that trades in multiple simultaneous agendas. And I suggest that it is the child's introduction to pretense. Numerous scholars have commented that the ability to hold multiple simultaneous representations of something is a defining feature of pretense.

Shared Intentions/Joint Attention. At about 9 months of age, typically developing infants begin to point to things, give things to adults, share, and tease. They also begin to look to where adults are looking (joint visual attention), they adopt the feelings that the adult displays toward a novel person or object (social referencing), and they do what adults are doing with a novel object (imitation learning). Activities such as giving, pointing, and social referencing show an early sensitivity, on the part of the infant, to the psychological relations between other people and objects. For example, giving indicates a sensitivity to the adult's desire, social referencing to the adult's emotions, and pointing to the adult's state of attention.[31]

Pretense/Multiple Simultaneous Representations. Human subjective consciousness owes a great deal to pretense. It is the first clear indicator that the infant is acquiring the capacity to decouple from the world of reality-based interactions. Pretense is the ability to simultaneously hold multiple representations of the same object or act.[32] Pretend play is different from other kinds of play such as running, jumping, shaking things, wrestling, or chasing someone. For example, after around 16 months of age, a child might begin to put a doll to bed and tell it to go to sleep instead of lying

---

29. Stern, *Interpersonal World of the Infant*, p. 221.
30. Ibid., p. 214.
31. Henry M. Wellman, "Early Understanding of Mind: The Normal Case," In S. Baron-Cohen, H. Tager-Flusberg, and D. J. Cohen (eds.), *Understanding Other Minds: Perspectives from Autism* (Oxford: Basil Blackwell, 1993).
32. Alan M. Leslie, "Pretense and Representation: The Origins of 'Theory of Mind,'" *Psychological Review*, 1987, 94, 412–426; R. Peter Hobson, "Through Feeling and Sight to Self and Symbol," in U. Neisser (ed.), *The Perceived Self: Ecological and Interpersonal Sources of Self Knowledge* (Cambridge: Cambridge University Press, 1993), pp. 254–279.

on the bed herself and pretending to sleep.[33] Pretense is exemplified by social scripts, such as pouring a cup of tea, that can have arisen only out of shared understandings concerning role relationships, episodic structures, and conventionalized attitudes toward objects and events.[34]

This is an extraordinary ability on the part of such a young organism. At the developmental point when the young of all other species are struggling just to get their representations of the world right, the human 16-month-old is busy engaging in fantasy play! Without this scaffolding, this incipient ability to decouple from the immediacy of the physical world and imagine another one, there would be no space for a future analog 'I' or metaphor 'me' to wander in.

Theory of Mind/Shared Mental States. This is the second transcendental moment referred to earlier. If all has gone well up to this point, the child is poised to be reborn as a metaphorical being. This is a nontrivial event that few of us explicitly remember. We owe a debt of gratitude to Helen Keller for her rendering:

> Before my teacher came to me, I did not know that I am. I lived in a world that was a no-world. I cannot hope to describe adequately that unconscious, yet conscious time of nothingness. I did not know that I knew aught, or that I lived or acted or desired.[35]

As was described earlier, theory of mind is manifested by the ability to construe the self and others in terms of theoretical concepts such as beliefs, desires, thoughts, and memories. The prototypical test for this is the False Belief test, where, between the ages of 3 and 4, typically developing children begin to indicate that they understand others can have a wrong belief about the world. Theory of mind also includes other measures of imaginative mental life that are related to Jaynes's view of consciousness.

There is the Appearance–Reality test, for example, which measures the child's ability to distinguish between what an object is and what it looks

33. Jerome Kagan, *The Second Year: The Emergence of Self-Awareness* (Cambridge, MA: Harvard University Press, 1981) p. 88.
34. Michel Deleau, "Communication and the Development of Symbolic Play: The Need for A Pragmatic Perspective," in J. Nadel and L. Camaioni (eds.), *New Perspectives in Early Communicative Development* (London: Routledge, 1993), pp. 97–116.
35. Helen Keller, *The World I Live In* (New York, NY: The Century Co., 1904), p. 113.

like.[36] The Source of Knowledge Task assesses the child's understanding of the relationship between the knowledge they have and the means by which they acquired that knowledge.[37] The Deception in Children task is a variant of the False Belief task in which a desired reward hinges on not telling the truth about something.[38] By 4 years of age children are beginning to conceptualize human behavior in terms of mental states, but they do not yet think of mental activity as being a continuous flow of content, or stream of consciousness. Only 5 percent of 3-year-olds attribute any mental activity to a sitting person. By age 7 this becomes 95%.[39]

Autism, Bicamerality, and Mental States

Critics of Julian Jaynes often find it difficult to believe that ancient people could have language and not be in possession of the rich mental life that is common today. I would like to make a suggestion illustrating how the topics we have just looked at might inform this issue. It has to do with autistic people, their use of language, and their difficulty with theory of mind concepts. Many autistic people become competent in language use and can function in the world. They often excel in the technical world, which is not surprising because the deficit is supposed to be a social one. Autistic people are competent at using nouns and verbs to refer to things and changes in the state of things. So why is it such a problem to use the same sentence structure to refer to mental states?

I suggest that this inability is what we would expect if the child had missed participating in interpersonal affect attunements in the first year of life. Recall that what is implicitly referred to during acts of affect attunement are internal feeling states, not the overt actions. If the child participated only in the indexing of external objects and events and never shared behavior in which feeling states are traded, then she may simply have no way of knowing what is being talked about when, at about 3 years of age, people begin to talk about mental states.

---

36. John H. Flavell, "The Development of Children's Knowledge About the Appearance–Reality Distinction," *American Psychologist*, 1986, 41, 4, 418–425.
37. Josef Perner, *Understanding the Representational Mind* (Cambridge, MA: MIT Press, 1993), p. 151.
38. Ibid., p. 193.
39. John H. Flavell, Frances L. Green, and Eleanor R. Flavell, "Children's Understanding of the Stream of Consciousness," *Child Development*, 1993, 64, 387–398.

This is not to say that bicameral people were autistic. Rather, it illustrates one possible way in which language and theory of mind capabilities can be independent of one another.

REVIEW

The purpose of this chapter has been to explore the role of child development in Julian Jaynes's theory of consciousness. There were two main goals in this exploration. One was to identify developmental milestones that contribute to the adult form of subjective consciousness. The other was to see what a developmental theory could contribute to understanding the nature of consciousness in the ancient world.

The Conscious Self

The developmental pathway to consciousness was examined by looking at five species-specific milestones in the first seven years of life. These milestones were linked to unique propensities of the human infant to attentively couple with his or her caregiver. These couplings were linked to the ability to share affect, experience, and intentions during the first year of life. Subsequently, in the second year, we see the onset of pretense in the form of reenacted social scripts. This demonstrates the internalization of routine interpersonal experiences between the child and the caregiver. And lastly, the child acquires the ability to share mental states via the development of a theory of mind.

The Ancient World

There were four observations that help us to understand how Bronze Age people could have had a mentality so different from our own. The observations were that executive skills are independent of theory-of-mind skills; executive skills precede theory-of-mind skills developmentally; the extent of executive skills is culturally specified; and theory-of-mind development is facilitated by challenging social interactions. These observations lend plausibility to the notion that cultures can exist by emphasizing primarily (or exclusively) executive skills. And, further, that it is the social context that determines the need to create a narrative self that is populated with mental state terms.

Summary

Julian Jaynes had begun work on a developmental component to his theory of consciousness. Woodward and Tower, in their review of Jaynes's life and thought, report that a chapter on this topic would have likely been included in a second volume that he had planned to write. Sadly, he did not have the opportunity to do that.[40]

We can only speculate on what such a developmental theory would look like. But I feel we are on secure ground by emphasizing the capacities of the human infant to affectively attune with his or her caregiver. As we have seen, these attunements make it possible for the partners to reference internal feeling states. It is this mechanism that allows that which is private to become public and nameable. And nameable things are potentially a topic of discourse. When such discourse is directed back at the infant the seemingly impossible happens; subjective states become objective entities, and through this objectification human consciousness is born.

To the extent that these suggestions are valid, they are just the beginning. All of the behaviors discussed earlier are expressed in varying degrees by individuals and favored or not favored by cultural norms. Some cultures do not emphasize face-to-face communication with their infants, for example. And in many traditional societies explicit instruction is not part of the learning experience of the young. Even within American and European communities — where face-to-face communication and explicit teaching are common — there are variations. These variables in child rearing raise questions about the adult form of consciousness. Is it all or none when it appears, for example? Or do subtle differences in the milestones we have looked at have predictable consequences on the degree or character of consciousness?

Beyond achieving a better understanding of the role of each developmental stage on consciousness, there is also the issue of how to use this understanding in fields outside of psychology. To fully understand the

---

40. William R. Woodward and June F. Tower, "Julian Jaynes: Introducing His Life and Thought," in Marcel Kuijsten (ed.), *Reflections on the Dawn of Consciousness* (Henderson, NV: Julian Jaynes Society, 2006).

origins of consciousness, the aspects of child development discussed in this chapter need to find their way into the methodologies of other fields such ethnology, anthropology, and archeology. This must be done if we are ever to realize the suggestion Jaynes made when he said that what we need is a paleontology of consciousness "in which we can discern stratum by stratum how this metaphored world we call subjective consciousness was built up and under what particular social pressures."[41] But that is a task for another essay.

---

41. Jaynes, *Origin of Consciousness*, p. 216.

CHAPTER 12

The Origin of Consciousness, Gains and Losses:
Walker Percy vs. Julian Jaynes

LAURA MOONEYHAM WHITE

IN 1977, TWO YEARS AFTER THE PUBLICATION of Walker Percy's collection of essays on language and our existential situation, *The Message in the Bottle*, the Princeton psychologist Julian Jaynes published his startling theory about the origin of human consciousness in his *The Origin of Consciousness in the Breakdown of the Bicameral Mind*. Neither of these thinkers about consciousness and language, Percy or Jaynes, has been influenced by the other, but nonetheless there is an extraordinary consanguinity between their positions.[1] Beyond the striking parallels between their ideas, moreover, we find an even more interesting divergence, for though Jaynes and Percy agree in many essentials about the nature of both language and consciousness, Jaynes holds to a materialist interpretation of events, events which for Percy cry out for metaphysical explanation. To analyze, as this essay will do, both the convergences and the disjunctions between the theories and rhetorical approaches of Jaynes and Percy is to illuminate two strikingly similar contemporary systems of belief, one rigorously devoted to transcendent explanations, the other rigorously devoted to the undermining of the same.

Jaynes holds that human consciousness, which he defines as our awareness of ourselves as selves, began at a much less distant date than

First published in *Language and Communication*, 1993, 13, 3. Copyright 1993, Elsevier Ltd. Reprinted with permission.
1. In a personal communication (February 9, 1992), Jaynes confirmed that he is not familiar with the works of Walker Percy (1916–1990); Percy cannot, of course, also confirm that he had not read Jaynes but there is no reference to Jaynes in Percy's writings.

most theories of consciousness presume. According to Jaynes, consciousness began to develop in human history roughly 3,000 years ago; by 700 or 800 B.C., almost all of the Indo-European world had become conscious. Jaynes claims that consciousness is generated by language, but not by any sort of language. Since human language predates the development of consciousness by at least 50,000 years, Jaynes asks us to consider that there "could have been at one time human beings who did most of the things we do — speak, understand, perceive, solve problems — but who were without consciousness."[2] What such preconscious people lacked were the defining elements of consciousness as Jaynes sees it: first, a spatial quality or mind-space in which we "see" ourselves introspecting; second, an "analog I" which functions in consciousness as the agent of this mental kind of seeing (that is, a metaphoric self we automatically construct to move about in mind-space concentrating on one thing or another); and third, the capacity to narrate, to fit all events into the past and the future, to read time spatially. Such characteristics allow Jaynes to define consciousness as an "analog of what we call the real world ... built up with a vocabulary ... whose terms are all metaphors or analogs of behavior in the physical world."[3] If consciousness is essentially the operant of this linguistic and metaphoric function, then consciousness must have developed after the human evolution of language.

But not all language-users have been conscious. Jaynes explores such texts as the *Iliad* and the Old Testament prophetic book of Amos to demonstrate that ancient people did not seem to introspect on their actions. He sees in Achilles, for example, an example of non-introspective humankind, a man who seems to have no language for events in the mind and whose actions are all initiated by divine *fiat*:

> volition, planning and initiative is organized with no consciousness whatever and then 'told' to the individual in his familiar language, sometimes with the visual aura of a familiar friend or authority figure or 'god', or sometimes as a voice alone. [An] individual [like Achilles] obeyed these hallucinated voices because he could not 'see' what to do by himself.[4]

2. Julian Jaynes, "Consciousness and the Voices of the Mind," *Canadian Psychology*, 1986, 27, 128-137; reprinted in Marcel Kuijsten (ed.) *The Julian Jaynes Collection* (Henderson, NV: Julian Jaynes Society, 2012).
3. Ibid., p. 132.
4. Julian Jaynes, *The Origin of Consciousness in the Breakdown of the Bicameral Mind* (Boston: Houghton Mifflin, 1976), p. 75.

Jaynes proposes that these hallucinated voices constituted all primitive religious experience, all the gods, omens, and visions of ancient people, and that these hallucinations were simply interiorized ancestral commands issuing from the vestigial speech centers of the right hemisphere. The voices of the gods came from the right hemisphere and told the slave-like left hemisphere what to do in any surprising situation that could not be directed by habit or conditioned behavior. Both hemispheres, god and slave, were unconscious, unaware of self.

This model Jaynes calls the bicameral mind, a mentality which provided rigid social control for small theocratic societies. Only small societies rigidly controlled by theocratic authority could operate for long with such a mentality, however, and more complex social organizations made the continuation of bicamerality impossible. When catastrophes engulfed the Mediterranean world in the second millennium B.C. and vast hordes of displaced peoples migrated and fought over territory, the precarious bicameral mind collapsed and self-consciousness began. In the social chaos that followed the eruption of Thera and the enormous uprooting of once-stable populations, the gods could not tell one what to do, for one's hallucinations would either lead one to fight the threatening stranger or would proliferate into a babble of conflicting voices. The development of writing during this period likewise weakened the bicameral mentality because as it "weakens the auditory hallucinations, ... the word of the god — his commands — becomes silent, located in a controllable location rather than an ubiquitous power with immediate obedience."[5] Voices multiply, then fall silent, as we develop an interiorized consciousness to replace bicameral authority.

Consciousness is generated in this transitional period by an increasing metaphorization of experience. Jaynes demonstrates how one can see the invention and learning of consciousness on the basis of metaphor and analogy by tracing in ancient Greek the transition in meanings of such words as *phrenes*, *kardia*, *psyche* and *thumos*. Each of these terms develops from simple objective referents, as in the oldest parts of the *Iliad*, to metaphoric descriptions of mental functions, as in the subjectively conscious text of the *Odyssey*.[6] *Thumos*, for example, one of the most common

5. Ibid., p. 209.
6. Jaynes, "Voices of the Mind," p. 127.

terms in the *Iliad* which refers to human function, begins as a referent for the externally observable activity or movement of a person: "one warrior aiming a spear in the right place causes the *thumos* or activity of the other to cease."[7]   As bicamerality weakens, the term begins to describe sensations felt internally; *thumos* then comes to refer to "a mass of internal sensations in response to environmental crises," particularly the stress response of the sympathetic nervous system and its freeing of adrenalin.[8] The pattern of sensation appropriates the term for the activity of stress-generated movement, and thus it becomes *thumos* which give strength to a warrior in battle. Some of the most recent parts of the *Iliad* also testify to an even later stage in the development of the term, as *thumos* becomes a more subjective word:

> We see [this developing subjectivity] in the unvoiced metaphor of the *thumos* as like a container: in several passages, *menos* or vigor is 'put' in someone's *thumos*. ... The *thumos* is also implicitly compared to a person: it is not Ajax who is zealous to fight but his *thumos*; nor is it Aeneas who rejoices but his *thumos*. ... If not a god, it is the *thumos* that most often 'urges' a man into action. And as if it were another person, a man may speak to his *thumos*, and may hear from it what he is to say, or have it reply to him even as a god. All these metaphors are extremely important. Saying that the internal sensations of large circulatory and muscular changes are a thing into which strength can be put is to generate an imagined 'space', here located always in the chest, which is the forerunner of the mind-space of contemporary consciousness. And to compare the function of that sensation to that of another person ... is to begin those metaphor processes that will later become the analog 'I'.[9]

Thumos ultimately becomes an entirely subjective term; by the time of the *Odyssey*, it becomes the mental function or the bodily sense of recognition. Thus, the old nurse of Odysseus recognizes him by his scars because a god has "put" that recognition in her *thumos*.[10] For Jaynes, then, the history of language as a movement from concrete terms to metaphorical ones is also the history of the development of consciousness.

---

7. Jaynes, *Origin of Consciousness*, p. 262.
8. Ibid.
9. Ibid., pp. 262–263.
10. Ibid., pp. 274–275.

Percy, too, understands consciousness as a product of language. In his *The Message in the Bottle*, Percy describes how his obsession to understand the human existential and linguistic predicament returned him repeatedly to the figure of Helen Keller as a child, joining in her mind the cold liquid pouring on her one hand with the letters signed to her by Annie Sullivan on her other, joining them and knowing that water is "water":

> For a long time I had believed and I still believe that if one had an inkling of what happened in the well-house in Alabama in the space of a few minutes, one would know more about the *phenomenon* of language and about man himself than is contained in all the works of behaviorists, linguists, and German philosophers.[11]

What has happened, according to Percy's recasting of the American linguist Pierce, is the delta phenomenon: an irreducible triad of self, object, and sign, a metaphysical leap into symbol mongering. Curiously, like Jaynes, Percy seems to believe that language does not immediately lead to self-consciousness. Helen, like the unfallen Adam in the garden, spends her first day with language in an exuberant round of naming; only several weeks later do abstract and metaphorical thoughts begin.

In *The Story of My Life*, Helen recalls how puzzled she was by the word "love." Miss Sullivan tells Helen that "love" is in her heart, and though Helen is aware for the first time of her own heartbeats, she cannot read her teacher's meaning: "her words puzzled me very much because I did not then understand anything unless I touched it." But two days later, when Helen is laboring at a sorting exercise with different shaped beads, Miss Sullivan touches her forehead and spells "Think" — "In a flash I knew that the word was the name of the process that was going on in my head. This was my first conscious perception of an abstract idea." A moment later, and Helen has come to an understanding of that first abstraction that had eluded her, "love": "the beautiful truth burst upon my mind — I felt that there were invisible lines stretched between my spirit and the spirits of others."[12]

In *Lost in the Cosmos*, Percy considers the human history of language use and proposes an ontogenetic parallel. Perhaps, Percy theorizes, we

---

11. Walker Percy, *The Message in the Bottle* (New York: Farrar, Straus & Giroux, 1975), pp. 35–36.
12. Helen Keller, *The Story of My Life* (New York: Doubleday, 1954), pp. 30–31.

used language in a non-abstract and unfallen way before the metaphorical and abstract brought us to full human consciousness and our anxiety-
soaked dilemmas:

> From the moment the signifying self turned inward and became con-
> scious of itself, trouble began as the sparks flew up. No one knows
> how such a state of affairs came to pass [but] does ontogenesis shed
> any light here? The two-year-old comes bursting into the world of
> signs like a child on Christmas morning. ... For him, signifying the
> signified is like unwrapping a gift. What about the four-year-old?
> By now he should be a sovereign and native resident of his world, ...
> at home in Eden. Gesell [of the world famous Gesell Institute] ...
> describes him [as] "rather a joy. His enthusiasm, his exuberance, his
> willingness to go more than halfway to meet others in a spirit of fun
> are all extremely refreshing." ... The four-year old is a concelebrant of
> the world and even of his own peers. The seven-year-old? Something
> has happened in the interval. [Again, Gesell]: "More aware of and
> withdrawn into self ... self-conscious about own body ... protects self
> by withdrawal ... apt to expect too much of self."[13]

Language brings us the joy of naming, but at some point we try to name
ourselves, or try to say what we are not. Then language turns in on itself
and we are henceforth lost in the pits of selfhood.

Percy then shares with Jaynes the assumption that because of language and consciousness a radical discontinuity lies between all other
biological forms (including preconscious, "good animal" human beings)
and language-using humans. As Percy notes of Helen's breakthrough —
and by extension of the entire human breakthrough into symbolification
— "it was something new under the sun, evolutionarily speaking."[14] In a
grand hyperbolic sweep, Percy will claim in *Lost in the Cosmos* that "there
is a sense in which it can be said that, given two mammals extraordinarily
similar in organic structure and genetic code, and given that one species
has made the breakthrough into the triadic behavior [of symbolification]
and the other has not, there is, semiotically speaking, more difference
between the two than there is between the dyadic animal and the planet

13. Walker Percy, *Lost in the Cosmos* (New York: Farrar, Straus & Giroux, 1983), p. 108.
14. Percy, *Message in the Bottle*, p. 39.

Saturn."[15] Percy can make this claim because other primates, like Saturn, are governed entirely by stimulus-response relationships. The human being as wielder of language inhabits a conscious world which cannot be explained by the dyadic relationships of behavioral conditioning.

Jaynes too posits an entire break between the preconscious realm which evolution and behaviorism can explain and the conscious world which supersedes the mechanistic claims of either Darwin or Skinner. At the McMaster-Bauer Symposium on Consciousness in 1983, Jaynes was asked if he was a behaviorist; his reply confirms this break: "I am a strict behaviorist up to 1000 B.C. when consciousness develops in the one species that has a syntactic language, namely, ourselves."[16] This belief in discontinuity, in an absolute break between conscious human beings and other forms of life, has garnered Jaynes an inordinate amount of criticism from his fellow scientists, as one might expect. Jonathan Miller, for instance, attacks Jaynes on the grounds that he is in a long line of writers "committed to the belief that the cognitive structure of preliterate man [the 'so-called primitive mind'] is quite different from that of his 'civilized counterpart'."[17] Miller lists Vico, Tyler, Hallpike and Sir James Frazer as such authors, but concludes his list with the anthropologist Lévy-Bruhl and his "prelogical mentality." This inclusion of Lévy-Bruhl is damning by association, of course, since Lévy-Bruhl's ideas about a great divide between primitive and civilized man have notoriously been employed by the Nazis and others as support for genocide.[18] W. T. Jones, one of Jaynes's most thoroughgoing critics, likewise attacks Jaynes on the score of his belief in a great divide. He critiques the discontinuity required by Jaynes's theory by identifying it as a sign of Jaynes's bias for "abrupt, dramatic and radical change." Jones holds that this bias "shows up in Jaynes's references to a 'huge alteration in human mentality' and to 'dramatic change', in his liking for the expression 'de nova' and even in the title of his book."[19]

---

15. Ibid., p. 97.

16. Jaynes, "Voices of the Mind," p. 142.

17. Jonathan Miller, "Primitive Thoughts," *Canadian Psychology*, 1986, 27, 155–157.

18. Percy himself carefully distances himself from Lévy-Bruhl in *The Message in the Bottle*: "Lévy-Bruhl's categories of 'prelogical thought' are not, in my opinion, a genetic stage of psychic evolution but simply a mode of symbolic behavior to which a denizen of Western culture is as apt to fall prey as a Bororo" (p. 206n).

19. W. T. Jones, "Julian Jaynes and the Bicameral Mind: A Case Study in the Sociology of Belief," *Philosophy of the Social Sciences*, 1982, 12, 153–171.

What Jones identifies as discontinuity bias in Jaynes, Walker Percy would identify as continuity bias in Jones himself. Percy repeatedly derides scientists such as Jones for their refusal to consider the possibility that nature and history are not seamless propositions. As Percy explained to Linda Hobson in an interview, the "main dogma" of most scientists

> is that they will not tolerate discontinuity. But there's no reason why there shouldn't be discontinuity. What matters is truth ... The whole burden of my non-fiction is to suggest that man is [such] a discontinuity. That's very offensive to scientists, let alone drag in the notion of God and all the rest. Just to suggest that man is different is shocking to the scientists. I say that man is the only alien we know about.[20]

The curious thing about Jaynes's position, as opposed to Percy's, is that he is convinced that discontinuity exists in history and yet rules out any addition "from outside of this closed system to account for something so different as consciousness."[21] In a brief two pages early in his book, Jaynes excludes from consideration what he terms "metaphysical imposition." Within a page of acknowledging that it is a fact that "all life evolved to a certain point, and then in ourselves turned a right angle and simply exploded in a different direction," Jaynes drags in the spiritualism of Alfred Wallace, the co-originator of the theory of natural selection, to ridicule the search for metaphysical explanations and then concludes that endeavors like Wallace's séances "were not acceptable to the scientific establishment. To explain consciousness by metaphysical imposition seemed to be stepping outside the rules of natural science. And that indeed was the problem, how to explain consciousness in terms of natural science alone."[22]

The simple past tense of the preceding passage obscures our knowing that Jaynes himself sees the problem as exactly circumscribed by these same bounds of natural science. No more will surface in the book about gods or God as a possible source of consciousness; rather, Jaynes's quest for a materialistic answer will lead him to his monumental critique of religion, his assertion that all religious impulses are merely nostalgic

---

20. Linda W. Hobson, "The Study of Consciousness: An Interview with Walker Percy," *Georgia Review*, 1981, 43, 1–19.
21. Jaynes, *Origin of Consciousness*, p. 9.
22. Ibid., p. 10.

vestiges of our own bicameral auditory hallucinations, the voices we called gods but which were in reality only emanating from our right hemispheres. Jaynes, then, will tolerate one sort of discontinuity, but not discontinuities which require a metaphysical explanation. He and Percy nonetheless share a belief in a radical change undergone by humanity as it developed consciousness in the wake of its development of language.

Percy and Jaynes not only agree about the generative power language has for consciousness, but also, in some ways, about the essentially social and intersubjective nature of language itself. Jaynes posits that one vital factor contributed to the origin of consciousness in the traumatic age of great migrations in the second millennium B.C., i.e., encounters between strangers.

> [I]n the forced violent intermingling of peoples from different na-
> tions, different gods, the observation that strangers, even though
> looking like oneself, spoke differently, had opposite opinions, and be-
> haved differently might lead to the supposition of something inside
> of them that was different ... It is thus a possibility that before an
> individual man had an interior self, he unconsciously first posited it
> in others, particularly contradictory strangers, as the thing that caused
> their different and bewildering behavior.[23]

The metaphorical mind-space Jaynes identifies as the hallmark of consciousness may owe its existence in part to our inference of mind-space in others; if so, consciousness derives from social interchange: "we may first suppose other consciousnesses, and then infer our own by generalization."[24]

This socially derived part of Jaynes's theory, however, is not particularly central to his claims. Not so for Percy. For Percy, there is no understanding possible of either language or consciousness without a social dimension. Percy argues that any attempt to describe the nature of language must include a recognition of the shared reflection which occurs in any given linguistic act between the namer and the hearer. Symbolization, a creative and wholly human process, by definition involves an Other. As Percy states in *The Message in the Bottle*:

---

23. Ibid., p. 217.
24. Ibid.

the second person is required as an element not merely in the genetic event of learning language but as the *indispensable and enduring condition of all symbolic behavior.* The very act of symbolic formulation, whether it be language, logic, art or even thinking, is of its very nature for a *someone else.* Even Robinson Crusoe, writing in his journal after twenty years on the island, is nonetheless performing a through-and through social and intersubjective act.[25]

Thus both Percy and Jaynes share a belief in the social grounds of language use. Though the principle of language as social exchange is more vital to Percy, both Percy and Jaynes thus seem to dismiss the premises embedded in transformational grammar and recent semiotics which require that sign-systems be understood apart from the user. For Jaynes, consciousness began in human history when increasingly complex social relationships created the need for an "analog I," a self-conscious entity that could conceal or dissemble to others and to itself. For Percy, language is also at heart social; the essential linguistic activity for Percy *is* intersubjectivity, a mediated act which requires an other to be complete.

The parallels between Jaynes's and Percy's thinking about consciousness extend further. Given the shared belief that human beings were once preconscious, it should not surprise that both Jaynes and Percy reveal a presiding interest in vestiges of preconsciousness in contemporary life. Jaynes surveys such contemporary phenomena as schizophrenia, hypnotism, speaking in tongues, possession, mediums, and poetry,[26] exploring each as a remnant of bicameral mentality. As we could expect, Jaynes views religion as the "most obvious and important carry-over from the previous mentality" of bicamerality.[27] As we developed consciousness, Jaynes argues, the voices of the gods multiplied into a babel of confusion, then grew into an unintelligible murmuring, and then into silence. But our thirst for divine authority remains despite the loss of our hallucinated voices:

---

25. Percy, *Message in the Bottle*, p. 200 (Percy's emphases).
26. Judith Weissman's "Vision, Madness and Morality: Poetry and the Theory of the Bicameral Mind" has extended Jaynes's analysis of poetry as a bicameral vestige in her survey of the English literary tradition from Milton to Yeats, finding in English poets a hunger after divine voices and bicameral authority. Coleridge's "Kubla Kahn" becomes under the terms of this analysis the consummate expression of the yearning for the bicameral voice.
27. Jaynes, *Origin of Consciousness*, pp. 317–318.

as the slow withdrawing tide of divine voices ... strands more and more of the population on the sands of subjective uncertainties, the variety of technique by which man attempts to make contact with his lost ocean of authority becomes extended. Prophets, poets, oracles, diviners, status cults, mediums, astrologers, inspired saints, demon possession, Tarot cards, Ouija boards, popes, and peyote are all the residue of bicamerality that was progressively narrowed down as un-certainty piled upon uncertainty.[28]

The rhetorical strategy of this list incidentally reveals Jaynes's hostility towards organized religion; that "popes" follow "Ouija boards" and pre-cede "peyote" reveals that for Jaynes, all forms of questing after tran-scendence are equivalent — equally compelling, equally misguided. The religious imperative is inescapable but doomed as chimerical.

Omen-seeking, prophecy, and schizophrenia, some of the bicameral vestiges Jaynes explores, are omnipresent in Percy's novels. Yet the reli-gious impulse is not one after old phantoms for Percy. For Percy, a move-ment towards omens or prophecy or schizophrenia is almost always a movement towards real discovery. To be irrationally convinced that the increasing population of Jews in North Carolina augurs the end of time, or to be equally certain that God will give one a sign about His presence if one descends into a cave and simply waits God out, is in Percy's world to be onto the search. When Father Smith tells Tom More in *The Thana-tos Syndrome*[29] that the Jews are a sign that cannot be subsumed, he is not only implicitly condemning the Nazi attempt to eradicate Jews from the human family but also pointing to Jews as a sign before all people of God's existence and of the ineradicable value of individual human life. The portentous life, therefore, filled with omens or merely hunches, leads in Percy's fiction to revelation. It goes without saying, perhaps, that for Percy, the religious search is not nostalgic or illusory, but is rather a search that has for its object a real transcendent entity, God. Though Percy is always coy about his religious meaning, he nonetheless gives us to understand that the religious quest has the attainable end of God, not a hallucination.[30] In Jaynes's world, omens and religious searches only

---

28. Ibid., p. 320.
29. Walker Percy, *The Thanatos Syndrome* (New York: Farrar, Straus & Giroux, 1987).
30. Percy can be downright precious in his indirection about God. In *Lost in the Cosmos*, for example, the Incarnation is explained obliquely as an incident in which because we have acted like foolish

indicate our past god-driven (or more precisely, right-hemisphere-driven) history; we are merely seeking after now-vanished neurological authority.

And yet Jaynes is not himself immune to the religious imperative; even as he acknowledges that humankind cannot relinquish its fascination with some *mysterium tremendum*, he includes himself: "*none* of us can escape ... a patterning of self and numinous other ... in times of our darkest distress."[31]   In some sense, Jaynes's own theory stands as a substitute for religion. Towards the end of his book, Jaynes writes of "scientisms," which he defines as "clusters of ideas which come together into creeds of belief, scientific mythologies which fill the very felt void left by the divorce of science and religion in our own time"[32]:

> They share with religions many of their most obvious characteristics: a rational splendor that explains everything, a charismatic leader or succession of leaders who are highly visible and beyond criticism, a series of canonical texts which are somehow outside the usual arena of scientific criticism, certain gestures of idea and rituals of interpretation, and a requirement of total commitment.[33]

Jaynes identifies Darwinism, Marxism, Freudianism, and behaviorism as such scientisms. Jaynes concludes his discussion of scientisms, however, with the ingenuous assertion that his own essay "is no exception."[34]

---

cats caught up in trees, an unidentified "someone" who loves us is required "to make as big a fool of himself to rescue us" (p. 248).

31. Jaynes, *Origin of Consciousness*, p. 318 (Jaynes's emphasis). Jaynes's own mysterious moment provided much of the direction for his theorizing about consciousness. In *The Origin of Consciousness in the Breakdown of the Bicameral Mind*, Jaynes tells of a moment of the sort of "darkest distress" he later identifies as inescapably propelling us into contacts with the numinous (p. 318). He had been under stress for some period of time, "studying and autistically pondering some of the problems of this book, particularly the question of what knowledge is and how we can know anything at all. ... One afternoon I lay down in intellectual despair on the couch. Suddenly, out of an absolute quiet, there came a firm, distinct loud voice from my upper right which said, 'Include the knower in the known!' It lugged me to my feet absurdly exclaiming, 'Hello?' looking for whoever was in the room. ... I do not take this nebulous profundity as divinely inspired, but I do think it is similar to what was heard by those who have in the past claimed such special selection" (p. 86). The wisdom which Jaynes hallucinated (if indeed the experience was a hallucination) — "Include the knower in the known" — exactly undoes scientific claims of total objectivity, claims Jaynes himself sees as invalid. He would certainly agree, for example, that Lovejoy's paradox of the thinking behaviorist is a real and not an insubstantial conundrum. Consciousness is our only vehicle for understanding the world (the known); our status as subjective knowers must never be forgotten.

32. Ibid., p. 441.

33. Ibid.

34. Ibid., p. 443.

W. T. Jones, again, has a harsh verdict against Jaynes, particularly against this admission, which he has seized upon as crucial evidence of the unscientific nature of Jaynes's ideas. He speaks of confronting Jaynes with the sentence — "and this essay is no exception" — at a colloquium at the California Institute of Technology in 1978: "he evaded me. That he did so is hardly surprising, for he cannot want to face the implications of admitting that his book is a scientism. In the whole book, up to this final page, he has written in a way that leads every reader to assume that Jaynes expects his assertions to be treated by scientific, not visionary, criteria. If, as he was finishing it, it occurred to him that he had produced not a scientific treatise but a visionary tract, no wonder this discovery was acknowledged in such an offhand way."[35] Jones's implied expectation, that scientific and visionary discourse keep themselves clearly delineated from each other, is reminiscent of C. P. Snow's *The Two Cultures: The Scientific Revolution,* in which Snow argues that imaginative and scientific languages are wholly distinct modes of communication. Jones, like Snow, plainly prefers the language of science over the language of art, imagination, and vision.

But this distinction is almost certainly misguided. As we have known at least since Thomas Kuhn's *The Structure of Scientific Revolutions,* the history of science has been shaped by presiding myths or paradigms of belief, paradigms analogous to Jaynes's scientisms. Thus the generative myths of science are kin to the imaginative enterprise of discovery on which an author such as Percy sends forth his protagonists. Percy's fiction has always operated on the principle that to find out, to know, is the charge to both the scientist and the writer, and that scientist and writer may be the same figure. As Lewis Lawson has commented, "for Percy, scientific research, medical diagnosis, and fiction writing are essentially identical activities."[36]

As for Jones, he may be himself guilty of a rival scientism, here scientism as Percy would define the term. In an interview, Percy explained his understanding of how science becomes religion: "instead of seeing science as one valid way of knowing, [a scientist prone to scientism]

---

35. Jones, *The Bicameral Mind,* pp. 170n-171n.
36. Lewis A. Lawson, *Following Percy: Essays on Walker Percy's Work* (New York: Whitson Press, Troy, 1988), p. 237.

elevates science to an omniscient way of approaching reality. He denies
any serious reality to any other way of knowing. I think that's going to
lead him into trouble. Scientism is dangerous."[37] Percy expands on the
danger of objectivity as creed in *Lost in the Cosmos*: "while the scientific method may be officially neutral toward God, scientism, an attitude
which extrapolates from the objectivity of the scientific method to an all-
construing transcending objectivism, cannot be neutral. There is no room
in the Cosmos for an absolutely transcending objective mind and an
absolutely transcending God."[38] Jaynes's admission of his own scientism,
then, rather than obviating the value of his ideas as no longer within the
realm of pure science, as Jones would have it, rather is at least a cleareyed
recognition of the necessary relationship between any comprehensive
scientific theory and belief. At issue between Jaynes and Percy, therefore,
is not a divide between pure science and fictional adventuring but instead
a rivalry between different systems of belief. Both are theologies, though
Jaynes's is a secular theology which insists on the impossibility of "metaphysical imposition." "Secular theology" is Jones's term for Jaynes's ideas,
and Jones means it to sting:

> 'theology' because, like the great theological works of past ages, it
> presents a vision of the world as a whole, ... 'secular' both because this
> vision is confined to what St. Augustine called 'the earthly city' and
> also because it is composed in a language that looks scientific, rather
> than in the language of ecstatic mysticism or formal theology.[39]

Jones plainly would anoint as exempt from the charge of secular theology
some kinds of scientific discourse, those which, unlike Jaynes's, admit of
no discontinuities. Some secular theologies are more equal than others.

One indication of theological thinking is a given system of understanding, scientific or not, can no doubt be found in the presence of
lapsarian logic. Both Jaynes and Percy offer us variations on the myth
of the fall.[40] In Jaynes's reworking of the fall, unconscious bicamerality
assumes many aspects of paradisial perfection. In most versions of the

---

37. Hobson, *Interview with Walker Percy*, p. 13.
38. Percy, *Lost in the Cosmos*, pp. 165–166.
39. Jones, *The Bicameral Mind*, p. 170.
40. Jones's arguments can also be viewed as participating in a variant fall myth. To fall for Jones is to
give into the shoddy thinking of mysticism. Edenic purity is found in objectivity unsullied by mythic
imperatives while east of Eden is reached by meddling with discontinuities.

fall, humankind lived in peace and perfection, following only the dictates of God or gods. Similarly, bicameral human beings lived without any awareness of anxiety, for when stressful situations arose, they had only to listen to the hallucinated voices inside their heads which told them what to do. As Adam and Eve lived in innocence, unaware of right or wrong, so too did bicameral humanity, who followed the dictates of the gods and thus had no need for guilt or shame. These bicameral people could neither reflect upon their past or future actions nor upon the possible consequences of those actions; therefore, they were without the moral consciousness which makes guilt possible. Jaynes states flatly that "there [was] no such thing as morality in the bicameral world."[41] As with prelapsarian human beings, the actions of the bicamerally minded were neither good nor evil: they simply were.

In the Biblical story of the Fall, Adam and Eve are seduced by the serpent to eat of the fruit of the Tree of Knowledge of Good and Evil; it tells them that the knowledge gained thereby will make them as gods themselves. They partake of the fruit against God's will, and even as their mouths are stained with its juice, they know guilt and shame. God, angered at their disobedience, expels Adam and Eve from the Garden of Eden, and thus is humankind expelled from grace. By the lights of Jaynes's theory, the transition to consciousness from the bicameral mind is akin to Adam and Eve's tasting of the fruit of the Tree of Knowledge. Jaynes himself makes the parallel explicit and offers a reading of the third chapter of Genesis which proceeds along lines coincident with his theory:

> The Hebrew *arum*, meaning crafty or deceitful, surely a subjective conscious word, is only used three or four times throughout the entire Old Testament. It is used here to describe the source of the temptation. The ability to deceive, we remember, is one of the hallmarks of consciousness. The serpent promises that "you shall be like the elohim themselves, knowing good and evil" (Genesis 3:5), a quality that only subjective conscious man is capable of. And when these first humans had eaten of the tree of knowledge, suddenly "the eyes of both of them were opened," their analog eyes in their metaphored mind-space, "and they knew that they were naked" (Genesis 3:7), or had autoscopic visions and were narratizing, seeing themselves as others see them. And

---

41. Jaynes, "Voices of the Mind," p. 143.

so is their sorrow "greatly multiplied" (Genesis 3:16) and they are cast out from the garden where He-who-is could be seen and talked with like another man.[42]

The development of consciousness allows people to reflect upon their actions, to narrate and temporalize those actions, and to realize that those actions may have moral significance. The tasting of consciousness, then, Jaynes understands as an essentially linguistic event and, like the tasting of good and evil, an irrevocable one. Bicameral, Edenic paradise was lost, as was direct communication with the gods.

W. H. Auden tells us that almost every imaginer either urges himself or herself backwards to Eden or forward to Utopia or Zion:

> Our dream picture of the Happy Place where suffering and evil are unknown [comes in two models], the Edens and the New Jerusalems. Though it is possible for the same individual to imagine both ... I suspect that between the Arcadian whose favorite daydream is of Eden, and the Utopian whose favorite daydream is of New Jerusalem there is a characterological gulf as unbridgeable as that between Blake's Prolifics and Devourers.[43]

Jaynes is plainly one who understands the human yearning for Eden, the Eden of bicameral innocence. He writes of our longings for a return to that lost organization of human mentality, a return to "lost certainty and splendour."[44] Jones believes, in fact, that Jaynes speaks for himself when he describes the "yearning for divine volition and service [which] is with us still,"[45] of our "nostalgic anguish" which we feel for lost bicamerality.[46] Even schizophrenia, seen from Jaynes's perspective as a vestige of bicamerality, is the anguishing state it is only because the relapse to bicamerality

> is only partial. The learnings that make up a subjective consciousness are powerful and never totally suppressed. And thus the terror and the fury, the agony and the despair. ... The lack of cultural support and

---

42. Jaynes, *Origin of Consciousness*, p. 299.
43. W. H. Auden, "Dingley Dell and the Fleet," in W. H. Auden, *The Dyer's Hand and Other Essays* (New York: Random House, 1962), pp. 407–428.
44. Jaynes, *Origin of Consciousness*, pp. 444–445.
45. Ibid., p. 313.
46. Ibid., 1976, p. 297.

definition for the voices [heard by schizophrenics] ... provide a social withdrawal from the behavior of the *absolutely* social individual of bicameral societies. ... [W]ithout this source of security, ... living with hallucinations that are unacceptable and denied as unreal by those around him, the florid schizophrenic is in an opposite world to that of the god-owned laborers of Marduk. ... [He] is a mind bared to his environment, waiting on gods in a godless world.[47]

Jones, in fact, asserts that Jaynes's discussion of schizophrenia is held in terms "reminiscent of R. D. Laing's thesis that schizophrenics are the only sane people in our insane world."[48] Jones goes on to say that "Jaynes, it would seem, holds that we would all be better off if 'everyone' were once again schizophrenic, if we could somehow return to a bicameral society which had not yet been infected by the disease of thinking."[49]

Jaynes does not, in my opinion, intimate a position nearly as reactionary as this; he has in fact made elsewhere an explicit statement to the effect that he himself feels no such longing to return to bicamerality, that he would in fact "shudder" at such a return.[50] Nonetheless, Jaynes does seem at some points in his book to describe introspection as a sort of pathological development in human history. For instance, instead of describing humanity's move towards consciousness as liberating, Jaynes calls it "the slow inexorable profaning of our species."[51] And no less an eminence than Northrop Frye recognized this tendency in Jaynes to disvalue consciousness. After surveying Jaynes's argument and admitting the fascination of that argument's revolutionary appeal, Frye points out that Jaynes's ideas provoke a disturbing reflection: "seeing what a ghastly mess our egocentric consciousness has got us into, perhaps the sooner we get back to ... hallucinations the better." Frye expands his discussion of Jaynes to consider the cultural ramifications of this way of thinking, what he terms "one of the major cultural trends of our time":

It is widely felt that our present form of consciousness, with its ego center, has become increasingly psychotic, incapable of dealing with the world, and that we must develop a more intensified form of

47. Ibid., 1976, p. 432 (Jaynes's emphasis).
48. Jones, *The Bicameral Mind*, p. 166.
49. Ibid., p. 167.
50. Personal communication with Julian Jaynes, February 9, 1992.
51. Jaynes, *Origin of Consciousness*, p. 437.

consciousness, recapturing many of … Jaynes' 'bicameral' features, if we are to survive the present century.[52]

Frye evidently has little sympathy with such a position which would hold that consciousness is a "late … and on the whole regrettable arrival on the human scene"[53] rather than the wellspring of all our essentially human endeavors and achievements: art, philosophy, religion and science. The ground of this deprecatory perspective on consciousness, that is, a dislike or distrust of consciousness, has been held by many modern and post-modern thinkers and artists besides Jaynes, among them Sartre, Nietzsche, Faulkner, Pynchon, Freud, and Lacan, so much so that we might identify such an ill opinion of consciousness as a peculiarly modern ideology.

Walker Percy, however, does not participate in this ideology; in fact, he stands in direct opposition to it, finding such verdicts against conscious-ness not only naïve but also potentially dangerous. While Percy too reads the myth of the fall as a fall into consciousness and symbol-mongering, Percy does not long to undo our fallen position by abolishing conscious-ness or the subjective use of language.[54] In his last novel, *The Thanatos Syndrome*, Percy allows the enunciation of the position that conscious-ness is like a disease to come from the character of Bob Comeaux, one of a team of conniving villain-scientists out to save American civilization by suppressing our neocortical functions. Adulterating the water supply with heavy sodium, Comeaux and his fellow conspirators hope to recre-ate a peaceable kingdom by doing away with consciousness itself. In the following scene, Comeaux attempts to seduce the protagonist, Dr. Tom More, with his vision:

> Okay, try this for size. What we have here is a philosophical question … What do you think of this hypothesis, which is gaining ground among psychologists, anthropologists, neurologists, to mention a few disciplines — as well as among academics and in liberal circles — even among our best novelists! — Kurt Vonnegut wrote a book set-ting forth this very thesis. … The hypothesis, Tom, … is that at least

---

52. Northrop Frye, "The View from Here," in R. D. Denham, (ed.), *Myth and Metaphor* (Charlot-tesville: University Press of Virginia), pp. 63–78.
53. Jones, *The Bicameral Mind*, p. 171.
54. Percy's fall myth is specifically a myth of language. As he told Phil McCombs, "words are like the original sin, the fall of man" (Phil McCombs, "Century of Thanatos: Walker Percy and his 'Sub-versive' Message," *Southern Review*, 1988, 24, pp. 808–824).

a segment of the human neocortex and of consciousness itself is not only an aberration of evolution but is also the scourge and curse of life on this earth, the source of wars, insanities, perversions — in short, those very pathologies which are peculiar to *Homo sapiens*. As Vonnegut put it ... the only trouble with *Homo sapiens* is that parts of our brains are too fucking big.[55]

What's remarkable about the Blue Boy project (this the code name for the spiking of the water supply) is that it in fact seems to undo the human propensities for the very "wars, insanities [and] perversions" Comeaux laments. Comeaux can boast of impressive reductions in violence and psychological difficulties: teenage suicide is down by 95 percent; wife-beating by 73 percent; assault and battery by 85 percent; child abuse by 87 percent; hospital admissions for depression, chemical dependence, and anxiety by 79 percent. A host of assorted human ills and vicious proclivities have likewise undergone dramatic attrition. What could possibly be wrong with a social program that can lay claim to such extraordinary and beneficial results?

A great deal, actually. Percy's position is that the cost is essentially that of the human soul. We explore the particular dimensions of this soul-loss in the novel with Dr. Tom More, psychoanalyst and soul-doctor, who discovers that members of his community, most of his patients, and even his wife, all drinkers of the sodium-laced water, share certain symptoms. All have lost the "familiar anxieties, terrors, panics, [and] phobias' and now exhibit a 'curious flatness of tone."[56] They demonstrate a radical indifference to cultural context, the past and putative future which both Jaynes and Percy stress must surround any event with an implied narrative; as More tells us, "Ask them out of the blue; Where is Schenectady? and if they know, they'll tell you — without asking you why you want to know."[57]

This sort of "regression from a stressful human existence to a peaceable animal existence"[58] also includes a reversion to a bestial sexuality, as women present rearward for intercourse with the disinterestedness

---

55. Percy, *Thanatos Syndrome*, pp. 194–195. That of all the potential authorities Comeaux could choose to cite in support of this view that consciousness is dangerous, Vonnegut is chosen, tells us volumes about Percy's conviction that such a view has become the common cant.

56. Ibid., p. 68.

57. Ibid., p. 69.

58. Ibid., p. 180.

of simple physical need. Heavy sodium, among other things, drastically reduces the frequency of a woman's estrus, so that hormonal urges and, in consequence, mating, become far less common. Sexual activity becomes emotionless and casual, as casual as in the sexual practices of the higher primates. As Jaynes has noted in a 1982 essay on the effect of consciousness on emotions, such mating, "in contrast to ourselves, is casual and almost minimal, with observations of mating in gibbons, chimpanzees, orangutans, and gorillas in the wild being extremely rare."[59] Jaynes forecasts the emotionless participation in sex we see in Percy's drugged and regressive characters, for Jaynes connects the erotic with the conscious capacity to narrate, to tell ourselves a story about our presence in time. Narration makes fantasy possible. Preconscious humans were not obsessed by sexuality, Jaynes argues: "All classicists will agree with this, that all Mycenean and Minoan art, in particular before 1000 B.C., is what seems to us as severely chaste"; "… tomb and wall paintings, sculpture and the writings of bicameral civilizations rarely if ever have any sexual references."[60] But after the advent of human consciousness, the erotic begins to make its claim upon human attention: "About 700 B.C., Greek and Etruscan art is rampant with sexual references, very definitely demonstrating that sexual feelings were a new and profound concern in human development in these regions. We can perhaps appreciate this change in ourselves if we try to imagine what our sexual lives would be like if we could not fantasize about sexual behavior."[61]

The sexually abused and sodium-dosed children at Belle Ame Academy in Percy's novel have lost that capacity to narrate about themselves and have therefore lost all sense of shame, all sense of what should be either morally perverse or erotically exciting. As Tom More surveys the six photographs which document the sexual abuse at Belle Ame, he is struck by the demeanor of the children's faces. One child being subjected to fellatio by an adult male seems in countenance merely "agreeable and incurious."[62] In another picture, a young girl is being penetrated by the chief villain, Van Dorn; she "is gazing at the camera, almost dutifully,

---

59. Julian Jaynes, "A Two-Tiered Theory of Emotions: Affect and Feeling, *Behavior and Brain Sciences,* 1982, 5, 434–435; reprinted in Kuijsten (ed.), *The Julian Jaynes Collection.*
60. Ibid.
61. Ibid.
62. Percy, *Thanatos Syndrome,* p. 298.

like a cheerleader in a yearbook photo, as if to signify that all is well"[63] Another photograph is a group shot of junior-high age boys witnessing an act of cunnilingus: "Two or three, instead of paying attention to the tableau, are mugging a bit for the camera, as if they were bored, yet withal polite."[64] Another child in yet another appalling picture seems to have a "demure, even prissy expression."[65] What is remarkable about these photographs is how eloquently they testify to the needfulness of consciousness for the emotions of guilt, shame, or desire. Percy and Jaynes concur that without consciousness, sex is a mildly entertaining physical activity, either at best or worst.

The most pressing loss of the heavy-sodium drinkers in *The Thanatos Syndrome*, however, is not sexual emotions but rather language. Tom More notices that his patients no longer use language subjectively. They forego the more or less complete sentences of conscious speech and employ instead the two-word fragments "reminiscent of the early fragmentary telepathic sentences of a three-year-old, or perhaps the two-word chimp utterances described by primatologists — 'Tickle Washoe,' 'More bananas.'"[66] Even the deplorable Bob Comeaux cannot hide the loss of complex language skills in his drugged subjects (ACT language scores have dropped badly), but Comeaux is not disturbed by this development. Bragging to Tom More, Comeaux explains that "these kids are way past comic books and *Star Wars*. They're into graphic and binary communication — which after all is a lot more accurate than once upon a time there lived a wicked queen."[67] "Binary communication" More translates as "two-word sentences," and we are to infer that a world driven by such deficient linguistic aptitudes would be a world not worth the living in. In fact, Percy does not need the horrors of child abuse at Belle Ame to complete his argument against those who would dispense with consciousness; the revelations those pornographic photographs supply about what the villain-scientists have been up to constitute a sort of rhetorical piling on against the jejune and dangerous position of the consciousness-haters.

63. Ibid.
64. Ibid., p. 299.
65. Ibid., p. 298.
66. Ibid., p. 69.
67. Ibid., p. 197.

And here Percy again diverges in emphasis from Jaynes, for though Percy is keenly aware of the lure of nostalgia, he nonetheless repudiates those who yearn for a recreated Eden of preconsciousness. Lawson has argued that Percy's Edenic nostalgia is closely reined in by his awareness of that nostalgia's moral threat. Speaking of the earlier Tom More of *Love in the Ruins*, Lawson points out that Percy vehemently disapproves of his protagonist's harkenings back to Eden.[68] More's choice of bourbon, Early Times, reveals More's "nostalgia for that greatest aesthetic repetition, Eden."[69] More's moral fault in that novel is his desire to "alter man's basic nature by eliminating his sense of alienation. He does not wish to improve man's estate so much as to restore Paradise Estates."[70] More in *Love in the Ruins* falls prey to the same evil which holds Comeaux, Van Dorn and company in sway, the desire to provide a scientific solution to the problems of humanness by undoing that humanness itself. The Tom More of *The Thanatos Syndrome* is a much wiser character. He knows something about the tremendous wrongness of taking away consciousness, even if consciousness is responsible for all our fears and sin. The Tom More of *The Thanatos Syndrome* has given up drinking Early Times and now drinks Jack Daniels.[71]

It does Jaynes credit that he too recognizes the impossibility of a return to Eden and bicameral innocence; his characterization of humankind's presiding desire for such a return is never accompanied by an intimation that such a return is possible. The fall into consciousness is irreversible, and because the gods were never more than hallucinations, Jaynes's longing for transcendent experience must remain, he believes, unsatisfied. Unlike Jaynes, Percy does not wish for the innocence of preconsciousness or the simplicity of dyadic language, yet Percy is not kept

68. Francois Pitavy has also written about Percy's distrust of Edenic nostalgia. In "Walker Percy's Brave New World," she contrasts Percy in this respect to Faulkner and Fitzgerald: "Unlike Faulkner, who went back to the foundation of the city in the first prologue of *Requiem for a Nun*, or Fitzgerald, who recreated the original moment of the American dream at the end of *The Great Gatsby* in the vision of the Dutch sailors, Walker Percy need not hark back to the origins and attempt to retrieve that moment of splendor when the dream still appeared possible. ... The undercurrent of nostalgia that runs through Faulkner and Fitzgerald does not run through Percy" (Francois Pitavy, "Walker Percy's Brave New World," in J. N. Gretlund and K.-H. Westarp (eds.), *Walker Percy: Novelist and Philosopher* (Jackson: University Press of Mississippi, 1991), pp. 177–188.
69. Lewis A. Lawson, "Walker Percy's Prodigal Son," in J. D. Crowley and S. M. Crowley (eds.), *Critical Essays on Walker Percy* (Boston: G. K. Hall, 1989), pp. 243–258.
70. Ibid., p. 253.
71. Percy, *Thanatos Syndrome*, p. 21.

from transcendent desires. Percy's theology allows himself a hope Jaynes's secular theology will not permit, for Percy's Catholicism holds that our fall into consciousness may be redeemed, not by a return to bicamerality, but by a god whose voice comes from beyond the hemispheres. If Jaynes is right, Percy's thirst after God is merely a primitive vestige of earlier bicameral mentality and Percy's hopes are doomed. If Percy is right, the longing to hear the voice of God may be one capable of satisfaction.

CHAPTER 13

Echoes of the Gods:
Toward a Jaynesian Understanding of Rhetoric

TED REMINGTON

I F JULIAN JAYNES HAD DONE NOTHING but write Chapter 2 of Book I of *The Origin of Consciousness in the Breakdown of the Bicameral Mind* (*OC* hereafter), rhetoricians would be in his debt. In this chapter, Jaynes offers a detailed explanation of how metaphor — a preoccupation of rhetoric from its beginnings as a discipline in ancient Athens — works on a tactical, cognitive level. Even without the broader context of his argument in *OC* regarding metaphor's role in creating consciousness, Jaynes offers rhetoricians a helpful vocabulary with which to talk and think about metaphor, one that builds on work done in the twentieth century by students of rhetoric, particularly I. A. Richards, whose *The Philosophy of Rhetoric* is one of the most influential works on rhetoric that have appeared in the last 100 years. Like Jaynes, Richards was preoccupied not only with what he saw as an impoverished vocabulary for the working of metaphor, but of the importance of metaphor to thought.

Of course, Jaynes's discussion of metaphor is but the groundwork for his argument that human consciousness is a relatively recent phenomenon intimately tied to language use and metaphor. If Jaynes's specific thoughts on the workings of metaphor are valuable in and of themselves to rhetoricians, the larger use to which Jaynes puts them offers untold riches to those of us who wish to more fully understand the role rhetoric plays in the world.

In what follows, I suggest we can see Jaynes's treatment of metaphor as a continuation of a line of thought emerging from Richards's *The*

Philosophy of Rhetoric. While barely mentioning Richards in *OC*, Jaynes advances two of Richards's main arguments: that metaphor plays a much more central role in thought than it is traditionally given and that a more exact vocabulary is necessary to understand how metaphor works as a way of structuring our understanding of the world.

Next, I point to ways in which Jaynes advances Richards's thought significantly, particularly in his discussion of the role of the paraphrand in metaphor. This, I suggest, puts an even greater emphasis on the rhetorical nature of metaphor.

After suggesting that Jaynes is expanding and developing ideas that are present but not fully explored in Richards's work, I sketch out a way in which the results of this process can be brought to bear on some of the underlying concerns Richards attempts to address. Specifically, I look at the way in which understanding how meaning is made metaphorically can help us come to more productive "study of misunderstanding and its remedies" (which is, for Richards, the defining concern of rhetoric). I suggest that this is achieved by using Jaynes's insights to think about ideology — what it is and how it is created.

I end by pointing out work already being done that provides guidance in the development of this project, specifically in the writings of cognitive linguist George Lakoff and philosopher Mark Johnson, as well as those who have used their insights to think about ideology. Such work, even when not overtly invoking Jaynes, shows the same interdisciplinary spirit of Jaynes and shares Jaynes's conviction that metaphor is tied to our embodied existence. While much remains to be done, particularly in a more mindful application of Jaynes's specific ideas to rhetoric, there is reason to be hopeful about the benefits of a Jaynesian approach to rhetoric.

Julian Jaynes: Some Necessary Background

Any discussion of Jaynes's notion of the metaphorical nature of consciousness must begin with a disclaimer about what exactly Jaynes does (and does not) mean by the term consciousness. A review of responses to Jaynes's work reveals how much ink has been spilled critiquing Jaynes without a clear understanding of the particular aspect of mental activity

Jaynes refers to as consciousness. For anyone new to Jaynes, this must be grasped before delving into the details of his theories. For those familiar with Jaynes, a reminder of the key defining aspects of consciousness will still prove helpful.

Very briefly, Jaynes does not mean that human beings before 1200 B.C. were not aware of their surroundings, did not feel or think, did not communicate, or were unable to make basic judgments about the world around them. In short, Jaynes does not posit a world of zombies, mindlessly building the pyramids of Egypt, founding the city of Babylon, or fighting the Trojan War. This misconception comes from assuming that "consciousness" is simply another word for "awake."

But as Jaynes points out, consciousness, like metaphor, is a concept for which we have a paucity of terms. Many layers of mental activity are often subsumed under the umbrella of "consciousness," from those that we share with virtually any animal, regardless of how simple, to those that are uniquely human. Jaynes devotes the entirety of the first chapter of *OC* defining in detail what consciousness (in his usage) is not. He points out that consciousness is not necessary for forming concepts, learning, thinking, reasoning, speaking, listening, etc. What is consciousness, then?

Jaynes lays this out in the second chapter of *OC*, along with six important features of consciousness in this more restricted sense. Consciousness "is an analog of what is called the real world. It is built up with a vocabulary or lexical field whose terms are all metaphors or analogs of behavior in the physical world. Its reality is of the same order as mathematics."[1] Consciousness involves spatialization — the ability to create a mind-space in which we can imaginatively be places or see things that are not present, and in which we turn abstractions (such as time) into entities that take up space. Consciousness involves excerption — the way in which we think of large concepts or entities (e.g., "city" or "last summer") as a collection of specifics (skyscrapers, cars, people; beach, sun, swimming). Third, consciousness involves an "analog 'I'" — a sort of virtual self that we can imaginatively place within our own mind-space (e.g., imagining swimming in the ocean as we actually sit at a desk typing). Fourth, in addition to an analog 'I', consciousness

---

1. Julian Jaynes, *The Origin of Consciousness in the Breakdown of the Bicameral Mind* (Boston: Houghton Mifflin, 1976), p. 55.

involves a "metaphor 'me'," which is imaginatively looking at our analog 'I' from the outside (e.g., imagining watching ourselves swimming in the ocean rather than imagining actually doing it). Fifth, consciousness turns experience into narrative. We see our lives as a story. Unlike any other living thing, we understand our life as a journey from birth to death, a tale in which we are the main character. More specifically, we assign causes to events in our world, seeing existence as a continual linking of cause and effect. Finally, consciousness involves conciliation, in which we consciously assimilate new experiences into preexisting notions of the way the world works.[2]

Jaynes's notions of consciousness were, and continue to be, revolutionary. However, I argue that at least some small part of Jaynes's innovative treatment of metaphor as the means by which consciousness is created was anticipated 40 years previous to the publication of *OC*, in the work of the scholar of literature and rhetoric, I. A. Richards, particularly in his book *The Philosophy of Rhetoric*.

I. A. Richards: Someone Lend Me a Tenor

I. A. Richards's *The Philosophy of Rhetoric* is made up of the text of five lectures given by Richards at Bryn Mawr College in 1936. Given the expansiveness of the title, it might surprise readers to see how much of the lectures are devoted to seemingly technical issues of how words create meaning, and particularly how metaphors work (the last two lectures are wholly devoted to metaphor). But Richards's seemingly narrow focus provides him a way of getting at the crux of what rhetoric is all about: "a study of misunderstanding and its remedies."[3] The humane ends of rhetoric — to allow us to live more harmoniously with one another — are tied to the tactics of word use. Indeed, at the beginning of his second lecture, Richards points out that it is a fatal mistake for rhetoric to simply assume explanations of how words create meaning and move on to larger issues. The nature of meaning lies at the heart of rhetoric, and any attempt to formulate the "philosophy of rhetoric" must look deeply into this issue.

2. Ibid., pp. 59–65.
3. I. A. Richards, *The Philosophy of Rhetoric* (Oxford: Oxford University Press, 1936), p. 3.

In fact, Richards's approach to the concept of "meaning" bears a number of similarities to Jaynes's approach to the concept of "consciousness." In both cases, the concepts are ones that are all too often taken as givens. When they are not, they are explained in ways that rely on simplistic, outmoded thinking. Both terms must be unpacked with care and examined, a process that quickly reveals profound connections among thought, language, and society.

A full explanation of Richards's theory of meaning lies beyond the scope of this essay, but a brief sketch of his main points will help us to not only understand his treatment of metaphor, but to see how Richards anticipates Jaynes in a number of interesting ways.

Richards's main objection is to what he termed "Proper Meaning Superstition," the idea that "a word has a meaning of its own (ideally, only one) independent of and controlling its use and the purpose for which it should be uttered."[4] Words, Richards points out, have meaning only within contexts. Most obviously, a word means something given the other words immediately around it (e.g., a sentence). But Richards is after bigger game than this obvious point. Words are affected by other words that may not be present. What's more, these meanings are not fixed. Outside of highly technical language, words have meanings which shift and change.[5] Against those who bemoan this uncertainty inherent in language, Richards celebrates this as language's essential power. In short, language is a system of moving parts, interconnected in ways not at all obvious. To do its work, it cannot and does not remain static.

One might still say this is an obvious point that offers us little of value. Sure, words can mean lots of things. "Bat" can be a flying mammal or a wooden club (noun A/noun B). It can be a wooden club, or it can be what one does with the club (noun/verb). All well and good. But what does this mean for rhetoric?

Just about everything, says Richards. The common notion that words are (or at least should be) stable units of meaning poisons the act of interpreting what others say; it

---

4. Ibid., p. 11.
5. Ibid., pp. 74–75.

takes the senses of an author's words to be things we know before we read him, fixed factors with which he has to build up the meaning of his sentences as a mosaic is put together of discrete independent tesserae. Instead, they are the resultants which we arrive at only through the interplay of the interpretative possibilities of the whole utterance. In brief, we have to guess them and we guess much better when we realize we are guessing and watch out for indication, than when we think we know.[6]

The illusion that words have some superhuman ability to possess stable meaning takes the humanity out of the act of interpretation — and magnifies rather than lessens the possibility of misunderstanding.

What does this have to do with metaphor? Again, the answer is a great deal. Metaphor is no longer some "special use" of language that deviates from the norm (a fallacy that emerges from the Proper Meaning Superstition). On the contrary, metaphor *is* the norm. By studying metaphor, we study meaning. This is why Richards's exploration of the way human beings create meaning culminates in a lengthy meditation on metaphor, a meditation that, I argue, we see developed even further in Jaynes.

In the first of the pair of metaphor-focused lectures that end *The Philosophy of Rhetoric*, Richards questions assumptions about metaphor in the same way he questioned the assumptions about the meaning of words earlier in the work. In this case, the focus is not on the Proper Meaning Superstition, but three of Aristotle's beliefs about metaphor: 1) that metaphor relies on an ability to see resemblances that some possess and others do not, 2) that this skill to see resemblances alone, of all the verbal arts, cannot be taught, and 3) that metaphor is a peculiar, nonstandard use of language.[7]

On the contrary, Richards notes that metaphor pervades all language, and that terms for all mental abstractions are ultimately traceable to metaphor. In common usage, "metaphor" refers to linguistic figures that stand out obviously as figurative. For example, if I say, "The coming year gallops toward us at breakneck speed," I am obviously using metaphor to compare the year with a horse. The uncommon nature of the comparison

---

6. Ibid., p. 55.
7. Ibid., pp. 89–90.

marks this as metaphoric language. But if I use the phrase, "The year ahead … ," I am also using a metaphor. I am comparing time to a spatial relation, in which a certain period of time lies off at some distance from where we are now (the present moment being metaphorically represented as a current location). The fact that this second phrase uses a "dead" metaphor — one so common that we do not (usually) note its metaphorical nature does not mean that it is not a metaphor. We cannot speak about the world without using metaphor, whether we are aware of it or not. The startling but inescapable conclusion to this is that "the mind and all its doings are fictions."[8]

Here we already see a connection between Richards and Jaynes, who says that the thing we refer to as "I" is a metaphorical construct. But the connection goes deeper. Metaphor is not only omnipresent in our language; it is omnipresent in our thoughts. Richards says, "*Thought* is metaphoric, and proceeds by comparison, and the metaphors of language derive therefrom" [Richards's emphasis].[9] Here again we see a connection to Jaynes, who argues that our mental processes themselves are metaphorical in nature.

Finally, we have Richards's best-known contribution to the study of metaphor: his terminology for the functions of parts of a metaphor. Richards notes that one reason we have difficulty thinking deeply about metaphor and how it functions to structure our thought is that we lack a clear set of terms to talk about metaphor. The term "metaphor" itself refers to an entire unit of meaning; its constituent parts have no name. To rectify this, Richards coins the terms *vehicle, tenor,* and *ground*.[10] It is here where we see the most obvious connection to Jaynes's work — the one connection that Jaynes himself seems to be aware of — although as I've suggested it is a specific connection between the two men that comes from a much broader shared vision of metaphor's centrality to the human experience. We now turn to a closer, tactical examination of this connection.

---

8. Ibid., p. 91.
9. Ibid., p. 94.
10. Ibid., pp. 96, 117.

'I' Is a Metaphor

Like Richards, Jaynes sees a need for a more exact vocabulary with which to talk about metaphor and, again like Richards, coins terms to meet this need. Despite what seems a clear link to and extension of Richards's project in his Chapter 2 of *OC*, Jaynes barely acknowledges this, referring to Richards a single time, and that in a footnote. After introducing the terms *metaphier* and *metaphrand*, Jaynes simply says in a note that "this distinction is not connotatively the same as I. A. Richards' 'tenor' and 'vehicle'."[11] His objection is that such terms "make the matter too literary." He repeats this objection in identical language in at least two lectures given after the publication of *OC*, saying that while his terminology is "similar" to that of Richards, the latter's terms are "more suitable to poetry than to philosophical analysis."[12]

What exactly this means is left unexplained, and it seems an odd description of terms introduced in a work titled *The Philosophy of Rhetoric*. Perhaps Jaynes encountered these terms out of their original context; vehicle and tenor, despite Richards coining them in a work specifically about how metaphor operates beyond the realm of poetry, have likely been more often encountered in primers on literary criticism than in studies of philosophy or rhetoric (let alone psychology). Without the crucial context of the rest of *The Philosophy of Rhetoric*, the terms might seem like a narrowly utilitarian set of labels for use by undergraduate English majors. As we have established, however, Richards's project is much broader than that, and we are left puzzled and perhaps frustrated that Jaynes himself did not grasp the degree to which he and Richards were kindred spirits. With the benefit of hindsight, however, we can see Jaynes is thinking along Richardian lines while also appreciating the significant and original contributions Jaynes makes to their shared project.

To better understand both the similarities and distinctions between Richardardian and Jaynesian vocabularies about metaphor, let's look at a specific example. To make our task a bit more straightforward, we'll

---

11. Jaynes, *Origin of Consciousness*, p. 49.
12. Julian Jaynes, "Four Hypotheses on the Origin of Mind," and "Consciousness and the Voices of the Mind," in Marcel Kuijsten (ed.) *The Julian Jaynes Collection* (Henderson, NV: Julian Jaynes Society, 2012).

use the metaphor Jaynes himself uses when introducing his terminology: "The snow blankets the earth."[13]

As both Richards and Jaynes note, we can easily identify this statement as a metaphor, but getting beyond that to examine how the metaphor works proves more difficult, largely because, despite thinkers from Aristotle forward providing reams of commentary on how metaphor works, we have lacked a vocabulary with which to talk about the internal workings of a given metaphor. Both Richards and Jaynes remedy this, and both identify the first step as distinguishing between the term being used figuratively in the metaphor and the concept being described by that figure. In our example, the term being used figuratively is "blankets," and the concept being described is the way the snow is covering the ground.

In Richards's terminology, the term "blanket" is the *vehicle*, and the way the snow covers the earth is the *tenor*. Jaynes uses the term *metaphier* for the term "blanket" and *metaphrand* for the way the snow covers the earth. One might prefer Jaynes's terms to Richards's or vice versa for aesthetic reasons, but they essentially do the same thing: label the two distinct parts of a metaphor.

But as helpful as such labels are, they don't get us to the beating heart of a metaphor: the new meaning it creates via the use of the vehicle/ metaphier and tenor/metaphrand. We now enter much more subjective, but much more interesting, territory, and one where we are even more in need of exact terminology.

Specifically, we'd like to be able to talk about how these two parts of the metaphor interact to create meaning. In our example, the metaphor is used to get at some similarity between a blanket and the manner in which the snow is covering the earth — something that would be difficult or impossible to quite capture in language used literally.

For Richards, what's needed is a term that denotes the shared characteristics of the vehicle and the tenor, and he coins the term *ground* to do that. A blanket and snow on the earth are different in many ways, but in others they are the same, and it is this collection of samenesses that make up the Richardian concept of *ground*. These shared qualities are not utterly objective (if they were, we might not be in need of a metaphor to

---

13. Jaynes's actual example is "The snow blankets the ground." I've taken a small liberty with the wording to avoid confusion with Richards's use of "ground."

express them), but the fuzziness of this category does not mean we cannot name it.

However, perhaps because of the inherent vagueness of the concept, *ground* is a term that Richards spends much less time unpacking and explaining than he does with vehicle and tenor. As we will see, it's not as exact as we might wish.

While not describing what he is doing as developing and refining Richards's term *ground*, Jaynes does just that. Where Richards conceptualizes the new meaning generated by a metaphor as a straightforward intersection of shared qualities of the vehicle and tenor, Jaynes sees a more complicated dance taking place. Jaynes replaces the single term *ground* with two: *paraphier* and *paraphrand*. At first blush, this might seem mere tweaking for its own sake, but for Jaynes, the resulting clarity of these terms helps explain not only how we use metaphor, but who we are.

Returning to our specific example, Jaynes's term *paraphier* refers to qualities we associate with blankets. As with ground, this list will vary from person to person, but would likely include such ideas as warmth, coziness, bed, sleep, domesticity, night, waking, etc. When we use the metaphor "the snow blankets the earth," we are not simply pointing to a shared set of commonalities between a blanket and the way the snow covers the earth. Rather, we are mapping the qualities we associate with blankets (i.e., paraphiers) onto the way the snow covers the earth (the metaphrand). The result is a new way of thinking or feeling about the way the snow covers the ground. These constitute the new meaning created by the metaphor, and to this Jaynes gives the name *paraphrands*.

This can be a difficult concept to grasp, so Jaynes offers us some examples. When we map our associations with blankets onto the way the snow covers the earth, we might associate the earth itself with a sleeping person, waiting for the morning (the spring), when it will get out from under the covers. The earth is personified as a human being, with all the inherent associations that carries.

"The snow blankets the earth."	
Richards	Jaynes
"Blanket" = **Vehicle**	"Blanket" = **Metaphier**
Way the snow covers the earth = **Tenor**	Way the snow covers the earth = **Metaphrand**
The common characteristics of a blanket and the way the snow covers the earth = **Ground**	Qualities we associate with blankets = **Paraphiers**
	Generated ideas (e.g. of earth "sleeping" and then awakening in spring) = **Paraphrands**

It's important to recognize the significant way this understanding of metaphor is distinct from that of Richards (even though it is in many ways a continuation of Richards's line of thinking). For Richards, metaphors work by pointing to unnoticed relationships of similarity. From a Jaynesian perspective, metaphor creates similarity by making connections that did not exist before. For Richards, metaphor is descriptive; for Jaynes, it is constructive. Metaphor creates by mapping associations with a concrete, known entity (e.g. a blanket) onto another entity (the quality of snow on the earth) to create a meaning that would not exist without the metaphor.

To put it slightly differently, a Jaynesian metaphor creates a new understanding of the metaphrand by directing us to understand it in relation to something else. It uses existing knowledge and attitudes of the audience to create a new understanding of the metaphrand — not simply to point out something simply waiting to be discovered. This understanding is not value neutral. Even with a pedestrian, generic example of "The snow blankets the earth," we see that the implied personification of the earth carries with it a host of assumed attitudes.

Jaynes's understanding of metaphor is, oddly enough, more thoroughly rhetorical than that of Richards. It identifies the mechanisms through which metaphor changes the way we understand the world. Of course, this is particularly important for Jaynes in that our very sense of self, our "I," is a paraphrand — not a preexisting entity that we found a way to refer to, but a creation of the metaphoric process.

We could say that if, as Aristotle notes,[14] an enthymeme is a rhetorical or informal adaptation of a syllogism that leaves the major premise unstated, a metaphor makes an argument that is even more informal (and, as a result, more vague), relying on only stating a form of minor premise, asking the audience to come to the conclusion themselves. Using our current example, we might look at how the same concept can be expressed in each of these three forms:

Syllogism:

The snow blankets the earth. (minor premise)
Blankets cover sleeping things. (major premise)
Therefore, the earth is a sleeping thing. (conclusion)

Enthymeme:

The snow blankets the earth.
Blankets cover sleeping things. (unstated)
Therefore, the earth is a sleeping thing.

Metaphor:

The snow blankets the earth.
Blankets cover sleeping things. (unstated)
The earth is a sleeping thing. (unstated)

Of course, both the power and limitation of metaphor is that there are a number of ways in which an audience could "fill in" the unstated major premise and conclusion. However, if a certain metaphor is used repeatedly in a way in which the major premise and conclusion become commonplace understandings (i.e., if it becomes a "dead" metaphor), the major premise and conclusion can start to be taken as self-evident assumptions rather than assertions. And, by this mechanism, we simply "know" what we mean when referring to our analog I's and metaphor me's, having forgotten that these are assertions about the nature of the world, not self-evident, objective realities.

---

14. W. Rhys Roberts (trans.), *Aristotle's Rhetoric and Poetics* (New York: Random House, 1954), pp. 22, 1355a.

Metaphor, Rhetoric, and (False) Consciousness

I've just made the case that Jaynes offers us a powerful way of thinking about metaphor. While it parallels the work of Richards in many ways, it is even more robust. This is not, as Jaynes himself claims, because Richards's concerns and ways of thinking about metaphor were too "literary." On the contrary, Richards takes up the topic of metaphor specifically because of its centrality to communication and thought itself, not as a matter of aesthetics. Richards's claim is that expanding the way we think about metaphor beyond the realm of overtly figurative language helps us better deal with "misunderstanding and its remedies." In other words, it makes us better students of rhetoric. I've argued that Jaynes's discussion of metaphor and the role it plays in creating consciousness is not only consistent with Richards, but actually goes further in linking the project of understanding metaphor with a better study of rhetoric.

However, Jaynes does not address this. We must take the insights Jaynes offers us and then mindfully return to the underlying rhetorical concerns that motivated Richards to take up these issues in *The Philosophy of Rhetoric* and see what the results are. And that is the topic to which I now turn.

It's beyond the scope of this essay to go into great detail about this. Indeed, it is beyond my abilities at present. But what I can do is offer a sketch of what form this practice might take. After the highly tactical and detailed comparison of the ways Richards and Jaynes approach metaphor, our pace will now pick up and I will paint with a broader brush. My hope is, however, that this will still offer some guidance to students of rhetoric, metaphor, and/or consciousness about profitable areas to begin exploring.

Summed up as briefly as possible, the key term is *ideology*,[15] specifically the role of metaphor in creating it.

Like rhetoric, ideology is a concept that Jaynes does not take up in any detail, but about which his ideas imply a great deal. Specifically, I

---

15. Despite the somewhat glib subtitle of this section, I should make clear that I do not use the term "ideology" in the narrow sense of some Marxian thinking as "false consciousness," but in a much more general way as a set of beliefs, assumptions, or values that guide social behavior. As will become clear, it would make no more sense to call ideology "false consciousness" than it would be to call consciousness (in the Jaynesian sense) itself false.

suggest the following: the breakdown of the bicameral mind might not only have led to the birth of consciousness, but to ideology as well. Perhaps one cannot even separate the two.

As Jaynes notes, the social purpose of the bicameral voices he posits was to ensure stability — the voices spoke with the authority of leaders or gods, providing at least the sensation of direct relationship with the entities that guided the social world. Fully conscious beings would no longer have such an experience of having these entities inside themselves, constantly present and ready to intervene and give direction when needed. Yet, a means of maintaining social order remained.

In other words, the creation of what Jaynes calls the "analog I" and "metaphor me" needed a social structure to inhabit. Fully conscious humans were able to stand outside themselves and observe their behavior, project themselves forward and backward in time, and place themselves imaginatively into the mind-space of others. Such abilities provided advantages, but they also threatened social order. Freed from the inner voices that directed them to do things they might not necessarily choose of their own volition, particularly things that might benefit the collective at the expense of the individual (e.g., go to war on behalf of a king, toil in fields for the sake of creating food others would eat, etc.), these new owners of their very own analog I's and metaphor me's needed another method by which they could maintain social organizations, particularly given that one of the very reasons given by Jaynes for the breakdown of bicamerality was the increasing size and complexity of the social sphere in which humans operated.

What to do? I suggest that the response to this was the creation of ideology — a symbolic construction of social relationships that dealt with the increasing complexity of human interaction by creating metaphorical spaces, spaces structured by and around abstract concepts such as "kingship," "family," and "law" in which these abstractions were understood via metaphor. As conscious individuals stood apart from themselves and observed their own actions, they did not see themselves simply moving around the physical space around them, but also around a world in which there existed things like "kingship," "family," and "law" — a world in which these were realities not simply in terms of specific individuals, but as ideas, concepts, values, and social norms. Such entities had the same level of reality as the analog 'I' and metaphor 'me' — they provided the setting in which these entities moved.

Of course, in saying that ideology was created as a response to the breakdown of bicamerality, I do not mean that leaders in, say, Archaic Greece sat down and said to one another, "By Zeus! These hoplites and farmers are starting to think for themselves! We had better come up with a way to control these folks!" Rather, what we often term "ideology" was a natural result of the breakdown of bicamerality, created via language use in tandem with the creation of the idea of the autonomous "self" as a way of representing the social world this self inhabited. Without something like this process happening, I have difficulty imagining the ability of large and complex social organizations to survive the breakdown of the bicameral mind, particularly when the survival of these organizations might depend on the willing performing of actions by individuals that are not in their immediate best interest. It's one thing for a soldier to walk toward likely slaughter if he hears Athena commanding him to do so; it's quite another for this soldier to do so with full consciousness, including the ability to imagine himself lying hacked to pieces a few moments in the future. With only his own consciousness guiding him, ideas like duty to a king or the value of bravery or the deathlessness of honor must be understood to be absolutely real.

The creation of ideology in this understanding is part of the project of creating consciousness in the Jaynesian sense — involving excerption to create abstract entities that make up the mind-space through which our analog I's and metaphor me's roam, allowing us to see our lives as coherent narratives into which new experiences are conciliated.

We might pause for a moment to touch on Jaynes's idea of the close relationship between bicamerality and schizophrenia. If we grant that individuals with schizophrenia are, like our bicameral ancestors, hearing voices that direct them to do or say things, we might also note that the reason this condition is considered an illness that can prevent sufferers from fully participating in society is that those with this condition often speak and act in ways that violate the metaphorically constructed boundaries we have around what is normal speech and behavior in certain instances and what is not. On a certain level, it is the schizophrenic individual's inability to fully inhabit the ideologies in which we live that marks them as in some sense disabled or at least different from the norm. In a society in which very few hear these voices, they become idiosyncratic in their admonitions (although, as Jaynes notes, they often tellingly relate to issues of authority and right behavior). Rather than performing a function of social stability, they have the opposite effect. In a world in which social status, relationships, and behavior are defined by collectively created symbolic realities we name "ideologies," those who still hear the voices have a difficult time navigating the social world they inhabit.

Lest we think we've strayed too far from our starting point — the deep connections between Richards and Jaynes — it's worth noting that although Richards also does not use the term "ideology," *The Philosophy of Rhetoric* closes by linking the study of how metaphor works with the way in which language orders our social world, invoking the very sorts of concerns implicit in the concept of ideology. Richards says that the true work of words "is to restore life itself to order."[16] Pointing out that the stakes in figuring out how metaphor works go well beyond narrowly literary concerns, Richards says that the workings of metaphor "enter into the ways we envisage all our most important problems. For example, into the question of belief. Must we believe what an utterance says if we are to understand it fully?"[17] He goes on to say that "a command of the interpretation of metaphors … can go deeper still into the control of the world that we make for ourselves to live in."[18]

This, I believe, begins to get at how a "Jaynesian rhetoric" can help us become better students of "misunderstanding and its remedies." Jaynes's ideas about metaphor, particularly when tied to his ideas about the centrality of metaphor in consciousness, go beyond those of Richards in helping us understand the ways in which language structures our inner world, including our internalized conception of the social world around us. It becomes a central task of rhetoric to map out this landscape created by language, revealing the ways certain uses of language create a perception of an objective and necessary social reality that is in fact built on metaphors — particularly the paraphrands that result from certain

---

16. Richards, *Philosophy of Rhetoric*, p. 134.
17. Ibid. One might note, by the way, the interesting parallel between this statement and Jaynes's assertion that "to hear is in a certain sense to obey." Both Richards and Jaynes suggest the link between simply comprehending language and having one's thoughts shaped by it is a strong one.
18. Ibid., p. 135.

metaphors. As students of general semantics remind us, the map is not the territory itself. Jaynes's ideas help provide rhetoric with both concepts and a vocabulary that help point this out and discuss the dangers of taking map for territory in particular cases.

Metaphors We Be By: Cognitive Linguistics and a Jaynesian Rhetoric

If the fairly vague hypothesis I've just made has any merit, the next step is to think about what this would look like a bit more specifically. What would a Jaynesian rhetoric, focused on the intimate connection between thought and metaphor and linking this to the concept of ideology broadly defined, do?

Again, space precludes an extensive exploration of this here, but I suggest there is already some work done that hints at the potential fruitfulness of this approach.

In his essay, "The Metaphoric Origins of Objectivity, Subjectivity, and Consciousness in the Direct Perception of Reality,"[19] Stanley Mulaik notes the affinities between Jaynes's conception of metaphor and that put forward by linguist George Lakoff and philosopher Mark Johnson. In their book *Metaphors We Live By*, as well as in much subsequent writing both as a team and individually, Lakoff and Johnson set out a notion of metaphor as grounded in bodily experience. According to Lakoff and Johnson, a great deal of the way we think about abstract concepts stems from metaphors we use in relation to them. So, for example, the phrase "as we look ahead to next year" reveals a conceptualizing of time as a physical space. Saying, "I felt really down last week" equates another abstraction, an emotional state, with physical orientation.

This close connection between how metaphor works and embodied existence is, as Mulaik notes, something that separates the thinking on metaphor of Jaynes, Lakoff, and Johnson from most other models. But as grounded in our embodied existence as metaphor is, according to Lakoff and Johnson, this in no way suggests that metaphor does not shape our most abstract thinking. On the contrary, it suggests that our most abstract thinking is grounded, via metaphor, to our embodied experience.

---

19. Stanley A. Mulaik, "The Metaphoric Origins of Objectivity, Subjectivity, and Consciousness in the Direct Perception of Reality," *Philosophy of Science*, 1995, 62, 2, 283–303.

Mulaik's essay details some of the philosophical ramifications of an embodied understanding of metaphor, focusing on issues of objectivity and subjectivity. Lakoff and Johnson themselves touch on this in *Metaphors We Live By*, and develop their thought further in *Philosophy in the Flesh*, in which they trace the basic world views of several major strands of Western philosophy and the disagreements among them back to root metaphors used to understand concepts such as the self, mind, knowing, and existence — metaphors that are rooted in embodied experience.

This, I suggest, is not only consistent with a Jaynesian approach to metaphor, but also with the notion that ideology is the name we give to the metaphorical terrain inhabited by our analog I's and metaphor me's. When we discuss concepts like *work*, *the people*, *property*, or *liberty*, (terms rhetorical scholar Michael Calvin McGee called *ideographs*[20] — links between rhetorical practice and ideology) we do so via metaphor. We have no other way of thinking about such abstract, generalized concepts. We begin to see a specific way in which, as Richards suggests in his lectures, the tactical study of how we make meaning is ultimately necessary to understand how we think and talk about the kinds of issues we normally think of as the topics of rhetorical acts, and how better understanding of metaphor's role in this process could, hopefully, lead to a better understanding of conflicts.

Lakoff himself has done work that begins to get at this in his more overtly political writings using his take on metaphor to develop the idea of interpretive frames and then applying them to political thinking and speaking. For example, in his book *Moral Politics*, Lakoff traces the implications of what he sees as the two specific and competing versions of the nation-as-family metaphor that lie at the center of American political discourse: the "strict father" and "nurturing parent" models of morality. He has addressed how such metaphors play out when used to understand the abstract notion of freedom in *Whose Freedom?: The Battle Over America's Most Important Idea*. He's even penned works that could be described as rhetorical primers in how to use language to influence ideological debates in briefer and unapologetically partisan works such

---

20. Michael Calvin McGee, "The 'Ideograph': A Link between Rhetoric and Ideology," *Quarterly Journal of Speech*, 1980, 66, 1, 1–16.

as *Don't Think of an Elephant!: Know Your Values and Frame the Debate* and *Thinking Points: Communicating Our American Values and Vision.*

Some helpful work overtly addressing the linking of metaphor as understood as an aspect of our embodied experience with ideology has already been done by James Underhill in his book *Creating Worldviews: Metaphor, Ideology and Language.* Coming to the issue from the perspective of linguistics, Underhill thoughtfully explores the consequences of a view of metaphor as something that both shapes our thinking and emerges from our embodied existence on ideology. Underhill focuses on Lakoff and Johnson's work as a starting point, and although he doesn't mention Jaynes specifically, we've noted the degree to which Lakoff and Johnson's view of metaphor is consistent with Jaynes's. Underhill notes, to give just one example, that apparently innocent terms such as "upper class" and "lower class" contain obvious connections to directional metaphors linked with our bodily existence. He goes on to note that abstract concepts such as "time," "desire," and "anger," while corresponding to things we experience physically, are only perceived themselves in ways that are constructed by language (Jaynes would surely add "I-ness" to this list).

Much of Underhill's study in the book is how different languages (Czech, German, French) have been used in specific ways to order political and social thought in particular contexts. This is an expected approach by someone interested in comparative linguistics, although as Underhill himself notes, this is only one vector that might be taken. He identifies four general approaches to metaphor beyond the relatively recent cognitive linguistic model epitomized by Lakoff and Johnson: the philosophical, the linguistic, the poetic, and the rhetorical. Underhill's point is not that a cognitive linguistic model of metaphor trumps or subsumes the other four. On the contrary, his point is that the various approaches to metaphor ought be examined for common threads and that this examination should proceed on the presumption that no one account of metaphor will tell us all we need to know about it.

And that is what is so promising about his work — and what ties it to the project of juxtaposing Jaynes's ideas about metaphor with the field of rhetoric: beyond whatever specific contributions he makes to the specific case studies he takes up, Underhill suggests metaphor is something that must be understood interdisciplinarily even as we work with it within particular traditions.

Jaynes, a consummate interdisciplinarian while always grounding his work in psychology, would agree. Indeed, Jaynes can only explain the specific case of the "analog I" and "metaphor me" by drawing on psychology, psychiatry, classics, literary studies, religious studies, archaeology, anthropology, as well as a host of other approaches. That is the particular genius of Julian Jaynes — an ability to think about a topic like consciousness in both highly tactical and extraordinary broad ways, and to approach it from a variety of perspectives while creating a coherent vision from these perspectives.

In his expansiveness, Jaynes's work serves as an invitation for rhetoricians, linguists, psychologists, anthropologists, political scientists, historians, and many more to freely blend various perspectives. More than this, Jaynes's work serves as a potential site where such blending can happen (as evidenced by the wide range of disciplines represented in this volume).

Conclusion

The small contribution in forwarding the project sketched above made by this essay is simply to note the already existing similarities between Jaynes's project and the work of one of the most influential students of rhetoric in the twentieth century, I. A. Richards — similarities that go well beyond simply the shared project of naming parts of a metaphor. Additionally, I've suggested that even to the extent that they differ, Jaynes's work develops rather than contradicts or supersedes that of Richards. I then suggested that one way to move their shared project ahead yet further would be to look at ideology as the metaphorically-created terrain in which our analog I's and metaphor me's move about in time and space. I ended by suggesting that the confluence of Richardian and Jaynesian thinking is consistent with some work already being done in the realm of metaphor and ideology, particularly that coming out of cognitive linguistics, particularly the work of Lakoff and Johnson.

Richards closes *The Philosophy of Rhetoric* with a moving statement of hope for an interdisciplinary study of not only metaphor but how such a study can lead to a better life:

> It is an old dream that in time psychology might be able to tell us so much about our minds that we would at last become able to discover with some certainty what we mean by our words and how we mean it. An opposite or complementary dream is that with enough improvement in Rhetoric we may in time learn so much about words that they will tell us how our minds work. It seems modest and reasonable to combine these dreams and hope that a patient persistence with the problems of Rhetoric may, while exposing the causes and modes of the misinterpretation of words, also throw light upon and suggest a remedial discipline for deeper and more grievous disorders; that as the small and local errors in our everyday misunderstandings with language are models in miniature of the greater errors which disturb the development of our personalities, their study may also show us more about how these large scale disasters may be avoided.[21]

I believe that, whether he fully recognized it or not, Julian Jaynes has moved us closer to realizing this dream of a consilience between psychology and rhetoric and has given us some of the tools needed to bring it more nearly to fruition.

---

21. Richards, *Philosophy of Rhetoric*, pp. 136–137.

CHAPTER 14

Souls, Gods, Kings, and Mountains: Julian Jaynes's Theory of the Bicameral Mind in Tibet, Part One

TODD GIBSON

THE RELEVANCE OF JULIAN JAYNES'S THEORY of the bicameral mind to the history of religion in Tibet may not be immediately apparent to either readers of Jaynes's work or Tibetologists. The former may object that if the dawning of consciousness across the Old World happened, according to Jaynes, around the first millennium B.C.E., what could his theory possibly have to do with Tibetan history and civilization, which flowered not until the beginning of the seventh century of our era? Those whose primary field of study is Tibet may also wonder (with some justification) whether the Tibetological world really needs yet another comprehensive theoretical framework, with accompanying jargon, to compete with the dozens of others already being used to describe the situation on the Tibetan plateau.

To begin with, it must be stated that this essay is not a Procrustean attempt to fit the data we have from Tibet into a Jaynesian framework; rather, it stems from the discovery that the approaches Jaynes took in his investigations, as well as certain of his insights into religious history, can be profitably applied to the Tibetan situation, and that his hypotheses can provide possible explanations for otherwise enigmatic aspects of Tibetan culture. Further, Jaynes's theory differs from most popular academic paradigms in that it is based on logic and empirical evidence, drawn from fields as disparate as neuroscience and the Greek classics, clinical psychiatry and the Hebrew Bible. To use a more appropriate Herculean metaphor, the floodwaters of his ideas may help to wash clean the Augean stables of long-accumulated but malodorous academic assumptions.

The theory, though far-ranging, has four main interrelated ideas, all of which have some relevance to Tibet. Briefly put, these are 1) that the human capacities for introspection and for long-term narratization of past and future (which Jaynes calls "consciousness") depend on a sense of a self, which is a social construct based on the use of language that allows the creation of a metaphoric "inner space" of the mind. Jaynes attempts to demonstrate this by logical analysis of what consciousness is and is not. 2) This "self," being rooted in language, is not innate to the human brain, but is a cultural rather than biological development, and, crucially, this development took place within historical time. 3) Before this transformation, humanity did not make decisions based on a sense of weighing alternatives within a conceptualized mind-space, but were rather ordered around by the voices of "gods," which were auditory (and sometimes visual) hallucinations. 4) These hallucinations, perhaps similar to those experienced by modern schizophrenics, or children with imaginary companions, were probably produced in the speech areas of the right hemisphere of the brain, with the left hemisphere acting as intermediary.[1]

Jaynes's first idea is perhaps not as revolutionary to those scholars of Tibet who have even a little background in Buddhist philosophy as it seems to have been among religious philosophers and theoretical psychologists in the Western traditions.[2] For those familiar with the dialectics of the Madhyamika school of Buddhism, the coherence and clarity of Jaynes's analysis of consciousness should be graspable without too much difficulty (it should be mentioned, however, that the end result of his logic is not precisely the same as that of the Madhyamika's, which fact might be fertile ground for comparative study). While the implications of the fact that Buddhism largely agrees with Jaynes (and some other

---

1. Research has also shown that even in modern times, the hearing of guiding voices is far from being restricted to schizophrenics or to children. See Kuijsten (2006) for a summary. See also Hamilton, 2006.

2. Many of the objections to Jaynes's theory have stemmed from a failure to grasp what exactly he means by consciousness. He stipulates at the beginning of his work that "consciousness" is not to be understood as the sum total of mental functioning, as the term is commonly used in Western psychology (and sometimes in Buddhist studies as well), but rather the "introspective" ability of humanity, which is dependent on the creation of a "self" standing apart from its surroundings in time and space. Similarly, "subjective" in his work (and in this one) refers simply to the mind that employs this reflective capacity. If this is not well understood, the rest of his theory is difficult to absorb.

recent Western philosophers) on the strictly artificially-constructed and metaphor-based character of the "self" are interesting and perhaps even crucial for comparative cultural history, they are far too extensive to be discussed here.[3]

It is obviously the second and third of Jaynes's postulates that are of most immediate interest to the historian of Tibetan religions, and it is in considering them that Tibetology may contribute to the evaluation of the theory of bicamerality. This is because, in the course of developing his theory, Jaynes's historical evidence was limited almost exclusively to the early civilizations of the Near East, Egypt, and Greece; India and China are merely mentioned in passing, and there is little more on the pre-Columbian civilizations of the New World. In one way, this is fortunate, as it provides an opportunity to test whether Jaynes's theories have any bearing on data from cultures he was unfamiliar with.[4]

THE LANGUAGE OF MENTATION IN TIBET[5]

The investigation of archaic language is key to the historical aspects of Jaynes's theory; it is clear that any investigation into religious mentality must include attempts to understand the language that expresses it, in as close as possible to its own context. First of all, it must be recognized that fixed, one-word-to-one-word translations (calques) of old religious documents are more often than not impossible, especially in the sphere of religion, and attempts to reduce every word to another current in the translator's own language unfailingly results in a game in which inter-changeable conceptual beads can be strung along threads of preconceived ideas. To counter this tendency, the investigator must be able to hold

---

3. In the Tibetan context, Gyatso (1999) has begun to address some of these implications within the idiom of contemporary Western academic discourse.
4. Michael Carr has published a number of Sinological studies that can be related to Jaynes's theory (see below n. 8), but the early civilizations of Iran and India evidently remain unexamined by anyone familiar with his work.
5. Most of what follows in this section is derived from the present writer's earlier investigations in this area (Gibson, 1991, pp. 69–104). I know of no other systematic analyses along these lines in the Tibetan sphere except for similar recent work by Walter (2009, pp. 79–164). After Jaynes, I am using the word "mentational" to describe language that deals with even the basic functioning of what we call mind, as the available alternatives (e.g. "psychological" or "mental") have misleading connotations.

several tentative meanings in his mind simultaneously without immediately committing to any.[6]

Such a process is doubly necessary when attempting to translate across a long period of historical time. The meaning of a given religious term must not be assumed to be static, as it may shift with changes in a society's religious needs or mentational sophistication. To assume that connotations of a word which exist in a given time period also were valid in earlier times is a common error among religious historians; here it will be called "katachronization."[7] Avoiding this assumption when tracing the common themes found in multivalent words, one can gain crucial knowledge of the development of both the language and the culture of the people who used it.[8]

In *The Origin of Consciousness*, Jaynes, following in the footsteps of classicists such as Adkins (1970) uses Ancient Greek to trace the development of consciousness, as that language has (like Chinese, if to a much lesser degree) an extensive and well-chronologized literature, starting with the *Iliad*, which betrays little, if any, of the language of subjective consciousness,[9] and ending in the writings of Solon (sixth century B.C.E.), to whom Jaynes attributes the first real statement of the subjective conscious mind in Europe.[10]

In the *Iliad*, the heroes are not men making conscious choices. Their motivations are strictly on the somatic level: they are caused to act by somatic impulses, which are described by words such as *thumos* (according to Adkins "the hot, swirling, surging … sensations produced by

---

6. O'Flaherty (1980, pp. 17–61) observes that words in the *Rig Veda* dealing with fluids bear a whole spectrum of meanings quite inadequately rendered by literal translation, and discusses some of the difficulties raised by this.

7. Panikkar (1977, p. 24) uses the Greek roots to coin an important distinction between anachronism and katachronism: "The former means to introduce old and obsolete notions into contemporary situations; the latter means to interpret a thing of the past with inadequate categories of the present day." The most commonly cited "anachronism," the "striking of the clock" in Shakespeare's *Julius Caesar*, should thus be considered a katachronism.

8. Owing to the very long and more easily datable written tradition, Sinologists especially have been able to utilize this approach with great profit. As examples of recent work, Carr (2006, pp. 357–84, and 1989) traces the usage of various words from oracle bones to Classical Chinese to account for apparently unconnected meanings.

9. Adkins (1970, p. 16) puts it bluntly, if perhaps too simply: "Homer has no non-material language." Jaynes (1976, pp 67–83) has expanded on this theme with more nuance; I have attempted to distill the latter's argument for the sake of brevity.

10. Jaynes, 1976, pp. 255–292.

feelings of anger and other violent impulses"[11]), *phrenes* (physical sensations based on respiration), and *etor* (centered in the stomach).[12] These words for internal sensations and drives (Jaynes calls them "preconscious hypostases") continue to appear as motivating forces for quite a while in Greek literature. However, in situations where the reactions provoked by these drives are inadequate to the situation (Agamemnon stealing Achilles's mistress, Paris meeting Menelaus in combat), and the heroes experience what we in modern times would call the stress of cognitive dissonance, gods appear to them and tell them the course of action they should follow.

Over time, though, the Greek gods fade away, except as the subjects of myth, and no longer offer direct counsel to humanity; simultaneously, the vocabulary of motivation in Greece changes. Gradually, *thumos*, *phrenes*, and *etor* are subordinated to new terms, which more closely approximate our own understanding of the word "mind." The most notable of these is *noos / nous*, which originated in the word *noeein* (to see, in a strictly literal sense). Using the metaphor of "seeing" inside their own, invented, mind "space," the Greeks become capable of subjective, conscious deliberation. (Another important word, *psyche*, will be mentioned below.)

Before examining the development of the vocabulary of subjectivity in Tibet, it might be useful to deal with an objection to this approach, to wit: we cannot prove an absence of the subjective mind by its absence in written records. If the earliest written records in a language deal with matters such as record-keeping for purposes of commerce, for example, one might not expect to find much concern with the vocabulary of human motivation, or that of religion. This is quite true, and the purpose of this section is certainly not to demonstrate that subjectivity in Jaynes's sense did not exist in ancient Tibet. On the other hand, if we can employ Jaynes's methods and trace some of the vocabulary of mentation which does exist back to its earliest usage, avoiding, as he has, katachronic assumptions, we might gain some deeper insight into the development of

---

11. Adkins, 1970, p. 17. The similarity with the Tibetan concept of *gtum mo* (pronounced *tu mo*), a fierce heat derived from the practice of internal yoga, is arresting.

12. It is crucial to keep in mind that to translate these early somatically-based terms with words such as "mind," with perhaps a footnote saying that the early Greeks believed mind to be in the stomach, completely misstates the issue. The case is rather that these words gradually developed associations that were not as connected to their earlier, more concrete meanings.

both the Tibetan language and Tibetan religion than if we assume, as so many have, that ancient Tibetans conceived of the world and their place in it in more or less the same way we do, or even in the same way that they do now.

We must start by saying that the modern Tibetan language is definitely conscious in Jaynesian terms; it has a rich language of mentation that presupposes both an objectification of mental events and processes and, necessarily, a viewer that stands apart from them. This language was largely inherited from the Indic Buddhist tradition, which had already been conscious for at least a millennium before it came to Tibet in a significant way, producing during that time a variety of sophisticated analyses of mental functioning unmatched in the Western intellectual world until the last two centuries. But what about the Tibetan language before Buddhism?

If we attempt to understand the psychology of ancient Tibet through examination of the earliest examples of the written Tibetan language that have come down to us, we might be disappointed to find that things are not nearly as clearly cut as in China or Ancient Greece. It is immediately apparent that most of even the oldest existing Tibetan literature has been heavily influenced by Buddhist terminology. This should not be surprising, since Buddhism came to Tibet during the same era that it became literate — and an international power — with the cultural exchanges that inevitably accompanied those changes in status. There is the further difficulty that we know little about the linguistic makeup of the peoples who inhabited the Tibetan plateau before the Tibetan consolidation, and how this may have influenced the vocabulary of the modern Tibetan language.

There are, however, a very few sources which seem to show comparatively little influence of Buddhist mentational vocabulary, and which provide some space for theorizing about the development of subjective consciousness in early Tibet. One of these sources is the corpus of stone inscriptions from the Imperial period. These are usually held to be among the oldest existing specimens of written Tibetan. Another source consists of the documents discovered in the famous depository at Dunhuang. Although almost all of these are probably more recent than the Imperial period and the inscriptions, and in general show a good deal of Buddhist influence, many of them do seem to preserve archaic language usage. A caution here is that many of these documents also contain material translated from other languages, and religious or mentational vocabulary in them may reflect attempts to match words that already existed in the Tibetan language with borrowed ideas.

A third source is the literature of the Bon tradition. Although the historical development of Bon is controversial among Tibetologists, in the context of the present investigation, it is enough to note that some of the literature that has come down to us in today's self-described Bonpo tradition includes important terms dealing with human mentation that are not derivable from formal Indic Buddhist doctrine, and are in fact sometimes anomalous to it. This alone, of course, does not demonstrate their antiquity: it would not, for example preempt the possibility that such terms were borrowed from cultural spheres other than the Indic. Since, however, they also appear in some of the earliest datable sources from both inside and outside of the Bon tradition, and, as will be seen, several of them have clearly undergone changes in meaning consonant with an increasing subjectivity in Tibetan society, their currency in Tibet prior to the widespread acceptance of Indic Buddhism can be at least usefully examined.

Again, a caveat: it has been asserted that honorific terms in the modern Tibetan language, bearing both social and religious significance, were deliberate inventions by the Imperial Tibetan ruling class, imposed on the commoners in order to establish themselves on a level of divinity. There is no real evidence for such an assumption (or at least those who assert it have offered very little), and it should be clear that such statements typify a "religion as confidence game" mindset, typical of a cynical materialist approach to the history of religion but highly prejudicial to open-minded investigation.

Glo ba (pronounced *lowa*)[13]

There is one very clear — if not very dramatic — example of a Tibetan term which initially seems to have had a somatic referent, but which later

---

13. Tibetan words are transcribed with the Wylie system; their modern pronunciation is supplied in parentheses. It is usually held that, at some point in history, now-silent letters in Tibetan words were pronounced, but Tibetan historical linguistics has not progressed to the point where any theories about when or why they became silent can be expressed with confidence.

came to take on a subjective meaning, an example, moreover, that closely parallels the Greek *phrenes*.[14] The word *glo*, in modern Tibetan refers to the lungs, and in earlier language, we may surmise, the feelings associated with changing patterns of breath. In the Old Tibetan inscriptions we find the phrase *glo ba nye*, which might literally be translated as "near to the lungs" but which from context clearly means to be in favor with the emperor, or, as we might say "close to his heart." The same phrase (and its opposite, *glo ba ring*) also occurs in the so-called *Annals* of Dunhuang, among the oldest of the manuscripts found there. In modern Tibetan the phrase is attested as meaning "intimate, near, dear"[15] and "friendly, amiable,"[16] but the word in this phrase is now spelled *blo*, and retains no somatic connotation whatsoever: in fact, *blo* is often used in Buddhism to signify the purely intellectual and analytic aspect of mind. This evident segue of meaning from the somatic to the ultra-subjective indicates at the very least that the intellect, considered in isolation, was not fixed into the Tibetan conceptual world even as late as the Imperial Period.[17]

Thugs (tuk)

This word is often translated as "mind" even when occurring in such Old Tibetan material as inscriptions dated to the reign of Trisong Detsen (755–797).[18] This is perhaps not unjustifiable given that it is used in modern colloquial Tibetan as an honorific, as Jaeschke says, "whenever mental qualities are spoken of in respectful language."[19] Nevertheless, we must decide if the word *thugs* had at the time of the inscription all or at least most of the characteristics we associate with the English word "mind." If it does not, then it is purely a katachronic imposition to use it.

The latter seems to be the case. In the inscription, the emperor is described as having a *thugs*, which may have qualities of strength (*thugs stobs*) and firmness (*thugs brtan*), as well as the capacity to "diminish"

14. See Jaynes's treatment of *phrenes* in 1976, pp. 263–65.
15. Roerich, 1983–7, Vol. 6, p. 260.
16. Das, 1989, p. 903.
17. A good illustration of the pre-subjective use of *glo / blo* comes in a modern Tibetan phrase for disappointment or depression: *blo pham*. Using the *glo* spelling it would literally mean "defeat of the lungs," very evocative of the physical sensations and respiratory changes inseparable from those emotions.
18. The examples are drawn from the Lhasa Zhol inscription and the inscription at the emperor's tomb.
19. Jaeschke, 1980, p. 232.

under adverse circumstances (*thugs snyung*).[20] In these phrases, *thugs* does not seem to connote any sort of subjectivity or capacity for interiorized thought whatever;[21] like the Greek *thumos*, it seems not to rise above the level of what we might call somatic-emotional reactivity. If, as seems likely then, *thugs* gradually incorporated the connotations of "mind," and this process was not complete at the time of Trisong Detsen, we might search for a somatic-based term that it could have developed from, and for that we might turn to Buddhism. Like many honorific terms, *thugs* also has a field of religious meaning in modern Tibetan; it is sometimes used as an honorific for *sems* (*sem*), which in turn is often a calque for the Indic *citta* — a generalized term for mentational processes which is more justifiably, if still roughly, translated as "mind."[22]

Now, in much Buddhist literature, particularly in the Vajrayana, *thugs / sems / citta* is associated with the heart area of the body. It might be thought, therefore, that thugs was at first simply a Tibetan honorific for "heart" (the common word is *snying*, pronounced *nying*). Its evolution, in other words, would have paralleled the development of heart/ mind words in other languages.[23]

This possibility we will keep in mind as we explore further, but there are problems with such a straightforward conception. To begin with, *snying* and *sems* are not used interchangeably in either Buddhist philosophy or colloquial Tibetan; nor am I aware of any non-Buddhist material that explicitly associates the *thugs* with the heart. Again, in modern Buddhist

20. As has been previously pointed out (Gibson, 1991, p. 90 n. 40), the modern honorific word for "illness," *snyung*, probably comes from this usage. See also Walter (2009, p. 140 n. 30).
21. See Gibson (1991 pp. 90–91) and also Walter (2009, p. 273 n. 35). There is, however, one phrase in the Zhol inscription (*thugs sgam*, "deep *thugs*") which suggests that the metaphorical associations necessary for subjectivity were at least beginning to take root.
22. It has also, however, developed more specific and quite sophisticated levels of Buddhistic meaning. As an example, H. V. Guenther (1989, p. 258 n. 49) translates *thugs* as "cognitive dynamics" and says that it is "a structure of meaning that infuses the whole texture of experience and gives it the character of situatedness." He is in agreement with most commentators on Tibetan Buddhism that a simple translation as "mind" is wholly inadequate to cover the specific semantic fields of *thugs* in modern Tibetan Buddhist philosophy; Norbu and Lipman, for example (Mañjuśrīmitra, 1986), use the term "primordial experience" to translate *thugs*, and the preface to this work contains a thorough critique of calque translations of Buddhist mentational terms.
23. The Chinese *xin* is an obvious example, on which in this context see Carr (1983), but there is also modern Thai, which has a rich vocabulary (over 300 words) of feeling/emotion/social interaction based the term *jai*, "heart" coupled with an adjective or adjectival phrase. See Moore (2006) for the best single source in English. The Homeric Greek term for heart-area sensation, *kradie* (whence the English "cardiac"), never seems to have developed into a broader, more subjective term of mentation, although it did develop a metaphorical "inner space" that could be "looked into."

usage, *thugs* is not used to mean the fleshy heart, even that of social or
religious superiors. On the contrary, for example, even in the modern
context of a high lama's cremation, if the heart survives the fire as a relic,
it is not referred to as the lama's *thugs*. It may in fact be the case that the
association of *thugs* with the nexus of feeling in the chest area, and the
later placement of mentational attributes there may be in great part if not
entirely due to the influence of Buddhism.[24] That this is a possibility has
already been hinted at by the shifting usage of *glo* discussed above, which
in early days seems to have been the attributed location of some feelings
we (and the Tibetans) now associate with the heart.

There is another inscription which shows a slightly different aspect of
thugs. On the west face of the temple inscription at Zhwa'i Lhakhang, an
inscription attributed to Tridé Songtsen,[25] a younger son of the emperor
mentioned above, discusses a succession crisis that ensued at the death of
his elder brother. It reads:

> When the *thugs* of my father and elder brother had successively been
> flawed, before I had received the Dominion, there was disorder, and a
> contention of evil influences. The monk Ting nge 'dzin, through his acu-
> men, offered beneficial counsel, and caused the disturbances to end.[26]

This passage illustrates the idea that the *thugs* of the king was something that could be flawed, and that this flaw was something that could
have serious repercussions on the imperial succession. "Mind" would be
a conceivable translation here, if two consecutive kings had been insane,
but history provides us no indication of this. While it is a fact that his
elder son met an untimely end, which could conceivably imply forcible
removal from the throne for reasons of insanity, there is no indication
whatever that Trisong Detsen himself was in any way unbalanced, and

---

24. Appropriation of pre-existing local religious terms to serve in a Buddhist context is known to have happened in China; see note 50 below.
25. Richardson, 1985, p. 47. Another warning: this inscription is one that some (e.g. Beckwith, 2011, p. 1) consider post-Imperial, although on what grounds is as yet unknown to me.
26. *Yab dang gcen thugs nongs brtud par byung ba'I rjes / nga chab srid ma bzhes pa'i skabs su kha cig phan phun dang / gdon stson pa dag yod pa dang / ban de ting nge 'dzin kyis nyam drod zin nas / dpend pa'i bk(a') gros gsold / khrag khrug myed par byas.* See Gibson (1991, pp. 152–57) for a critical discussion of earlier translations of this inscription. See also Walter (2009, p. 273 n. 35, 282 n. 52). *Nongs* commonly appears in the *Annals* as a word for death, but only for royalty other than the emperor (Richardson, 1952, pp. 143–44; Hill, 2008, pp. 72–73), and not preceded by *thugs*. Further, it is generally accepted that Trisong Detsen was still alive after he abdicated.

even if he had been, this would not have been widely advertised on a stone inscription at a Buddhist monastery, during or after the Imperial period. The inscription, whatever its date, is thus another context in which the use of "mind" is not adequate.

There is still another semantic field of *thugs* that needs to be considered, one which seems to have even less to do with "mind."

In the well-studied Dunhuang document P.T. 1042, *thugs* is found repeatedly in a description of the funeral procedures for dead emperors. In this document, the corpse of the emperor is called *thugs spur*, and there are accessories for the funeral service called *thugs gur* (tent of the *thugs*) and *thugs glud* (ransom of the *thugs*). It might be thought at first glance that these are mere honorifics, but a thorough reading of the text makes this untenable. Lalou (1952) translated *thugs* throughout as "âme," thus avoiding having to grapple with a more profound meaning,[27] but Haarh, analyzing the same document,[28] more cautiously considers *thugs* to be a "potential essence," "with an unknown charge or content." Stein, devoting close attention to the *thugs* in this context, suggested that the imperial funeral rites included an animation of the tent of the *thugs* by the descent or arrival of the *thugs* (*thugs 'bebs*).[29]

The most recent (and thorough) examination of early Tibetan funeral practices takes up a large part of John Bellezza's massive work on ancient Tibetan civilization.[30] He accepts Stein's interpretation of the summoning of the *thugs* in P.T. 1042, but also discusses another funerary tradition preserved in the Bon tradition which uses *thugs* in a way comparable to the Dunhuang material (more will be said on this below). Unfortunately,

---

27. The concept of "soul" in the Western tradition is logically vague, but usually implies an entity residing in but separate from the body, and surviving the body after death. This is quite different from the original meaning of the Greek *psyche* (whence Western concepts of soul originated), and the history of the Greek word's evolution is far from clear (Dodds, 1984, esp. pp. 138–39, 212–15, and Jaynes, 1976, pp. 288–292). It moreover carries a huge weight of connotations from its association with Christian doctrine. While it is useful in some contexts as a very provisional translation, it would be better not to use it in discussions of non-Western belief systems when any amount of precision is desired.

28. Haarh, 1969, pp. 373–4.

29. Stein, 1970, pp. 171 and 178 n. 22. Stein notes a "Sino-Vietnamese" parallel to the *thugs gur*, and, regarding the *thugs gyi zhal* (an image of the deceased rather than the "repast of the *thugs*" as Haarh thought), refers to the Chinese practice of summoning the "spirit" of the deceased into a funeral effigy or tablet, on which see note 88 below, and Part Two of this paper.

30. Bellezza, 2008.

he too translates *thugs* as "mind," although it is clear that the word is a poor match with its context.

These scholars' interpretation of the role of the *thugs* in the imperial funeral seems to have been shared by the author of a nineteenth century Bonpo history which has become available since Stein wrote and which also contains a description of a Tibetan emperor's funeral. The relevant passage relates how the presiding Bonpo priest "summoned the *nam shes*, and caused the *thugs* to descend."[31] This passage is of interest in the present context not as much for the alleged historicity of the episode, as for its juxtaposition of *thugs* with another term unquestionably derived from Indic Buddhism (*rnam shes*, an abbreviation for *rnam par shes pa*, a calque translation of the Sanskrit *vijñāna*[32]). This passage demonstrates that "mind" cannot be what was meant in this context, and that *thugs* had its own separate associations. Parenthetically, it also shows that the modern Bonpo tradition in some cases preserves archaic terminology, even if it is no longer well understood or relevant.[33]

Both P.T. 1042 and the Bonpo materials Bellezza treats are almost certainly of a later date than the inscriptions of Trisong Detsen. If we operate under the common assumption that we have to chronologize concepts according to the date they appear in texts, i.e., that the older a text is, the older are the concepts found in it, we would have to accept the proposition that the proto-"mind" of the *btsanpo* seen in the inscription developed into the crypto-"soul" of the funeral documents. This way of thinking, which admittedly can be a useful deterrent to katachronization, is probably not valid in this instance.

The evidence for this comes with the probable connection between the *thugs* in this last, funereal, sense, and its homonym *thug*, the black cylindrical standard, often made of yak hair and usually topped by a trident, that was often displayed for apotropaic purposes on the roofs of

---

31. Bkra shis Rgyal mtshan, 1977, p. 324; Karmay, 2005, p. 102. The phrase is *rnam shes bkug thugs phab*.
32. *Vijñāna* has been understood in various ways by the various Buddhist schools. Here it is enough to note that it connotes the culminating stage of the mind's reaction to its environment, and that in this passage, it refers to that aspect of mental functioning which continues after the death of the body.
33. In the modern Bonpo funeral (see below) *thugs* no longer plays any part at all. The word's presence in the *Legs bshad mdzod* seems to show that Bkra shis Rgyal mtshan, happily, employed a relatively light editorial hand with his source material. In the present writer's opinion, this is typical of many Bonpo scholars, who seem to respect their sources even when not understanding them fully.

monasteries in Tibet,[34] and which is visually quite similar to the Turko-Mongol *tuq*, another yak- or horse-hair banner carried in war and believed to be connected to ancestral spirits.[35] The word *tuq* eventually came to refer to both the standard itself and the ancestral and martial power that it embodied,[36] just as the Mongolian *onggot* refers simultaneously to a small image kept in the yurt and the spirits of a clan.[37]

The Turkic word *tuq* probably had its origins in the Old Chinese *tu*.[38] This word is attested from the Zhou Dynasty (1121–221 B.C.E.) as referring to "both military emblems and banners placed on coffins."[39] It need hardly be said that both meanings could be relevant not only to the Altaic *tuq*, but also in the context of early Tibetan imperial religion.

This connection, coupled with the difficulties with the *thugs* / heart connection noted above, shows that the *thugs* of the funeral document was in all probability already current when Indic Buddhism became a force at the Tibetan court, and was first appropriated by the Buddhists to express their idea of that which passes from one life to the next (of honorific people, anyway), and, later, to be used as an honorific for *sems*.

34. On the Tibetan *thug*, see Norbu (1995, p. 130). For an illustration, see *Bod rgya tshig mdzod chen mo*, plates following p. 3294.
35. On the Turko-Mongol *sülde tuq*, see Heissig (1980, pp. 84 seq.), Tatár (1990), and Kler (1957). The Mongolian *tuq* can easily be viewed by image-searching "Mongolian banner" on the internet. According to Vladimirtsov (Kler, op. cit. p. 98), Chinggis Khan's *tuq* was held to be the abode of a protective spirit, and it is said that after his death, his "soul" resided there; no Mongolian word is given for "soul," but probably the word is *süü*; see note 36.
36. Tatár, 1990, p. 335. Personal communication from Jack Weatherford, February 2014: "*Tug* is the word for banner. *Suu* was the word for charisma, genius, heavenly mandate. The soul had several parts with their own fates after death, but this part remained with the family and the place of its location (adding the ending *d* made it a place) was *suld tuq*. Thus the two words became more or less synonymous …. These are all flexible, particularly over a period of 800 years." (cf. Skrynnikova, 1992/3, p. 55). For comparison's sake, one may note that, whatever its ultimate provenance, the Tibetan word *rlung rta* now popularly refers to both a vital force and the banner that is its emblem.
37. Heissig, 1980, pp. 11–17.
38. Györgi Kara, personal communication, 1990; Karlgren (1964, p. 266, n. 1016b: "d'ok / duok / tu and d'og / d'au / tao – banner, streamer.") A connection between the Tibetan *thug* / *thugs* and the Altaic *tuq* would seem to be in accord with Beckwith's hypothesis (2011, p. 169), based on comparative historical linguistics, of a migration of Old Tibetan speakers from the northeastern limits of the Tibetan plateau, where these religious concepts had been in play for a very long time (Tátar, 1990, pp. 33 seq.). The connection might imply that the migration took place centuries before the foundation of the Tibetan Empire, and before the proto-Tibetans accepted any complex of religious beliefs based on the subjective individual mind, as there is no indication at all that *tuq* ever evolved (or was appropriated) in a similar way to become a generalized term for mentational processes among Turkic or Mongol speakers. Beckwith (op. cit., p. 169) suggests Late Antiquity as the most likely period for the migration, and this also seems to fit rather well.
39. *Chung wen ta tz'u tien*, 1973, Vol. 7, p. 11351. It may be of some interest that Jaynes has placed the probable advent of consciousness in China to the Zhou period; see discussion in Carr (2006, pp. 347 ff.).

Thugs thus provides a fascinating Tibetan example of the weakness of using a single translation — "mind" — across a long historical era. In its earliest detectable usage, *thugs* was too basic to justify such a translation, while in its current contexts, it is the word "mind" that is too simplistic. Although specialists in religious philosophy might find it hard to accept that a modern Tibetan word that in other contexts is now used to express some of the most subtle concepts to come out of Tibetan Buddhism originated in the funeral practices surrounding rulers of the medieval steppe, it is difficult if not impossible to come up with an alternative theory that fits the facts as well; to the best of the present writer's knowledge, no other etymology for the word has ever been proposed.[40]

Bla (la)

A particularly difficult term found in the oldest Tibetan material is *bla*. In the Old Tibetan sources, it already encompasses a number of apparently disparate meanings. The origin of the word is a conundrum. The *Mahāvyutpatti*, an early Buddhist attempt to standardize Sanskrit-to-Tibetan translation, renders *bla* with the Sanskrit *pati*: "king, lord, master," or, alternately "superior, above."[41] These two senses of the word could conceivably account for a great part of the word's occurrences in the very early material, but there is a third context in which neither of these semantic sets is adequate.

Based on a particular modern usage, *bla* has (like *thugs*) been rendered by some scholars of Tibet as "soul"; again, a term perhaps suitably nebulous for a concept previously little understood, but, again, not an adequate translation in serious historical investigations. This usage of *bla* is now chiefly preserved in the context of a ritual which is performed by modern specialists in both the Bonpo and Nyingmapa Buddhist traditions, the

---

40. There is, however, one interesting case in which a more archaic use of *thugs* may have survived in modern Tibetan Buddhism, seen in the institution of the *ma 'das sprul sku*, in which a lama names the child who is to be his "rebirth" before the lama has passed away. In such cases, it is usually said to be the *thugs* that is transferred from one body to another. Calkowski (2013) has discussed the issue of the *ma 'das sprul sku* systematically; what is especially interesting in her presentation are the rather convoluted, overly intellectualized justifications for this tradition, which is anomalous to the well-developed theory of death and rebirth widely accepted (albeit with a number of variants) in Tibetan Buddhism since about the thirteenth century (see Cuevas, 2003, 39–68). On the other hand, transference of the *thugs* to a successor either living or dead, seems quite suggestive of the passage of royal authority across generations during the Tibetan Imperial period.
41. Karmay, 2009d, p. 311.

so-called "summoning the *bla*."[42] This is undertaken when a person who has experienced severe stress in terms of shocking events or frightening incidents exhibits symptoms including insomnia and fearful waking from sleep, weakness, apathy, and extreme mental perturbation — what in modern jargon we might call shock or traumatic disorder — which can lead to coma, and eventually, in some cases, death. The ritual is meant to call the *bla* back, either into the body of the patient, or perhaps into a concrete talisman such as a piece of turquoise.[43] In a modern frame of reference, it could be said that the "summoning of the *bla*" is meant to restore the normal psychological and social functioning of an individual.[44] In sum, *bla* is best considered a functional or instrumental rather than an ontological concept;[45] it will be useful to keep this in mind rather than to immediately become lost in postulating some sort of supernatural phantom entity.

We have no certain way of knowing how old the *bla*-summoning ritual is, however; no early texts have been found, and the *Mahavyutpatti* does not provide a Sanskrit term that would conceivably be used in such a context. This latter fact is not an argument against the existence of the word in the context of early Tibetan religion, though. It should be noted that *bla* finds no place in any formal Indo-Tibetan Buddhist analysis of mental functioning, which suggests that this specific meaning of the word was thought to be a poor fit with its doctrine. The Bon religion, on the other hand, has preserved a tradition in which *bla* is linked to two other components of human existence: *srog* (*sok*, vital force) and *dbugs* (*ook*, breath).[46] This triad seems to be based on a very simple sort of empirical observation, involving no intellectual or doctrinal superstructure, so it may well represent a very old linguistic stage of mentational

---

42. Treated in detail in Karmay, 2009d.
43. For comparable beliefs and practices among the Mongols, see Chiodo (1996); another Mongolian "soul" word, *sünesü*, is employed in this context; the origin and development of mentational and "soul" concepts in Mongolian is in urgent need of investigation.
44. Here a comparison might be drawn with a Chinese "soul" word, *po*. Like *tu*, it first appeared in the Zhou Dynasty, and connoted, among other things, the psychological integration of an individual. If it was lost, the person would exhibit what we would call mental dissociation (Yu, 1987, p. 371). The thorough — and ongoing — analysis of "soul" words in Sinology should serve as a humbling example for Tibetologists who still use the English word with no further clarification.
45. Gibson, 1991 p. 96; see also Walter (2009, p. 107) on the *bla* as a "guiding power" within an individual, though he seems to accept this meaning only in relation to later literature.
46. Karmay, 2009d, p. 311; unfortunately, no sources for this tradition are cited.

awareness, perhaps comparable to the earliest examples of Greek mentioned above.[47]

The Bon tradition as it exists today, though, has also attempted to place the *bla* in a larger theory of mentation. This theory discusses the necessity of bringing three aspects of the human mind together after death to ensure its liberation: the *bla*, the *yid*, and the *sems*. This schema dates back to (at least) the fourteenth century *Gzi brjid*, and is still in use among modern Bonpos.[48] Now, *yid* and *sems* are integral parts of the Indic Buddhist description of mentation (usually translating the Sanskrit *manas* and *citta* respectively), and a similar triad of terms can be found in the teachings of the Yogacara school,[49] but instead of *bla*, Yogacara uses *rnam shes*, the Tibetan calque of the Indic *vijñāna* mentioned above.[50] This similarity surely indicates a borrowing from one set of religious concepts to the other, and the indications are that in this case the direction was from Indic Buddhist to Bonpo rather than the other way around.[51]

---

47. Hill (2009, p. 560) mentions an Old Tibetan document which has the "*brla*" moving throughout the body. Here, however, the unusual spelling might reflect that the word is being used as a translation from some foreign term, part of a sophisticated analysis of energy flow the likes of which were already present, for example, in China (the text deals with moxibustion). Karmay (2009d, p. 314 n. 23) does note a much later Buddhist text by Nyang ral Nyi ma 'Od zer which similarly has the *bla* shifting according to the time of day and month.

48. *Gzi brjid* (1978, Vol. 3, p. 55, p. 368), Snellgrove (2010, pp. 117, 121, 160); see also *Bon skyong* (Vol. 1, p. 368), Norbu (1995, pp. 254–55), Karmay, (2009d, p. 312), Bellezza (2008, p. 363).

49. A brief description of these three aspects of mentation as seen by the Yogacara, taken from the writings of Khenpo Ngag dbang Dpal bzang (*Gzhi khregs chod skabs* p. 32) will sum them up for those not familiar with this school. *Sems* is the aspect of mind which conceives of objects of mental activity as external, *yid* is an organizing capability, which moves over these objects "like a king moves over a country," and *rnam shes* is that which cognizes the objects as individual things.

50. This is not the only case we have of what seems to be an early indigenous term being replaced with an Indic Buddhist one as that religion became more established. Another Chinese "soul" word, *hun*, sometimes coupled with the *po* mentioned above, was at times used in early Chinese Buddhism to denote something which passes from life to life, but later, as this was seen to be in contradiction with Buddhist orthodoxy, it was replaced by several alternate terms intended to render the Indic *vijñāna*. See Park (2012, pp. 151–195) for a thorough discussion. By contrast, Tambiah (1970, pp. 223 seq.) discusses a Thai folk ritual by which the *khwan* of an individual is restored, either in rites of passage or after traumatic events, enabling his reintegration as a functioning member of society; in Thai religion, however, the *khwan* has never been conflated with the *winjan* (also clearly derived from an Indic original), and it is the latter that passes across existences and may become a ghost. The former is in the province of village elders; the latter, that of monks.

51. There is also a possibility that the triune found in the later Bonpo tradition is an adaptation of the Yogacara system, developed independently of, and perhaps even before, the triumph of the Indic Buddhist schools in Tibet. If this were the case, it may well be that an earlier conception of *bla* served as a bridge to the Indic Buddhist system in the same way that *hun* did in China. It could even be speculated that the Bonpo system was taken outright from an early Chinese (or Inner Asian) version of Yogacara, with *bla* in this instance employed as a calque for *hun* (or some equivalent in an Inner Asian language).

How the word *bla* might fit into the history of mentation in Tibet will be discussed further. First, however, a crucial concept in early Tibetan religion must be mentioned in passing.

Sku bla (ku la)

The importance of this term in understanding the cult surrounding the Tibetan Emperor was first brought to light in Ariane Macdonald's ground breaking work of 1971. Although aspects of her treatment of the *sku bla* are not without controversy, the field of Tibetology owes a great deal to her isolation of the concept. A more detailed approach to understanding the *sku bla* will appear as this work progresses; here, a simple working definition will be proposed.

Sku is a term which appears in the oldest written Tibetan documents. Like *thugs*, its modern usages fall into the categories of either honorific language or Buddhist philosophy. In the former, it is used to refer to anything associated with the physical form of exalted personages, while in the latter, it was chosen to translate the Sanskrit *kâya*, which expresses ideas both subtle and profound, so that translators of Buddhist texts have had difficulty rendering *sku* into English. While there is no single word adequate to convey all of its nuances in Buddhism, attempts have included "Gestalt," "dimension," "mode of being," and "embodiment." Although both *kâya* and *sku* have sometimes been rendered as "body," this is only even possible because of the very broad semantic coverage of the English word; in neither Old Tibetan nor modern Buddhist usage can *sku* be understood merely as a substantive body of flesh.[52] In the Old Tibetan context, it may perhaps best, though still perhaps inadequately, be rendered as "sacred presence"; this phrase is sufficiently broad to allow more detailed investigation, while not inviting a fall into any preconceptions, either religious or intellectualistic. Thus, coupling the term with our previous delineation of *bla*, we may provisionally consider the *sku bla* as "the capability or capacity for sacred presence"; in terms of the Tibetan kingship, it is that which enables the ruler to function in his sacral role. This stopgap definition will play out against the facts as we can discern them in some surprising ways in the following sections.

---

52. For example, as mentioned above, the corpse of the *btsanpo* was never called *sku*, but rather *spur* or *thugs spur*.

Lha (lha)

Lha is clearly related to *bla*; even leaving aside the phonological similarity, this can be seen in the fact that the words are polysemous in the
same general directions. Both can connote something above, or superior
(spatially or qualitatively as well as socially), and both have a particular
meaning primarily of interest to scholars of religion. In this last sense,
bla, as we have seen, seems at first to have simply referred to basic mental
functioning or capacity, but later seems to have become some sort of entity
manipulable by ritual and usually located within a human individual, but
also capable in folk belief of residing in external objects, (where, however,
it does not exhibit sentience). In the Bonpo tradition (but not the Indic
Buddhist) it was adapted to refer to a component of man's mentation,
though this may have been in response to a non-Indic Buddhist model.

Lha, on the other hand, seems generally to refer to something external, a sacred power residing outside the individual. In some Old Tibetan
material, it can refer to not only the emperor, but also the ruling aristocracy, in both present and past manifestations (i.e. they could be *lha* both
while alive and after their deaths).[53] It was chosen to represent the Indic
Sanskrit *deva* by the early Buddhist translators, which has led to its cus-
tomary translation as "deity" or "god," but, again, this can be misleading
except as a shorthand term.

While the *bla* in the modern religious sense seems to be a matter, in
(slightly distorting) modern terminology, of an individual's own psycho-
somatic makeup, the *lha* is evidently a term to be shared by a society. A
lha as an object of religious worship may have an etiology or genealogy, a
place in a cosmology, a history across time, and even a personality; none of
these attach to the *bla*. In Jaynesian terms, one might thus call the *bla* pre-
mythological, while the *lha* as "deity" is mythological: necessarily associated with a subjective mind. This comparison is meant to indicate a trend,
as there are many cases when the two words are used interchangeably.[54]

---

53. Jaynes's theory, of course, holds that the first "gods" of humanity everywhere were precisely
ancestral voices originating in the speech areas of the brain. Walter (2009, pp. 113 seq.) properly
emphasizes the ancestral-spirit meaning of the word in the Old Tibetan material, which is often
ignored because of the too-ready translation of *lha* by "god," implying something abstract and oth-
erworldly. The conclusions he draws from this, however, are quite different from those of this paper.
54. Samuel (1993, esp. pp. 441–2) has theorized that *bla* and *lha* originated in a single field of meaning which gradually bifurcated under the influence of increased political centralization. This is an
important perception; though the present essay would consider the prime cause of the reification

Bka' (ka)

The final word to be considered here, also found in the earliest writings, is *bka'*. It deals with speech, so it is not inevitably associated with mentation, but it, like *thugs*, seems to have undergone a shift in meaning so that its early connotations were not seen as completely compatible with later intentions. In modern Tibetan, the word can commonly mean "command," or "sacred word," and it is also used as an honorific prefix for speech-related words, as it was already in Old Tibetan. It might be expected, given the discussion of *thugs* above, that modern Tibetan Buddhism would employ the word to designate religious speech, and indeed the collected teachings of Śākyamuni Buddha (and Shenrab Miwo, the putative founder of Bon) are called *bka' 'gyur* (*ka gyur*), the "translated Word." However, in modern times, the speech of holy beings, as well as the general notion of speech as sacred utterance, is not commonly rendered with *bka'* but rather the completely unrelated word *gsungs* (*sung*). *Bka'* in modern honorific speech seems to be a vestige of a time when the word was used purely to denote verbal utterances from a higher (*bla / lha*) sphere, with connotations of complete dominion or infallibility.[55] Its relevance to the subject of this essay will become apparent later.

To summarize this section: while it is at present simply not possible to trace the development of the vocabulary of mentation in the Tibetan language as cleanly as scholars of ancient Greek have been able to do for that language, using their approach has yielded some insights which should be thought-provoking, and which will be valuable in re-examining early Tibetan religion as a whole.

---

into "inner" *bla* and "outer" *lha* a shift from a pre-subjective or proto-subjective to a subjective mentality, a changing political situation would probably have been one of the causes of this shift. The difference between the intent of his formulation and mine may be negligible.

55. This can be most clearly seen in the compound *ka nyen* (*bka' nyan*), literally, "hearing the *ka'*," but meaning "obedient." If taken literally, the term would imply no mental "space" or deliberation between the hearing and the obeying; according to Jaynes, this would have been a characteristic of bicameral man.

Tibetan Word (Wylie Transcription)	Modern Pronunciation	Proposed Early Meanings	Modern Definitions
thugs	tuk	1) funeral and war banner or standard 2) hereditary ancestral power	1) mind-related honorific 2) mind, cognitive dynamics, primordial experience, etc.
glo / blo	lo	breath-related emotional affects	intellect
sku	ku	sacred presence	1) body-related honorific 2) dimension, embodiment, Gestalt, etc.
bla	la	1) upper, above, superior 2) individual mental capacity or capability	1) upper, above, superior 2) component of mental functioning 3) "spirit", "soul"
lha	lha	beneficent ancestors (or other numina)	1) superior 2) upper realms of cosmos 3) deity
sku bla / lha	ku / lha	that which catalyzes the presence of the sacred	mountain deity
bka'	ka	"divine" extrapersonal speech	1) speech-related honorific 2) command, order
gnyan (po) (see below)	nyen	quality of divine voices	1) (n) mountain spirit 2) (adj) fierce, solemn, awesome, exalted, revered, mighty, essential, etc.

Table 1. Summary of Tibetan words.

THE SACRAL KINGSHIP IN TIBET

The association of religious sacrality and political power is at once one of the oldest and most enduring themes in mankind's history, so much so that to call it an *Ur*-belief of mankind has real significance: as Jaynes has reiterated, all over Mesopotamia, cities were built centered on the house of a god (what we would call an idol, on which more in Part Two of this article), with smaller neighboring houses for the human kings and subsidiary priests.[56] In Egypt, on the other hand, the kings were themselves the gods.

---

56. The same system prevailed among the earliest Greeks. In the records of the Mycenean state, the word for the head of state is *wanax*; in later Greek, this word is used only for gods. The later Greek word for king is *basileus*, but in the Greek of the Linear B records, *basileus* merely denotes the ranking servant of the *wanax*. (Jaynes, 1976, p. 80).

Directly following from this is another feature of the sacral kingship documented in many civilizations of antiquity, which is that dead kings became living gods.[57] Jaynes's explanation for this phenomenon is again, that, for some time after a king's death, his hallucinated voice would continue to be heard by his subjects (or perhaps at least to his successor), and ascribed to his continuing presence. This does not mean that each dead king retained his individual identity after death; in Egypt, each dead king became in turn the god Osiris.[58]

If the investigation of the Tibetan vocabulary of mind is complex, attempting to discover the nature of the early Tibetan sacral kingship is even more so. As a result of the investigations of Haarh, Macdonald, Stein, et. al., it has become clear that later Tibetan accounts of the kingship, written centuries after its fall, do not provide a complete picture, and often betray the agendas of their authors. These are commonly either to establish legitimating family or religious lineages stemming from the time of Tibet's greatness, or, alternatively, to show that the culture of Tibet before the triumph of Buddhism was cruel, barbarous, and without value. Even if attempts had been made to write without bias, however, it would be unwise to assume that later traditions, particularly those involving extinct institutions (here, the imperial cult), could have been preserved completely uncorrupted; even the earliest Buddhist and Bonpo scholars, like those of modern academia, would have tried to interpret the beliefs and practices of the Imperial (and pre-Imperial) era in terms of intellectual categories they were familiar and comfortable with, resulting in varying degrees of distortion. This essay will therefore not assume factuality in any of the later Tibetan sources' accounts of the Imperial Era. Nevertheless, it would seem to be unnecessary to dismiss their perspectives on early religious practices altogether, being as they were only centuries away from the raw data, so to speak (as opposed to over a millennium in our case), as long as we are wary of katachronism.

Another important point that seems to have been largely overlooked is that, just as religious vocabulary certainly underwent some of the changes discussed above, so did the institution of the sacral kingship

---

57. Again, this is such a widespread phenomenon that there is no reason to attribute its presence in Tibet (discussed below) to any particular outside influence, whether that of China or of Central Eurasia.
58. Jaynes (2006) discusses the Osiris myth in relation to a mural on the wall of Tutankhamen's tomb.

itself. It would be more than a little rash to assume that there was a fixed set of religious and cultural beliefs and practices associated with the Tibetan emperor that remained unchanged over two centuries of exposure to not only Indic Buddhism, but also other ideologies and mores from some of the most varied and sophisticated civilizations in Asia (and beyond). Simply put, we cannot safely say that the sacral kingship that prevailed at the end of the empire, even in regards to its central rituals and terminology, was the same as at its beginning. It is appropriate to remember that we are aiming at a moving target.[59]

It seems impossible that Tibet was ever a strictly bicameral realm in Jaynesian terms. Even the major cities of early Inner Eurasia were probably not of such size in antiquity as to require the rigid social pyramids typical of the early Sumerian and Egyptian kingdoms that Jaynes uses as his templates. Further, from a very early date, the nomadic and semi-nomadic populations of Inner Eurasia seem to have used a command-and-control structure based on the taking of oaths rather than on a strict organizational hierarchy.[60] What is to be investigated in the following sections is more modest: whether the early kings and emperors of the Tibetan plateau, as well as their subjects, retained some connection to the pre-subjective mind that was crucial for the functioning of the kingdom.

The Centrality of the Sku Bla

The importance of the *sku bla* to the sacral kingship in Tibet was first drawn out by Macdonald; since her time, although there has been some disagreement with her interpretations, it seems to have been generally accepted that a discussion of the *sku bla* is a necessary part of understanding the Tibetan sacral kingship. The *sku bla* is mentioned in several Dunhuang documents that are late or post-Imperial, as well as in one inscription, found in Kongpo.[61] According to Macdonald's reading of one of the former, P.T. 1047, the *sku bla* protect(s) the emperor and ministers

---

59. That different mythologies surrounded the Tibetan emperor is indisputable. See, for example, Karmay (2009c) which discusses several of these, only two or three of which survived intelligibly to the post-Imperial era; Haarh (1969, pp. 171–230) has discussed the later versions of these in detail. There is no reason that differing viewpoints could not have existed simultaneously during the Empire.
60. Beckwith has studied this sort of kingship the most thoroughly; see particularly his forthcoming contribution, and the bibliography contained therein.
61. Some have doubted that this inscription is authentically from the Imperial Era, though again, on what grounds is presently unknown to the present writer. The reference to the *sku bla* it contains

if content, but abandons them if unhappy. In the latter case, misfortunes will befall the realm. More will be said on this below.

Kings and Mountains

Another aspect of Macdonald's theory was the connection between the *sku bla* of the Tibetan emperor with mountains. The association of kings and mountains is both ancient and widespread. Jaynes (1976, p. 143) notes that in the tomb of the first historical king yet discovered (from the Middle Eastern Mesolithic culture called Natufian, dating to about 9000 B.C.E.), the king's body was oriented so that his head, propped on a stone pillow, faced the peak of Mount Hermon.[62] The basalt stele on which the Code of Hammurabi is engraved depicts Hammurabi supplicating the god Marduk, who is seated on a mountain (Jaynes, op. cit. p. 199). Hittite sculptures at the outdoor shrine of Yazilikaya depict mountains crowned with headdresses associated with deities (Jaynes, op. cit, p. 153). The Avestan *yasht* which deals with the *xwarenah* (royal glory) of the king begins with a list of mountains.[63] In the context of these Near Eastern civilizations, Jaynes suggests that mountains' sacrality may have been associated with their role in triggering the hallucinatory voices of the kings, and congruence here with the evidence from Tibet will be discussed below.

In Asia, the myth of the First King's descent from heaven onto the top of a mountain is found in Japan and Korea,[64] and in the Old Turkic inscriptions,[65] the *qaqan* is described as "heaven-like and heaven born," though no mountains are mentioned. While the myth of the first king's descent from heaven was a major part of the royal mythology in Tibet, it is important to keep in mind that in Macdonald's reading, the sacrality of the mountain was not merely due to its function as a ladder or stairway from above: in some way the *sku bla* actually were (or was, there are no number markers) the mountains themselves, as in the ancient

---

is moreover very hard to make sense of. See Hill (2013) for the most recent translation as well as a critical evaluation of some of the previous ones.

62. The orientation of the corpse within the tomb (or probable orientation, if the tomb has already been looted) might be something for archaeologists excavating Tibetan tomb sites in the future to be aware of.

63. Malandra, 1983, p. 89. Malandra notes the connection but does not attempt to explain it.

64. Waida, 1973.

65. Tekin, 1968, p. 261.

Near East.[66] She draws support for this theory in works from the later religious traditions of Tibet, which identify major mountains of the Tibetan plateau with so-called *sku lha*.[67] It is well known that Tibetans have preserved a belief in certain landmarks as being deeply associated with the *bla*: there are *bla*-mountains, *bla*-lakes, etc., which are intimately tied up with an individual's or a region's welfare.[68] This may be a vestige of a time when elements of the landscape were felt to be deeply bound up with a ruler's (or a people's) well-being, to the extent that their fates were felt to mirror each other.[69] No gratuitous supernatural entities such as "souls" or "gods" need be interposed here; at its most basic level, the *sku bla* may have simply been any mountain which served, by its very qualities of endurance, stability, and perhaps its dominance of the landscape, to reinforce what we would perhaps call the psychological capacity of the leader, whether this was a clan elder or village headman. Perhaps only later, when the elders and headmen became sacral kings and emperors, ruling over large groups of disparate peoples, was it necessary for the chief's *bla* to become a *sku bla*, an independent being with a mythology and an increasingly complex set of ritual procedures surrounding it. This transition may be difficult for modern scholarship to appreciate, accustomed as it is to either seek involved and unnecessary theoretical explanations, or to label such phenomena as "animism" (and then disregard them).[70]

---

66. It is crucial to recognize that the myth of the descent of the first king onto the mountain is not inseparable from the belief in mountains themselves as sacred. On the contrary, the latter seems rather to provide a subjective mythological rationale for the former, one which is moreover quite useful in a political ideology. Based on the similarities of the myth with that of other Northern Asiatic cultures, one might speculate that, like the *thugs*, the myth came to the plateau with the proto-Tibetans. On the other hand, of course, the possibility cannot be dismissed that it preceded them, and that it simply reflects increasing subjectivity and/or political sophistication among earlier denizens of the plateau.

67. Macdonald, 1971, pp. 303 seq.; Karmay, 2009a, p. 437.

68. The eleventh century Muslim writer Mahmud Kāšgarī writes disparagingly about the religious sensibilities of the pre-Islamic Turks of Inner Asia: "The Infidels — may God destroy them! — call the sky *tängri*; also anything that is imposing they call *tängri*, such as a great mountain or a tree, and they bow down to such things." (Dankoff, 1975, p. 70).

69. The ultimate expression of this affect may be found in Tibetan folklore in which someone's *bla* is tied up with an external object to the extent that destroying the object, even unbeknownst to that person, will cause his death. For two examples, see O'Connor (1975, pp. 103–115 and 147–157). This motif is also found in the Gesar Epic (David-Neel, 1987, pp. 101, 174).

70. The words in the 121st Psalm ("I will lift my eyes unto the hills, whence cometh my help"), are, because of their provenance, seldom taken to indicate a belief in "animistic mountain deities." The word "animism" itself is a prime example of the superciliousness certain scholars bring to the subject of religion. It is almost never defined by those who use it, and it is generally dependent on the notion

Objections have been raised to the association of the *sku bla* with mountains; the absence of a clear and definite connection between the two in authentically Imperial-era texts is one.[71] There may be some validity to this objection, but to reject the connection entirely would leave those who do so in the position of having to account for its consistent acceptance in the later tradition, which they have not yet done.

The presence of *sku bla* in various locales outside of Tibet, is another objection, but this might be just a matter of the term being used to translate a similar religious concept in another language. Many of the Old Tibetan documents in which the term appears are translations or paraphrases of foreign originals.

It is also true that there are a few mentions of the *sku bla / lha* in which no seeming connection with mountains can be gleaned, as will be detailed in Part Two.

It seems best, therefore, to accept that the association of *sku bla* with mountains is, while valid, perhaps not exclusive of other possibilities. It may well be that the term came to have different referents during the evolution of the sacral kingship.

Relationship of the Sku Bla to Jaynes's Theory

The relationship of the *sku bla* to Jaynes's theory comes in its association with the adjective *gnyan po* (*nyenpo*).[72] According to one of the Dunhuang manuscripts mentioned above (P.T. 1047), whether or not the *sku bla* was *gnyan po* or not was important to the functioning of the kingdom. This word has been a thorn in the side of translators for a long time. Words used to translate it in its modern context are wide-ranging: "cruel, fierce,

of "soul" (which is vague and slippery enough in itself — see note 27), and, more importantly, it implicitly assumes that the substantial differences in so-called "soul" (and other) conceptions among varied non- or pre-literate people are insignificant enough to be ignored, which is simply absurd. It is thus employed as a condescending, shorthand way of avoiding the questions that these non-literate traditions raise, and should never be used by conscientious historians of religion, betraying as it does either a bias towards scriptural monotheism (see note 68) or an intellectual laziness. See Bolle (1987) for a brief summary of the issue.

71. Walter, 2009, pp. 230–31.

72. Karmay, 2009, p. 435. According to Walter (2009, p. 151), *gnyanpo* is in fact the only adjective associated with the *sku bla* in the Old Tibetan material. The association of *sku bla / lha* and *gnyanpo* has also been retained into modern times in the Gesar epic; see Norbu (1995, p. 9 n. 45) and Stein (1959, p. 184).

severe";[73] "powerful";[74] "rigid, solemn, serious";[75] "dignified";[76] "exalted";[77] "awesome, revered";[78] and "essential, of great value or utility, mighty."[79] Few of these definitions seem to match very well the situation at hand, in which the *sku bla* being *gnyan po* was a favorable state of affairs, and many of them seem to be entirely circumstantial, based on the phrase where they are found. Certainly there is no single English word that seems to cover all of its contexts in modern Tibetan. Making things even more complicated is the fact that in the contemporary traditions of both Bon and Buddhism, there is a class of extrahuman beings called *gnyan* (*nyen*) who are often associated with mountains.[80]

However, in the light of Jaynes's theory, there is a simple explanation for this multivalence. Substitute, for a moment, an adjective based on the homonymous verb *nyan* (*nyen*) "to hear," for *gnyan*, and the phrase *sku bla gnyan po* allows an entirely different, but altogether cogent, interpretation: the *sku bla* was at once the bicameral voice guiding the king, and the object that stimulated it.[81] The voice that guided the king was either heard by him or not. If the king could hear it, he could function as a sacral presence; if not, there was a problem for him, and by extension, for those he ruled. One might note that all of the translations of *gnyan* cited above could fit very well in describing a god-like bicameral voice; some of the modern contexts of the word in which a connotation of audibility can be surmised will be discussed in Part Two.

It might be objected that the existence of *gnyan* as a class of deities distinct from other classes might invalidate this proposal. Furthermore, in much of this literature, the *gnyan* are associated with features such as rocks and trees more than mountains. Yet, as most students of the subject

---

73. Das, 1989, p. 401.
74. Norbu, 1995, pp. 51, 67.
75. Snellgrove, 2010, p. 309.
76. Karmay, 1972, pp. 43, 225.
77. Karmay, 1972, pp. 65, 239.
78. Karmay, 2009a, p. 443.
79. Bellezza, 2008, p. 811.
80. Discussed in Karmay (2009a, pp. 441–447). According to Karmay, the *gnyan* are closely connected to another, rather obscure, class of spirit called *ma sangs* (*ma sang*) who are popularly believed to have governed Tibet at a certain period in in prehistory. At times, Karmay says, the two are identified, while at others, the *ma sangs* have *gnyan* as an epithet, like the *sku bla*. Haarh (1969, pp. 297–8) believes the *ma sangs* to have been deified ancestors.
81. Again, while at present we are talking about mountains, there is no reason that the bicameral voices of the rulers could not have been triggered by other objects, as will be seen in Part Two.

are aware, the literature of the "eight classes of spirit being" (*lha srin sde brgyad*) is a later attempt to impose some order on the huge variety of non-corporeal beings found in post-Imperial Tibetan culture. Though some of these named types do seem to have loose sets of characteristics consistently attributed to them, these are far from fixed from source to source, and the etiologies ascribed to them are far from consistent. Many or most of these names (*gnyan* among them) do not seem to appear unequivocally in Old Tibetan materials as defined categories of spirit being,[82] and some of them that do (as *lha* above) are used as calque translations for categories of such beings that are found in Indic Buddhist mythology, and have, or had, native Tibetan meanings not reflected in these Indic calques.

A similar case may shed some additional light. In an earlier work,[83] the present author attempted to demonstrate that the mythology of the *btsan* (*tsen*), another class of spirit being found in later Tibetan religion, almost certainly developed towards the end of or after the Imperial period, and the characteristics attributed to this spirit being were a reflection of the qualities embodied above all in the *btsanpo*, the Emperor of Tibet. *Btsanpo* was, as *gnyanpo* seems to have been, originally an adjective descriptive of a sacred quality; the former was associated with the unusual powers of the emperor, and the latter with anything that had the capability to serve as a cue for the auditory guides of the leaders, (and also perhaps their peoples). Only later were they both reified into distinct classes of divinities, with all their accompanying lore.[84]

The Continuing Presence of the Dead King

In *The Origin of Consciousness*, Jaynes sees funeral practices originating in the continued hearing of hallucinated voices after the person they were

---

82. Macdonald (1971, p. 304) cites one example in an Old Tibetan document which she takes to indicate *nyen* as a type of spirit-being ("*bdagi smon lam du go lha gnyan thams cad la 'us la phyag 'chal lo*"), but it is more likely an adjective modifying *go lha*, about which see more in Part Two. The same is true of Stein's reading (1959, p. 205) of *ma sang gnyan* as referring to two groups of beings.
83. Gibson, 1991, especially pp. 217–45.
84. Gibson, 1991, esp. pp. 218–219. A reiteration of my arguments is not possible in this space, but the years since that work have seen the appearance of no evidence that would make my conclusions untenable. Karmay (2009b, pp. 365–66) independently reached the same historical conclusion regarding the *gyalpo* (*rgyal po*), a closely related group of spirits. See also Walter (2009, p. 59 n. 50 and pp. 241 seq., in particular p. 247).

associated with in life has died. Accepting his premise for the moment, it is clear that there would be two factors which would have been very important to the survivors: ensuring that such voices either 1) ceased altogether, or 2) remained helpful and benevolent protective "ancestral spirits" (in the Tibetan context *lha*) rather than becoming threatening "ghosts" (*'dre*). As Bellezza notes,[85] much of Tibetan funeral ritual could be viewed as being aimed at these three goals; the funeral literature of Bon makes frequent references to the importance of separating the dead (*shi ba*) from the living (*gson pa*). He further states that "The armature of ritual performances functions to prevent the deceased from returning to his or her former home and relatives, and wrecking [sic] havoc in the world of the living."

In the funeral rites of the Bonpo tradition prevailing today,[86] the goal is liberation or emancipation from the world, in the Buddhist sense. As mentioned above, it is considered crucial to bring together the *la*, *yid*, and *sems* in order to liberate the individual at death, with each of these three components of mentation having its own ultimate destination. As a prelude to the ritual procedures, the *bla* (or the *rnam shes*)[87] is summoned into a tablet, called a *byang bu* (*jangbu*), perhaps comparable to the effigies or personal effects that filled the same purpose in the Dunhuang documents.[88] There it is offered a variety of gifts (it becomes "like a king") before the presiding Bonpo confronts the forces detrimental to its liberation, and then guides it on its way.

Bellezza's recent exploration of an alternative set of funerary rituals, however, has brought to light a variation on this procedure perhaps relevant to the present exploration.[89] The *Mu cho'i khrom 'dur* is an early Tibetan funerary tradition (eleventh century?) which preserves a vocabulary quite different from the normative. Bellezza accepts that the texts of this tradition do not represent an unadulterated Imperial-era source; he believes they have been reworked in response to changing

---

85. Bellezza, 2008, p. 364.
86. See Kværne (1985) for a complete description of a modern Bonpo funeral procedure.
87. Kværne's informants for the work cited immediately above used the Indic Buddhist *rnam shes* in place of *bla*.
88. Here a comparison can be drawn with ancestral tablets used in China, with the significant difference that the Tibetan tablets are destroyed after the funeral, which is supposed to effect the definitive separation of the deceased from the living. See Yu (1987, p. 369) and Bellezza (2008, p. 555 n. 718).
89. The following is drawn from Bellezza (2008, esp. pp. 367–68).

social conditions. He also notes that "the cultural setting behind [the ritual performances] is no longer well understood," and that the Bonpo assert that "the demise of the ... tradition occurred over a period of many centuries through a process of attenuation." Nevertheless, he claims, "the revamping of the ... tradition was not radical enough to expunge many of the archaisms still found in its literature."

One of these archaisms is the final destination of the departed. In the prevailing Bonpo tradition, as mentioned above, the Buddhist model of complete liberation from existence is employed. In the *Mu cho khrom 'dur* literature, however, the desired destination of the deceased is the Dga' yul, the "Country of Joy," where he is reunited with his ancestors.

Another archaism comes in the use of mentational vocabulary. In the prevailing Bonpo tradition, as mentioned above, *thugs* does not occur at all, but only *bla*, *yid*, and *sems*. In the archaic tradition as described in the *Mu cho khrom 'dur*, *sems* is left out; only *bla* and the *yid* are manipulated. However, in an alternately employed pairing within this same tradition the *thugs* (sometimes spelled *thug*) is summoned as in Pelliot 1042, but here it is paired with the *bka'*.[90] Bellezza believes that the *bka'* here appears to be tantamount to the *bla*, while the *thugs* is equivalent to the *yid*.[91]

---

90. As, to my knowledge, this pairing has not appeared in the scholarly literature before Bellezza's work, I reproduce relevant passages here. My translations are definitely provisional; as I suspect Bellezza's to be the same, I have not included them.

p. 615, xvii : *gshin rje'i bla sgram ma bres na / bka' thugs stong khams 'gugs thabs med /* "If the *bla sgram* of the lords of death is not spread out, there is no way to summon the *bka'* (and?) *thugs* of (from?) the empty realm."

p. 619, ii: *da lta sku lus phung po g.yar po la / mi rtag khrom pa'I rkyen ngan 'jigs / sku lus phung po bdud kyis bshig / bka' thug gri bog shed dmar 'khor /* "Now, the borrowed heap of the body's remainder has been destroyed by a gathering of impermanent bad causes. The heap of the body's remainder has been destroyed by Death, and the red power of death circles the *bka' thug*.

p. 619, iii: *bka' thug gral du (+ma) pheb tshe / yab gdung chen sras po rigs kyi bu / khyod kyi bka' ni nam (= gnam) gyi gang (= gung) na 'bod / thugs ni bar snang gling nas skyabs / brla (mod. = bla) ni na rag rtsang so snyags /* "When the *bka'* (and?) *thug* are/is (not) set in order, child of good family, son of the great paternal clan, your *bka'* calls out in the high point of space, the thugs protects from (?) the middle sphere, and the *bla* hastens *rtsang so* to hell."

p. 621, i: *dang po bla khor ma 'khor na / bka' thugs phab pa'I rten med pa'i (= pas) / khar tsang bla 'khor rten du bzhengs /* "If the *bla*-circle is not established first, there will be no receptacle for the descent of the *bka' thugs*. Therefore, the *bla*-circle was established yesterday."

91. Bellezza, 2008, pp. 363–364. In note 717 (op. cit. p. 554) he sees a "self-evident" parallel between the *bka'* (= *thugs*) / *bla* (= *yid*) pairing with the Chinese *hun* / *po* concepts mentioned above, but the present writer finds this not so obvious (why is *bka'* used at all?) and a little oversimple, though the subject is worthy of more detailed investigation. The possibility I have suggested above, that the *bka'* was the voice of the *bla* / *lha* might find a comparable pairing elsewhere; see Jaynes (1976, pp. 189–94). Given the paucity of source material for comparison, it is even possible that *bka' thug* simply referred to a *thug* that had a quality of *bka'*, on which more in Part Two.

Nevertheless, he says, it is not clear why these two bipartite systems exist, and notes that the components are sometimes mixed, "as if their historical pedigree and significance had been lost by the time the funerary texts were written down in their present form."

It is, in fact, very difficult to know what is intended by *bka'* in this context, as it seems to appear in no funerary documents outside of this particular tradition. Nevertheless, it is highly unlikely that it is a completely arbitrary insertion. While we could simply dismiss the *Mu cho khrom 'dur* texts as hopelessly corrupt and indecipherable, we might also consider whether there was a way that a divine voice, the voice of a *lha* (recall that the definition includes ancestral spirits) could be made to manifest at a funeral ceremony.

One possibility is that the ancestor spoke through an intermediary. Sinologists have studied exhaustively[92] an ancient ceremony, already archaic by the Han Dynasty, in which a lineal descendent of the deceased in some sense embodied him, receiving offerings and speaking on his behalf. In the earliest era, before the practice had become decadent, it is directly stated that the voice was that of the deceased; perhaps the "personator" was acting as some sort of spirit medium.[93]

On the Tibetan side, we do not have any direct testimony of such a practice; nevertheless, if we turn again to the *Legs bshad mdzod's* description of the conflict between the Buddhists and the Bonpos at the emperor Mune Tsenpo's funeral, we see such an extraneous voice playing a major role:[94]

> Mune reigned for one year and seven months, and in the seventeenth [year], he was poisoned by his mother and died. The *bandes* [Buddhist priests] performing the ritual for the deceased, did not draw forth the *bla*, which, entering and residing in various people, made them speak against their will [literally with "bursting lungs" *glo brdol*]. Since the *bandes* [Buddhist monks] had no evocation ritual, they took the Bon (ritual) as a model, but the common people of Tibet were aware of

---

92. See Carr (2006, esp. pp. 364–90) for a discussion of the extensive scholarship on this matter. The modern Chinese "spirit tablets" representing ancestors mentioned above probably originated in this practice.
93. Carr (2006, p. 389–90) notes that the descriptions of the formal and dignified bearing of the personator, who may have still been a child, contrast sharply with the frenzies of other spirit mediums attested for that era, who are moreover named with a different word.
94. The following translation is from Gibson (1991, pp. 154–55).

this and did not believe in it from the beginning. Then Dranpa Nam mkha' summoned the *rnam shes* and caused the *thugs* to descend, and the lord Trisong, also believing in Bon said, "If there are no evocation rituals for the dead, they cannot be brought forth from the abode of the dead."[95]

The upshot of this passage seems to be that, as a result of an irregular funeral ceremony, what modern psychology might call a sort of negative possession or mass hysteria occurred among the spectators, with unintended people acting as personators or "channels" of the deceased.[96] The above account cannot, obviously, be taken at face value, as it is clearly part of the large Bon vs. Chos wonder contest literature.[97] Nevertheless, the passage gives the impression that the use of *bka'* in the *Mu cho khrom 'dur* might not have been simply haphazard, but seems to have had some basis in archaic belief. Here we might recall that other names for shamanic practitioners in later Tibet included *bka' babs pa* (kabapa, to whom the *bka'* descends) and *lha babs pa* (likewise for *lha*), *lha bka' ma* (lhakama, for females) or even *lha yi bka' babs pa*,[98] and that ancestral spirits are among those invoked by them. The question of so-called shamans in Tibet is a

95. Bkra shis rgyal mtshan, (1977, p. 324): *chab srid lo gcig dang zla ba bdun du mdzad de bcu bdun pa la yum gyis dug stang ste 'das so / de ban des 'dur bas bla ma bkug ste / mi rnams kyi khong tu zhugs nas glo brdol gyi btam smra bar byed la / ban de la 'dur phug med pas bon la dpe blangs pa bod 'bangs rnams kyis shes nas gzod yid ma ches so / der dran pa nam khas rnam shes bkug thugs phab pas / rje khri srong yang bon la thugs ches nas gshin 'dur gyi bon med nag shin po gnas mi 'brong bar 'dug gsungs* / Karmay's translation (1972, p. 102) is much the same as mine, but he renders the key phrase here as "The Buddhists tried the 'evocation ritual', but failed to summon the spirit (*bla*). It would enter someone and babble." He offers no explanation.
96. For those who find this improbable, the present writer offers an experience he had in a rural Thai village, where two villagers drowned in a shallow, not-very-threatening fish pond on two successive days; this was considered very inauspicious. Soon after the funeral ceremonies, another villager began speaking in a voice that was widely attributed to one of the deceased, detailing further procedures he wanted done. He was "possessed" for about two hours. Regardless of how one views such occurrences, there does not appear to be any real reason that twenty-first century Thai villagers should be considered any more susceptible to them than medieval Tibetans.
97. In an earlier contribution (2004), the present author suggested that all the ever-more-elaborate stories of miracle contests between Bonpos and Buddhists that appear in the later literatures of these traditions may have stemmed from an actual conflict between Indic Buddhists and some practitioners of non-Indic-Buddhist traditions (whatever one chooses to call them) over funerary procedures at the death of Mune, which may in turn be the same spiritual crisis referred to in the inscription at Zhwa'i Lhakhang mentioned above (again, whether or not this inscription is genuinely from Imperial times is not crucial to this hypothesis). Given the importance of the *btsanpo's* sacral position in the Empire, it is understandable that concrete issues such as the proper performance of funerals would have had considerably more urgency for the Tibetan people of the time than doctrinal disputes.
98. Snellgrove, 2010, p. 24; Bellezza, 2008, p. 443; see also citations of Tibetan works in Norbu (1995, p. 279 n. 5).

large one, though, and deserves to be discussed separately. This will be done in Part 2.

The Decline of the Tibetan Sacral Kingship

In *The Origin of Consciousness*, Jaynes attributes the decline of bicamerality and its replacement by subjectivity in Greece and the Near East to several causes, some of which are not relevant to the situation in Tibet. These included the fundamental instability of bicameral kingdoms, which were based on a strict hierarchy of authority, which might easily be shaken by novel situations such as increasing contact with other peoples, who followed different god-voices. The spread of literacy would have been another factor working against bicamerality, as writing would have reduced the dependence on hallucinated voices for guidance. The chaotic conditions prevailing in the Eastern Mediterranean and Near East after the eruption of the Thera volcano and the so-called "Dorian invasions" may have contributed to a situation in which bicamerality collapsed suddenly and traumatically across the whole region; in the completely unprecedented circumstances of that era, the voices of past experience would have grown increasingly more erratic and untrustworthy. As a rudderless subjectivity took root, those individuals who still had bicameral capabilities would have at first been honored and their pronouncements recorded, but, as their guiding voices passed from undependability to incoherence and finally into seeming madness, they would have been, as were the *nabiim* among the Hebrews, first ostracized and then eliminated, leaving societies to yearn for their vanished gods, either clinging to written records of past god-voices or resorting to methods such as divination and astrology to fill the void.

As far as we know, the Tibetan plateau never experienced a catastrophe on the scale of the Thera eruption, and its comparative geographical isolation and sparser population undoubtedly contributed to its ability to create and retain a distinctive mentality and culture, which seems (as will be seen in Part Two) to have included more durable links to the pre-subjective mind than some of its neighbors. Nevertheless, some of the same influences that in Jaynes's view would have contributed to the gradual replacement of bicamerality by subjectivity were also present in

Tibet, starting with the Imperial period. Writing was one. Tibet's rapid military expansion in all directions from the Tibetan plateau would also have made political authority more diffuse, and made a personal connection to the *btsanpo* and any special qualities associated with him both infeasible and increasingly irrelevant.

There are a few signs that these qualities were becoming weaker. One of them is the anxiety (mentioned above in connection with P.T. 1047) that the *sku bla* of the *btsanpo* was not always being heard by him. It is pertinent that this manuscript deals with divination, the use of which Jaynes sees as intensifying wherever bicameral voices were in decline.

On another level, the myth of the death of the pre-historic emperor Drigum, as carried down in the so-called Tibetan *Chronicle*,[99] tells of a mad ruler whose insanity was first triggered by a verbal misunderstanding altogether trivial to a modern subjective mentality. This flaw led to an inability to master himself, which in turn caused him to provoke a catastrophic conflict with one of his subjects, in the course of which his *bla* left him, resulting in his death. Such a myth is very suggestive of the psychological fragility of pre-subjective rulers.[100]

The introduction of Indic Buddhism on a large scale was undoubtedly another factor that radically changed the early Tibetan outlook. Although we can be sure that Buddhism would have found itself in conflict with some pre-Buddhist norms (mass sacrifices at royal funerals being an obvious example, mentioned in some later Tibetan historical works), and that Trisong Detsen attempted to replace whatever model(s) of the sacral kingship had preceded him with one based on a Buddhist paradigm, it is

---

99. This story has understandably drawn quite a bit of scholarly interest; see Dotson (2011, p. 88 n. 18) for a partial list of studies. It must be emphasized, however, that the *Chronicle* cannot be considered in the least historical, being a weaving together of sacral kingship legends from most of the cultures surrounding Tibet in the early medieval period. Haarh (1969, p. 156), followed by Dotson (op. cit., pp. 90–91) has discerned influence of the Ramayāna in the *Chronicle*, and Takeuchi (1985) has found borrowings from the Grand Historian of China there. Dotson (op. cit. p. 95 n. 43) has also perceived elements of the "First Story" typical of the Central Asiatic Cultural Complex (on which see Beckwith, 2009, pp. 1–2), and Hummel (1974) has demonstrated convincing similarities between the Drigum story and the myth of Osiris, which may have come to Inner Asia with other elements of Hellenistic culture such as medicine, art, and the revival of religious imagery discussed in Part Two.
100. Haarh (1969, p 330) has properly emphasized that, under the mythological trappings, the story of Drigum is at bottom about the inability of the King Drigum to rule because of insanity, and how his successors dealt with the problems this caused. Dotson (2011, pp. 87 seq.) has discussed the theme of the sacrally flawed ruler's inability to function found in Frazer's *Golden Bough*, and the influence it might have had on such early scholars of the Tibetan kingship as Tucci; Jaynes's theory provides a lucid *raison d'etre* for this myth.

difficult to gain a clear picture of how such a conflict would have played itself out. Later sources frame this in terms of a struggle between Buddhism and Bon, but these sources are highly colored and not easy to sift for historical fact relevant to the issue at hand.[101]

Equally important in the present writer's view, however, is the fact that Buddhism has been from its beginning a subjective religion. It arose in India in an era when subjectivity was spreading across Eurasia, and the *śramana-s* in India were abandoning society and living in solitude in an attempt to grapple with the existential problems the new mentality had brought with it. Unlike those of the Near Eastern religions, therefore, its elite never sought certainty in the recorded commands of past gods. While it did not deny the existence of non-material beings, it has traditionally viewed such beings as harmful or helpful to worldly pursuits, but not ultimately relevant to the religion's primary purpose; thus Buddhism has a long record of adapting itself to religious and cultural mindsets very different from the Indic. The efforts to establish Buddhism as the religion of the Tibetan court would of course have brought to the fore economic and political controversies as well, but these are concerns largely irrelevant to the present essay.

---

101. The probable conflict between the existing tradition and the Buddhists over the Imperial funeral, which may have crystallized with Mune Tsenpo's death, has already been mentioned. A proclamation preserved in an early Buddhist account of early Tibet (Dpa' bo gtsug lag 'Phreng ba, 1980, Vol. *Ja*, p. 55) purportedly dating from the reign of Trisong Detsen, talks about the conflict between the supplication and rituals of the *sku lha* with those of Buddhism, and people's apprehension that the new religion would result in degradation of the *btsanpo's* sacred presence (*sku*) and the weakening of the government associated with it, as well as causing famine and disease. This source has earlier been discussed by both Tucci (1950, p. 48), and Macdonald (1971, p 308), but the latter's translation is much preferable; see discussion in Gibson (1991, pp. 149–52). In the present author's view, the fact that the proclamation does not label the opposition to Trisong Detsen as "Bonpo," but instead mentions only the cult of the *sku lha* strengthens the case for its authenticity. Besides buttressing the case for the *sku bla's* importance, however, it does not contribute much to the present exploration.

On the other hand, in the legends carried down by the Bonpo tradition (Bkra shis Rgyal Mtshan, 1977, p. 319; Karmay, 1972, p 99, 266; see also Blo gros Rgyal mtshan, 1974, pp. 55–56), it is said that during Trisong Detsen's rule, the mountain divinities of the ruler (here called *rje'i mgur lha*) turned away from Tibet in response to "unclean" Tantric Buddhist rites, resulting in misfortune for the country. This "departure of the gods" is similar to that which Jaynes documents in the literature of the Near East, and might well indicate the failure of the bicameral voices which had earlier been associated with mountains, although this occurrence need not be dated to precisely the time of Trisong Detsen, as this polemical passage would suggest. It is also possible that the descriptions of the early Tibetan courts found in these same Bonpo sources, in which representatives of pre-Buddhist traditions held exalted positions — inspiring Tucci (1955, p. 197) to describe the emperors as "sacred but inert symbols" — are exaggerated memories of a period in which religious specialists were increasingly filling the sacral role once played by the *btsanpo* himself. See Blo gros Rgyal mtshan (op.cit., pp. 115–17) for the Tibetan, translated e.g. in Gibson (1991, pp. 133–36), and Bellezza, (2008, p. 286).

We can only speculate on how the earliest representatives of Indic Buddhism in Tibet might have reacted to a sacral kingship based on the qualities of a bicameral ruler. It is more than likely, however, that by the time of Trisong Detsen, those qualities had already declined, and that the *btsanpo-s* were walking through the institutional roles created centuries before, their meaning disappearing or already lost. It does seem that Trisong Detsen himself had little enough faith in those roles to consider a radically new ideology as a basis by which the Empire could be sustained. Any residual bicameral guiding voices the *btsanpo-s* still might have heard might have been seen as a challenge by a politically ambitious Buddhism, but this would in any case have become a moot point when the Empire collapsed.

This collapse undoubtedly left not only a political vacuum, but also a huge religious one. In the absence of a central religious figure, local traditions would have again become more important. With the disappearance of institutional Buddhism and the decline in international contacts, the links to subjective mentality would have been weakened, allowing for the revival and strengthening of practices and institutions that were based in the pre-subjective or proto-subjective mind. The lineages of the nascent Bonpo tradition were usually clan-based, which might imply a hereditary ability for bicameral functioning was being nurtured,[102] while the practices of the so-called "Causal Bon," which included divination and astrology (and perhaps elaborate funerals), would have taken on new importance, as what had probably previously been the exclusive province of the court became much more widely disseminated.

Nevertheless, it seems that in some cases, those claiming direct connections with the *lha* in this period were as unintelligible and unreliable as their Greek and Hebrew counterparts in the immediate post-bicameral world. Martin[103] has discussed four spirit-guides of this period who claimed divine revelation, but whose pronouncements seem neither rational nor inspired (though this may be also partially due to the hostility of the Buddhist writers who described them). In this respect, it might be remarked that there is now, among the Rnyingmapa "Ancient" school of Buddhism, a fairly strict set of criteria governing the authenticity of *gter*

---

102. This may also a contributing factor to the family-based succession of the Khon Sa skya tradition.
103. Martin, 1996.

ston-s (*tertöns*), the visionaries who may be one of the last Tibetan links to the pre-subjective era.

This part of the essay has examined the profitability of analyzing Tibetan linguistics and ancient Tibetan history through the lens provided by Julian Jaynes's bicameral theory. Part Two will examine possible vestiges of the pre-subjective era in more recent Tibetan religion.

References

Adkins, A.W.H. 1970. *From the Many to the One: A Study of Personality and Views of Human Nature in the Context of Ancient Greek Society, Values, and Beliefs*. Ithaca: Cornell University Press.

Bacot, Jacques, Frederick W. Thomas, and Gustave-Charles Toussaint. 1940. *Documents de Touen-houang Relatifs a L'Histoire du Tibet*. Paris: Librarie Orientaliste Paul Geuthner.

Beckwith, Christopher I. 2011. "The Central Eurasian Culture Complex in the Tibetan Empire: The Imperial Cult and Early Buddhism," in Ruth Erken (ed.), *1000 Jahre asiatisch-europäische Begegnung*. Frankfurt: Peter Lang, 221–238.

_____ 2011. "On Zhangzhung and Bon," in *Emerging Bon: The Formation of Bon Tradition in Tibet at the Turn of the First Millenium A.D.*, International Association of Tibetan Studies, Konigswinter, 164–184.

_____ 2009. *Empires of the Silk Road*. Princeton: Princeton University Press.

Bellezza, John Vincent. 2008. *Zhang Zhung: Foundations of Civilization in Tibet*. Vienna: Verlag der Osterrreichischen Akademie der Wissenschaften.

Bkra shis Rgyal mtshan, Shar Rdza. 1977. *Legs bshad rin po che'i mdzod*. Dolanji.

Blo gros Rgyal mtshan, Khyung po. 1974. *Rgyal rabs bon kyi 'byung gnas*. In *Three Sources for a History of Bon*. Dolanji.

Bod rgya tshig mdzod chen mo. 1993. Beijing: Mi rigs dpe skrun khang.

Bolle, Kees. 1987. "Animism and Animatism." In Mircea Eliade (ed.), *The Encyclopedia of Religion*. New York: MacMillan, 296–302.

Bon skyong sgrub thabs bskang gsol bcas. 1972. 2 Vols. New Thobgyal.

Calkowski, Marcia. 2013. "Arriving Ahead of Time: The *ma 'das sprul sku and issues of sprul sku* Personhood." *Journal of the International Association of Tibetan Studies*, 7, 340–362.

Carr, Michael. 2006. The Shi 'Corpse/Personator' Ceremony in Early China." In Marcel Kuijsten (ed.), *Reflections on the Dawn of Consciousness*. Henderson, NV: Julian Jaynes Society, 343–416.

_____ 1989, " The **k'og* (考) 'To Dead Father' Hypothesis." *Review of Liberal Arts*, 77, 51–117. Summarized in Carr, "Shi 'Corpse/Personator' Ceremony."

_____ 1983, "Sidelights on *Xin* (心) 'Heart', 'Mind' in the *Shijing*." [Abstract in] *Proceedings of the 31st International Congress of Human Sciences in Asia and North Africa, Tokyo and Kyoto*, 24–26. Summarized in Carr, "Shi 'Corpse/Personator' Ceremony."

_____1985. "Personation of the Dead in Ancient China." *Computational Analyses of Asian and African Languages*, 24, 1–107.

_____1985. "Big Heads in Old Chinese." Paper presented at the 18th International Conference on Sino-Tibetan Linguistics, Bangkok, August 27–29. Summarized in Carr, "Shi 'Corpse/Personator' Ceremony."

Chiodo, Elisabetta. 1996. "The Jarud Mongol Ritual 'Calling the Soul with the Breast.'" *Zentralasiatische Studien*, 26, 153–71.

Chung wen ta tz'u tien. 1973. (comp. Lin Yin, Kao Ming, et. al.) Research Institute of Chinese Culture, 10 Vols. Taipei.

Cuevas, Brian. 2003. *The Hidden History of the Tibetan Book of the Dead*. Oxford: Oxford University Press.

Dankoff, Robert. 1975. "Kāśgarī on the Beliefs and Superstitions of the Turks." *Journal of the American Oriental Society*, 95, 68–80.

Das, Sarat Chandra. 1989. *Tibetan-English Dictionary*. Kathmandu: Ratna Pustak Bhandar.

David-Neel, Alexandra, and Lama Yongden. 1987. *The Superhuman Life of Gesar of Ling.* Boston: Shambhala.

Dodds, E.R. 1984. *The Greeks and the Irrational.* Berkeley: University of California Press.

Dotson, Brandon. 2011. "Theorizing the King: Implicit and Explicit Sources for the Study of the Tibetan Sacred Kingship." *Revue d'Etudes Tibètaines,* XXI, 83–103.

Eliade, Mircea. 1964. *Shamanism: Archaic Techniques of Ecstasy.* London: Routledge and Kegan Paul.

Gibson, Todd. 2004. "Two Figures in the Early Great Perfection." *Tibet Journal,* XXIX, 4 (Winter), 72–91.

_____ 1991. "From *btsan po* to *btsan*: The Demonization of the Tibetan Sacral Kingship." Doctoral dissertation, Indiana University, Bloomington.

Gtsug lag Phreng ba, Dpa' bo. 1980. *Mkhas pa'i Dga' ston.* Delhi.

Guenther, H. V. 1989. *From Reductionism to Creativity: rDzogs-chen and the New Sciences of Mind.* Boston: Shambhala Publications.

_____ 1977. *Tibetan Buddhism in Western Perpective.* Emeryville, CA: Dharma Publishing.

Gyatso, Janet. 1999. *Apparitions of the Self: The Secret Autobiography of a Tibetan Visionary.* Princeton: Princeton University Press.

Haarh, Erik. 1969. *The Yar lung Dynasty.* Copenhagen: G.E.C. Gad's Forlag.

Hamilton, John. 2006. "Auditory Hallucinations in Nonverbal Quadriplegics." In Marcel Kuijsten (ed.), *Reflections on the Dawn of Consciousness.* Henderson, NV: Julian Jaynes Society, 141–168.

Heissig, Walter. 1984. "Shaman Myth and Clan Epic." In Mihály Hoppál (ed.), *Shamanism in Eurasia.* Gottingen, Germany: Edition Herodot, GmbH, 319–24.

Heller, Amy. 2003. "The Archaeology of Funeral Rituals as Revealed by Tibetan Tombs of the 8th to 9th century." In *Êrān und Anêrān, Studies Presented to Boris Il'ic Marshak on the Occasion of his 70th Birthday,* Libreria Editrice Cafoscarina.

Hill, Nathan. 2013. "A New Interpretation of the Mythological Incipit of the Kongpo Inscription." In K. Tropper and C. Scherrer-Schaub (eds.), *Tibetan Inscriptions: Proceedings of a Panel Held at the Twelfth Seminar of the International Association for Tibetan Studies, Vancouver 2010.* Leiden: Brill.

_____ 2009, Review of Michael Walter, *Buddhism and Empire: The Political and Religious Culture of Early Tibet,* in *Journal of the Royal Asiatic Society of Great Britain and Ireland,* Third Series 20 (4), 559–62.

_____ 2008, "Verba moriendi in the Old Tibetan Annals." In Christopher Beckwith (ed.), *Medieval Tibeto-Burman Languages III, Tibetan Studies: Proceedings of the Eleventh Seminar of the International Association of Tibetan Studies, Konigswinter, 2006.* International Institute for Tibetan and Buddhist Studies, 71–86.

Hummel, Seigbert. 1974, 1975. "The Osiris Myth in Tibet." *Central Asiatic Journal,* 23–29; 199–201.

Jaeschke, Heinrich A. 1980. *Tibetan Dictionary.* Delhi: Motilal Banarsidass.

Jaynes, Julian. 2006. "The Meaning of King Tut." In Marcel Kuijsten (ed.), *Reflections on the Dawn of Consciousness.* Henderson, NV: Julian Jaynes Society, 297–303.

_____ 1976, *The Origin of Consciousness in the Breakdown of the Bicameral Mind.* Boston: Houghton Mifflin.

Karlgren, Bernhard. 1964. *Grammatica Serica Recensa.* Göteborg, Sweden: Museum of Far Eastern Antiquities.

Karmay, Samten Gyaltsen, 2009a, "The Cult of Mountain Deities and its Political Significance." In *The Arrow and the Spindle.* Kathmandu: Mandala Book Point, 432–50. Reprint of an article in *Reflections of the Mountain.* Vienna: Verlag der Osterreichischen Akademie der Wissenschaften, 1996, 59–65.

_____ 2009b. "The Man and the Ox: A Ritual for Offering the *glud*." In *The Arrow and the Spindle.* Kathmandu: Mandala Book Point, 339–79 [translation of an article in *Journal Asiatique,* XXIII, 1995, pp. 162–207].

_____ 2009c. "The Origin Myth of the First King of Tibet as Revealed in the Can lnga." In *The Arrow and the Spindle,* Kathmandu: Mandala Book Point, 282–309. Reprint of an article in P. Kvaerne (ed.), *Tibetan Studies,* Vol. 1, Oslo: The Institute of Comparative Research in Human Culture, 1994, 408–29.

_____ 2009d. "The Soul and the Turquoise: A Ritual for Recalling the *bla*." In *The Arrow and the Spindle.* Kathmandu: Mandala Book Point, 310–338. Translation of "L'âme et la turquoise: un rituel tibétaine," *L'Ethnographie,* LXXXIII, No. 3–4, 1987, 97–130.

_____ 1972. *A Treasury of Good Sayings*. London: Oxford University Press.

Kler, P. Josef. 1957. "Die Windpferdefahne oder das k'î-mori bei den Ordos-Mongolen." *Oriens*, Vol. 10, No. 1, 90–106.

Kuijsten, Marcel (ed.). 2012. *The Julian Jaynes Collection*. Henderson, NV: Julian Jaynes Society.

_____ 2006. "Consciousness, Hallucinations, and the Bicameral Mind: Three Decades of New Research." In Marcel Kuijsten (ed.), *Reflections on the Dawn of Consciousness*. Henderson, NV: Julian Jaynes Society, 95–140.

_____ 2006b, (ed.), *Reflections on the Dawn of Consciousness: Julian Jaynes's Bicameral Mind Theory Revisited*. Henderson, NV: Julian Jaynes Society.

Kvaerne, Per. 1985. *Tibet Bon Religion: A Death Ritual of the Tibetan Bonpos*. Iconography of Religions XIII, Leiden: E.J. Brill.

Lalou, Marcelle. 1952. "Rituel Bon-po des funerailles royales" *Journal Asiatique*, 339–61.

Macdonald, Ariane. 1971. "Une lecture des Pelliot tibétain 1286, 1287, 1038, 1047, et 1290. Essai sur la formation et l'emploi des mythes politiques dans la religion royale de Sron-bcan sgam-po," in *Etudes tibétaines dédiées à la mèmoire de Marcelle Lalou*. Paris, 190–391.

Malandra, William. 1983. *An Introduction to Ancient Iranian Religion*. Minneapolis: University of Minnesota Press.

Mañjušrimîtra. 1986. *Primordial Experience* (Translation of Rdo la gser zhun, by Namkhai Norbu and Kennard Lipman). Bosto: Shambhala.

Martin, Dan. 1996. "The Star King and the Four Children of Pehar: Popular Religious Movements of 11th to 12th-Century Tibet." *Acta Orientala Hungaricae*, 49, 171–95.

Moore, Christopher G. 2006. *Heart Talk*, third edition. Bangkok: Heaven Lake Press.

Ngag dbang Dpal bzang. *Gzhi khregs chod skabs kyi zin bris bstan pa'i nyi ma'i zhal lung snyan rgyud chu bo'i bcud 'dus* (no publication data available)

Norbu, Namkhai. 2009. *The Light of Kailash*, Vol. 1. Arcidosso: Shang Shung Publications.

_____ 1995. *Drung, Deu, and Bon*. Dharamsala: Library of Tibetan Works and Archives.

O'Connor, W.F. 2006. *Folk Tales from Tibet*. Varanasi: Pilgrims Books.

O'Flaherty, Wendy Doniger. 1980. *Women, Androgynes, and other Mythical Beasts*. Chicago: University Press.

Panikkar, Raimundo. 1977. *Mantramanjari: The Vedic Experience*. Berkeley: University of California Press.

Park, Jungnok. 2012. *How Buddhism Acquired a Soul on the Way to China* (Oxford Centre for Buddhist Studies Monographs). Sheffield: Equinox Publications.

Richardson, Hugh. 1985. *A Corpus of Early Tibetan Inscriptions*. Hertford, England: Royal Asiatic Society.

_____1952. "Tibetan Inscriptions at Zva-hi Lha Khang, Part I." *Journal of the Royal Asiatic Society*.

Roerich, Nicholas. 1983–7. *Tibetan-Russian-English Dictionary*, Moscow: Central Department of Oriental Literature.

Samuel, Geoffrey. 1993. *Civilized Shamans: Buddhism in Tibetan Societies*. Washington, D.C.: Smithsonian University Press.

Skrynnikova, T.D. 1992/3. "Sülde — The Basic Idea of the Chinggis Khan Cult." *Acta Orientala Scientiarum Hungaricae*, Vol. 46, No. 1, 51–59.

Snellgrove, David (ed.). 2010. *The Nine Ways of Bon: Excerpts from gZi-brjid*. Bangkok: Orchid Press. First published by Oxford University Press, 1967.

Stein, R.A. "Une document ancient relative aux rites funéraires des bonpo tibétaines." *Journal Asiatique*, 155–85.

_____ 1959, *Recherches sur L'épopée et le barde au Tibet*. Paris.

Tambiah, Stanley. 1970. *Buddhism and the Spirit Cults in North-East Thailand*. London: Cambridge University Press.

Takeuchi, Tsuguhito. 1985. "A Passage from the Shih chi in the Old Tibetan Chronicle." In Barbara Aziz and Matthew Kapstein (eds.), *Soundings in Tibetan Civilization*. New Delhi: Manohar, 135–45.

Tatár, Maria Magdolna. 1990. "New Data about the Cult of Cinggis Qan's Standard." In Bernt Brendemoen (ed.), *Altaica Osloensia: Proceedings of the 32nd Meeting of the Permanent International Altaistic Conference*. Oslo: Universitest Forlaget, 325–38.

Tekin, Talát. 1968. *A Grammar of Orkhon Turkic*. Bloomington: Indiana University Publications.

Tucci, Giuseppe. 1955. "The Secret Characters of the Kings of Ancient Tibet." *East and West*, Vol. 6, No. 3, 197–205.

———— 1950, *Tombs of the Tibetan Kings*. Rome: Serie Orientale Roma I.

Waida, Manabu. 1973. "Symbolism of 'Descent' in Tibetan Sacred Kingship and Some East Asian Parallels." *Numen*, 60–78.

Walter, Michael. 2009. *Buddhism and Empire: The Political and Religious Culture of Early Tibet*. Leiden: Brill.

Yu, Ying-shih. 1987. "O Soul, Come Back! A Study in the Changing Conception of the Soul." *Harvard Journal of Asiatic Studies*, Vol. 47, 2, 363–95.

CHAPTER 15

Listening for Ancient Voices:
Julian Jaynes's Theory of the Bicameral Mind in Tibet, Part Two

TODD GIBSON

I T IS LIKELY THAT READERS OF THIS ESSAY unfamiliar with Jaynes will have mentally rebelled against some of the conclusions drawn in Part One, if for no other reason than they are so far outside the usual approaches to Tibet's early history (though it seems to the present writer that the intellectual framework employed here is no more different from the several others currently in vogue than these are from each other). Nevertheless, without having read *The Origin of Consciousness*, it is understandable that one night consider this point of view (and Jaynes's theory itself) merely speculative: amusing and mildly plausible (or perhaps even completely fanciful), but not backed by any sort of hard evidence. Is there, for example, any direct evidence at all of neurologically-produced voices in post-Imperial Tibetan religious life?

As it happens, there is a lot.

Oracles and Shamans in Tibet

To Jaynes, human oracles that channeled divine voices, as did the priestesses at Delphi, were "subjectivity's umbilical cord reaching back into the sustaining unsubjective past,"[1] and it is the well-documented history of the Greek oracles that provided him a template to compare

---

1. Julian Jaynes, *The Origin of Consciousness in the Breakdown of the Bicameral Mind* (Boston: Houghton-Mifflin, 1976), p. 326.

with similar phenomena in the modern world. Looking at this history, Jaynes traces a decline in the institution of oracles in Greece through several stages.[2] At first, he believes, oracular power was tied to certain landscapes, where anyone that visited could hear hallucinated voices. Gradually, however, the power could only be realized by certain people whose particular psychological temperament allowed them to function as channels to the gods. Later these mediums had to be trained, and still later had to go through increasingly complex induction procedures before they could function. Finally, their pronouncements became garbled, and had to be interpreted by priests.

Jaynes, as noted in Part One, limited himself to data from the Western and Near Eastern world. He would doubtless have considered the tradition of Inner Asian (including Tibetan) shamans and possessed oracles as relevant to his theory, but he might have been daunted by the sheer volume of material available to evaluate.

The very question of the shamanic is one that has invited a good deal of discussion and controversy.[3] In the first place, it has seemed impossible even to find a definition of the word "shaman" that is suitable for every context. Some have insisted that the term be used only in the narrowest sense, i.e. referring to the specialist religious practitioners among the Tungus in Siberia, while others have posited that "shamanism" is the original religion of all mankind,[4] and still others have used the term in a very broad way within an anthropological context, in order to point out certain trends and commonalities in varied contexts.[5] In this essay, too, it is used in a very broad way, to speak of Inner Asian religious specialists recognized by their society as having direct contact with the extrahuman; this would include oracles and possessed mediums as well as the

---

2. Ibid., p. 321–332.

3. For those unfamiliar with the literature, but interested in the Tibetan aspects of the question, one might begin with Samuel (2005) particularly the introduction to that volume and the chapter titled "Shamanism, Bon, and Tibetan Religion," including its fairly comprehensive (though now a bit dated) bibliography.

4. Eliade (1964) is by far the most erudite of those who hold to this position, but his case is based on assumptions that are dubious at best, such as that beliefs in a celestial god and ascent to heaven are primordial cultural universals.

5. Samuel (1993), for example, uses the term to indicate an approach to religion that is based on the spiritual abilities and experiences of individual practitioners, as opposed to a text-based, "clerical" approach.

so-called clan shamans and professional healers usually seen as typical of
Inner Asia.

In Tibet itself, the history of both clan shamanic and oracular institutions is vexingly thorny. To begin with, we have no idea how old so-called
"shamanic" functioning on the Tibetan plateau actually is,[6] or what its
earliest cultural idiom(s) might have been,[7] and only the haziest notions
of how these idioms may have changed over time.

Further, shamanic religion in many of the forms it survives in modern
Inner Asia (or survived until recently) shows strong influences from both
Buddhism[8] and the Inner Asian sacral kingship.[9] The connection of the
shamanic and the Tibetan sacral kingship in particular seems quite extensive. The present writer has previously explored[10] the possibility that
the Tibetan *btsanpo* might have had supernormal powers that could be
labelled "shamanic" in a modern anthropological framework, though the
cultural idiom(s) used to explain these powers at the time of the Empire
(if indeed there was one beyond their self-evident existence) remains in
doubt.[11] Nevertheless, there seems to be a strong connection between

---

6. Macdonald (1971, pp. 275) notes the presence of a group called *mu sman* in the Old Tibetan
documents, and believes these were female shamans.

7. By "cultural idiom," I mean the terminology that the society used to express what was happening to the specialist practitioner: spirit possession, celestial flight, medium for the departed, etc. It
should of course be kept in mind that all such categories are merely provisional, and that, as Samuel
points out (2005a, pp. 73–74), more than one may be present at the same time.

8. The present author has noted (1997) that most of the names used for modern-day shamanic practitioners in Inner Asia originate in Buddhist culture, even among those peoples who have since con-
verted to Islam. The Tungusic word *shaman* itself, from which the word in all European languages
is derived, probably comes from the Sogdian or Chinese version of the Indic *śramāna* (Eliade, 1964,
pp. 496 seq.; no convincing alternative has yet been proposed).

9. There has long been speculation on an early "shamanic aristocracy" on the steppes (Heissig, 1980,
p. 114, n. 2; Voigt, 1984, p. 18 n. 17). Waida (1976) has seen similarities between modern-day shamanic initiations among Siberian peoples such as the Buriat and Samoyed and the medieval Turkic
enthronement ceremony described in historical sources, and concluded that the Turkic *qagans* were
shamans. Rosen (2009) describes Inner Asian artistic techniques, and motifs associated with Inner
Asian shamans, on an early crown of the Silla Dynasty, and concludes that those kings, too, were
shamans. These suppositions are certainly possible or even likely, but not certain; it may also be that
the later shamanic initiations simply took the enthronement ceremonies as an authorization model
after the institution of sacral kingship in the steppes declined. There is even one Islamic source, the
Tabaqat-i-nasiri, which has an extensive description of Chinggis Qan himself acting as a possessed
oracle (Boyle, 1972, p. 81); such a description seems to appear nowhere else, but see Znamenski
(2011, pp. 140–41) for a modern Mongolian political leader who also claimed such powers.

10. Gibson, 1991; see also Walter, 2009, p. 98.

11. The Sherpas studied by Ortner (1989, pp. 52–53) used the word *ongchermu* for supernormal force
directed towards political ends: "Rolwa Dorje was very *ongchermu*. The people did not want to obey
him. But … he twisted an iron rod into a knot. And people were scared." The word *btsanpo* might
easily be substituted for *ongchermu* here. Walter (2009, p. 59 n. 50, p. 63 n. 62) has since compared

the *btsanpo* as war leader and the modern State Oracle of Tibet, even
beyond the obvious fact that the oracle channels a spirit classed as a *rgyalpo*, "king."[12] A brief description of the trance of the oracle's medium
will make the point clear, as well as providing an illustration of Jaynes's
paradigm.[13]

> The monk who is the medium for the oracle spirits dresses in a loose
> costume of brocade and silk, covered with a jerkin styled like ancient
> Tibetan mail. Banner and flags are attached to his back, and another
> cloth covers his front. The medium also wears a golden mirror on his
> breast, and carries a long sword and a quiver of arrows. The invocation
> begins with chanting and music, and the medium begins to enter the
> trance. His face becomes distorted and balloons out, and the left side
> of the face slips below the right.[14] The skin draws tight on the skull,
> and the medium assumes a distant look. As another round of invoca-
> tion begins, the medium exhibits signs such as hyperventilation, gag-
> ging, shaking, or convulsions … His face assumes a dark red color …[15]

> At these symptoms of possession, the attendants place a helmet on
> the oracle's head.[16] The helmet is three feet high, and is said to weigh
> upwards of sixty pounds. As soon as it is secured, the possessed me-
> dium begins to move, springing back up as if the helmet were weight-
> less. He performs a ritual dance … and steps to the right of the Dalai
> Lama's throne in order to answer a question. He … receives three
> more questions. After a further *'chams* dance, the oracle delivers the

---

the *btsanpo* to the Nordic *berserker*, from the other geographical extreme of the Central Eurasian
Cultural Complex.

12. On the post-Imperial displacement of the term *btsanpo* "emperor" by *rgyalpo* "king," see Beckwith (1993, 14–15 n. 10). *Btsanpo*, being a title which connoted supreme power, was unacceptable
to prevailing ideas of *sangha* — state relationships in Buddhism. In post-Imperial mythology, both
btsan and *rgyalpo* spirits are wrathful and martial, and they share many other characteristics.

13. Taken from Gibson (1991, pp. 61–63). This description is based on accounts by Nebesky-
Wojkowitz (1975, pp. 429–31), Avedon (1984, pp. 191–99), and Harrer (1954, pp. 203–205).

14. This lateralization of facial muscles is congruent with Jaynes's theory of hemispherical division of
brain function. Compare this to an account of a negatory (involuntary) possession in Japan, in which
the left side of the face undergoes contractions (Jaynes, 1976, pp. 350–351).

15. This is taken to be an indication of possession by a wrathful spirit; a peaceful spirit causes the
face to turn white.

16. It may be recalled that, in Old Tibetan writings, the helmet (*dbu rmog*) of the emperor was
held to be an important attribute of his authority. Scholars such as Macdonald and Tucci believed
that the imperial helmet was a "symbol" of the emperor's power, but this may be too rationalistic.
Perhaps the *dbu rmog* was none other than a heavy helmet that the *btsanpo* would wear in order to
demonstrate his supernatural qualities. See discussion in Gibson (1991, pp. 74–76); mentioned also
by Walter (2009, p. 98 and especially p. 281 n. 49).

answers in verse, in a high, hollow voice, at times straining his me-
andering mouth to produce the proper sounds, then looking up to
ascertain that he has been understood.

Taken as a whole, this séance is similar to Jaynes's description of the
Delphic oracle in its final stage. Although the superhuman strength of
Nechung was evidently not paralleled at Delphi, the lengthy and involved induction process, including music and multiple supplications to
the possessing entity, the violent contortions of the medium, the limited
intelligibility of its replies, and their interpretation by trained specialists,
are marks, for Jaynes, of an oracular institution on its last legs; we can
only wonder how Nechung's séances might have played out in earlier
centuries. Given the change in the society which surrounded it before
the Chinese invasion, the future of the institution is by no means certain,
but it is striking that the institution of State Oracle in Tibet has already
outlasted that of Greece by eighteen centuries.[17]

The Question of Idols

Here, a short digression is in order. Undoubtedly because of the per-
vasive if unconscious influence of Western monotheistic religions and
Greek intellectual trends, as well as the European (Protestant) Enlightenment's disdain for and ridicule of (Roman Catholic) religious images, the
terms "idol" and "icon" generally and from the start may invoke negative
reactions. Even today many scholars of literary religions which employ
statuary or icons often approach the subject apologetically, if at all; many
prefer to remain wholly in the realm of religious ideas, regarding the use
of images as the domain of the *hoi polloi*.[18]   More subtle, but possibly
even more damaging to an accurate understanding of religious imagery,
is the katachronistic (but generally unstated) assumption that ancient or
even medieval peoples had the same understanding of images as modern
rationalistic intellectuals, viz. that they are, at best, mere "representations"

---

17. The Delphic oracle ceased to function soon after Delphi was ransacked by the Christian emperor
Constantine in 360 C.E.
18. As Geoffrey Samuel has reminded me, this is of course not true in anthropological studies of
religion, which tend to approach the topic more evenhandedly; I thank him for this and several
other helpful suggestions.

of transcendent deities.[19] This tendency must be seen through if we are to investigate the history of such phenomena in a thorough manner; it is very much to Jaynes's credit that he provides a well-developed rationale for the presence and significance of images in religion, falling into neither credulity nor cynicism and condescension.

Idols play an important role in Jaynes's schema of the transition from the bicameral to the subjective mind in religion, which can only be summarized here. In the context of his theory, idols can be seen as effigies which replaced the earlier human remains, such as the body of the king, or of ancestors,[20] which, as seen above, originally aided in triggering bicameral voices. It is crucial to absorb the idea that in the truly bicameral era, idols might have served to prompt what we would call hallucinations, but what to their devotees were the actual voices of the gods themselves. It follows that the figures were not seen to be receptacles of the gods, as modern rationalism might have it, but divinities in and of themselves. As direct evidence for this theory, Jaynes cites the Old Testament, which mentions a type of idol called *terap* that had the power of speech, and quotes remarkable testimony from the *conquistadores* concerning the speech of Inca idols.[21]

Societies in which hearing the voices of idols was common or universal, according to Jaynes, would have been a feature of the earliest period of recorded history, before the collapse of the bicameral mind and the advent of subjective consciousness. Idols from later days, such as those that pervaded every corner of the later Greek and Roman worlds, were probably not, in most cases, expressions of continuing bicamerality but rather attempts to re-establish a direct contact with voices that were already

---

19. Stove (2006, pp. 286–87) tells a wry story about two Virgin Marys competing for lucrative pilgrim traffic in eleventh century France — a difficult situation to account for if they were only surrogates or representations of the same deity, as orthodox doctrine would have it.
20. Here again, it is easy to imagine the Mongolian *onggot* figurines having had such a function.
21. Jaynes, 1976, pp. 174–75. Jaynes hypothesizes that subjective consciousness may have come to the New World much later than to the Old. Even in the Near East, though, we have a source from the early Islamic period, the *Kitāb Al-Asnam*, testifying to an oracular idol on the Arabian peninsula (Hisham Ibn Al-Kalbi, 1952, p. 35):
> My young camels were startled by the blood of sacrifice
> Offered around Su'ayr where Yaqdum
> And Yadkhur go on pilgrimage, and stand before it in fear and awe,
> Motionless and silent, awaiting its oracular voice.

When, or how long, this idol was worshipped is not mentioned in the *Kitāb*, and the contents of its pronouncements are not detailed. Needless to say, Islam considered such idols abominations (though not because of their association with blood sacrifice).

fading or gone. In the Egypt of the Hellenistic period, for example, there were manuals of instruction on how to animate images to enable them to speak and prophesy.[22] Nevertheless, as the godlike voices of the right brain grew dormant, and finally disappeared altogether, the utility of religious images continued to decline in the West, and in those modern faiths that still employ them, they are never seen as conterminous with the divine, though they still can invoke numinous awe among the faithful, and in some cases the sense of communion with a sacral reality.

The history of religious imagery in Asia is stunningly varied. Until the onset of Islam, there seems to have been no sense that worship of images was in any way negative, so all types of imagery were everywhere on the continent from Bamiyan to Kamakura, ranging from the crude but esthetically powerful statues of ancestors found among the Sulawesi to the artistic marvel of the dancing Shiva Natraj in the National Museum at Delhi, and we may assume that levels of interpretation as to their nature and function varied according to the subjectivity and cultural sophistication of their worshippers. Nevertheless, it is clear that the belief in the power of certain individual images remains an active part of religion in the few remaining pockets of traditional Asia.[23]

In the Tibetan context, the most prominent sacred images are of course those connected with the Buddhist religion. Buddhism, being a very subjective, "conscious," religion, would have considered such images from the beginning as representations rather than deities in themselves, and their usual name in Tibetan — *sku 'dra* — indicates their status as

---

22. Jaynes, 1976, p. 332. See also Strickmann, "L'icône animée" (1996, pp. 165–74). Strickmann notes the outright chicanery sometimes associated with such efforts, which was doubtless one cause for the scorn that much of the Greek intellectual world and, later, the European Enlightenment held for idols. Jaynes mentions in passing (1976, p. 333) that during this period there seems to have been a minor cult centered on the cult of severed heads, which were held to have the power of oracular speech; on this practice see also Ogden (2001, pp. 208–15). In the Asian context we may recall not only the postmortem laughter of Ong Khan's head in *The Secret History of the Mongols* (de Rachewiltz, 2006, pp. 110–11), but also the preserved heads of Branka Dpal gyi Yon tan in Tibet (Shakabpa, 1984, p. 51; Richardson, 1998, pp. 69–70; thanks to Dan Martin for the latter citation), and Tairo no Masakado in Japan (Samuel, 2005b, p. 110); both of the latter were considered "protective spirits." Here Jaynes's theory provides a plausible rationale for a practice which would otherwise be considered either distortion on the part of early historians, raconteur's fantasy, or simply inexplicable lunacy.

23. As an example, one need look no further than the so-called Erawan Brahma (image searchable), an image in the heart of the wealthiest shopping district in Bangkok, which still sees a day-long busy traffic of supplicants seeking (and evidently being granted) favors. There are probably thousands of Brahma images in spirit houses across Thailand, but this one in particular is undoubtedly paramount in popular esteem.

a mere likeness or facsimile of the sacred presence (*sku*). Nevertheless, the first images of Śakyamuni were certainly of Greek inspiration, and thus part of the Hellenistic revival of idols and icons mentioned above. Further, the consecration process of such images shows that even today they are held to have some power or life of their own above and beyond the merely symbolic.[24] One very interesting aspect of this consecration is that it is considered incomplete until the stage of "opening the eyes."[25] Could this be an explanation for the passages in Old Tibetan materials which mention "opening the eyes" of the *sku bla*, as well as for the lists of edibles that were to be supplied to them?[26] Here, obviously, the images would not have been statues of Śakyamuni Buddha, but if idols or icons of some sort were considered *sku bla* (a possibility according to our provisional definition), their worship might have allowed the sacred presence of the *btsanpo* to be felt at a distance; possibly they might have acted as cues for bicameral voices, but this function may have already been eroded. They might well have accompanied the emperor (or his generals) on military campaigns, as images of the ancestors were carried into battle in ancient China,[27] or as the Mongols carried their ancestral *tuq-s*.[28] If this were the case, it would also help explain the post-Imperial tradition that Pehar, the spirit protector of Samye and advisor to the Tibetan government in latter days, was captured on a military expedition to the northeast. If there is any historical basis to this tradition at all, perhaps

---

24. See Bentor (2004) for a succinct summary of Indo-Tibetan Buddhist procedures. Strickmann (1996, pp. 165–74) points out interesting parallels between Hellenistic and Buddhist consecration rituals.
25. See Strickmann (1996, pp. 177 seq.), Bentor (2004, pp. 208–209), Gombrich (1971, pp. 103–43), et. al. The eyes of idols during the earliest period of their history were generally created disproportionally large. Countless idols that consist of merely a trunk and a pair of eyes have been uncovered in Mesopotamia (see illustrations in Jaynes, 1976, pp. 168–171); these bear visual comparison with the Tibetan *thog lcags* figurines shown in Norbu (2009, pp. 173–174), though nothing of the latter's history can be established. Many idols of Sumerian gods have huge eyes (Jaynes, op. cit.). Recent discoveries at Sanxingdui in Sichuan province in China, dating from the twelfth to eleventh centuries B.C.E., included forty bronze masks with exaggerated eyes, as well as large isolated bronze eyes, probably meant to be attached to wooden effigies (Carr, 2006, pp. 398–403). As Strickmann notes (1996, p. 189) perhaps the ultimate testimony to the power of eyes to provoke the appearance of life in the inert are those that gaze from the tops of the mountainous stupas of Svāyāmbhunāth (and Bauddhanath) in Kathmandu.
26. Cited by Walter (2009, p. 99). Jaynes (1976, pp. 179–180) notes that lists of very ordinary foodstuffs meant to be offered to idols have been found in ancient cuneiform tablets.
27. See Carr, 1988, p. 37 seq.; 2006, p. 380.
28. For an interesting account of the use of banners in twentieth century Mongol warfare, see Tatár (1990, p. 328). This episode is also mentioned in Znamenski (2011, p. 140).

Pehar was originally a sacred image (or mask?) that embodied the *bla* of the Bhata Hor ruler and his people.[29]

Before leaving the subject, it must be mentioned that even certain Buddhist images in Tibet were credited with the power of speech. References to these *gsung byon ma* ("those to whom speech comes") occur sporadically throughout, for example, Buddhist pilgrim guides,[30] but the present writer has never seen the subject treated in detail by either Tibetan or foreign writers. There is, however, an interesting event found in the biography of a fourteenth century Tibetan Buddhist master who, in response to his patrons' lack of faith, granted the power of speech to images of several wrathful protective spirits. Of special relevance is the fact that after this happened, the statues became known as "*gnyan*": the same adjective used for the Tibetan emperor's *sku bla* discussed in Part One.[31]

Bicameral Voices in Later Tibet

In an earlier contribution,[32] the present author described a particular modality of the *bla*-concept which seems to be a close fit with Jaynes's theory of guidance by bicameral voices. In Tibetan mythology, there is a term, *dgra lha*, which would ordinarily be pronounced "*dra lha*," and translates literally as "enemy god." Rather than constituting a class of deity, as is often supposed, it is used as a general term for spirit beings that have a protective function; thus both *btsan* and *rgyalpo* spirits may be referred to as *dgra lha*. However, as Snellgrove noted long ago, "the meaning of … *enemy god*, for a divinity whose protection one expects,

---

29. The *Sba bzhed* (Stein, 1961, pp. 36–42) and Nyang ral Nyi ma 'Od zer's *Chos byung* (pp. 466–76), some of the earliest examples of Buddhist historiography from post-Imperial Tibet, contain long lists of "protective deities" that the Tibetan emperors caused to reside at Samye; most of their names are unknown to Buddhist scholars today. Perhaps these were local idols, brought to what was meant to be the new center of sacral power of the Empire. One may recall that at the same time the Tibetan Empire was beginning to expand, the Ka'aba in Mecca, the sacral center of the Arabian Peninsula, was reputed to have contained 360 idols, and so was religiously a neutral ground where trade could be carried on peacefully.
30. See for example Wylie (1962, p. 71) and Dowman (1988, pp. 46, 135). Bentor (2004, p. 200) also mentions "numerous stories" of Buddha-images in Thailand speaking to their worshippers.
31. Stearns (2007, p. 417), translates the word as "fierce," but since the statues earned the epithet only after they started to speak, it is clear that it was their ability to be heard that was the cause for it. Images of wrathful deities appearing fierce would hardly be "astonishing."
32. Gibson, 1985; see also Gibson, 1991, pp. 256–263.

seems rather unsatisfactory."[33] He further noted that the term is pronounced "drapla"; this is more in keeping with another spelling, *sgra bla*. The word *sgra* means "sound"; the present writer therefore proposed that the term originally referred to an audible manifestation of an individual's capacity for psychological integration — in other words, a hallucinated bicameral voice. Since that article's appearance, much more information has come to light on the subject, including much more Bonpo literature in which the *sgra bla* spelling is the more common. Karmay[34] has noted its "frequent occurrence," and Norbu[35] says the same, and insists on the *sgra* spelling's primacy, saying that it "is based on a very deep principle ... of the most ancient Bon tradition," although he does not explicitly tie it to voices. Bellezza refers consistently to *sgra bla / dgra lha* throughout the volume cited in Part One, and Clemente[36] follows his Bonpo source material in using this spelling, even though the deities he discusses are definitely mythological, in the sense used above, and martial in character.

Even more recently, however, still another alternate spelling has been discussed, one which moreover dates as far back as the Dunhuang material.[37] In these documents the term is rendered *dgra bla*, and, according to Berounsky, the term refers to warlike deities.[38] Berounsky has further translated and discussed a manuscript that predates the Bonpo sources used by the above scholars[39] in which the *dgra bla* spelling is used, but here seems to refer to a vital force of one's foes that could be ritually captured (*dgra bla srub*) and then used against him. He makes the valid point that in Old Tibetan material *dgra* sometimes means "war" instead of strictly "enemy," so that the translation could be "warrior spirits," and argues that the *dgra* spelling should be considered more accurate because

---

33. Snellgrove, 2010, p. 258 n. 20. It is very much to Snellgrove's credit that he did not "correct" the spelling he found to make it accord with the Buddhist concept.
34. Karmay, 1998, p. 257 n. 54
35. Nobu, 1995, pp. 60–62.
36. Clemente, 1994.
37. The following discussion is based on Berounsky (2009, pp. 22–23, 50).
38. In recent times, an interpretation of the term based on the *dgra bla* spelling has come into vogue with some Buddhist teachers, with a (clearly contrived) meaning of "above the enemy," and so "beyond aggression" (cf. Trungpa, 2007, p. 103). This is a distortion of the intent of the term as found in the early materials, but it provides a more contemporary illustration of how Buddhist clerics and scholars sometimes "edit" received concepts to fit them into frames of reference they are more comfortable with, just as their non-ecclesiastical counterparts (both Tibetan and otherwise) sometimes do.
39. This is the *G.yag ru dgra chos kyis shug mgon dgra brub chung ba gris kha mtshon bsyur* by Dpon gsas khyung rgod rtsal (b. 1175).

the character of these beings is in all cases that of "fighting gods."[40] He does not attempt to deal with the common Bonpo *sgra* spelling, saying merely that its significance "is not easy to elucidate." Nor does he comment on the shift from *bla* to *lha* in the Buddhist sources.

Again, if we were to hold strictly to the maxim that the earliest available written documents must preserve the earliest conceptions, we would be forced to conclude that the *sgra bla* spelling is indeed a later contrivance on the part of the Bonpos (though that would still leave us the task of accounting for it). On the other hand, it is easily possible, even likely, that a concept of *sgra / dgra bla* was present in Tibetan culture before it became literate, so the preference for the *dgra* spelling in the Old Tibetan material may simply reflect the disappearance of bicameral voices, so that the original meaning of the term was no longer commonly understood. Alternatively, it may have come about as a result of Indic Buddhism's rejection of such voices as legitimate spiritual guides: the *sgra* spelling is never found in Buddhist texts.[41]

Whatever the case, there is no lack of evidence that the term retains significant auditory as opposed to martial associations. Bellezza says that of all the supernatural entities in the spiritual world of the prevailing Bonpo lha yi bka' babs shamanic tradition, it is the *sgra bla* with whom they have the most contact.[42] Each of the six ancestral clans of Bonpo mythology is said to have its own *sgra bla*, which is congruent with Jaynes's concept of early bicameral voices as expressing the accumulated experience of small human groups.

Nonetheless, it is in another context the term is found that is of paramount interest in this connection; this is the notion of the *sgra bla / dgra lha* as one of "five original deities" ('*go ba'i lha lnga*, also sometimes translated as "five deities of the head") said to be born with human beings;

---

40. It may be splitting hairs to mention that Nebesky (1975, pp. 330–31) mentions a group of thirteen *dgra lha* supplicated in a *lha bsangs* text which includes at least three female deities whose duties include melting butter, supporting the pillars of the house, and aiding in the birth of children. None of these is fierce or bears weapons.

41. On the other hand, one might also propose an overlap of the two meanings during a certain period in the term's history. Norbu, (1995, p. 61) based on sources unavailable to the present writer, makes the interesting claim that the *thug*, the Tibetan apotropaic standard discussed in Part One, is the receptacle of the *sgra bla*. Perhaps Kublai Khan (1215–1294) was looking at a *tuq* when he "heard from afar / Ancestral voices prophesying war" (the lines are from Coleridge's "Xanadu"), and perhaps this is the significance of *bka' thug* in the *Mu cho khrom dur*.

42. Bellezza, 2008, p. 443.

according to Mumford, this belief is still current among some ethnic Tibetans in Nepal.[43] The earliest literary work on these five, most often taken as authoritative in the Buddhist tradition, seems to be that composed by the *terton* Grwa pa Mngon shes (1012–1090).[44] His work lists the following five spirits: *srog lha* (life-force deity) *pho lha* (male deity), *ma lha* (female deity), *yul lha* (local deity), and *dgra lha*.[45] Each of these deities is stated to occupy a particular part of the body; in the case of the *dgra lha*, in Grwa pa Mngon shes's work, as almost always elsewhere, it is on the right shoulder.[46] It is relevant that Macdonald cites later source material which assumes the identity of the *sku bla / lha* and the *'go ba'i lha*,[47] and that in a work on the *'go ba'i lha* by the Fifth Dalai Lama, it is only the *dgra lha* (again, located on the right shoulder) that retains the epithet *gnyanpo*.[48] And it surely cannot be sheer coincidence that the meaning of the last Tibetan emperor's (unofficial) name, Glang dar ma, contains words that in the language of Zhang Zhung (an ancient language of the Tibetan plateau), mean "voice" and "shoulder";[49] the name could mean "the one with a shoulder voice." The Emperor's proper name was U'i dum ten, and the later Buddhist tradition (but not the Bonpo) remembers him as being anti-Buddhist, but this defamation could have been due to a proclivity for following the voice of his *sku bla* rather than the advice of Buddhist ministers.[50]

---

43. See Mumford, 1989, p. 118 n. 1. Mumford's informants, however, listed only four spirits. Further, some of them reported that only high-born males were born with them (though his female informants evidently did not share that view).

44. Grwapa Mngon shes, 1976, pp. 361–99.

45. Other sources show some slight variation in the names of the five, but all sets include the *dgra lha*; see also Macdonald (1971, p. 301 n. 407); Tucci (1980, p. 193).

46. There is some indication that the perceived "location" of hallucinated voices may be tied to the divided hemispherical functioning of the brain. While this is not altogether consistent among schizophrenics, many patients have reported associating good voices with the upper right, and bad ones with the lower left (see Jaynes, 1976, pp. 86, 89–90), but also Jaynes (2006, p. 86), Kuijsten (2006, pp. 103, 121), Hamilton (2006, pp. 150–51), and Mumford (1989, p. 129).

47. Macdonald (1971, pp. 299–302). While there is no indication at all that the *sku bla* of the Imperial Period was considered in any way fivefold, the individual *lha* in the system described (or likely invented) by Grwa pa Mngon shes can be seen as aspects of the individual's basic "psychological" constitution earlier subsumed under the term *bla*.

48. Norbu, 1995, p. 67.

49. Martin, 2010, pp. 65, 112: *glang* = voice, sound, *dar* = shoulder, upper arm. His name has often been related to the Tibetan word *glang* "ox," but none of these folk etymologies makes any sense.

50. Parenthetically, the unofficial name of another emperor, Sad na leg, could be translated from Zhang Zhung as "existing in the ancestral spirit" (Gibson, 1991, p. 158 n. 55). Norbu (1995, p. 25) believes that the names of the ancient mythic kings of Tibet are in the Zhang Zhung language, but he does not mention the cases of the historical rulers established here.

There is artistic as well as textual evidence in recent Tibetan culture for an audible spirit guide perceived to be located on the shoulder. It may hardly be necessary to mention in this connection that Milarepa, one of the best-known figures in Tibetan Buddhism, is almost invariably depicted cupping his hand to his right ear.[51] According to Stein, the gesture is typical of not only Milarepa, but also 'Brug pa Kun legs and other poet-saints of the *Bka' rgyud* schools.[52] In Stein's still-definitive study of the Gesar epic, there are several depictions of the bards of the Gesar epic, who are (or formerly were) often in trance when they recite the epic, in which they are cupping their hands to their ears as if listening for divine inspiration.[53] Stein says, "The … gesture is characteristic of the epic hero, when identified with the bard or when receiving revelations from the gods."[54]

Even now, other residual bicameral voices are still not wholly extinct in the Tibetan cultural world. One modern-day documentation of an auditory spirit guide comes from Bhutan. In the Bumthang region of that country, there is a form of divination in which the diviner makes a pact with a spirit called the *Pang lha Gomo*. After a grueling occult rite, this spirit is supposed to take up residence on the shoulder of the diviner, ready to help and protect him. To quote Kunzang Choden: "Although *Pang lha* worshippers are viewed with suspicion and skepticism they are sought after for their powers of divination. The accuracy of their divination is attributed to the spirit sitting on the shoulder of the worshipper and whispering divinations."[55] Which shoulder is not specified.

The Bon tradition up until lately seems to have carried on a tradition of cultivating a bicameral voice through the medium of an effigy as part of a process of medical diagnosis. Lopön Tenzin Namdak describes the practice as follows:

> … you take a small piece of birch wood and make a kind of little doll, practice and recite mantras while doing visualization. You make nice

51. An image search for "Milarepa" will suffice to illustrate this.
52. Stein, 1980, p. 272. The Tibetan word used to describe the inspired songs of Milarepa and other poet-saints is mgur (gur), as distinct from ordinary songs which are called glu (lu). As noted in Part One, the mountain deities of the early emperors are sometimes referred to in Bon sources by the name mgur lha.
53. Stein, 1959, pp. 350–51 and 361.
54. Stein, 1980, p. 272.
55. Kunzang Choden, 2009, pp. 316–317.

clothes for the doll, and keep it warm, keeping it just under your collar on your right so it can talk in your ear. ... when you are ready, it can speak. Other people can't hear it, but you can, and in the best case, you hear it speaking directly into your ear, telling you how to cure the patient and what to do. ... Now this is very rare; even Bonpo doctors find it difficult to access this text because there was one lama who used it a lot, but the little doll talked too much and said too many things, so he had to burn it.[56]

And here, with the tale of a tiny homunculus chattering into a physician's ear, we must close the door to the arcane chamber of archaic mentation, and return to the world of subjectivity.

Concluding Thoughts

This essay had its beginnings in an attempt to see if a new theory that its writer found intriguing had any relevance to the field of study that most interested him, i.e. the history of religions in Tibet. It now seems plain that it does.

As stated in the introduction to Part One, one should not regard the connections discovered here as an attempt to "prove" Jaynes's theory of the bicameral mind. Although his theory certainly accounts for the whole of the data presented here more concisely and cleanly than any alternative yet proposed, in the end, theories are only theories, and the most we can hope from them is that they widen and deepen our understanding in a meaningful way until a better one comes along.

Nevertheless, the weight of the evidence gathered here should compel a new approach to some very old problems in the field of Tibetology. At the very least, for example, the systematic examination of important words in the light of the possibility of a change in a culture's subjectivity should, in the future, give pause to scholars who use hackneyed and demonstrably inadequate religious terminology that merely reinforces reductive and unproductive ways of thinking. Likewise, a strong case has been made that living extrapersonal voices directed, and still sometimes direct, the Tibetan religious world. One may or may not choose to regard these voices as vestiges of a time when they were a vital form of social

---

56. Lopön Tenzin Namdak in Ermakov, 2008, pp. 612–613.

guidance at the highest level; still, it seems that any attempt to deal comprehensively and in good faith with Tibetan religious history must take them, and the bicameral theory, into account.

Nor has this modest contribution exhausted all that might be said; on the contrary, it has raised any number of questions, major and minor, that deserve further exploration by Tibetan specialists. Why, for example, is the epithet that implies a special ability in an emperor of Tibet found in the language of Zhang Zhung, and not in Tibetan? Can the repeated pattern of semantic shift accompanied by a slightly different spelling (*glo / blo, thug / thugs, bla / lha, gnyan / nyan, sgra / dgra*) reveal anything about the development (or creation) of the written or spoken Tibetan languages? Conversely, does the presence of evident bicameral ability in not only a ruler but also in many of his subjects long after most of the surrounding world had definitively made the switch to subjectivity have any implications for Jaynes's theory?

A personal comment from a broader perspective: many of us who are not Tibetan were drawn to the field of Tibetology because we felt there was something compelling about a culture that has managed, perhaps uniquely and certainly to the highest degree, to preserve some of the most archaic features of humanity's common experience side by side with a keenly-developed understanding of the human mind, a circumstance serendipitously expressed in Geoffrey Samuel's book title *Civilized Shamans*. *The Origin of Consciousness* provides the first model ever proposed that brings the scientific empiricism of both clinical and neurological psychology together with a philosophy of mind and data from the history of religions to provide a coherent account of how this auspicious coincidence might have come about, and, just as importantly, offers one more line of approach that versatile scholars can keep in their investigative toolboxes.

Nevertheless, my purpose in writing this essay has not been to "explain" distinctive features of Tibetan religious culture and history, and still less to explain them away. There is always a danger of trivialization when scholarship attempts to treat profound or esoteric topics. It would be a pity if its readers took away from this treatise the idea that, after all, Tibetan religion, with the possible exception of Buddhist philosophy, is "just" a matter of anachronistic hallucinations, and hence insanity; this is true only in the sense that a string quartet by Mozart is "just" the sound of horsehair scraped over sheep intestine, and hence noise. To turn away from the snowy heights of a new perspective and then, hemmed in by the dark and narrow gorges of presupposition and habitual patterns of thought, to descend to the hot crowded plains of mere dogmatic scholasticism is to betray both the scholarly endeavor, and, more broadly, the continuing search for understanding that is the inseparable companion of the post-bicameral mind.

On the other hand, neither has the purpose here been to initiate a new trend; it would equally be a pity if Tibet became, in the popular imagination, a "right-brain" culture, in contrast to the heartless, left-brain intellectual world of the West. Such a conception, being just another in a long line of tropes that have romanticized Tibet, is in the end just as reductive as the first, and just as barren: if the Tibetans had not had an acute and flexible intellectual tradition to rely on, it is unlikely that the distinctive resonance of the land and its people could have survived the cacophony of the modern world's competing subjective voices as long as it has. If one looks for a broader message from this essay at all, it might be that we should follow the Tibetan example, and continue to listen humbly for ancient voices of inspiration and guidance even as we use our intellects to weigh their value.

References

Avedon, Richard. 1984. *In Exile From the Land of Snows.* New York: Knopf.

Beckwith, Christopher I. 1993. *The Tibetan Empire in Central Asia: A History of the Struggle for Great Power Among Tibetans, Turks, Arabs and Chinese in the Early Middle Ages.* Princeton: Princeton University Press.

Bellezza, John Vincent. 2008. *Zhang Zhung: Foundations of Civilization in Tibet.* Vienna: Verlag der Osterrreichischen Akademie der Wissenschaften.

Bentor, Yael. 2004. "The Consecration of a Buddha Image." In Donald Lopez (ed.), *Buddhist Scriptures.* London: Penguin. pp. 200–211.

Berounsky, Daniel. 2009. "'Soul of Enemy' and Warrior Deities (*dgra bla*): Two Tibetan Myths on Primordial Battle." In *Mongolo-Tibetica Pragensia: Ethnolinguistics, Sociolinguistics, Religion and Culture,* Vol. 2, No. 2 (Special Commemorative Volume in honour of Associate Professor J. Lubsangdorji on his 70th birthday). Prague: Charles University.

Boyle, John Andrew. 1972. "Turkic and Mongol Shamanism in the Middle Ages." *Folklore,* 177–93.

Choden, Kunzang. 2009. "The Malevolent Spirits of the Tsang Valley (Bumthang) — A Bhutanese Account." In Françoise Pommaret and Jean-Luc Achard (eds.), *Tibetan Studies in Honor of Samten Karmay.* Dharamshala: Amnye Machen Institute. H.P., 313–340.

Clemente, Adriano. 1994. "The *Sgra bla*, Gods of the Ancestors of Gshen-rab Mi-bo According to the *Sgra Bla gso sbyong* from the *Gzi brjid.*" In *Tibetan Studies: Proceedings of the International Association for Tibetan Studies, Fagernes 1992,* Oslo: The Institute for Comparative Research in Human Culture, Vol. 1, pp. 127–136.

De Rachewiltz, Igor. 2006. *The Secret History of the Mongols*. Leiden: Brill.

Dowman, Keith. 1988. *Power Places of Central Tibet: The Pilgrim's Guide*. London: Routledge and Kegan Paul.

Eliade, Mircea. 1964. *Shamanism: Archaic Techniques of Ecstasy*. London: Routledge and Kegan Paul.

Ermakov, Dmitry. 2008. *Bö and Bon*. Kathmandu: Vajra Publications.

Gibson, Todd. 2004. "Notes on the History of the Shamanic in Tibet and Inner Asia." *Numen*, 44 (1), 39–59.

———— 1991. "From *btsan po* to *btsan*: the Demonization of the Tibetan Sacral Kingship." Ph.D. Dissertation, Indiana University, Bloomington.

———— 1985. "*Dgra-lha*: A Re-examination." *Journal of the Tibet Society*, 67–72.

Gombrich, Richard. 1971. *Precept and Practice*. Oxford University Press.

Grwa pa Mngon shes. 1976. *Bla ma rig 'dzin rgya mtsho mkha' gros chos skyong srung ma rnams dang phas kyi lha lnga'i skyobs pa'i man ngag gdams pa* in *Rin chen Gter mdzod*. Vol. 70 (*tho*), 361–99.

Harrer, Heinrich. 1954. *Seven Years in Tibet*. New York: E.P. Dutton.

Heissig, Walter. 1984. "Shaman Myth and Clan Epic." In Mihály Hoppál (ed.), *Shamanism in Eurasia*. Gottingen, Germany: Edition Herodot, GmbH, 319–24.

———— 1980. *Religions of Mongolia*. London: Routledge and Kegan Paul.

Jaynes, Julian. 2006. "Verbal Hallucinations and Preconscious Mentality." In Marcel Kuijsten (ed.) *Reflections on the Dawn of Consciousness*. Henderson, NV: Julian Jaynes Society, 75–94.

Karmay, Samten Gyaltsen. 1998. "The Appearance of the Little Black-headed Man." In S.G. Karmay (ed.), *The Arrow and the Spindle*. Kathmandu: Mandala Book Point, 245-281. Reprint of an article in *Journal Asiatique*, CCLXXIV, 1986, pp. 79–138.

———— 1972. *A Treasury of Good Sayings*, London: Oxford University Press.

Ibn Al-Kalbi, Hisham. 1952. *The Book of Idols: Being A Translation from the Arabic of the Kitab Al-Asnam*. Trans. by Nabih Amin Faris. Princeton: Princeton University Press.

Kuijsten, Marcel (ed.). 2012. *The Julian Jaynes Collection*. Henderson, NV: Julian Jaynes Society.

————, 2006. "Consciousness, Hallucinations, and the Bicameral Mind: Three Decades of New Research," in M. Kuijsten (ed.), *Reflections on the Dawn of Consciousness*. Henderson, NV: Julian Jaynes Society, 95–140.

———— 2006b. (ed.), *Reflections on the Dawn of Consciousness: Julian Jaynes's Bicameral Mind Theory Revisited*. Henderson, NV: Julian Jaynes Society.

Martin, Dan. 2010. "Zhang-zhung Dictionary." *Revue d'Etudes Tibétaines* XVIII, 5–253.

Macdonald, Ariane. 1971. "Une lecture des Pelliot tibétain 1286, 1287, 1038, 1047, et 1290. Essai sur la formation et l'emploi des mythes politiques dans la religion royale de Sron-bcan sgam-po," in *Etudes tibétaines dédiées à la mèmoire de Marcelle Lalou*. Paris, 190–391.

Mumford, Stan. 1989. *Himalayan Dialogue: Tibetan Lamas and Gurung Shamans in Nepal*. University of Wisconsin, Madison.

Nebesky-Wojkowitz, René de. 1975. *Oracles and Demons of Tibet: The Cult and Iconography of the Tibetan Protective Deities*. Graz, Austria: Akademische Druck-u. Verlagsanstalt.

Norbu, Namkhai. 2009. *The Light of Kailash*, Vol. 1. Arcidosso, Italy: Shang Shung Publications.

———— 1995. *Drung, Deu, and Bon*. Dharamsala, India: Library of Tibetan Works and Archives.

Nyi ma 'Od zer, Nyang ral. 1979. *Chos 'byung me tog snying po sbrang rtsi'i bcud*. Paro.

Ogden, Daniel. 2001. *Greek and Roman Necromancy*. Princeton: Princeton University Press.

Ortner, Sherry. 1989. *High Religion: A Cultural and Political History of Sherpa Buddhism*. Princeton: Princeton University Press.

Richardson, Hugh. 1998. *High Peaks, Pure Earth*. Chicago: Serindia Publications.

Rosén, Staffan. 2009. "Korea and the Silk Roads." *The Silk Road*, Vol. 6, No. 2, 3–14.

Samuel, Geoffrey. 2005a. "Buddhism and the State in Eighth Century Tibet." In G. Samuel, *Tantric Revisionings: New Understandings of Tibetan Buddhism and Indian Religion*. Delhi: Motilal Banarsidass, 94–115. First published in Henk Blezer (ed.), *Religion and Secular Culture in Tibet: Proceedings of the 9th Seminar of the International Association of Tibetan Studies*. Leiden: Brill, 2000, pp. 1–16.

———— 2005b. "Shamanism, Bon, and Tibetan Religion." In G. Samuel, *Tantric Revisionings: New Understandings of Tibetan Buddhism and Indian Religion*. Delhi: Motilal Banarsidass. First published in Charles Ramble and Martin Brauen (eds.), *Anthropology of Tibet and the Himalaya.* Ethnological Museum of the University of Zurich, 1993, pp. 318–30.

———— 1993, *Civilized Shamans: Buddhism in Tibetan Societies.* Smithsonian University Press, Washington, D.C.

Shakabpa, Tsepon W.D. 1984. *Tibet: A Political History.* New York: Potala Publications.

Snellgrove, David (ed.). 2010. *The Nine Ways of Bon: Excerpts from gZi-brjid.* Bangkok: Orchid Press. First published by Oxford University Press, 1967.

Stearns, Cyrus. 2007. *King of the Empty Plain.* Ithaca, New York: Snow Lion Publications.

Stein, R.A. 1972. *Tibetan Civilization.* Stanford, CA: Stanford University Press.

———— 1961. *Une chronique ancienne de bSam yas: Sba bzhed.* Paris: Publications de l'Institut des Hautes Études Chinoises.

———— 1959. *Recherches sur L'épopée et le barde au Tibet.* Paris: Publications de l'Institut des Hautes Études Chinoises.

Stove, David. 2006. "The Oracles and their Cessation." In Marcel Kuijsten (ed.), *Reflections on the Dawn of Consciousness: Julian Jaynes's Bicameral Mind Theory Revisited.* Henderson, NV: Julian Jaynes Society, 267–94.

Strickmann, Michel. 1996. *Mantras et mandarins: Le bouddhisme tantrique en Chine.* Mayenne, France: Éditions Gallimard.

Tatár, Maria Magdolna. 1990. "New Data about the Cult of Cinggis Qan's Standard." In Bernt Brendemoen (ed.), *Altaica Osloensia: Proceedings of the 32nd Meeting of the Permanent International Altaistic Conference.* Oslo: Universitest Forlaget, 325–38.

Trungpa, Chogyam. 2007. *Shambhala: Sacred Path of the Warrior.* Boston: Shambhala Publications.

Tucci, Giuseppe. 1980. *The Religions of Tibet.* Berkeley: University of California Press.

Voigt, Vilmos. 1984. "Shaman – Person or Word?" In Mihály Hoppál (ed.), *Shamanism in Eurasia.* Gottingen, Germany: Edition Herodot, GmbH, 13–20.

Waida, Manabu. 1976. "Notes on Sacred Kinship in Central Asia." *Numen*, 179–90.

Walter, Michael. 2009. *Buddhism and Empire: The Political and Religious Culture of Early Tibet.* Leiden: Brill.

Wylie, Turrell. 1962. *The Geography of Tibet According to the 'Dzam-gling-rgyas-bshad.* Serie Orientale Roma XXV, ISMEO. Rome.

Znamenski, Andrei. 2011. *Red Shambhala: Magic, Prophecy, and Geopolitics in the Heart of Asia.* Wheaton, Illinois: Quest Books.

CHAPTER 16

Vico and Jaynes:
Neurocultural and Cognitive Operations
in the Origin of Consciousness

ROBERT E. HASKELL

IN THE TIME OF THE BEGINNING OF THE HUMAN SPECIES it is possible "there existed a race of men who spoke, judged, reasoned, solved problems, indeed did most of the things that we do but who were not conscious at all"; that "most men at one time, throughout the day, were hearing poetry ... composed and spoken within their own minds," and that "poetry ... was the language of the gods." These words may seem to be from Vico's *New Science*; they are, however, from *The Origin of Consciousness in the Breakdown of the Bicameral Mind*, by Julian Jaynes, a psychologist who has become widely known for his theory of consciousness since the book appeared in January 1977.[1] Giambattista Vico (1668–1744), however was never one of his authors. A review of the literature on Vico in English shows occasional citings of Jaynes,[2] usually with the suggestion that his ideas on consciousness and on language may be pertinent to Vico's work.

This paper will first explore significant parallels between Vico and Jaynes; second, suggest the equivalence of the mind of Vico's "first men"

First published in *New Vico Studies*, 1993, 11, 24–51. Reprinted with permission.
1. Hereinafter abbreviated as *OC*, followed by the page number. References to the *New Science* will be *NS*, followed by the page number. While Vico is most noted for his social and historical theory, the scope of this paper is largely confined to his contributions to psychological phenomena. A further limitation: it is not possible in this short space to emphasize the many differences between Vico and Jaynes. I wish to acknowledge my gratitude to Dr. Jaynes for reading and discussing my accuracy in rendering his bicameral theory in a near-final draft of this manuscript.
2. Danesi, 1986, 1987, 1989; Gardner, 1976; Haskell, 1978, 1987b; Singer, 1976.

with Jaynes's bicameral mind; third, and what is perhaps more important, it will suggest that Jaynes's theory of consciousness and its evidential base generally support Vico's historical theory of mental development.[3]

Jaynes's theory of the origin of consciousness and the breakdown of the bicameral mind can be outlined as follows: (1) Humans were not always conscious beings; (2) prior to the origin of consciousness the "mind" was bicameral, i.e., by analogy with the term as it is used in political science, divided into two "houses" or parts; (3) consciousness (as we understand it) arose from interaction with culture and society; (4) consciousness was fundamentally formed by language, particularly by metaphor and analogy; (5) consciousness began somewhere around 1400-600 B.C.; (6) during the bicameral stage, the human species hallucinated voices that they took to be the voices of gods; and (7) consciousness has a neurological substrate.[4]

Methodologically, Jaynes's approach can be characterized in four parts: (1) a historical analysis of ancient texts which are considered to be valid historical documents describing the human experience; (2) the study of language and philology; (3) the study of the differential functions associated with the brain's left and right cerebral hemispheres; and (4) the study of pathological and other anomalous cognitive phenomena. (Those in the humanities may find the analysis of ancient texts and philology not unusual methodologies, but for a psychologist they are quite unusual.) One important difference between Vico and Jaynes should be noted. Despite Jaynes's use of ancient texts as data, Jaynes, unlike Vico, is

---

3. While the literature on Vico is replete with insightful comparative articles (e.g., Mora, 1976a; Verene, 1976a), a comparative course is not without its risks. Tagliacozzo (1976) observed that while many resemblances to Vico are substantive, others may be purely coincidental. Others have lamented that Vico is often used instrumentally (Battistini, 1981; Kiernan, 1986; Lilla, 1986). Mora (1976b) characterized some similarities as "amazing." Vico's mental dictionary common to all people (*NS*: 144; 161) would perhaps predict such amazing resemblances; Cotroneo (1969) and Faucci (1969) suggest similarities of Vico to scholars before him. To I. A. Richards (1936), comparative studies are "interactive metaphors" writ large, with the potential to provide insights into both terms of the comparison.

4. It seems prudent here to cite Jaynes's 1986c succinct explanation of his use of the term *consciousness*, since it has a nearly all-meaningful nature in psychology and philosophy: "'conscious expereience' with its episodic memory is precisely what I call consciousness ... I prefer to remain with consciousness as Locke and Descartes ... would define it, as what is introspectible." Elsewhere Jaynes says it is "All our introspective experience, including retrospection and imagination" (1982, 434). In this regard, he says a more precise title for his 1976 book would be *The Origin of Conscious Experience in the Breakdown of the Bicameral Mind*.

an empiricist in the sense of valuing empirical data and sound methodology, as well as clear and distinct, *intelligible* ideas.[5]

Vico's First Men and Jaynes's Bicameral Mind

For Vico, the history of the world is divided into three ages: that of
gods, heroes, and men, each respectively corresponding to three natures
of the human species: divine, heroic, and human. This paper will be concerned with only the first age and the first natures that we are told were
all sensation and totally lacking in reflection, that is, consciousness. It is
likewise Jaynes's bicameral thesis that early humans were not conscious
as we know it; further, they hallucinated voices that they mistook for
voices of gods.

In the beginning of humanity, for both Vico and Jaynes, human perception emanated from within and was based upon bodily sensations.
Vico's first men "were all robust sense and vigourous imagination" (*NS:*
375) who "at first feel without perceiving" (*NS:* 218). For Jaynes: "Bicameral men did not imagine; they experienced" (*OC:* 371). Indeed, for both
Vico and Jaynes, prior to the time of consciousness as we know it, the
first humans were "almost all *body* and almost no reflection" (*NS:* 819, my
italics). Jaynes says, "The conscious psyche is imprisoned in the *body* as in
a tomb" (*OC:* 291, my italics). Thus for Vico and Jaynes the mentality of
early man was confined within the body structure.

According to Vico, "The first [men] were divine, or, as the Greeks
would say, theocratic, in which men believed that everything was commanded by the gods" (*NS:* 925), "that the early gentile peoples ... were
poets who spoke in poetic characters ... formed by their imagination"
(*NS:* 34). In this regard, Jaynes concludes, "I shall state my thesis plain.

---

5. It is particularly interesting to note, given the centrality of Vico's epistemological *verum-factum*
principle of the convertability of the *true and the made*, that Jaynes experienced a nearly identical
insight: that of the human construction of knowledge. Jaynes recounts that while lying down, one
afternoon, in intellectual despair, "Suddenly, out of an absolute quiet, there came a firm distinct loud
voice from my upper right which said, '*Include the knower in the known*'" (*OC:* 86, my italics). Jaynes
does not elaborate on this Vichian-like *verum-factum* epistemological principle, nor apply it to his
own analysis. In discussion with Jaynes, he said he simply used this auditory episode to illustrate that
normal contemporary people hear such hallucinated voices, as indeed the literature attests (Jaynes,
1976a, 1990; Singer, 1973). Though Jaynes does not intend any epistemological implications for his
own work, it is reasonable to expect that such a profoundly experienced concept is implicit in his
work. It could certainly be suggested that, at the least, Jaynes's entire thesis of the bicameral mind in
the evolution of consciousness implies including the knower in the known.

The first poets were gods. Poetry began with the bicameral mind. The god side of our ancient mentality, at least in a certain period of history, usually or perhaps always spoke in verse" (*OC*: 361). In the Vico litera-ture an often-cited example is that the first men sensed or imagined the sound of thunder to be an angry god: "it was believed that the thun-dering sky was Jove" (*NS*: 383). Jaynes maintains, "Generations ago, we would understand thunderstorms perhaps as the roaring and rumbling about in battle of superhuman gods" (*OC*: 52). For Vico, there was an "age of gods, in which gentiles believed they lived under divine govern-ments and everything was *commanded* them by auspices and oracles (*NS*: 31, my italics). It is in this age that the first men hallucinated thunder to be Jove, and hence "heard" what was for them the first Word.[6]

It is significant that in the Vico literature the primary metaphor used in discussing imagination is *visual*, the *image* rather than *auditory* or *hearing*. Indeed, in the *New Science*, the word "hearing" is never used. However, Vico does say "later men were unable to enter into the imagi-nations of the first men ... which made them *think they saw gods* (*NS*: 399, my italics). It seems reasonable to say that since these "first men" hallucinated visually they hallucinated auditorially as well.

With the exception of transmuting sensory experience of the thun-dering sky into Jove, Vico does not appear at first glance to suggest that the first men hallucinated actual voices, as the Jaynesian bicameral thesis indicates. In fact, the *New Science*, with one exception, does not refer to the first men "hearing" at all. Instead Vico uses the concept of imagina-tion, a term which he appears to use generically for all sensory phenom-ena. It will be suggested here that at the time of the beginning Vico's first men did in fact not merely imagine (in the modern "rationalized" or intelligible sense, at least) the voices of the gods, but hallucinated or heard them in their minds, a kind of inner speech. "For speech was born in *mute* times as *mental* ... language, which ... existed before vocal or articulate [language] ... [Which] was a fantastic speech making use of

---

6. Recognizing the fundamental transformative nature of this event in Vico's *New Science*, Verene (1976a), says, "All the original powers of mind that are manifest in the various forms of poetic wisdom are present in this initial act. It is this act that must be sought out and followed in its de-velopment if we are to grasp the origin point of any nation" (419), that "it is from the initial act of forming the thunder as Jove that human consciousness is born" (418). (A kind of "Big Bang" theory of consciousness [Haskell, 1987b], as it were.)

physical substances endowed with life and most of them imagined to be divine" (*NS*: 401). [Which] "was *almost entirely* mute" (*NS*: 446, my italics). Further, the first or divine language was, "understood only by God; men know of it only what has *been revealed* to them. .... *this has been by internal speech to their minds as the proper expression of a God all mind*" (*NS*: 948, my italics); he says that the first men "had not yet heard a *human voice*" (*NS*: 454, my italics), implying that they had heard a non-human or god voice. He also asserts, "Whatever these men saw, imagined, *or even made or did themselves* they believed to be Jove" (*NS*: 379, italics added), that is, the gods. In referencing the Heroic language, Vico says that Homer "mentions a more ancient language and calls it 'the language of the gods'" (*NS*: 174). Moreover, Vico seems to suggest that the mental activity of the first men was "*for the most part*" (*NS*: 34, italics added) images, clearly implying that other sensory activity, including auditory activity, was likely present.

The italicized words and phrases of these Vico quotations are significant for the present thesis. From all that had been said above, it is thus being suggested that Vico's concept of imagination as it applies to the first men includes hallucinations of auditory phenomena and that the first of the first men heard voices and thought them to be the voices of gods. Certainly Vico would not have excluded such an important sense modality.

According to Jaynes: "The presence of voices which had to be obeyed were the absolute prerequisite to the conscious stage of mind in which it is the self that is responsible and can debate within itself ..." (*OC*: 79). "The gods were in no sense 'figments of the imagination' of anyone. They were man's volition. They occupied his nervous system, probably his right hemisphere, and from stores of admonitory and perceptive experience transmuted this experience into articulated speech which told man what to do" (*OC*: 203). It follows then that consciousness was born of hallucination.[7]

Vico and Jaynes seem to hold similar views on the everyday function of the voices of the gods. Vico says of these first men that they "no sooner

---

7. A hallucination is a *sensory* experience, auditory, visual, etc., which does not referentially exist external to the individual. Technically speaking, the first men experiencing thunder as anger or Jove was not a hallucination but a delusion since the sensory experience was based on a distortion of an external event. Experientially, the transmutation of thunder into a feeling of anger is what Werner and Kaplan (1963) in their classic but infrequently cited work call a holophrastic phenomenon, i.e., just as a verbal insult may be experienced as a "slap in the face." They also discuss in seminal detail the process of Vichian-like inner speech.

imagine than they believe" (*NS*: 376), where to believe is to act; similarly, according to Jaynes, in the time of the beginning: "The gods take the place of consciousness. ... The beginnings of action are not in conscious plans, reasoning and motives; they are in actions and speeches of gods" (*OC*: 72); "volition came as a voice that was in the nature of a neurological command, *in which the command and the action were not separated*, in which to hear was to obey (*OC*: 99, my italics). Hence internal voices, not individual volition, initiated behavior.

Vico's notion of imagination includes memory as a generative base. On this he says "imagination is nothing but extended or compounded memory" (*NS*: 211), which suggests that Vico's concept of imagination has at its disposal more memory stores than "consciousness" has in its immediate grasp. Jaynes, too, in explaining hallucination emphasizes the role of memory. He says: "Hallucination often seems *to have access to more memories and knowledge* than the patient [does consciously] — even as did the gods of antiquity" (*OC*: 412, my italics). Vico further says, of the first men, "they must have had marvelously strong memories" (*NS*: 819). According to Vico, "Memory thus has three different aspects: memory when it remembers things, imagination when it alters or imitates them, and invention when it gives them a new turn or puts them into proper arrangement and relationship. For these reasons the theological poets called Memory the mother of the Muses" (ibid.). Jaynes, too, sees the beginnings of conscious memory as being linked to the Muses. He avers, "It is possible that the oral tradition in Greece was an immense benefit in its demand that 'Apollo' or the 'muses' in the right hemisphere becomes the source of memory" (*OC*: 219).[8] In the Jaynesian bicameral age, as in the Vichian age of the gods or the first men, humans had no sense of

---

8. Verene (1976b; 1981) insightfully points out and examines the significance of memory or *memoria* in Vico's concept of imagination, or what he calls *fantasia*. According to Jaynes: "Men who did not live in a frame of past happenings, who did not have 'lifetimes' in our sense, and who could not reminisce because they were not conscious ..." (*OC*: 371) "Reminiscent memory (or episodic memory, as it is sometimes called), in sharp contrast to habit retention (or semantic memory), is new to the world with consciousness" (*OC*: 457). Research on memory has always been a significant area in psychology. Most of the research, however, has been largely on what is called memory span at a point in time, not on everyday memory or memory of the past. Ulric Neisser, the father of modern cognitive psychology (1967), laments this in *Memory Observed: Remembering in Natural Contexts*: "Shouldn't memory have something to do with the past?" (1982, 7). From Verene's (1981) extensive analysis of Vico's "concept" of *memoria*, it is clear that further examination of the philosophy and psychology of memory as well as of imagery may prove useful.

time. "The theological poets," says Vico, "gave beginnings to chronology" (*NS*: 732). Jaynes suggests, in one of his descriptions of what he considers to be a vestige of the bicameral mind, that "The sense of time ... is ... diminished ... in the bicameral mind" (*OC*: 391).

Vico and Jaynes describe similar conditions that lead to the initiation of imagined and hallucinated gods. The stimulus to hallucinating is stress, largely internally generated. We find Vico suggesting: "it was fear which created gods in the world; not fear awakened in men by other men, but fear awakened in themselves" (*NS*: 382). In like manner, Jaynes suggests: "Anything that could not be dealt with on the basis of habit, any conflict between work and fatigue, between attack and flight, any choice between whom to obey or what to do, anything that required any decision at all was sufficient to cause an auditory hallucination" (*OC*: 93). Jaynes points out that stress is what often induces hallucinations in schizophrenics.

One of Vico's insights was to suggest that the development of mind was dependent on cultural events, as indicated in his well-known principle, "The order of ideas must follow the order of institutions" (*NS*: 238). Though Jaynes is a psychologist, he does not maintain a simple maturational or intrapsychic perspective of mental development; he is, in effect, more of a social psychologist. Construing "institutions" in a more anthropological sense, Jaynes maintains: "The creation of such a [conscious] self is the product of culture" (*OC*: 79). Jaynes points out that: "The brain is more capable of being organized by the environment than we have hitherto supposed, and therefore could have undergone such a change from bicameral to conscious man mostly on the basis of learning and culture" (*OC*: 106). Throughout *Origin*, Jaynes describes how changes in consciousness and language paralleled changes in institutions.

Discovery of Metaphor and Language: First Cognitive (Tropological) Operations

Fundamental to this comparative analysis of Vico and Jaynes is language and the concept of metaphor. Jaynes maintains that language preceded consciousness; in Vichian terms, language preceded the age of reflection. Unlike most contemporary linguists, Jaynes maintains (1976b) that language developed in the late Pleistocene period (from 70,000 B.C.);

he says "the implications of such a position are extremely serious" (*OC*: 66). Jaynes, like Vico, considers metaphor to be fundamental to consciousness and language. Vico says: "All the first tropes are corollaries of this poetic logic. The most luminous and therefore the most necessary and frequent is metaphor" (*NS*: 404), and that "every metaphor ... is a fable in brief" (ibid.). Moreover, the fables, i.e., myths, are "true narrations" (*NS*: 408), not simply allegories. Such narrations were the first fables or myths. Thus, "the first age of the world occupied itself with the primary operation of the human mind (*NS*: 496), which was metaphorical, or tropological transformation.

Among the many implications of this discovery of metaphor as a fundamental cognitive operation is that it reverses those views which maintain that (a) metaphor is a figure of speech, an ornamental rhetorical device, and (b) that poetic speech developed after prose.[9] Thus Vico says that the "poetic style arose before the rational or philosophical universals" (*NS*: 460). Like Vico, Jaynes sees the birth of metaphor as issuing from the illustration of the first men's apprehension of thunder, "as the rumbling about in battle of superhuman gods" (*OC*: 52). For Jaynes, too, "metaphor is not a mere extra trick of language ... it is the very constructive ground of language (*OC*: 48). More than this, Jaynes maintains, "Consciousness *is* the work of lexical metaphor" (*OC*: 58, my italics).

It is the common sense of the current nations, so to speak, that figurative language followed literal language; that figurative or poetic speech is a special case of literal language. Vico and Jaynes, however, maintain that figurative language evolved first. Vico says: "these expressions of the first nations later became figurative when, with the further development

---

9. Like Vico, Jaynes "reads" previous evidence quite differently than most other scholars, whom, both men maintain, have imposed the epistemology of their own times on the evidence. Jaynes says: "It is generally agreed that the ancient Egyptian language, like the Sumerian, was concrete from the first to last. To maintain that it is expressing abstract thoughts would seem to me an intrusion of the modern idea that men have always been the same" (*OC*: 186), and: "When the Memphite Theology speaks of the tongue or voices as that from which everything was created, I suspect that the very word 'created' may also be a modern imposition, and the more proper translation might be *commanded*" (ibid.). Jaynes points out other areas of unwarranted impositions (see *OC*: 184). This imposition of a modern epistemology upon translations of works that may not have been based on such an epistemology, this "conceit of scholars," to turn a Vichian phrase, is a serious epistemological issue, one that, as I have suggested (Haskell, 1978, 1987b), may have implications in the translations of Vico's *New Science*, especially given his "new" epistemological stance. Like Vico, Jaynes, in his bicameral theory, calls for a radical departure in understanding many human mental phenomena. The work of both men engenders an epistemological paradigm shift.

of the human mind, words were invented ... (*NS*: 409). Jaynes says: "In early times, language and its referents climbed up from the *concrete to the abstract* on the steps of metaphors" (*OC*: 51, my italics).[10] For Vico and Jaynes, then, metaphor was a cognitive operation before it was a linguistic device.[11]

Vico and Jaynes hold similar views of the evolution of some of the parts of language, though they differ on the particulars, with each differing radically from their respective peers on language development. For example, both maintain that nouns were a late development and that verbs came after nouns. From his linguistic analysis of ancient texts Vico found that the parts of speech evolved in particular ways. "[Our theory] gives us ... the order in which the parts of speech arose, and consequently the natural causes of syntax" (*NS*: 454). Vico lays out the developmental order of the parts of speech. First there were interjections formed from intense passions, then came pronouns, then particles and prepositions, then nouns, and last came verbs (*NS*: 447–58).

Jaynes (1976b) maintains that first came "calls" formed from feelings of danger, then modifiers, prepositions, life-nouns, and thing-nouns, then verbs, and last articles and conjunctions. Further, he says, "That the differentiation of vocal qualifiers had to precede the invention of nouns which they modified, rather than the reverse" (*OC*: 132). Both view verbs as evolving similarly: Vico says, "verbs must have begun as imperatives" (*NS*: 453); Jaynes (1976b) suggests that verbs evolved out of, "were common among the first modifiers and commands" (320). Each linguistic change paralleled cultural changes. Jaynes suggests that "just as the age of modifiers coincides with the making of much superior tools, so the age of nouns for animals coincides with the beginning of drawing animals

---

10. Like Vico, Jaynes sees language development in children as paralleling language development historically. Jaynes (1976b) suggests that despite the outdated nineteenth-century Biogenetic Law of ontogeny recapitulating phylogeny, "it is nevertheless proper to ask whether or not the sequence of language development in the child in any way resembles its sequence in the species as a whole" (323).
11. In previous works (Haskell, 1978, 1987b), I suggested Vico was, in effect, a cognitive psychologist and as such was concerned with cognitive operations. Vico says, "the first age of the world occupied itself with the primary operation of the human mind" (*NS*: 496) and that the primary operation to which he refers is metaphorical operations. As a consequence, I suggest that he was the first to "discover" metaphor to be a fundamental cognitive operation, rather than a simple literary device. In recent years there has been a new literature in psychology finally viewing metaphoric and analogical reasoning as important cognitive and learning operations. (See, e.g., Honeck and Hoffman, 1980; Lakoff and Johnson, 1980; Vosniadou and Ortony, 1989). For a theory of equivalence transformations that reference Vico's notion of sensory topics, see Haskell (1989).

on walls of caves ..." (*OC*: 133). In Vichian fashion, he says that each new stage of words created new perceptions which resulted in important cultural and institutional changes.[12]

Vico, like Jaynes, seems to suggest that for the first men the hiero-glyphs (pictures) may have been a stimulus for hallucinating auditory voices. He says, "the first nations *spoke* in hieroglyphs" (*NS*: 435). "This axiom is the principle of the hieroglyphs by which all nations *spoke* in the time of their first barbarism" (*NS*: 226); "all nations began to *speak* by writing" (*NS*: 429, my italics). Jaynes suggests that just as bicameral man hallucinated voices of gods from cuneiform characters, and thus begin reading. He says that reading "had become in later bicameral times a matter of *hearing* cuneiform" (*OC:* 247) "rather than visual reading of syllables in our sense" (*OC*: 182). In addition, both Vico and Jaynes view language as evolving out of a kind of "Piagetian" action schema. "Speech," says Vico, "stands as it were midway between mind and body" (*NS*: 1045) "the many abstract terms in which language now abound ... came to it from the body" (*NS*: 699). In like manner, Jaynes says, "All the proce-dures of consciousness are based upon ... metaphors and analogies with behavior ... there is no operation in consciousness that did not occur in behavior first" (*OC*: 450). By way of example, Jaynes maintains that "con-sciousness is constantly fitting things into a story, putting a before and an after around any event. This feature is an analog of our physical selves moving about through a physical world with its spatial successiveness which becomes the successiveness of time in mind-space" (*OC*: 450).

Both Vico and Jaynes see consciousness, in part, as a means to solve a social problem — communication. Vico says "articulate" speech was formed "in order to make certain of one another's wills" (*NS*: 1030). Jaynes also suggests that as social groups increased in size social order based upon hallucinated voices became more difficult, because there came to be too many competing voices of gods. Thus, a form of social control that was based on a means of inter-person communication be-came necessary.

---

12. For an early and insightful exposition of how the four major tropes are related to major institu-tional and cultural changes, see White (1976).

Discovery of the True Homer: Mind and Consciousness

Homer, the (ostensible) author of the *Iliad* and the *Odyssey*, was for both Vico and Jaynes formative in the development of their ideas. Contrary to the historically traditional view, they both maintain that (a) Homer was not the sole author of the *Iliad* and the *Odyssey*, (b) the *Iliad* and the *Odyssey* were not epic poems in the modern sense but were in fact literal historical documents narrating the history of early man, but more importantly, therefore (c) within the *Iliad* and the *Odyssey* lay the "proof" of the origin of consciousness.[13]

For Vico the discovery of the true Homer, i.e., that the fables were true narrations, "cost us the research of a good twenty years" (*NS*: 338). According to Vico, the original histories were altered and corrupted, "and in their corrupt form finally came down to Homer" (*NS*: 808). "The first sages of the Greek world were the theological poets, who undoubtedly flourished before the heroic poets …" (*NS*: 199); "whence we must deny to Homer any kind of esoteric wisdom" (*NS*: 787), as Plato and others suggested. Jaynes's quest for consciousness also leads him to the discovery of the true Homer. In his quest for the nature of consciousness, he says (Jaynes, 1986a), "I traced it back until it disappeared in some of the works ascribed to Aristotle, and then in some of the Presocratics, and then it vanished in the *Iliad*" (146). He maintains that the gods in the *Iliad* and the *Odyssey* were not mere poetic devices as typically believed. To the contrary, he views the *Iliad* as a literal historical document, saying "We may regard the *Iliad* as standing at the great turning of the times, and a window back into those unsubjective times when every kingdom was a theocracy and every man the slave of voices heard whenever novel situations occurred" (*OC*: 83). Jaynes proposes that the *Iliad* be regarded, "as a psychological document of immense importance" (*OC*: 69).

---

13. From my personal discussions with Jaynes, it is clear that he had no knowledge of Vico before writing his 1976 book. He had been aware of Snell's *The Discovery of the Mind* (which also had many similarities to Vico's interpretation of Homer and the *Iliad*); he says in a footnote, "I was well along into the ideas and material of this chapter before knowing of Snell's parallel work on Homeric language. Our conclusions, however, are quite different" (*OC*: 71). It is not surprising that Jaynes did not know of Snell, let alone Vico: being a psychologist, as well as a solitary scholar, Jaynes was working far outside his field. However, given his early interest in the problem of consciousness and in philosophy and literature, it is not particularly surprising that he went to Greek texts. Vico, too, appears to have had precursors for the idea that Homer was not a single author (see Adams, 1935; Wellek, 1969). In addition to the Greek texts, Jaynes examines the ancient texts of numerous other cultures.

Prior to Vico, the claim that Homer was the author of the *Iliad* and the *Odyssey* had been questioned; however, it was not at that time a generally recognized or accepted notion. In any event, in analyzing these two ancient "poems," Vico states that the facts show clearly "that the Homer of the *Odyssey* was not the same as the Homer of the *Iliad*" (*NS*: 789). He continues to assert that, "The Homer who was the author of the *Iliad* preceded by many centuries the Homer who was the author of the *Odyssey*" (*NS*: 880); that Homer was in fact a collective author, "that the Greek peoples were themselves Homer" (*NS*: 875), that "Homer composed the *Iliad* in his youth, that is, when Greece was young ... he wrote the *Odyssey* in his old age, that is, when the spirits of Greece had been somewhat cooled by reflection" (*NS*: 879). Jaynes, too, concludes from his analysis of these epics documents that "The *Odyssey* followed the *Iliad* by at least a century or more, and like its predecessor, was the work of a succession of *aoidoi* rather than any one man" (*OC*: 272), that Homer was a collective person, not an individual.

Jaynes finds the two documents distinct not only linguistically but psychologically. Like Vico, he philologically analyzes the language of the *Iliad* and the *Odyssey*, and concludes that consciousness begins with the *Odyssey*. Again, like Vico, for Jaynes the important distinction is that Iliadic man was non-conscious; hence the complete absence in the *Iliad* of a word for "mind." Iliadic man "did not have subjectivity as we do; he had no awareness of the world, no internal mind-space to introspect upon" (*OC*: 75). In the *Iliad*, there is no volition, no free will, no soul, no plans, no motivations, few abstract nouns, and no ego; there was no private ambition, no private grudges, no private frustrations.[14] It is significant, too, that in the *Iliad* there are no secrets, falsehood, or deceit. It is generally recognized that to engage in deceit or to have a sense of irony requires reflective consciousness. Both Vico and Jaynes find no evidence of deceit or irony in early man. Vico says, "the first fables could not feign anything

---

14. An interesting example of the implications of a different epistemological approach to phenomena is the following: A bicameral perspective suggests that a concept of an 'other' developed before the concept of an 'I'. Since there is no 'interior self', Jaynes suggests quite a different twist on the old philosophical puzzle of the problem of other minds. "The tradition in philosophy that phrases the problem in the logic of inferring other minds from one's own has it the wrong way around. We may first unconsciously [sic] suppose other consciousness, and then infer our own by generalization" (*OC*: 217). Jaynes's perspective, like Vico's, tends to turn Western philosophy on its head, as great ideas often do.

false" (*NS*: 408). Secrecy and deceit presumably require consciousness. Of the trope irony, Vico says that it "could not have begun until the period of reflection" (ibid.), that is, consciousness. According to Jaynes, "The kind of deceit that is treachery ... is impossible for an animal or for a bicameral man" (*OC*: 219). Jaynes distinguishes between instrumental or short-term deceit and long-term deceit, which he defines as treachery. This distinction is important, since chimpanzees have been observed engaging in the former but not the latter. Long-term deceit requires a time orientation and introspection. Animals and bicameral man, says Jaynes, cannot engage in the latter (*OC*: 219).

In the *Odyssey*, on the other hand, is found the beginnings of consciousness, of the breakdown of the bicameral mind. Indeed, one finds there most of the attributes missing in the *Iliad*. In addition, the gods have become defensive and feeble. "In a word," says Jaynes, "Odysseus of the many devices is the hero of the new mentality of how to get along in a god-weakened world" (*OC*: 273). Consciousness began between 1400 and 600 B.C., Jaynes concludes, with its first explicit dictum to be found in the personage of Solon of Athens, who is attributed to have first advised: "Know thy self." With Solon, says Jaynes: "Suddenly we are in the modern subjective stage" (*OC*: 287). Vico also recognizes the kind of reason that Solon signifies (*NS*: 416). In this stage a poet now has to learn the gift of the Muses. Unlike Vico (*NS*: 414), however, Jaynes sees Solon as a real individual, not as a collective identity.

Vico's First Men, Bicamerality, and Neurology

As I indicted at the outset, empirical evidence from Jaynes's work can be seen as supporting Vico's theory of mind regarding the first of the first men, neurological evidence that Jaynes develops in support of his theory of the bicameral mind. Such neurological data seems to provide an inherent substrate for (a) hallucinated internal voices, and (b) poetic logic. Vico says of the first men: "It was by a *necessity of nature* that the first nations spoke in heroic verse" (*NS*: 833, my italics). "We find that the principle of these origins both of languages and of letters lies in the fact that the early gentile peoples, *by a demonstrated necessity of nature*, were poets" (*NS*: 34, my italics). Presumably, the poetic nature of the first men was genetically based. Because of the rather specialized character of this neurological evidence, I will outline it briefly before further demonstrating its significance to Vichian theory.

The neurological findings on what has come to be more widely known as "split brain" or "right brain/left brain" involves relative differential functions of the brain's two cerebral hemispheres or lobes. This differential functioning is also known as brain lateralization, i.e., each hemisphere tends to be associated with certain functions.[15] A familiar example: in most right-handed people the language function is located in the left temporal lobe in two basic areas, known as Broca's area and Wernicke's area. The corresponding areas on the right lobe are generally known as the "silent" areas. Though the language function is largely in the left lobe, the right hemisphere can understand language. Left-lobe functions have been generally associated with "linguistic/logical/analytical/scientific" processes, the right lobe with "artistic/spatial/emotive" processes, including the more symbolic and figurative aspects of language.[16] Current research suggests that the right hemisphere is more sensitive to the finer nuances of tone, inflection, and rhythm as well as to some aspects of music. It is also involved in the perception of the finer nuances of facial cues.

The two hemispheres are connected by bundles of fibers called commissures, of which the larger is the *corpus callosum*, the smaller, the *anterior commissure*. The anterior commissure connects the temporal lobe areas. It is by means of these commissures that information from each hemisphere is transferred to the other so input from the environment can be coordinated. Various experimental procedures have demonstrated that when the two hemispheres are disconnected either surgically or functionally, one of the hemispheres does not "know" what the other

---

15. Jaynes saw the significance of these neurological findings before this literature became widely cited. As much as these data seem to explain and support his theory of bicamerality, he points out that his theory does not stand or fall on the basis of them; he considers such evidence as a model of bicamerality. He is emphatic on not connecting consciousness directly to the material brain and its structures. It should be pointed out that much of the early and widely cited evidence on hemispheric functions has not stood the test of time. Jaynes's use of this evidence, however, remains basically sound. In one of the few citations to Jaynes's work in the Vichian literature, Gardner (1976) insightfully recognized and briefly noted this literature in relation to Vico.

16. It should be noted that findings cited here are stated as being "associated" with the hemispheres, rather than as a necessary consequence or the sole function of each structure. Research suggests that some functions may be the result of reciprocal inhibition or other effects of one hemisphere on the other and/or may vary according to the task (see Kitterle, 1991). Thus, technically, many functions cannot always be strictly attributed to a given hemisphere.

hemisphere is experiencing; hence the popular term for this neurological state is: "split brain."[17]

In terms of Vico's first men hallucinating voices of the gods, important here is Jaynes citing the classic experiments of the famous neurosurgeon, Wilder Penfield. Penfield electrically stimulated the hemispheres of patients who were kept awake during surgery (the brain does not feel pain). What he found was that stimulation of the right lobe "silent" areas often produced auditory hallucinations. These hallucinations tended to be voices, admonitory voices, sometimes of people unknown, sometimes of people known to the patients; and they were experienced as coming from various locations. Jaynes suggests that the silent areas on the right cerebral lobe had a function at an earlier stage in man that is now only vestigial.

In early man, says Jaynes, language evolved in only one hemisphere, "in order to leave the other free for language of the gods" (*OC*: 104). Jaynes concludes: "The gods were organizations of the central nervous system and can be regarded as personae in the sense of poignant consistencies through time ... (*OC*: 74). The hallucinated voices, Jaynes suggests, are transmitted via the anterior commissure, where the right lobe silent areas, under conditions of stress and agitation, organized and coded this sense data into "voices" which were then "heard" over the anterior commissure by the left or dominant linguistic hemisphere. "Here then," suggests Jaynes, "is the tiny bridge across which came the directions which built our civilization and founded the world's religions, where gods spoke to men and were obeyed because they were [at that time] human volition" (*OC*: 104–5).[18]

In the beginning, Vico's first men were not conscious in the modern sense. "*Men at first feel without perceiving*, then they perceive with

---

17. See Jaynes's Ch. 5 for his more detailed, but quite understandable, neurological analysis. See also Springer and Deutsch (1981) for a readable review of brain lateralization research. See also Gazzaniga, 1978, 1983, 1985, 1988; Kimura, 1967; Sperry, 1984. For more specialized neurophilosophical analysis of the brain and lateralization see Churchland, 1986; Kitterle, 1991.

18. It is instructive to note that the findings from the "split brain" research can be seen as supporting Vico on the issue of the voices of the gods commanding behavior and Jaynes's further hypothesis that these voices were man's *volition*. In Gazzaniga's (1988) research, he found that commands to the right hemisphere can elicit behaviors without left hemisphere awareness, leaving the subject not conscious of why they engaged in the behavior. By way of instantiation, Gazzaniga gives the case of a patient who, when the command "walk" was given to the right hemisphere, began to walk out of the testing area. When asked why the subject was leaving, the left hemisphere had to come up with a plausible reason. This kind of "non-volitional" (from a left hemisphere perspective) behavior is identical to subjects' explanations of behavior resulting from a post-hypnotic suggestion.

a troubled and agitated spirit, finally they reflect with a clear mind" (*NS*: 218, my italics). Yet presumably they were able to think and solve problems. Jaynes devotes considerable space in the first chapters of his book clarifying and demonstrating what consciousness is not; one of the things it is *not*, he says, is necessary for thinking. "One does one's thinking," he says, "before one knows what one is to think about ... thinking, then, is not consciousness" (*OC*: 39). For academic psychology the concept of "unconscious" processes has a long, controversial past, largely beginning with Freud. However, because of considerable experimental research on "non-consciousness" or parallel information processing, the idea of what are called higher order mental processes occurring on non-conscious levels has recently become generally accepted. More recently, some researchers are speculating that many non-conscious operations can be explained in terms of right hemisphere associated functions, and that Freud's concept of the unconscious may be equated with the right hemipshere.[19]

A great deal of the "split brain" literature demonstrates that the hemispheres may function autonomously, with each hemisphere unaware of the experience of the other. Thus, it appears that it may not at all be unreasonable to suggest, as do Vico and Jaynes, that in the early history of the species humans reasoned, voiced poetry,[20] judged, and solved problems — but were not conscious of it.

19. Galin, 1974. For selected literature on non-conscious processing, much of it experimentally generated, see Bowers and Meichenbaum, 1984; Dixon, 1981; Hilgard, 1977; Marcel, 1983a, 1983b, 1988; Piaget, 1973.
20. Vico (*NS*: 461, 288, 230) and Jaynes (*OC*: 364) note that early speech, that is, poetry, was in fact melodious singing, and both observed similar pathologies of language of brain-impaired individuals to the normal functioning of early man (*OC*: 365–68) and utilize such instances as support of their theories. In terms of hemispheric laterality, in the open brain stimulation procedure of Wilder Penfield, patients occasionally heard singing and music. It is significant to note that much of the musical function appears to be associated with right cerebral hemisphere functions; for example, as Jaynes explains, when sodium amytal is injected through the left carotid artery, inactivating the left hemisphere, where the language function is largely found, the person can no longer speak but can still sing. Jaynes suggests that during the breakdown of the bicameral mind singing served to stimulate those parts of the right hemisphere from which the divine auditory hallucinations originated, and that later the use of musical instruments and chanting served the same function. For a clear exposition of Vico in relation to the traditional singing to speaking to writing hypothesis, see Trabant (1991).

The Bicameral Mind, Gender, and Neurology

It is important in comparing Vico and Jaynes to make inquiry into what their theories maintain regarding gender. In one of the few references to gender in the English-language literature on Vico, Verene (1976b) suggests in a footnote that Vico rather "unflatteringly connects poetic language with the mentality of women" (303). The passage from Vico to which Verene refers deals with language: "Digressions were born of the grossness of the heroic minds, unable to confine themselves to those essential features of things that were to the purpose in hand, as we see to be naturally the case with the feeble-minded and above all with women" (*NS*: 457). In another passage, Vico says that the Homeric heroes "are like boys in the frivolity of their minds, like women in the vigor of their imaginations" (*NS*: 829), and elsewhere Corsano (1969) cites a passage from Vico's inaugural address: "Nothing is as antithetical to reason as the imaginative faculty. We can observe this antithesis in women. Since they are endowed with a strong imagination, reason, in them, is less active; consequently, they are more affected by potent and forceful passions than men" (427). On first glance, these passages certainly seem disparaging to women. What are scholars to make of Vico's *apparent* — to use today's phrase — "sexist" view of women?

One obvious approach to explain Vico's views is to lay it to a stereotypic cultural perception of women during this time, a kind of historicist explanation, as it were. But perhaps a more valid explanation lies in the neurological and lateralization research. Feminist ideology notwithstanding, this research tends to find consistent gender differences between male and female brain function, though as Gardner (1976) points out, in young children prior to the fourth through the eighth year of development, this asymmetry in lateralization is not prominent. It should therefore be stressed that when differences are found they tend to be of small magnitude.[21]

In any event, one of the basic gender differences appears to be that females are more bilateralized than males, that is, many functions distributed to both hemispheres. Since there is little gender disparity in childhood, much of the difference may be due to differential environmental

---

21. See Wood, Flowers, and Naylor, 1991.

pressures and socialization processes. There is evidence, though scant, that certain sections of the *corpus callosum* are larger in females than in males.[22] In other words, females may have more communication between the hemispheres and can apparently utilize both hemispheres for a given function; i.e., they are not as localized in their hemispheric functioning as males (this is not to say there are not some women whose brains are lateralized "like men" and vice-versa).

Thus it may not be coincidental that females may use their sensory imagination more than males, or at least have more potential access to it (as Vico suggests) and therefore be more responsive and open to affective and right-hemisphere associated stimuli. For example, there is evidence suggesting that females tend to be more perceptive of facial and linguistic cues. It is these cues that transmit much of the emotional content of speech. The perception of such cues appear to be largely right-hemisphere associated. It is interesting to note here that Vico mentions the first men as being sensitive to facial cues. He says that the first men "regarded every change to facial expression as a new face" (*NS*: 700). These lateralization gender differences are not lost on Jaynes. He clearly suggests that these neurological differences may be behind the historical fact that females constituted the majority of oracles, i.e., those who continued to hear the voices of the gods during the breakdown of the bicameral mind. Jaynes says that among the oracles "were those few but unknown number of weird and wonderful women known as the Sybils" (*OC*: 331). "Indeed, the majority of oracles and Sibyls at least in European cultures were women" (*OC*: 344).

Even today there are vestiges of the bicameral mind, and, it might be added, vestiges of the mentality of Vico's first men. As Jaynes says, "There is no reason not to think that the residuals of these different functions at least are present in the brain organization of contemporary man" (*OC*: 117). Thus modern man is still in the throes of the breakdown of the bicameral mind.

The bicameral mind evolved as a final stage in the evolution of language, and in this development in about 10,000 B.C. "lies the origin of civilization" (*OC*: 126). The voices of the gods began to end in about 2500 B.C. With the invention of writing and increased population

---

22. Springer and Deutsch, 1981; see esp. Waber, 1976, Witelson, 1976.

pressures the bicameral mind was weakened, and in this breakdown lies the origin of consciousness. The bicameral mind was also weakened by the increased complexity of cultures and commerce among them. Corresponding to this breakdown, in numerous texts and ancient tablets, including both testaments of the Bible, Jaynes finds repeated references to "being forsaken by one's gods." Jaynes quotes one example: "My god has forsaken me and disappeared, my goddess has failed me and keeps at a distance. The good angel who walked beside me has departed" (*OC*: 225). Jaynes points to the "hallucinogenic statuary that are mentioned throughout the Old Testament" (*OC*: 308) as vestiges of the bicameral period. For bicameral man, "The statue was not *of* a god ... but the god himself" (*OC*: 178). Vico says that the first men, like children, would "take inanimate things ... and talk to them as though they were living persons (*NS*: 375). For Jaynes, the Old Testament is a record of the "birth pangs" of a new consciousness.

With this breakdown and the loss of authorial voices to guide men, there developed a host of oracles and divinatory personages and phenomenon. The oracles in the first century B.C. have been estimated as at least ten in number around the Mediterranean world. According to Vico, "Every gentile nation had its own Sybil ... Sybils and oracles are the *most ancient institutions* of the gentile world" (*NS*: 381, my italics). Jaynes says it is only with the breakdown of the voices of the gods that religious prayer originated. "In the classical bicameral mind ... before its weakening ... I suggest there was no hesitancy in the hallucinated voices [of the gods] and no occasion for prayer" (*OC*: 228). "Prayers as the central important act of divine worship only became prominent after the gods are no longer speaking to man" (*OC*: 229). For Vico the first orations of the first men were prayers (*NS*: 955), and they were of a particular rhetorical nature. "The family fathers complained to the gods of the wrongs done to them ... and called the gods to bear witness to the justice of their causes" (ibid.).[23]

---

23. From a rhetorical perspective based on Vico's description of the first prayers, the origin of prayer can be viewed as being born in what Gresson (1977), in another context, has called the "rhetoric of protest." In the breakdown of the bicameral mind and the beginnings of reflection and their felt loss of communication with their gods, of their feeling abandoned by them, the first men can be said to have experienced the first sense of betrayal. (For a rhetorical analysis of the experience of betrayal in human affairs, see Gresson, 1982.)

What is more, the form of prayer is typically silent or "mute;" it is closer to internal speech and thus it could be advanced that silent prayer is a vestige of the hallucinated internal voices of the gods. In Vico there is the hint that this may be the case. In discussing speech being born in mute times, he claims "it is an eternal property of religions that they attach more importance to *meditation* than to speech" (*NS*: 401, my italics), that is, more oriented to the internal, mental, or imagined voice. From this perspective, then, meditative prayer is an attempt to re-experience the communion, to make contact with one's gods. For Jaynes, the breakdown of the bicameral mind is the beginning of the Paradise lost, the Fall from the Garden of Eden.[24]

Other major phenomena, along with various minor ones such as spiritual and demonic "possession," Jaynes sees as vestiges of bicameral voices: schizophrenia, hypnosis, and [visitation] dreaming. It is well known that many schizophrenics hallucinate voices. What is perhaps less well known is that more often than not these voices are admonitory; and they come from external locations, or from inside the person's head, or on occasion they seem to come from the schizophrenic's own mouth. Reviewing the literature, Jaynes marshals significant evidence that seems to support his thesis. For example, brain-wave recordings of schizophrenics compared to normal people show pronounced right-hemisphere activity. Jaynes also notes that a positron tomography study of auditorially hallucinating schizophrenics found increased glucose uptake in the right hemisphere during these episodes. More important perhaps is evidence from an autopsy of a small number of long-term schizophrenics indicating that their *corpus callosum* was significantly thicker than normals, suggesting perhaps more access to right-hemisphere associated phenomena.[25]

Conflict and stress seem to bring on hallucinations in many schizophrenics. As quoted above, Vico maintained that "it was fear which

---

24. Jaynes suggests that contributing to this breakdown was some sort of catastrophic geological event which occurred around 2100 B.C. Referring to ancient texts that relate a time when the Nile became dry and the sun was hidden (*OC*: 196), suggesting that this may have been due to a series of volcanic eruptions on the island of Thera, that geologists have estimated may have been 350 times more powerful than a hydrogen bomb explosion. Elsewhere (Jaynes, 1986c) he speculates that since about half of the world's population was killed during the bicameral period, the bicameral population may have been largely the victim of such circumstances. While this would have biogenetic implications, he more strongly believes in learning as the predominant mechanism of consciousness.
25. Beginning in 1999, numerous neuroimaging studies have demonstrated a right/left temporal lobe interaction during auditory hallucinations, confirming Jaynes's neurological model. — *Ed.*

created gods in the world; not fear awakened in men by other men, but fear awakened in men by themselves" (*NS*: 332). Jaynes suggests: "What we call schizophrenia ... began in human history as a relationship to the divine, and only around 400 B.C., came to be regarded as the incapacitating illness we know today" (*OC*: 407) "[that] before the second millennium B.C., everyone was schizophrenic" (*OC*: 405). By implication of this comparison, then, the first men can be characterized as schizophrenic-like.

Many schizophrenics are capable of great endurance and can often endure what for normals would be great pain. It is interesting in this regard to note that Jaynes (1985) suggests that much of the experience of pain is due to consciousness; that bicameral man did not experience pain as we know it. In what is perhaps the only time in the *New Science* that Vico mentions pain it is in relation to childbirth during the Heroic age, not the age of first men (*NS*: 994). Jaynes distinguishes between *sensory* and *conscious* pain. Jaynes argues that in languages and texts during the bicameral period there was no word for pain or hurt. In the early part of the *Iliad*, he says, despite the gory descriptions of bloody wounds and disembowelments, there is no mention of discomfort. In contrast, Jaynes points to Plato's *Philebus*, dating from about 350 B.C., where Plato discusses pain in the modern sense.[26]

In the phenomena known as hypnosis, the cognitive vestiges of the first men can be seen. In the Western world the hypnotic induction of a trance state has classically been induced by the voice commands of a hypnotist. The subject is told, "listen only to my voice." If trance is achieved, the subject then "obeys" the voice as if only the voice exists; for one of the defining characteristics of the trance state is to narrow consciousness, to render the subject unreflective. Research suggests that the hypnotic capacity is enhanced by the subject's capacity for imagination and for trusting the hypnotist. For the deep-trance subject, hearing the voice command and carrying out the command are nearly identical, the voice becomes the impetus for action, for what is commonly

---

26. Jaynes's position of sensory pain can be seen to be supported by Ernest Hilgard's Stanford University Hypnosis Laboratory research on pain (Hilgard and Hilgard, 1975), which found that pain was composed of two parts: sensory and suffering. Under hypnosis the concious "suffering" aspect was often eliminated or reduced, with the sensory pain still evident. The "pure" sensory experience of pain did not seem to bother subjects. Similar findings have been noted with subjects with brain implants for the control of pain.

called hypnotic suggestion. This automatic response derives from what Jaynes calls a "cognitive imperative," that is, from a time when the voice of the gods commanded and from when one's psychological identity was a community one, not individual. In Vichian terms, like the first men, hypnotic subjects "no sooner imagine than they believe" (*NS*: 376).

Jaynes believes that the phenomenon of responding to a commanding voice is vestigial, harking back to early man's hearing the authorial voices of the gods, the first cognitive imperative.[27] According to Vico: "There were three kinds of authority. The first divine ... the second heroic ... the third is human ... based on the trust placed in persons of experience" (*NS*: 942). Research on hypnotic induction procedures has demonstrated that the ability to induce compliance is related to the trust of the subject and the authority and status of the hypnotist. For example, a physician will have better success than a technician, even better if she or he wears a white lab coat; other hypnotists will have better success if they are wearing a tie. Finally, according to brain wave recordings, hypnosis appears to be associated with right hemisphere activity.

Vico does not mention dreaming in the *New Science*, nor apparently anywhere else in relation to the three ages of man. (If Vico's first men did "dream," as surely they did, what might their dreaming process have been?) Jaynes (1986a) examines dreaming in bicameral man: bicameral man did not "dream" in the modern sense. In fact, he says, [conscious] dreaming, like consciousness, begins only in the first millennium B.C. He notes that in the hieroglyphic record there are accounts of dreams dating back as far as 2650 B.C., but they are bicameral dreams.

Jaynes notes there are four dreams in the *Iliad*, though they are not labeled "dreams" since there is no word for dreaming in the *Iliad*. There are well-known dreams mentioned in the Old Testament, also bicameral, according to Jaynes. A bicameral dream is recognized by two basic characteristics: first, the content of the dream occurs exactly where the dreamer is — sleeping. The dream is not translocative, that is, it does not occur somewhere else. Second, the dreamer is doing exactly what he is

---

27. The laboratory research on hypnosis suggests that in the hypnotic "state," consciousness and context are narrowed so that the individual accepts induced realities uncritically, as though they were real. Given the restricted consciousness of Vico's first men, it is not unreasonable to suggest that what we call "hypnosis" is a vestige of the early state of human consciousness.

doing — sleeping; it is not vicarial, that is, the dream is not an imagined participation in another experience.

It is only after the *Iliad* that dreams become translocative and vicarial. Jaynes (1986a) regards this historical change in dreaming, "as one of the greatest confirmations ... of the central hypothesis of the origin of consciousness and the breakdown of the bicameral mind" (147). He further suggests there remains vestiges of the bicameral dreams in the modern age, noting Descartes' famous dream that had profound effects on his life.[28]

As noted earlier, there are many differences between Vico and Jaynes that cannot be developed here. The following, however, seems noteworthy. In Vico's "anthropological" description of the first men, he is systematic throughout his *New Science* in imagining the early sexual appetites, not only of the first males but also of the first females. In fact, it is basically only in this context that he describes the first females. The first men, he says, "must be supposed to have gone off into bestial wandering ... [in] the great forests of the earth ... pursuing the shy and indocile women" (*NS*: 301); they were, "nefarious in their frequent intercourse with their own mothers and daughters" (*NS*: 1099), just as there existed a "nefarious promiscuity of women" (*NS*: 985). The first men, and by implication, the first women, were under "the goading stimuli of bestial lust (which must ... have been extremely violent in such men) ... which took the form of forcibly seizing their women, who were naturally shy and unruly, dragging them into their caves, and, in order to have intercourse with them, keeping them there as perpetual lifelong companions" (*NS*: 1098). As the first stage of the first men developed, Vico says the first men "must have learned to hold in check the impulse of the *bodily* motion of lust" (*NS*: 1098, my italics). Adams (1935) remarked of his description of the

---

28. Jaynes had originally written two chapters on dreaming for *Origin*, but his publisher suggested deleting them because of the size of the manuscript. It should be noted that like hypnosis the study of dreams has not until recently been accepted in academic psychology (see Haskell, 1986). For research that could be interpreted to support Jaynes on dreaming, and, by implication, the dreaming of Vico's first men, the reader is particularly referred to the laboratory research on children's dreams (as well as his view on the cognitive importance of sleep mentation data); from a Vichian perspective, it would be in the dreams of children that we may see the vestiges of the mentality of the first men. The psychological literature on dreaming, imagination, imagery, and memory are significant areas that I think could be profitably applied to Vico's concept of imagination and Verene's concept of *fantasia* in relation to Vico.

state of existence of these first men that "Vico must have lived intensely in his primeval forest and its clearings, his theories as to what happened there are so distinct and elaborate" (187). Vico speaks of bestial violence during the times of the first men.

Jaynes, however, suggests that the bicameral period was a time of peaceful harmony (OC: 205). It was only in the breakdown of the bicameral mind that cruelty came into being. From his analysis of the evidence, he says that the "practice of cruelty as an attempt to rule by fear, is, I suggest, at the brink of subjective consciousness" (OC: 214). This and other differences between Vico and Jaynes can possibly be the consequences of either Vico's poetic anthropology regarding primitive man's original social state, or the consequences of Vico's descriptions being those during the initial breakdown of the bicameral mind (see n. 29, below).

It is uncertain upon what Vico founded these "imaginative" anthropological descriptions, but Jaynes is of a different opinion as to the sexuality of these bicameral or Vichian first men and women. In the Afterword of the second edition (1990) of *Origin*, Jaynes speculates that the sexuality of bicameral humans was not highly charged; only after the breakdown of the bicameral mind was sexuality a potent force. As evidence he presents two lines of research, citing, first, research on the anthropoid apes. In contrast to other primates, mating behavior of the anthropoid apes in their natural habitat appears to be so rare as to have baffled the early ethologists. Further, mating behavior is complex; it is not merely a physical or bodily phenomenon, nor does it build up like hunger or thirst; it is an act of imagination. Now when "human beings," says Jaynes, become "conscious about their mating behavior, can reminisce about it in the past and imagine it in the future, we are in a very different world, indeed, one that seems more familiar to us" (OC: 466). Vico can be read as saying the same thing; in describing the sexuality of the first men Vico uses the phrase: "the impulse of the *bodily motion* of lust" (NS: 1098, my italics), implying a kind of Jaynesian bicameral sexuality not enhanced by consciousness.

The second line of research supporting Jaynes's claim is as follows. Scholars of ancient history would agree, says Jaynes, that the murals and sculptures during what he calls the bicameral age, that is, before 1000 B.C., are chaste. Though there are exceptions, depictions with sexual references prior to this time are nearly non-existent. After 1000 B.C., there seems to be a veritable explosion of visual depictions of sexuality: ithyphallic satyrs, large stone phalli, naked female dancers, and later, brothels, apparently instituted by Solon of Athens in the fifth century B.C. Such rampant sexuality had to be controlled. According to Vico it was "frightful superstition" (ibid.) and fear of the gods that lead to control. Jaynes speculates that one way was to separate the sexes socially, which has been observed in many preliterate societies. Since males have more visible erectile tissue than females, something had to be done to inhibit the stimulation of sexual imagination (fantasy). Jaynes cites the example of the orthodox Muslim societies in which to expose female ankles or hair is a punishable offence.[29]

The Question of Religion

There is no recourse but to end this paper not only where it began, but upon that which much of its content is founded: the question of religion: more specifically, on the parallels between Vico and Jaynes on this issue. Vico clearly states, "the world of peoples began everywhere with religion. This will be the first of the three principles of this Science" (NS: 176);[30] and we find Jaynes suggesting — perhaps the first to suggest — that "The brain is organized in a religious fashion. Our mentalities have come out of a divine kind of mind."[31]

On one level Vico and Jaynes agree on the origin of religion, yet on another level there is certain divergence: the Catholic Christian religion. Without doubt, Vico believed in the reality of a true Christian God and a Providential history. According to Bergin and Fisch's invaluable introduction to the *New Science*, in order for Vico to maintain the belief in an

---

29. It is interesting to note that both Vico and Jaynes seem to assume a hyper-sexuality on the part of males, not females. Is this an example of Vico's "conceit of scholars," or more specifically, the conceit of male scholars? To the contrary, Mary Jane Sherfey (1996), a physician, has suggested that in early history the female sexual appetite was stronger than the male and therefore had to be controlled by the male in order to create and maintain social order.

30. Just as Vico suggests that the origin of nations began in multiple places, Jaynes speculates there were probably many bicameral theocracies spread throughout the world, rising up and then breaking down. He hints there may have been other bands of primate-like creatures who were neither bicameral or conscious. He does not imply that all humans at that time exhibited such behavior; rather he intends his theory to describe a norm (OC: 222). Similarly, Vico suggests that the *New Science* may not apply exactly to all nations, as it is only "perfect in its idea" (NS: 1096) and in principle.

31. In Rhodes, 1978 p. 78.

eternal one God, he had to separate the early Hebrew religion from that of other peoples in developing his theory (*NS*: B4). Only the Hebrews did not evolve through the three states of mental development. In contrast, Jaynes's theory of consciousness applies to all human kind. Moreover, in a reversal to Vico's distinction between the Hebrew and Christian peoples and all other peoples (*NS*: 167), Jaynes attributes Judaism with bicamerality and the movement to Christianity with consciousness.

In viewing the Christian Bible as a bicameral document, Jaynes says, "A full discussion here would specify how the attempted reformation of Judaism by Jesus can be considered as a new religion of conscious men rather than bicameral men" (*OC*: 318). He views the Old Testament as bicameral and the New Testament as reflecting the transition to conscious man. He compares the Book of Amos, dating from the eighth century B.C., with Ecclesiastes, dating from the second century B.C. "Amos is almost pure bicameral speech ... in Amos there are no words for mind or think or feel ..." whereas "Ecclesiastes is the opposite on all these points" (*OC*: 296). Jaynes says that the constant nostalgia and anguish found in biblical documents is in response to "the loss of bicamerality. ... This is what religion is" (*OC*: 297). With loss of the bicameral voices of the gods, in a sense: "We have become our own gods" (*OC*: 79). But this does not imply a Hegelian end of history. This narration of the first men and of the bicameral mind continues. We are "still in the arduous process of adjusting to our new mentality of consciousness" (Jaynes, 1986a, p. 139). In Vichian terms history recycles,[32] in Jaynesian terms evolution continues.[33]

References

Adams, Henry, P. 1935. *The Life and Writings of Giambattista Vico*. New York: Russell and Russell.
Berlin, Isaiah. 1976. "Vico and the Ideal of the Enlightenment." *Social Research*, 43: 640–53.
Battistini, Andrea. 1981. "Contemporary Trends in Vichian Studies." In G. Tagliacozzo (ed.), *Vico: Past and Present*. Atlantic Highlands, NJ: Humanities Press.

---

32. For a discussion of the idea of progress, historical cycles, and of providence in Vico's *New Science* by scholars within and outside the Vichian literature, see Berlin (1976), and Van Doren (1967), respectively.

33. This paper has outlined what I consider to be the main correspondences between Vico and Jaynes, along with only a few of the major differences. A more extended analysis between the two men remains to be done. There are, for example, correspondences and differences in the areas of the origins of law, morality, and economics, as well as in a time line for various developments.

Bowers, Kenneth S. and Donald Meichenbaum (eds.). 1984. *The Unconscious Reconsidered.* New York: Wiley-Interscience.

Churchland, Patricia A. 1986. *Neuro-Philosophy: Toward a Unified Science of the Mind/Brain.* Cambridge, MA: MIT Press.

Corsano, Antonia. 1969. "Vico and Mathematics." In G. Tagliacozzo and H.V. White (eds.), *Giambattista Vico: An International Symposium.* Baltimore: Johns Hopkins University Press.

Cotroneo, Girolamo. 1969. "A Renaissance Source of the Scienza nuova: Jean Bodin's Methodus." In G. Tagliacozzo and H.V. White (eds.), *Giambattista Vico: An International Symposium.* Baltimore: Johns Hopkins University Press.

Danesi, Marcel. 1986. "Language and the Origin of the Human Imagination: A Vichian Perspective." *New Vico Studies,* 4: 45–56.

_____ 1987. "A Vichian Footnote to Nietzsche's Views on the Cognitive Primacy of Metaphor: An Addendum to Schrift." *New Vico Studies,* 5: 157–64.

_____ 1989. "Vico and Chomsky: On the Nature of Creativity in Language." *New Vico Studies,* 7: 28–42.

Dixon, Norman F. 1981. *Pre-Conscious Processing.* New York: Wiley.

Faucci, Dario. 1969. "Vico and Grotius: Jurisconsults of Mankind." In G. Tagliacozzo and H.V. White (eds.) *Giambattista Vico: An International Symposium.* Baltimore: Johns Hopkins University Press.

Foulkes, David. 1985. *Dreaming: A Cognitive-Psychological Approach.* New York: Lawrence Erlbaum.

Galin, David. 1974. "Implications for Psychiatry of Left and Right Cerebral Specialization." *Archives of General Psychiatry,* 31: 572–83.

Gardner, Howard. 1976. "Vico's Theories of Knowledge in the Light of Contemporary Social Science." In G. Tagliacozzo and D.P. Verene (eds.), *Giambattista Vico's Science of Humanity.* Baltimore: Johns Hopkins University Press.

Gazzaniga, Michael S. 1985. *The Social Brain.* New York: Basic Books.

_____, Michael S. 1983. "Right Hemisphere Language Following Brain Bisection." *American Psychologist: A 20-Year Perspective,* 38: 525–37.

_____, Michael S. 1988. "Brain Modularity: Towards a Philosophy of Conscious Experience." In Anthony J. Marcel and Edoardo Bisiach (eds.), *Consciousness in Contemporary Science.* Oxford: Clarendon.

Gazzaniga, Michael S. and Joseph E. LeDoux. 1978. *The Integrated Mind.* New York: Plenum.

Gresson, Aaron. 1977. "Minority Epistemology and the Rhetoric of Creation." *Philosophy and Rhetoric,* 10: 244–62.

Gresson, Aaron. 1982. *The Dialectics of Betrayal: Sacrifice, Violation and the Oppressed.* Norwood, NJ: Ablex.

Haskell, Robert E. 1978. "Vichian Tropological Transformation: An Empirical Confirmation." Paper presented at the Vico/Venezia Conference, Venice, Italy (August 1978).

_____. 1985. "Thought-Things: Lévi-Strauss and the Modern Mind." *Semiotica: Journal of the International Association of Semiotics,* 55: 1–17.

_____ 1986. "Cognitive Psychology and Dream Research: Historical, Conceptual, and Epistemological Considerations." In R.E. Haskell (ed.), *Cognition and Dream Research* (also published as a special issue of *Journal of Mind and Behavior*). New York: Institution of Mind and Behavior.

_____ 1987. (ed.). *Cognition and Symbolic Structures: The Psychology of Metaphoric Transformation.* Norwood, NJ: Ablex.

_____ 1987. "Cognitive Psychology and the Problems of Symbolic Cognition." In R.E. Haskell (ed.), *Cognition and Symbolic Structures: The Psychology of Metaphoric Transformations.* Norwood, NJ: Ablex.

_____ 1987. "Giambattista Vico and the Discovery of Metaphoric Cognition." In R.E. Haskell (ed.), *Cognition and Symbolic Structures: The Psychology of Metaphoric Transformation.* Norwood, NJ: Ablex.

_____ 1989. "Analogical Transforms: A Cognitive Theory of Origin and Development of Equivalence Transformation, Parts I & II." *Metaphor and Symbolic Activity,* 4: 247–77.

_____ 1991. "An Analogical Methodology for the Analysis and Validation of Anomalous Cognitive and Linguistic Operations in Small Group (Fantasy Theme) Reports." *Small Group Research, An International Journal of Theory, Investigation, and Application*, 22: 443–74.

Hilgard, Ernest R. 1977. *Divided Consciousness: Multiple Controls in Human Thought and Action*. New York: Wiley Interscience.

Hilgard, Ernest R. and Josephine Hilgard. 1977. *Hypnosis in the Relief of Pain*. Los Altos, CA: William Kaufmann.

Honeck, Richard P. and Robert R. Hoffman (eds.). 1980. *Cognition and Figuration Language*. Hillsdale, NJ: Lawrence Erlbaum.

Jaynes, Julian. 1976. *The Origin of Consciousness in the Breakdown of the Bicameral Mind*. Boston: Houghton-Mifflin.

_____ 1976b. "The Evolution of Language in the Late Pleistocene." *Annals of the New York Academy of Sciences*, 280: 312–25. Reprinted in M. Kuijsten (ed.), *The Julian Jaynes Collection* (Henderson, NV: Julian Jaynes Society, 2012).

_____ 1982. "A Two-Tiered Theory of Emotions: Affect and Feeling." *Behavioral and Brain Sciences*, 3: 434–35. Reprinted in M. Kuijsten (ed.), *The Julian Jaynes Collection* (Henderson, NV: Julian Jaynes Society, 2012).

_____ 1985. "Sensory Pain and Conscious Pain." *Behavioral and Brain Sciences*, 8: 61–63. Reprinted in M. Kuijsten (ed.), *The Julian Jaynes Collection* (Henderson, NV: Julian Jaynes Society, 2012).

_____ 1986a. "Consciousness and the Voices of the Mind." *Canadian Psychology*, 27: 128–48. Reprinted in M. Kuijsten (ed.), *The Julian Jaynes Collection* (Henderson, NV: Julian Jaynes Society, 2012).

_____ 1986b. "McMaster-Bauer Symposium on Consciousness: Panel Discussion and Response." *Canadian Psychology*, 27.

_____ 1986c. "Hearing Voices and the Bicameral Mind." *Behavioral and Brain Sciences*, 9: 526–27. Reprinted in M. Kuijsten (ed.), *The Julian Jaynes Collection* (Henderson, NV: Julian Jaynes Society, 2012).

_____ 1990. "Verbal Hallucinations and Pre-Conscious Mentality." In M. Spitzer and B.A. Maher (eds.), *Philosophy and Psychopathology*. New York: Springer. Reprinted in M. Kuijsten (ed.), *Reflections on the Dawn of Consciousness* (Henderson, NV: Julian Jaynes Society, 2006).

Kiernan, Suzanne. 1986. "J.F. Lyotard's *The Postmodern Condition* and G.B. Vico's *De nostri temporis studiorum ratione*." *New Vico Studies*, 4: 101–12.

Kimura, Doreen. 1967. "Functional Asymmetry of the Brain in Dichotic Listening." *Cortex*, 3: 163–78.

Kitterle, Frederick L. (ed.). 1991. *Cerebral Laterality: Theory and Research*. Hillsdale, NJ: Lawrence Erlbaum.

Lakoff, George and Mark Johnson. 1980. *Metaphors We Live By*. Chicago: University of Chicago Press.

Lilla, Mark. 1986. "Backing into Vico: Recent Trends in American Philosophy." *New Vico Studies*, 4: 89–100.

Marcel, Anthony J. 1983a. "Conscious and Unconscious Perception: Experiments in Visual Masking and Word Recognition." *Cognitive Psychology*, 15: 197–237.

_____ 1983b. "Conscious and Unconscious Perception: An Approach to the Relations between Phenomenal Experience and Perceptual Processes." *Cognitive Psychology*, 15: 238–300.

Marcel, Anthony J. and Edoardo Bisiach (eds.). 1988. *Consciousness in Contemporary Science*. Oxford: Clarendon.

Mora, George. 1976a. "Vico, Piaget, and Genetic Epistemology." In G. Tagliacozzo and D.P. Verene (eds.), *Vico's Science of Humanity*. Baltimore: Johns Hopkins University Press.

Mora, George. 1976b. "Vico and Piaget: Parallels and Differences." *Social Research*, 43: 698–712.

Neisser, Ulric. 1967. *Cognitive Psychology*. New York: Appleton-Century-Crofts.

Neisser, Ulric (ed.). 1982. *Memory Observed: Remembering in Natural Contexts*. San Francisco: W. H. Freeman.

Piaget, Jean. 1973. "The Affective and the Cognitive Unconscious." *Journal of the American Psychoanalytic Association*, 21: 249–61.

Rhodes, Richard. 1978. "Alone in the Country of the Mind: When Did Humans Begin Thinking?" *Quest* (Jan./Feb.): 249–61.

Richards, Ivor A. 1936. *The Philosophy of Rhetoric*. London: Oxford University Press.

Sherfey, Mary Jane. 1966. "A Theory of Female Sexuality." In R. Morgan (ed.) *Sisterhood Is Powerful: An Anthology of Writings from the Women's Liberation Movement*. New York: Vintage Books

Singer, Jerome L. 1973. *The Child's World of Make-Believe*. New York: Academic Press.

———. 1976. "Vico's Insight and the Scientific Study of Consciousness." *Social Research*, 43: 713–26.

Snell, Bruno. 1973. *The Discovery of the Mind*. New York: Academic Press.

Sperry, Roger W. 1984. "Consciousness, Personal Identity, and the Divided Brain," *Psychologia* 22: 661–73.

Springer, Sally and George Deutsch. 1981. *Left Brain, Right Brain*. San Francisco: W.H. Freeman.

Stove, David C. 1989. "The Oracles and Their Cessation: A Tribute to Julian Jaynes." *Encounter* 72: 30–38. Reprinted in M. Kuijsten (ed.), *Reflections on the Dawn of Consciousness* (Henderson, NV: Julian Jaynes Society, 2006).

Tagliacozzo, Giorgio. 1976. "Introductory Remarks." *Social Research*, 43: 391–98.

Trabant, Jürgen. 1991. "Parlare cantando: Language Singing in Vico and Herder." *New Vico Studies*, 9: 1–16.

Van Doren, Charles. 1967. *The Ideas of Progress*. New York: Praeger.

Verene, Donald Phillip. 1976a. "Vico's Philosophy of Imagination." *Social Research*, 43: 410–33.

———. 1976b. "Vico's Science of Imaginative Universals and the Philosophy of Symbolic Forms." In G. Tagliacozzo and D.P. Verene (eds.), *Vico's Science of Humanity*. Baltimore: Johns Hopkins University Press.

———. 1981. *Vico's Science of Imagination*. Ithaca, NY: Cornell University Press.

Vico, Giambattista. 1970. *The New Science of Giambattista Vico*, trans. T.G. Bergin and M.H. Fisch. Ithaca, NY: Cornell University Press.

Vosniadou, Stella and Andrew Ortony (eds.). 1989. *Similarity and Analogical Reasoning*. New York: Cambridge University Press.

Waber, Deborah. 1976. "Sex Differences in Cognition: A Function of Maturation Rate?" *Science*, 192: 572–73.

Wellek, René. 1969. "The Supposed Influence of Vico on England and Scotland in the Eighteenth Century." In G. Tagliacozzo and H.V. White (eds.), *Giambattista Vico: An International Symposium*. Baltimore: Johns Hopkins University Press,.

Werner, Heinz and Bernard Kaplan. 1963. *Symbol Function: An Organismic Developmental Approach to Language and the Expression of Thought*. New York: Wiley.

White, Hayden. 1976. "The Tropics of History: The Deep Structure of the New Science." In G. Tagliacozzo and D.P. Verene (eds.), *Vico's Science of Humanity*. Baltimore: Johns Hopkins University Press.

Witelson, Sandra F. 1976. "Sex and the Single Hemisphere: Specialization of the Right Hemisphere for Spatial Processing," *Science*, 193: 425–27.

Wood, Frank B., D. Lynn Flowers, and Cecile E. Naylor. 1991. "Cerebral Laterality in Functional Neuroimaging." In Frederick L. Kitterle (ed.), *Cerebral Laterality: Theory and Research*. Hillsdale, NJ: Lawrence Erlbaum.

Index